The Revolutionary Gospel

The Revolutionary Gospel

Paul Lehmann and the Direction of Theology Today

Edited by

Nancy J. Duff
Ry O. Siggelkow
Brandon K. Watson

LEXINGTON BOOKS/FORTRESS ACADEMIC
Lanham • Boulder • New York • London

Published by Lexington Books/Fortress Academic
Lexington Books is an imprint of The Rowman & Littlefield Publishing Group, Inc.
4501 Forbes Boulevard, Suite 200, Lanham, Maryland 20706
www.rowman.com

86-90 Paul Street, London EC2A 4NE, United Kingdom

Copyright © 2022 by The Rowman & Littlefield Publishing Group, Inc.

All rights reserved. No part of this book may be reproduced in any form or by any electronic or mechanical means, including information storage and retrieval systems, without written permission from the publisher, except by a reviewer who may quote passages in a review.

British Library Cataloguing in Publication Information Available
Library of Congress Control Number: 2022035718
ISBN 978-1-9787-1224-9 (cloth: alk. paper) | ISBN 978-1-9787-1225-6 (electronic)

∞™ The paper used in this publication meets the minimum requirements of American National Standard for Information Sciences—Permanence of Paper for Printed Library Materials, ANSI/NISO Z39.48-1992.

To all those people—past, present, and future—who struggle to make and to keep human life human

Contents

Acknowledgments	xi
Editors' Note	xiii
Introduction	1

PART I: THE DIRECTION OF THEOLOGY TODAY	11
Chapter 1: The Direction of Theology Today (1946)	15
Chapter 2: Contextual Theology (1972)	25
Chapter 3: The Context of Theological Inquiry (1956)	31
Chapter 4: The Formative Power of Particularity (1963)	41
Chapter 5: The Dynamics of Reformation Ethics (1950)	55
Chapter 6: Barth and Brunner: The Dilemma of the Protestant Mind (1940)	63
Chapter 7: The Ant and the Emperor (1998)	77
Chapter 8: Theologians Who Have Influenced Me [Reinhold Niebuhr] (1970)	87
Chapter 9: Louise Pettibone Smith, Rudolf Bultmann, and Wellesley (1985)	97

PART II: THE REVOLUTIONARY DIMENSION OF THE GOSPEL	107
Chapter 10: The Shape of Theology for a World in Revolution (1965)	111

Chapter 11: Toward a Protestant Analysis of the Ethical Problem (1944)	121
Chapter 12: The Politics of Easter: A Political Celebration of Easter (1980)	141
Chapter 13: Piety, Power, and Politics: Church and Ministry Between Ratification and Resistance (1982)	155
Chapter 14: The Christian Faith and Civil Liberties (1952)	171
Chapter 15: Karl Barth, Theologian of Permanent Revolution (1972)	177
Chapter 16: Black Theology and "Christian" Theology (1975)	197
Chapter 17: The Transfiguration of Jesus and Revolutionary Politics (1975)	207

PART III: THE FUTURE OF THEOLOGY IN A POST-CHRISTIAN WORLD — 213

Chapter 18: Protestantism in a Post-Christian World (1962)	217
Chapter 19: For an Abrahamic People (1974)	227
Chapter 20: The Changing Course of a Corrective Theology (1956)	231
Chapter 21: Law as a Function of Forgiveness (1959)	255
Chapter 22: No Uncertain Sound! (1973)	267
Chapter 23: The Stranger Within the Gate: Two Stories for the American Conscience (1972)	273
Chapter 24: A Christian Alternative to Natural Law (1942)	281

PART IV: DIETRICH BONHOEFFER — 299

Chapter 25: Paul Lehmann's Initiative (1974) *Eberhard Bethge*	303
Chapter 26: Invitation and Contribution of Lehmann for a BBC Broadcast about Dietrich Bonhoeffer (1960)	305
Chapter 27: Dietrich Bonhoeffer: Some Vignettes of Remembrance and Interpretation (1984)	309
Chapter 28: Faith and Worldliness in Bonhoeffer's Thought (1967)	319
Chapter 29: Logos in a World Come of Age (1964)	333

Chapter 30: Dietrich Bonhoeffer and Paul Lehmann Correspondence (1938–1939)	345
Chapter 31: Dietrich Bonhoeffer: Four Theological Giants Influence Our Faith (1968)	359
Chapter 32: Bonhoeffer—Real or Counterfeit (1966)	373
Chapter 33: Called for Freedom (1947)	379
Scripture Index	387
Name Index	391
Subject Index	395
About the Editors	409

Acknowledgments

This project has taken many twists and turns over many years. When Ry Siggelkow, as a PhD student, suggested we edit a volume of Paul Lehmann's essays, we had no idea what kind of work lay before us. We are immeasurably grateful to Mike Gibson, our original editor at Fortress Press, who first recognized the importance of this project. When Fortress merged with Lexington Press, Gayla Freeman took over as editor. We are grateful to her for patience while we finished this work.

We would like to thank Philip G. Ziegler (Professor of Dogmatics at the University of Aberdeen) for his continuing interest in Paul Lehmann's work. His work on Lehmann's theology and ethics has helped cultivate interest in Lehmann's work among longstanding scholars as well as in a new generation of Christian theologians and ethicists. Early on he made suggestions for which essays he thought we should consider for this volume. We are also grateful to Christopher Morse (the Bonhoeffer Professor of Theology and Ethics Emeritus at Union Theological Seminary in New York City) and James F. Kay (the Joe R. Engle Professor of Homiletics and Liturgics Emeritus, and former Dean and Vice President of Academic Affairs at Princeton Theological Seminary). Each read a draft of the introduction to this book, making corrections and adding additional information. They encouraged us over the years, always believing in the significance of this project. We also thank James Kay for his careful reading of the text, making numerous corrections regarding typos. Our gratitude is extended to Raimundo César Barreto, Jr. (Associate Professor of World Christianity at Princeton Theological Seminary) who talked with us at length about Lehmann's connection with M. Richard Shaull, helping us more clearly to see Lehmann's connection to Brazil and influence on the development of Latin American liberation theology more broadly.

We are grateful to Wallace M. Alston (former pastor of Nassau Church and former Director of The Center of Theological Inquiry in Princeton, NJ, now retired) who, as executor of the Lehmann papers, gave us copyright permission to publish material from the Lehmann archives in the Wright Library at

Princeton Theological Seminary. We are grateful to Ken Henke (Curator of Special Collections and Archivist at the Wright Library, Princeton Seminary, now retired) and Kate Skrebutenas (reference librarian at the Wright Library, now retired) for their help in the archives as well as their work on copyright. We would also like to express our gratitude to Kait Dugan (director of the Center for Barth Studies at Princeton Theological Seminary) for scouring the Lehmann archives and finding the perfect cover photo for the book. Securing copyright for the essays was a more daunting—and expensive—task than we had anticipated. We thank all the publishers who gave us permission to reprint Lehmann's work, but most especially those who made the process easy. We are grateful to Judith Attride and Joy Crosley for typing several of the manuscripts, ensuring that Brandon Watson did not have to type them all. Finally, we thank our family members and friends who have gently asked how the project was going and who lent their support up to its completion.

Editors' Note

None of the essays in this collection have been abbreviated except for "Louise Pettibone Smith, Rudolf Bultmann, and Wellesley" in Part I and "A Christian Alternative to Natural Law" in Part III, where several pages were omitted due to the excessive length of each essay. These deletions are clearly marked in the footnotes. All of the essays in this volume remain in the form as originally written except for slight modifications in language. Occasionally, for instance, an overly long sentence has been broken into shorter ones. Also, generic language has been adjusted to reflect Paul Lehmann's commitment to inclusive language in his more recent work and to make his work more accessible to contemporary readers.

Introduction

Paul Lehmann's life spanned most of the twentieth century: born in Baltimore in 1906, he died at 87 on February 27 in New York City in 1994. But to those who knew him personally, his Old World manners seemed at times to belong to a different era. He wore a three-piece suit with a Phi Beta Kappa key to almost every occasion, even in the heat of a New York City summer while sorting through boxes of papers long stored in a colleague's office.[1] He and his wife, Marion, entertained friends in their small but elaborately decorated Manhattan apartment by delivering drinks to each guest one at a time on a silver tray. They had enormous appreciation for beautiful things, such as art, which covered the walls of their apartment, and music, represented by the baby grand piano that took up almost half the space of their living room. Nothing that involved Paul and Marion was ever simple but being a guest in their home was always an experience full of grace and charm.

In spite of his Old World manners, Lehmann was acutely aware of the theological, social, and political issues that pressed upon the age in which he lived. In her address at his funeral, Fleming Rutledge said that the day after his death she had found him in the newspaper, but not in the obituary column. Instead, she found him "in the news, where the human story is being told in all its terror and wonder every day."[2] Similarly, Christopher Morse has noted that Lehmann is unsurpassed among twentieth-century Christian theological ethicists "for having put the news back into the Good News of Gospel proclamation."[3] Even as he addressed political and social issues of his day in light of his theological convictions, reading Lehmann's work now, it often seems he was ahead of his time as his writings speak to the direction of theology today.[4]

Born in Baltimore on September 10, 1906, to Timothy Lehmann, a Russian-born German Evangelical pastor, and Martha Emilie Menzel, Paul Lehmann graduated with a B.S. from Ohio State University in 1927 and with a B.D. from Union Theological Seminary in New York City in 1930.[5] It was here where he became friends with Dietrich Bonhoeffer, who studied there as a Sloan Fellow in 1930–31. Lehmann earned a Th.D. from Union six years later with Reinhold Niebuhr as his advisor. He liked to tell his students that he had nearly finished his thesis (which compared Karl Barth and Albrecht Ritschl on forgiveness), when he decided it was inadequate and started over from the beginning. It was not a story any Ph.D. student really wanted to hear! After being awarded the Fog Traveling Fellowship, he was able to study with Emil Brunner at the University in Zürich and with Karl Barth in Bonn during the fateful year of 1932–33.

Lehmann held teaching positions at Elmhurst College in Illinois (1933–40), where his father had previously served as president; Eden Theological Seminary in Missouri (1940–41); and Wellesley College in Massachusetts (1941–46). After serving briefly (1946–47) as Associate Editor of Religious Books at Westminster Press, he joined the faculty of Princeton Theological Seminary in 1947 and remained there until 1956 when he left to teach at Harvard Divinity School (1956–63). In 1963, he returned to New York, joining the faculty at Union Theological Seminary. Three of the essays included in this volume represent his inaugural lectures at Harvard Divinity School, Princeton Theological Seminary, and Union Theological Seminary.[6]

The type of positions Lehmann held at these various schools testify to the breadth of his knowledge. He taught religion and philosophy; biblical and systematic theology; biblical literature, history, and interpretation; applied Christianity; systematic theology; and theology and ethics. This range of teaching responsibilities may, in part, reflect a time when theological studies were less specialized than today, and faculty were typically required to teach beyond a narrowly defined field, but they also reflect the breadth of his expertise in theological studies. Over the course of his career, he published four books: his dissertation, *Forgiveness: Decisive Issue in Protestant Thought* (Harper and Brothers, 1940); *Ethics in a Christian Context* (Harper & Row, 1963 and republished by Westminster John Knox Press, 2006); *Transfiguration of Politics:[The Presence and Power of Jesus of Nazareth in and Over Human Affairs]* (Harper & Row, 1975); and *The Decalogue and a Human Future: The Meaning of the Commandments for Making and Keeping Human Life Human* (Wm. B. Eerdmans, 1994).[7]

Lehmann was well known for his commitment to civil liberties. Having experienced and opposed McCarthyism, he was among the founders of the Emergency Civil Liberties Committee in 1951, when the American Civil Liberties Union (ACLU) refused to defend those accused of being communists.[8] James Kay believes "his opposition to McCarthyism and the national security state" stands as one of his greatest legacies.[9] He was also active in the Marxist-Christian dialogues of the late 1960s and as an ordained Presbyterian minister and member of Boston Presbytery, he was an enthusiastic participant in ecumenical conferences. Also, given the anti-immigration hysteria of our day, Lehmann's work with Louise Pettibone Smith, Rudolf Bultmann's translator at Wellesley College, on foreign born immigrants, especially Haitians, is noteworthy.

Paul Lehmann married Marion Nelle Lucks on August 29, 1929. They had one son, Peter, whose death at 26 resulted in a lifelong grief woven into their lives in an almost palpable manner.[10] Their heartache, however, did not make them bitter over the years. In spite of their grief, they both were, as the New Testament scholar, J. Louis Martyn, once described Paul, "other directed,"[11] a notable trait when receiving guests in their home or when interacting with staff who worked around them. When walking around the quadrangle of Union Seminary, long after he had retired, Lehmann could call mailroom staff as well as security guards by name and ask about members of their family, recalling past celebrations and tragedies. One security guard, who had worked the door of the building where Paul and Marion once lived, said that in cold weather they used to bring him cups of hot coffee. Lehmann also demonstrated this sense of being "other directed" when he encountered strangers. James Kay gives an account of Lehmann's habit of giving money to beggars he met on the streets of New York:

> He gave money to beggars without question, but never as a demeaning act of charity. One Sunday I accompanied him to church on Madison Avenue, and afterward, he told me to wait a moment. He walked half a block to a man without legs in a wheelchair. He gave the man some bills, then lingered and had a genuine conversation. There always had to be a conversation, recognizing the humanity in the beggar.[12]

His work, as James Kay has said, "represented a retrieval of Christian theology on behalf of a more human world."[13] These actions are consistent with one of the concepts most frequently associated with Lehmann's work: humanization.

The concept of "humanization" arises from Lehmann's understanding of God's activity as breaking into the world to create a space "for making and keeping human life human."[14] We, in turn, as "believers in Jesus Christ and members of his church"[15] are to engage in parabolic action that reflects the humanizing activity of God. Critics of Lehmann's use of "humanization" have tended to say that the concept represents a secular form of humanism or that the meaning of the word is vague because it was never clearly defined. Regarding the latter, Lehmann was alarmed that "being human" carried no readily identifiable meaning, believing that if we have to ask for a definition of what it means to be human, we are in worse shape than he feared. Furthermore, the charge that he was employing a secular form of humanism misses Lehmann's insistence on the theological grounding of "humanization" in the action of God.[16] Concern for "making and keeping human life human" stands as one of his most frequently quoted phrases and continues to be employed by former students. As Christopher Morse and others have noted, Lehmann's work "has nurtured in generations of students the discernment of God's humanizing action in the social controversies of current events."[17]

For those generations of students and colleagues who had the opportunity to hear him speak, Lehmann had a way of creating an atmosphere filled with erudition, humor, and insight even if not always with complete clarity. Many listeners were left enthralled *and* a bit puzzled, but eager to hear more and to read his work. Some of those who knew him personally were afraid that his written work would not have the same effect on those who never had the opportunity to hear him speak and that with his death interest in his work could wane. This, however, has not been the case. From September 2001 to July 2002, Philip Ziegler worked on Lehmann's papers at the Princeton Theological Seminary library. Never having heard Lehmann speak, he thoroughly understands what Lehmann's work is about and recognizes its significance.[18] Furthermore, there is a younger generation of scholars who are discovering Lehmann's work.

The three editors of this present volume of Paul Lehmann's essays represent two generations of scholars interested in his work, one who knew him personally and two who did not. Nancy Duff was Lehmann's student, beginning in 1974, the second year of her M.Div. program at Union Presbyterian Seminary in Richmond, where Lehmann served as a visiting professor. Later, Duff had frequent contact with him in her Ph.D. program at Union Theological Seminary in New York (as Paul and Marion lived in New York City in retirement), and she wrote her dissertation on his work.[19] Christopher Morse, also a former student and close friend of Lehmann's, served as her advisor, and James Cone, a former colleague of Lehmann, was the second reader of her thesis. She also studied under the New Testament scholar, J. Louis Martyn, who was Lehmann's colleague and close friend. She is ordained in the Presbyterian Church (USA) and taught theological ethics at Princeton Theological Seminary from 1990 until she retired in December 2020.

Ry Siggelkow and Brandon Watson represent the newest generation of theologians interested in Lehmann's work. As a doctoral student at Princeton Seminary (2011–2017), Ry Siggelkow was primarily exposed to Lehmann's theological progeny through his advisor Nancy Duff, and through classes and conversations with Beverly Gaventa and James Kay, both of whom served on his dissertation committee. Siggelkow was drawn to Lehmann's theology because of his contextual approach to theological ethics, his dynamic interpretation of Dietrich Bonhoeffer and Karl Barth, and his constructive theological engagement with the political revolutions of his time. Siggelkow looked for a common thread or tradition that could provide some theological unity to make sense of what James Kay has termed "The Union School." In the work of his teachers at Princeton, Siggelkow identified a distinctive, yet diverse, theological tradition that emerged out of Union Theological Seminary in the late 1960s through the influence of James Cone, J. Louis Martyn, Christopher Morse, Dorothee Sölle and especially Paul Lehmann. He also came to appreciate the impact Lehmann had on the development of Third World liberation theology, seen especially in Lehmann's influence on John Mackay and M. Richard Shaull in the United States, Rubem Alves, Sergio Arce, and Beatriz Melano Couch in Latin America, Alan Boesak in South Africa, and Kim Yong Bock in Korea. Siggelkow has spent many hours combing through the collection of Lehmann's papers at the Princeton Theological Seminary library, and he was the motivating force behind this current collection of essays. He is ordained in the Mennonite Church USA and currently serves as the director of the Leadership Center for Social Justice at United Theological Seminary of the Twin Cities.

As a graduate student at Princeton Seminary, Brandon Watson encountered Paul Lehmann's work as a research assistant for Nancy Duff. Spending time working in the Lehmann archives was formative for piecing together Lehmann's personal life, political involvement, and transatlantic relationships, truly seeing his liberative vision for humanity across all areas of life. These experiences had a lasting effect on his own theological development, giving language to the humanizing way in which theology and ethics play out in everyday life. Instead of asking how one's actions might fit within a principled ethical grid, one was led to ask from within the *koinonia*: "What am I, as a believer in Jesus Christ and a member of his church, to do?" During a PhD seminar on Lehmann's theology and ethics, he continued to work out the contextual nature of Lehmann's thought with a focus on Lehmann's doctoral dissertation, published as *Forgiveness*. On a comparative level, he focused significant attention on Lehmann's understanding of the God who is always "making and keeping human life human" coupled with Karl Barth's anthropology, which proved fruitful in a move toward a relational, theological anthropology. During this time, Brandon also studied with James Kay. Learning more about Lehmann's theological and personal influence on Kay was highly influential and enlightening. Currently, Brandon is a candidate for ordination in the Presbyterian Church (USA), works as an academic assistant in Systematic Theology at the Protestant University Wuppertal, and is a researcher at Heidelberg University, where he also recently completed his PhD.

We believe that Paul Lehmann's distinctive work in theology and theological ethics is significant for both the academy and the church today for a variety of reasons. First, he belonged to a generation of great theologians, and his work sheds light on theologians he knew personally whose work has had enormous impact on theological discussions in the 20th and now

21st centuries. Reinhold Niebuhr was his dissertation advisor and later colleague at Union Theological Seminary in New York. He was one of the first American theologians to read Karl Barth, his proficiency in German allowing him to read Barth's work before it was translated into English. (He grew up in a German-speaking family, only speaking English with regularity when he entered the first grade.) He studied with Emil Brunner, was one of Dietrich Bonhoeffer's close American friends, and he was a colleague and friend of Paul Tillich at Harvard. Later, at Union Seminary he was a colleague of James Cone, Dorothee Sölle, and Christopher Morse. This book includes some of Lehmann's essays that reflect on the theology of Karl Barth, Emil Brunner, Dietrich Bonhoeffer, Reinhold Niebuhr, and James Cone.

Second, Lehmann's Christian ethic is distinctively *theological*. While he never produced a systematic theology, Christian doctrine in the Reformed tradition undergirds all of Lehmann's theological editorial reflections, including his theological ethic. It should be noted that while Lehmann wanted to show that "the faith and thought of the Reformation provide insights into and ways of interpreting ethics which give creative meaning and direction to behavior,"[20] he also believed that the Reformers sometimes lost the courage of their own convictions. His work, therefore, never represents a wooden recitation of Reformed theology, but a willingness to set the theology of the Reformers in conversation with other forms of theology and with other disciplines, such as sociology, philosophy, literature, and poetry even as he always sought to preserve the integrity of theology, insisting as Karl Barth did, that no other discipline should be allowed to dictate theology's content or method.

Third, Lehmann's theological work is methodologically *contextual*. Lehmann viewed theology as the work of discernment of God's ongoing activity in the world. As such, theological reflection must be attentive to both the particular contexts out of which it emerges and the contexts in which God is active and human life is lived. The theologian cannot act as one who stands at a remove from the historical realities that give material shape to the pressing issues and questions of the present. Lehmann's contextual approach to theology is a good example of what his friend and former president of Princeton Seminary, John Mackay, famously called "theology from the road" as opposed to "theology from the balcony." While Lehmann's contextual approach to theology and ethics was not always well understood or accepted by the Euro-American academy, it had deep resonance among theologians throughout South America, South Africa, and Korea who because of their social location more readily saw the relevance of a theological methodology that created space for contextual analysis of colonialism and racism and concrete discernment of the presence and power of the activity of God in anticolonial revolutionary struggles.

Fourth, Lehmann addressed particular moral and political issues that continue to be the subject of theological debate today. He wrote essays on such topics as racism, civil liberties and civil rights, immigration, abortion, sexuality, war, revolution, and the task of prophetic truth-telling in a post-Christian context.[21] While deeply attuned to the contextual nature of theological ethics, his reflections on these perennial issues continue to hold insight for both the academy and the church today.

Finally, Lehmann's theology retains a contemporary relevance for the recent discussions about the place and function of "apocalyptic" in theology today. Influenced by the work of Ernst Käsemann and J. Louis Martyn, Lehmann sought to bring New Testament apocalyptic themes to bear on both theological ethics and political theology, with particular attention to the "revolutionary" dimension of the gospel.[22] The title of this book, *The Revolutionary Gospel*, points to the centrality of apocalyptic theology in Lehmann's work and his own distinctive political-theological appropriation of apocalyptic themes.

Essays in Part I of this collection indicate how the doctrine of God leads Lehmann to identify the contextual character of Christian theology and ethics. They also demonstrate the influence of Karl Barth, Reinhold Niebuhr, and Emil Brunner on Lehmann's work. His understanding of the revolutionary character of divine activity in the world is the focus of the essays in Part II. Part III takes its title from a 1962 essay, "Protestantism in a Post-Christian World," and also contains essays that focus on Karl Barth as well as two essays that focus on the issue of immigration. Finally, Part IV includes essays and letters concentrating on Dietrich Bonhoeffer, including a previously unpublished address given by Lehmann at the dedication of the Bonhoeffer Room at Union Theological Seminary in New York. That section, and the volume as a whole, concludes with a baccalaureate sermon, "Called for Freedom," delivered at the University of North Carolina in 1947. While the sermon is primarily concerned with the Pauline understanding of freedom in Galatians 5:1 and 13, it includes a reference to Bonhoeffer's poem, "Who Am I?" written from prison. References to Bonhoeffer's life and thought often punctuated Lehmann's work.

The subtitle of this book, "The Direction of Theology Today," comes from an essay Lehmann wrote in 1947. That essay compares and contrasts "liberalism" and "neo-orthodoxy," particularly on the issues of biblical authority and Christianity's relationship to history and culture. It concludes by identifying three arenas that Lehmann believed would shape the direction of theological thinking: (1) interpretation of the Bible, (2) divine revelation, and (3) the Christian life. These are, of course, sweeping and perennial theological issues that are addressed by numerous theologians. The reader of this collection of Lehmann's essays is invited to consider the *particular* way Lehmann describes these issues in the context of the times in which they were written and in light of the theological situation in which we find ourselves now.

When Lehmann began teaching at Princeton Theological Seminary in 1947, President John Mackay introduced him with the following words:

> Combining a passionate devotion to the theology of the Reformation, an awareness of current theological issues, a deep knowledge of and sensitivity to present-day social and ethical questions, together with an established reputation as a teacher and writer, Dr. Lehmann will bring to his chair the powers of a first-class theological mind and the concerns of a social thinker.[23]

We believe Lehmann's sensitivity to social and ethical questions, his readiness to consider current theological perspectives while remaining grounded in Reformation theology can, to paraphrase Lehmann himself, "provide insights into and ways of interpreting" theology and ethics, which "give creative meaning and direction" to Christian belief and behavior today.

NOTES

1. When Lehmann retired from Union Theological Seminary in New York in 1973, Christopher Morse allowed him to store numerous boxes of papers in his office at Union, where they remained until the summer of 1988, when Brite Divinity School of Texas Christian University in Fort Worth gave Nancy Duff a grant to spend a week in New York City, helping Lehmann sort through his papers. Those papers are now archived at the Wright Library of Princeton Theological Seminary. We gratefully acknowledge Wallace Alston for donating the Lehmann papers to Princeton and Doug Denne for beginning to catalog the Lehmann papers, as well as all those who have organized them over the years.

2. Fleming Rutledge, "A Tribute to Paul Louis Lehmann," (eulogy delivered at Lehmann's funeral at Nassau Presbyterian Church in Princeton, NJ, March 2, 1994), *The Princeton Seminary Bulletin* 15, no. 2 (1994): 165–169.

3. Christopher Morse, "Paul Lehmann as Nurturer of Theological Discernment," in *Explorations in Christian Theology and Ethics: Essays in Conversation with Paul Lehmann*, Philip G. Ziegler and Michelle J. Bartel, eds. (Farnham: Ashgate, 2009), 11. Christopher Morse is the Bonhoeffer Professor of Theology and Ethics, Emeritus at Union Theological Seminary in New York City. He was first a student, then colleague of Lehmann's at Union Seminary and then a life-long friend. He and James Kay were with Paul Lehmann when he died.

4. The phrase, "the direction of theology today," is the subtitle of this collection and the title of Part I. It was taken from a 1946 essay, which is the first entry below.

5. His B.D. thesis was titled "The Historical Relation of Barth's Theology to the Lutheran Doctrine of 'The Word of God'" and can be found in the Lehmann archives in Wright Library, Princeton Theological Seminary.

6. After retiring from Union Theological Seminary in 1974, Lehmann taught at various schools, including Union Presbyterian Seminary in Virginia (1974–76), Bryn Mawr College in Pennsylvania (1976–77), the University of California at Berkeley and San Francisco Theological Seminary (fall, 1976), and Moravian Theological Seminary, Bethlehem, PA (fall, 1977).

7. For an excellent analysis of each of these books, see Christopher Morse, "Paul Lehmann as Nurturer of Theological Discernment," in *Explorations in Christian Theology and Ethics: Essays in Conversation with Paul Lehmann*, eds. Philip G. Ziegler and Michelle J. Bartel (Farnham: Ashgate, 2009), 11–28. That volume also includes an essay by Nancy J. Duff, "The Commandments and the Common Life: Reflections on Paul Lehmann's *The Decalogue and a Human Future*" that describes how the *Decalogue* book made its way to publication and explains some of the more complex, and sometimes confusing, concepts in that book. Other contributors to that volume are Phillip Ziegler and Michelle Bartel (eds.), Sally Ann Brown, James F. Cubie, David E. Demson, Barry Harvey, Eunjoo Mary Kim, Christopher Morse, and Fleming Routledge. The volume also includes a bibliography of Lehmann's work.

8. Lehmann's obituary in the *New York Times* explains that the Emergency Civil Liberties Committee was "formed by 150 clergymen, educators and professional people to safeguard Constitutional rights." The obituary also notes that Lehmann "firmly rejected insinuations that some of its leaders acted as fronts for Communists." Wolfgang Saxon, "Rev. Paul L. Lehmann, 87, Dies; Theologian and Civil Libertarian," *New York Times Obituary Page*, March 2, 1994, Section B, Page 10.

9. This quotation was included in a fax from Barbara Chappel to Wolfgang Saxon at the *New York Times*. James F. Kay is the Joe R. Engle Professor of Homiletics and Liturgics, Emeritus, and former Dean and Vice President of Academic Affairs at Princeton Theological Seminary. He studied with Paul Lehmann when he was a Ph.D. student at Union Theological Seminary in New York and attended the last class Lehmann taught there.

10. The three of them, Paul, Marion, and Peter, are buried side by side in Witherspoon Cemetery in Princeton, New Jersey.

11. Fleming Rutledge, "A Tribute to Paul Louis Lehmann," 167.

12. James Kay, "Toward a More Human World: Paul Lehmann, 1906–1994," *Alumni/ae News: Princeton Theological Seminary* 32, no. 1 (Winter 1994): 23.

13. James Kay, "Toward a More Human World."

14. This phrase can be found throughout Lehmann's work. For early instances see Paul Lehmann, *Ethics in a Christian Context* (New York: Harper & Row, 1963), 138 and 316.

15. Lehmann identifies the fundamental question of Christian ethics as "What am I, as a believer in Jesus Christ and as a member of his church, to do?" Lehmann, *Ethics in a Christian Context*, 47.

16. "Humanization" refers first to the "humanizing activity of God," which in turn defines responsible human behavior. See Lehmann, *Ethics in a Christian Context*, 153.

17. Wolfgang Saxon, "The Rev. Paul Lehmann, 87, Dies: Theologian and Civil Libertarian," Obituaries, *New York Times*, March 2, 1994.

18. Ziegler's work on Lehmann's papers was part of his postdoctoral fellowship in "Public Theology in America" at Robert Wuthnow's Center for the Study of the Religion at Princeton University.

19. Duff's dissertation was later published as *Humanization and the Politics of God: The Koinonia Ethics of Paul Lehmann.* (Grand Rapids, MI: Eerdmans, 1992). See also, Nancy J. Duff, "Paul Louis Lehmann . . . ," *Theology Today* 53, no. 3 (October 1996): 360–369.

20. Lehmann, *Ethics in a Christian Context*, 14.

21. In a letter exchange with Ernst Käsemann about his *Transfiguration of Politics*, Lehmann expressed his profound indebtedness to Käsemann. Lehmann indicates that his constructive account of the revolutionary power of the gospel was a theological elaboration on the meaning of Käsemann's claim that "Jesus means freedom." The letter exchange is held in the Tübingen library.

22. For the significance of apocalyptic in Lehmann's theology, see Duff, *Humanization and the Politics of God*, 117–52; and Morse, "Paul Lehmann as Nurturer of Theological Discernment," 11–28.

23. John Mackay, "President's Page," *The Princeton Seminary Bulletin* 41, no. 1 (Summer 1947): 25.

PART I

The Direction of Theology Today

The essays in Part I are identified by the subtitle of this book and the title of its first essay: "the direction of theology today." While these essays span the decades from the 1940s to the 1980s, they carry significance for the direction of theology in the third decade of the twenty-first century. They introduce readers to methodological issues at stake in Lehmann's work and provide reflections on three theologians who influenced him: Karl Barth, Emil Brunner, and Reinhold Niebuhr.[1] Significantly, these theologians were not always in agreement with one another, making it impossible to label Lehmann's work as strictly belonging to a particular school of thought.

As one of the first Americans to read Karl Barth's work, Barth's influence on Lehmann is unmistakable. In his essay, "The Ant and the Emperor," he admits he was pleased to find his name among the "ants," so identified by Barth, who came to see him during a summer vacation. (This essay also explains why Lehmann frequently referred to Barth as "Carolus Magnus.") Christopher Morse, however, has rightly pointed out that Lehmann is only "superficially" classified as "Barthian."[2] Lehmann was also influenced by Reinhold Niebuhr, a family friend who later became his teacher at Union Theological Seminary in New York, and is someone he identifies as "a father in God" to him.[3] While Barth and Niebuhr often stood at odds with each other, Lehmann believed "there is more Barth in Niebuhr and more Niebuhr in Barth" than either of them recognized.[4] Lehmann disagreed with those who only take note of the contrast between Barth's Christocentric theology and Niebuhr's focus on theological anthropology, arguing for a Christological foundation for Niebuhr's work. He also rejected the stark divide that Barth had defined between his own work and that of Emil Brunner.[5]

Furthermore, Lehmann identified strengths and weaknesses of both liberal *and* dialectical theology even though his own theology is closer to the latter.[6]

Liberal theology, he says, sometimes confuses the divine with the best of human nature, while dialectical theology sometimes loses sight of creation in its insistence on the otherness of God.[7] He appreciates liberal theology's emphasis on God's activity in the *world*, while valuing dialectical theology's focus on *God's* activity in the world. In spite of being able to acknowledge the strengths and weaknesses of liberal and dialectical theology and being influenced by the work of theologians who disagreed with each other, Lehmann was not, as Morse points out, middle of the road.[8] While he never aligned himself uncritically with one theological perspective, he did not mince words when seeking to protect the integrity of the Christian faith, and the faith he defended is grounded in, although never woodenly restricted by, the theology of the Reformation. He often felt free to carry the Reformers' convictions in different directions and to different conclusions than they themselves did, but believed that his theology remained consistent with the Reformers' original claims.

Lehmann also entered constructive conversation with contemporary theological movements. While he did not always agree with liberation theology and could never have been identified as a feminist theologian, he read the works of liberation and feminist theologians carefully and allowed their critique to influence his work.[9] It may in part be because of his willingness to listen to a variety of theological voices that he was criticized from theologians from different perspectives:

> Opposing equally the repristination of tradition and the amnesia of modernity with respect to tradition's present day innovative import, Lehmann's thought has been criticized by conservatives as being too radical, and by radicals as being too conservative. Even the so-called neo-orthodox, or Barthians . . . have been suspicious of his politicizing emphasis, while the Liberationists more sympathetic to his leftist politics have tended to discount Lehmann's revolutionary claims as being too dependent upon divine agency.[10]

What others identified as a theological divide (his leftist politics and his dependence upon divine agency) go hand in hand in Lehmann's work as he focused on the dynamic (apocalyptic) nature of God's activity in the world. This dynamic character of divine activity influenced his method and language, making him insist that dialectical claims about God are more appropriate than strictly systematic ones. He also frequently punctuates his theological arguments with the words of poets, such as e. e. cummings and W. H. Auden, believing that while poetry cannot replace critical theological reflection, it sometimes expresses the truth about God that no other form of language can.

For Lehmann, the freedom of God, including God's radical transcendence *and* immanence is also best served by a key feature of his theology and ethics, that is, their essentially contextual nature.[11] One way to understand what Lehmann meant by the contextual nature of ethics is to contrast his work with the ethics proposed by Joseph Fletcher in *Situation Ethics: The New Morality*.[12] Published three years after Lehmann's *Ethics in a Christian Context*, many readers, who had not read both books, assumed that Fletcher's term, "situation ethics," and Lehman's term, "contextual ethics," meant the same thing. Although Lehmann and Fletcher shared a rejection of moral absolutes, their approaches to ethics are radically different. Fletcher's book proposes a Christian utilitarian ethic, replacing the greatest good with the New Testament concept of agape. Lehmann's ethics is *not* utilitarian, and he was highly critical of Fletcher's book, especially the inconsequential position Christology played in it.[13] Unlike Fletcher, Lehmann's ethic is grounded in Christian doctrine, making his a theological ethic rather than a Christian version of a philosophical approach to ethics.

Lehmann, in fact, insisted that no approach to ethics could be extracted from a typology and imposed on Christian faith and doctrine. The contextual character of ethics, he argued, arises in response to the question regarding the difference the life and teaching, death and resurrection, and exaltation and lordship of Christ make to responsible human action in the world.[14] God's action in the world cannot be captured in an absolute rule, law, or principle. Rather, as the writer of Lamentations knew (3:23), God's grace is new every morning, which means not only new in human awareness, but newly and dynamically presented to the particular situation in which we find ourselves. The dynamic, apocalyptic character of divine action that breaks into the world in the incarnation and continues to work to create a space where human life, as well as all creation, can flourish stands at the heart of all his work.[15]

The first five essays included in Part I ("The Direction of Theology Today," "Contextual Theology," "The Context of Theological Inquiry," "The Dynamics of Reformation Ethics," and "The Formative Power of Particularity") give accounts of Lehmann's understanding of Christian ethics, especially its contextual character, which arises from God's breaking into the world in Jesus Christ. The next four essays ("Barth and Brunner: The Dilemma of the Protestant Mind," "The Ant and the Emperor," "Theologians Who Have Influenced Me," and "The Christology of Reinhold Niebuhr") help readers understand Lehmann's theological method in relation to some of the theologians who influenced his work. It will become clear to readers that Lehmann never simply repeated what others said, but drew on various theological perspectives to serve what he believed was the single task of theology and ethics: "translating the language and conceptions of the tradition into their *human* reality and meaning."[16] The last essay, "Louise Pettibone Smith,

Rudolf Bultmann, and Wellesley," provides a delightful description of Louise Pettibone Smith, a professor of Biblical History, Literature and Interpretation at Wellesley College from 1915 to 1953, a translator of Rudolf Bultmann, and Co-Chair of the American Committee for Protection of the Foreign Born.

NOTES

1. Essays referring to James Cone and Dietrich Bonhoeffer are included in Parts III and IV.

2. Morse, "Paul Lehmann as Nurturer of Theological Discernment," 11.

3. Lehmann, "Theologians Who have Influenced Me," 87.

4. Lehmann, "Theologians Who have Influenced Me," 89.

5. Lehmann could, nevertheless, be critical of certain aspects of Niebuhr's theology. See Philip G. Ziegler, "Justification and Justice: The Promising *Problematique* of Protestant Ethics in the World of Paul L. Lehmann," *BThZ* 21, no. 1 (2004): esp. 143–147.

6. See, "The Direction of Theology Today," 15–24. While Lehmann used "dialectical theology" and "neo-orthodoxy" interchangeably in this essay, over time the former term became the more accurate one.

7. Lehmann, "Barth and Brunner: The Dilemma of the Protestant Mind," 63–76.

8. See Morse, "Paul Lehmann as Nurturer of Theological Discernment," 11.

9. For Lehmann's reflections on James Cone's theology, see "Black Theology and Christian Theology," 197–206.

10. Christopher Morse, "Paul Lehmann as Nurturer of Theological Discernment," 11.

11. In 1963, Lehmann published the book by which he is best known, *Ethics in a Christian Context* (New York: Harper & Row, 1963). In three parts ("Christian Faith and Christian Ethics," "Christian and Philosophical Thinking about Ethics," and "The Question of Conscience") he sets forth his Christian theological ethic.

12. Joseph Fletcher, *Situation Ethics: The New Morality* (Philadelphia: Westminster 1966).

13. See Paul Lehmann, "Review of Fletcher's *Situation Ethics*," *The Bulletin of the Episcopal Theological School* 59, no. 1 (1966): 25–27; not included here.

14. Lehmann, "The New Morality: A Sermon for Lent," *Dialogue* 5 (1966): 52; not included here. See also Duff, *Humanization and the Politics of God*, 60–162.

15. Paul L. Lehmann, *Transfiguration of Politics* (New York: Harper & Row, 1975), 80.

16. Lehmann, "Contextual Theology," 25–30.

Chapter 1

The Direction of Theology Today (1946)[1]

Last August, there was held in Cambridge, England, under the auspices of the Provisional Committee of the World Council of Churches, a Conference on International Affairs. We all know that the formal achievement of that conference was the creation of a *Commission* on International Affairs whose task it will be to relate, by study and by advisory counsel, the mind and the conscience of non-Roman Christendom to the critical issues and policies of the society of nations in its struggle to achieve unity and peace. But those who were present at that gathering have returned with oral reports of an *informal* achievement of the conference, which is certainly not less, and very likely even more important and far-reaching than the resolution creating the new commission. The word is that contrary to expectation, and quite without advance preparation, the Cambridge meeting was marked by an unanimity of mind and a unity of spirit with respect to the message and function of the church in the present cultural and social situation that were overwhelming and unique. Theological and ecclesiastical extremes were neither compromised nor repressed. To the astonishment of everyone, disruptive divisions were not at hand.

Now, of course, this does not mean that there are no theological issues, and that the day of theological controversy is gone forever. Certainly, it does not mean that Methodists have become Greek Orthodox and Greek Orthodox, Unitarian. Bishops have not resigned, and Presbyteries are not governing the churches. Indeed, the motives and expectations that have surrounded the appointment of the new Commission on International Affairs may be, and doubtless are and have been, ambiguous. But I should like to suggest that whatever may be the ultimate significance of the Cambridge Conference of August 1946, there is an immediate significance, which a responsible church and responsible Christians cannot ignore.

The Cambridge meeting may be regarded as a sign that a frontier has been crossed in the ongoing story of the Christian movement. Theologically that frontier can be said to have been crossed in the sense that the direction of theology today is toward constructive rather than polemical thinking. This does not mean that polemics have no constructive significance. Without polemics, there would have been no Christian movement, as the Corinthian letters and the Fourth Gospel sufficiently attest. Without polemics, there would have been no Protestant Reformation. Indeed, it was Erasmus' unwillingness to assume the responsibility of polemics that not only deprived the Reformation of his leadership but also deprived him of more far-reaching historical significance. And we shall not rightly understand the direction of theology today unless we take proper account of the polemical phase through which we have passed. But the peril of polemics is that the controversies aroused by disputation outlast their true occasion. The ground thus cleared is, then, apt to be reduced to shambles and new growth to be stifled in the growing. It is this peril, which requires us to refresh our minds about the principal theological controversy of our time so that we may rightly assess the constructive issues now beginning to emerge from that debate.

We have all heard tell of "liberalism" and of "neo-orthodoxy." But we have not always remembered that liberalism was itself a polemical theological movement and that neo-orthodoxy includes more than the dialectical theology of Barth and Brunner. It has, therefore, not infrequently turned out that both liberalism and neo-orthodoxy have been attacked where they ought to have been defended and defended where they ought to have been attacked. These errors are, of course, easier to recognize in retrospect. But they are not always easier to correct. Correction requires not only perspective, but also the crossing of a theological frontier.

Theological liberalism is essentially the position that the world and humanity have an independent and positive relation to the redemptive self-disclosure and activity of God in Jesus Christ. It is both recognized and emphasized that Christianity is a religion of redemption, uniquely centered in the person and work of Jesus of Nazareth and uniquely expressed in the faith and life of the community of believers, however diverse its institutional forms. Liberalism never denied that the world and everything in it was the work of God the Creator, and that humanity and all its works were deficient both in goodness and in power. But liberalism insisted that precisely because the world has been created and humans are creatures, the purpose and the will of God continued to be operative in both, despite defection and distortion.

In this insistence, liberalism was incontestably right. It was right for at least two reasons: one, constructive, the other, polemical. The constructive reason was that the doctrine of creation was an essential part of biblical and historic Christian faith. But the polemical reason was equally important. It was the responsibility for preserving the biblical and historic Christian faith from arbitrariness. Liberalism had to contend against arbitrariness, owing to pressure from two directions. On the one hand, there was the pressure from inside the Church; on the other, there was the pressure from outside the Church, exerted by an irreversible shift in cultural and social patterns. Actually, it was a matter of two sides of the same coin. For what was at stake were the nature of religious authority and the validity of religious judgments. Inside the Church, the claim was tenaciously, and not a little belligerently, made that religious authority was biblical authority and that an inerrant text not only defined the validity of religious judgments but also established religious judgments as the criteria for all other judgments as well. Nothing could be true religiously unless there was a corroborative biblical text. But neither could anything be true geologically, geographically, biologically, or any other way, if it contradicted the biblical text.

Outside the Church, it was contended that religious authority could not possibly be biblical authority, partly because religion was regarded as more inward and more universal than a written text, and partly because the increase of knowledge about the world, humanity, and society was too impressive to be devoured by the omnivorous claims that were being made in the name of the Bible.

Thus, a theological movement which was endeavoring to relate the vast range of new knowledge about created things to the long-acknowledged activity and purpose of God the Creator had to take the form of a "liberal" movement if Christianity was to be preserved from the stagnation of pursuing "the letter which killeth," while "the Spirit which giveth life" passed to other auspices than those of the Christian heritage and the Christian Church. If the Christian God is a God who "made known his ways to Moses, his acts to the people of Israel" (Ps. 103:7), and if history means anything at all, this was an inescapable responsibility. But it *was* polemical. Liberalism was and is, characteristically the protest against the arbitrariness of biblical authority and the isolation of Christianity from historical and cultural meaning.

Liberalism rescued the Bible from idolatry and irrelevance. But its polemics overshot the mark—polemics always do; this is alike their strength and weakness. And what it means is that polemics are neither to be avoided for the sake of tranquility, nor pursued for the sake of consistency. In exchange for textual literalism, liberalism offered textual criticism; and instead of isolating the Bible from significant cultural and social changes, liberalism underlined the continuity of human experience in the *Bible* with human experience *generally*. These exchanges saved the Bible from discard, but they did not allow the Bible to speak sufficiently of and for itself. A new polemic was called for if the Bible, which had been delivered from arbitrariness, were not to be rendered impotent. The cultural and social patterns of a world in which all authority was being radically re-examined and re-oriented could not be allowed to ignore the influence and wisdom of the Bible. But neither could such a world be allowed to mistake the wisdom and influence of the Bible for its own. To prevent this confusion and to make room for the Bible to speak its own word to a completely altered world was the true occasion and the true significance of the theological movement which we know as neo-orthodoxy.

This term was first applied to the "dialectical" or "crisis" theology associated with the names of Karl Barth and Emil Brunner. Such terms as "dialectical" and "crisis" are certainly not obviously "biblical." And certainly, since the Reformation, people had not been used to reading the Bible in a dialectical way. But as Barth and Brunner tried to preach the gospel and to think about what it meant, it became more and more clear to them that the Bible could *only* be read in a dialectical way.

Your dictionaries will tell you that "dialectic" has to do with "speaking between." That is to say, affirmations are made which, as *statements*, are in opposition to each other, but which, nevertheless, do not cancel each other out. Not all statements, of course, are dialectical statements. I cannot say, for example, about this paper from which I am reading, both that "it is white" *and* that "it is black." The situation, or object to which those statements refer, requires that they cannot both apply. They cancel each other out. But if I say, "Mr. X is a good person"; "Mr. X is a bad person"—both those statement *do*, in *fact*, apply to the situation or object to which they refer. We may soften the opposition between them by noting that Mr. X is more good than bad, or more bad than good. We may say that Mr. X is better today than yesterday and suspect that tomorrow he will behave worse than he has behaved today. But when all is said, the fact remains that Mr. X is both good and bad.

Thus, a dialectical situation is one about which one must say both "yes" and "no," a situation which requires both positive and negative affirmations if one is rightly to describe and understand it. "I believe in God," say you and say I. But if, in making that affirmation, we really give attention to what is going on, it is plain, is it not, that we always, at the same time, do *not* believe in him? And this also is plain, is it not, that we believe in God most surely when we ask most intensely concerning him? In other words, when the question *about* God becomes the question *of* God, when our asking for God becomes God's asking for us, then we know surely that what we believe is the truth, for both faith and life have lost all illusion and pretense.

Dialectical theology tries in this way to face the actual human situation in the midst of which the question of faith arises. It calls this situation a crisis situation. "The word crisis," according to Brunner, "has two meanings: first, it signifies the climax of an illness; second, it denotes a turning point in the progress of an enterprise or movement."[2] And while the accent falls upon the "turning point," the suggestion of "climax" is somehow always also kept in view. The point is that the course of events in an individual human life or in a cultural epoch ever and again moves toward a climax at which point a radical turnabout must come if the life of that individual or culture is to have meaning. A decision must be made between the shadow of death, which hovers over the old way, and the promise of life, which lies at the turn of the road.

Such decisions are familiar to us all, I am sure. They inspire the "creative minority," without which, as Professor Toynbee's monumental *Study of History* has shown, no civilization or culture can endure. They inform the skepticism of the youth who goes to college and finds that childhood religion simply will not reach, so that as an honest human being the youth simply must repudiate that faith for the sake of the truth and the life. They attended that night in Aldersgate without which the heritage of this institution would certainly be other than it is, if indeed, this institution would be at all. Such a decision, such a crisis situation confronted Barth as he stood in his little parish church in Safenwil, Switzerland, with the rather terrifying responsibility of saying something about the God of the Bible to a congregation shattered by the First World War. It was plain that somehow the pulpit, on which there was an open Bible from which preaching was done, must either become a relic of a bygone age or be the outpost of a new and living connection between the ways of the God about whom the Bible spoke and the confused, broken despairing ways of humanity.

In the theological seminary, Barth had been taught the liberal understanding of these things. But there seemed, in 1919, no way of moving from humans to God, for the ways of humanity, if not paralyzed, were badly marred. And if the important thing about the Bible was the continuity of deepening moral and religious sensitivity between the people of the Bible and the people to whom Barth had to preach, the Bible could only be as badly discredited as the people knew their own experience to be. Here was no abstract situation, compounded of a hundred and one possibilities to be weighed and sorted in reflective detachment. This was a very concrete situation, circumscribed as every concrete situation is. The demand is to act within the limits of the situation or to abandon it. The limits were imposed upon Barth; he did not make them. The Reformation had put the Bible open on the pulpit. And the urgency of the times, as it always does, had made the choice as simple as it was critical. One could only take up the Bible *again* and *afresh* or take up some other responsibility outside the Protestant Church. It is not strange that Barth should have described himself as being like a man ascending the dark and winding staircase of a church tower, and, reaching for the banister to steady himself, got hold of the bell rope instead.

Barth's rereading of the Bible led essentially to the discovery that the crisis of the war was at bottom the crisis of the world and that the crisis of the world was the crisis of one's separation from a God who could not be escaped. It is sin which separates humanity from God; and it is God who pursues people in their sin. That is why humans are perennially restless, and why people sooner or later experience this restlessness as a judgment upon them. It is exactly as Pascal's fragment puts it: "If man is not made for God, why is he only happy in God? If man is made for God, why is he so opposed to God?"[3]

But the Bible not only makes sin plain. It makes plain too that God forgives sin as well as judges it. Indeed, this judgment and forgiveness are, according to Barth, what the Bible is centrally about. This judgment and forgiveness are the central significance of the life, death, and resurrection of Jesus of Nazareth. And this judgment and forgiveness, humanly and divinely brought to humanity in and through Jesus of Nazareth, enable one to understand and to live in the crisis of one's situation. "I have often been asked," says Brunner:

> what the 'Dialectical Theology' is really driving at. The question can be easily answered. It is seeking to declare the Word of the Bible to the world . . . What the Word of God does is to expose the contradiction of human existence, then in grace to cover it . . . It is only by means of the contradiction between two ideas—God and man, grace and responsibility, holiness and love—that we can apprehend the contradictory truth that the eternal God enters time, or that the sinful man is declared just. Dialectical Theology is the mode of thinking which defends this paradoxical character, belonging to faith-knowledge, from the non-paradoxical speculation of reason, and vindicates it against the other.[4]

Thus, we may say, in a word, that dialectical theology is that theology which is concerned to interpret the contradictions of the Bible in their bearing upon the contradictions of human existence.

Dialectical theology is, in genesis and spirit, neo-orthodox rather than liberal. It began to read the Bible again from the standpoint of the insistence of the great Reformers that Scripture is the sole norm of Christian faith and life, and it has sought to state in a new way not only the great ideas of the Bible but the great doctrines of the heritage of the Christian faith. Liberalism also insisted emphatically upon the rereading of the Bible in the light of the teaching of the Reformers. Indeed, it is not too much to say that liberalism did as much to restore and retain the significance of the Bible for the cultural and religious situation of the nineteenth century as dialectical theology has done for the twentieth century. Yet if one considers more specifically the way in which the Bible and the Reformers were appealed to by each of these two movements, one comes in sight of the true relation between them and of certain emerging issues, which require a constructive, rather than a polemical theology.

So far as the Bible is concerned, the stress of liberalism lies upon the religion of Jesus and upon the long history of its emergence as the complete and perfect expression of the moral and religious quest. The Bible was studied with phenomenal zeal and prodigious knowledge in terms of the historical, cultural, and religious context of its *own* time. And though its distinctiveness was always kept in view, it was a superiority of degree rather than of kind. As for Jesus himself, it was the exemplary character of his life and death and teaching that commended him to the loyalty and emulation of the world rather than the substitutionary character of his death and resurrection. The latter was looked upon as an overstatement of the apostle Paul rather than as the key to the real significance of Jesus.

Dialectical theology, on the other hand, lays stress upon the uniqueness of the biblical message of salvation, upon Jesus as the object of faith and the lord of life rather than the supreme example and teacher, and finds the Pauline forms of thought a help rather than a hindrance in the understanding of the gospel. So far as the Reformation is concerned, liberalism was inclined to emphasize the religious and moral attitudes of the individual and the community of the Kingdom of God as operative everywhere where people of good will were broadening and deepening spiritual life and fellowship. Dialectical theology, on the other hand, finds the Reformation significant not because of its individualism but because of its understanding of the Bible, and the community of the Kingdom of God becomes the community of believers in the forgiving grace of God mediated by Word and sacrament.

How then, are these contrasts to be appraised? I venture to think that from the standpoint of the contribution of each to the meaning and the survival of the heritage of Christian faith both movements must be regarded as positive and indispensable. But the polemical relation of these two movements has been sufficiently intense as to suggest that the issue, which divides them, is very fundamental indeed. *This issue is the issue of the nature of the authority by which Christians think and live as believers in the world, and the relation of that authority to whatever else Christians think and do in the world.* Liberalism is "liberal" because its conception of this authority is broader than that of dialectical theology. It finds the insights of the Bible and of the great doctrines of the Church an indispensable guide to Christian thinking and living. But the validity of these insights is derived in the last analysis from their correspondence with the general moral and spiritual aspirations and achievements of humanity. The superlative excellence of Jesus, for instance, is established not so much because he is the revelation of the nature and the will of God but because the highest aspirations and deepest intuitions of people respond to and confirm this excellence. Indeed, liberalism insists that precisely in the assent of human life at its best to the excellence of Jesus, the God of Jesus is not less but more truly and more surely known.

Dialectical theology, on the other hand, is orthodox because its conception of the authority by which Christians think and live as believers in the world is at once narrower and more traditional than is the case with liberalism. The insights of the Bible and of the great doctrines of the Church are indispensable to Christian thinking and living not because they are the superlative but because they are the sole guide to such thinking and living. The validity of these insights is derived in the last analysis from what is believed to be the self-authenticating character of the revelation of God in Jesus Christ. This revelation is given content and meaning by the inner logic of biblical ideas, and it is assented to because of the activity of God, the Holy Spirit, rather than because of the highest aspirations and the deepest intuitions of humans. These aspirations and intuitions cannot authenticate revelation because of the contradictions of human nature and the paradoxical message of the Bible.

How can this understanding of Christianity be related in a positive way to human history and human culture? This is the point at which the polemics of dialectical theology seem to have overshot *their* mark. If liberalism, in rescuing the Bible from arbitrariness, gave too much away in failing to distinguish properly between what was "Christian" and what was "religious" and just plain "human-at-its-best," dialectical theology, in restoring the integrity and independence of the Bible, seems to have taken too much back, so that it is not clear that Christianity has any positive relation to human creativity at all. In its zeal to correct and preserve us from the errors of liberalism, neo-orthodoxy has encountered the peril of a new cultural isolation, which it was the great achievement of liberalism to have overcome. The remarkable aspect of the meeting at Cambridge last August was that this division over the *nature of the authority* by which Christians think and live as believers in the world and *the responsibility* of Christianity for the ongoing cultural and historical life of humanity was lifted above the level of the polemics and accepted as the common task of a common mind of the Christian movement. Theology has crossed a frontier. It is the line at which the issue of the authority and independence of the gospel has become the issue of the responsibility of believers in the gospel for the world.

As I survey the field of theological discussion today and try to reflect upon the constructive task of theology in the light of the polemical history through which we have passed, there are at least three pressing problems that will shape the direction of theological thinking. The first of these problems concerns the interpretation of the Bible. It may be identified by the contrast between biblical criticism and biblical theology. The issue is this: How shall what we know *now* about the inner logic of biblical faith be related to what we know *now* about the actual historical and cultural situation out of which the biblical record came? If we ignore, for example, the time, and place, and situation in which Genesis was written, we shall be in danger of imposing upon Genesis theological ideas that are actually not in Genesis but in ourselves. If, on the other hand, we localize Genesis too completely, we are in danger of missing its significance as revelation.

The second problem concerns the interpretation of revelation. It may be identified by the contrast between revelation as creation and revelation as saving knowledge. The issue is this: How shall what we know *now* about the depth and destructiveness of sin and the desperate urgency of the saving initiative of the grace of God in Christ be related to what we know *now* about the sustaining structures of nature and society within which both sin and grace are operative and apart from which sin and grace have no meaning at all? If God, for example, can be said to act in history, history and nature must, in some sense be revelatory. If they were not, the redemptive act of God in Jesus Christ would seem not to be historical. But if history and nature are revelatory, how shall we understand the special significance of what happened in the life, death, and resurrection of Jesus of Nazareth? In short, what is the relation of act to knowledge in revelation?

And finally, the third problem concerns the interpretation of the Christian life. It may be identified by the contrast between believing and doing. The issue is this: If the inner logic of biblical ideas focuses upon the redemptive significance of Jesus Christ, and if this significance is apprehended by faith, what difference does this faith make in the way in which we live in this kind of world? To put together something old with something new: What is the relation of justification to sanctification in a world of moral anarchy, psychoses, economic and political revolution? What seems to be called for here is a constructive re-statement of the doctrine of the Holy Spirit.

Even if these questions could be answered simply, it cannot lie within the scope of this discussion to answer them. If, however, the consideration of the polemical character of the theology of our time has prepared us with a sense *both* of the complexity and seriousness of our theological responsibility *and* of the resources of insight and faithfulness in our heritage of faith, we may look out with a clearer eye upon the direction of theology today and seek with patience to pursue it.

NOTES

1. Presented before the faculty and students at Duke Divinity School in Durham, North Carolina, December 5, 1946. Previously published in *The Duke Divinity School Bulletin* 11, no. 4 (1947): 67–76. It can also be found in *Union Seminary Quarterly Review* 3, no. 1 (1947): 3–10; reprinted with permission.
2. Emil Brunner, *Theology of Crisis* (New York: Charles Scribner's Sons, 1935), 1f.

3. Blaise Pascal, *Pensées*, translated by W. B. Trotter (New York: E. P. Dutton & Co, 1931), fragment 438.

4. Emil Brunner, *The Word and the World* (New York: Charles Scribner's Sons, 1931), 6–7.

Chapter 2

Contextual Theology (1972)[1]

There is more than one way to "do" systematic theology. But whatever method is followed, it must take with due seriousness the positivistic character of the relationship between the reality which theology seeks to describe and the *description* of this *reality* which theology offers. To do otherwise is to ignore the self-disclosing initiative of God, as the *subject* (not the object) of theology, and the intrinsic character of theology as *response* to God's initiative. The positivistic character of theology expresses the fact that theology and revelation are not identical. Affirmatively stated, the positivistic character of theology expresses the openness of theology to the concreteness, the diversity, and the freedom of God's self-disclosure. So, the radically experimental character of systematic theology is intrinsic to the integrity of its response to its subject. Sensitive to every mode of human knowledge and experience, systematic theology seeks to exhibit in, with, and under the activity of humanity, the particular activity of God. It is this formative power of God, as he gives shape to the life and doings of humanity, that provides systematic theology with its specific content. The formative power of God which gives place to humanity and puts humanity in its place in a world of God's making also gives to the doing of theology its positivistic occasion and significance.

I

If we ask whether there is a way of doing theology which takes due account of the *reality* that theology seeks to describe and the *description* of this reality which theology offers, we come upon a promising possibility. The method by which theology exhibits both its specific content and its positivistic occasion and significance is *contextual*. As a theological method, *contextualism* may be said to be that way of doing theology which seeks to explore and exhibit the dialectical relation between the *content* and the *setting* of theology. When Schleiermacher suggested that Christian doctrines are to be understood as accounts of Christian religious affections set forth in speech, and that they are limited to a particular time, he was emphasizing the dialectical relation between content and setting in the doing of theology, with special stress upon *contemporaneity*. When Barth moves from the concrete talk and language about God in the church to the analogy between the Word of God and the Trinity of God, he is emphasizing the dialectical relation between content and setting in the doing of theology, with special stress upon what is *concretely going on* (phenomenology). When the Reformers underlined the dynamic interrelation between word, spirit, and community of believers, as both content and setting in the doing of theology, they were emphasizing concrete relationships between both God and humanity and humanity and humanity as the central concerns of theology. In each case, what has gone before us is a lively and liberating sense of the *context* within which and with reference to which Christian theologians do their work.

A contextual method in theology is, thus, a response to the positivistic occasion and character of theology. It carries the doing of theology beyond the unfruitful dichotomies which have hitherto obtained between dogmatics and apologetics, between revelation and reason, Jesus Christ and history, content and communication, theology and culture, faith and ethics. These dichotomies have arisen when theology has become unsteady about its systematic task. At least thirty years ago, Barth refused to give theological status to the distinction between *ein Wort zur Sache* (content) and *ein Wort zur Lage* (situation). He was prophetically and proleptically correct. Prophetically, he knew that the integrity of theology was at stake in its faithful adherence to the dialectical interrelation between the self-disclosing activity of God and human apprehension and obedience to this activity. *Proleptically*, he was preparing theology for addressing itself to a situation marked by the collapse of idealism and the rise of cultural positivism. When systematic theology learns to be less ambivalent about its own positivistic character and more sensitive to a contextual way of doing its work, it will know how to deal at one and the same time with its own content and setting and with the ethos and the options posed by the human situation in which systematic theology must work.

II

Theology, if it is to be contextual, means, first and foremost, to be contemporary. Such a method in theology neither follows earlier models of thinking nor is completely novel. It seeks rather to regroup earlier procedures for new purposes. A contextual method for systematic theology concentrates attention upon the dynamic and dialectical relation between the *phenomenological* and the *referential* aspects of the theological task.

The *phenomenological* aspect of the theological task does not refer to philosophical phenomenology. It refers to the seriousness with which theology takes the concrete situation out of which it arises as a discipline of reflection and inquiry. The phenomenology of paramount immediacy and concreteness for the doing of theology is the empirical reality of the Christian community. The Christian community lives always in the present *out* of its past and fully *open* to the future. This is why the materials of theology are compounded of tradition and experimentation. It is precisely those elements of tradition which exhibit the greatest openness in their own present to the future which guide theology in the exercise of its own contemporary responsibility.

The *referential* aspect of a contextual approach safeguards theology against excessive positivistic pressure. It keeps the phenomenological aspect of the theological task from becoming epi-phenomenal, as when Paul van Buren, in *The Secular Meaning of the Gospel* (1963), leaves no room for "God language." In the special use which it makes of the referential aspect of theology, a contextual approach is intrinsically Protestant. The dialectical interrelation between the referential and the phenomenological aspects of theological reflection correspond with the dialectical interrelation between word, faith (church), and spirit. A contextual way of doing theology presupposes and responds to a dynamic authority which in the catholic tradition, particularly in its Roman form, succumbed to heteronomy. Such a dynamic authority may be described by saying that the criteria of a contextual theology are given by the reciprocity between its method and its findings.

One important consequence of this method for systematic theology is that the gap between the language and the content of theology, which has become so critical in our time, is not disposed of by jettisoning the language of liturgy or tradition. It will be recognized that traditional theological language (confessional, liturgical, doctrinal) has a referential as well as a functional significance. Whether this language is retained or abandoned depends upon the referential clarity and power with which this language functions.

Thus, systematic theology is free to make referential use or disuse of the language which the concrete life of the Christian community makes available to it. Systematic theology exercises this freedom in a twofold way. First, it takes up the language and the conceptualization that belong to the dynamic relation between tradition and its referent (that to which the tradition is a response). So, the formative elements of orthodoxy function as conceptual instruments of theological clarification. Whereas Paul Tillich, for example, and in a curiously similar way also Paul van Buren, affirm the intrinsic significance of the Christ symbol for systematic theology, contextual theology opens the way for the whole of orthodoxy in such a way as to exhibit the theological appropriateness and meaning of every formative element of the tradition, not simply of Christology.

In the second place, systematic theology based on a contextual model always engages in the translation of its language. Under this rubric, dogmatics and ethics become distinguishable perspectives upon a single task, not separate sections of a systematic whole. The single task is the task of translating the language and conceptions of the tradition into their *human* reality and meaning. A theology that fails in this enterprise of humanization has defaulted both upon its content and its setting. Such a humanization of theology is to be distinguished from the imperialism by which the theologian presumes to speak with authority in matters pertaining to other disciplines and arts. It is equally to be distinguished from the theologization of the human which is unable to distinguish between what God does to shape and to interpret what is human and what humanity, even at the highest levels of creativity, makes of itself and the world. Contextual theology aims at the humanization of theology in the sense of being open to every human enterprise while continuing to speak its own piece.

III

The contextual method for systematic theology exhibits at least three characteristic marks or criteria. First, such a method exposes the *confessional* character of theology. Here theological positivism is sharply at variance with all other forms of positivism. The line is a thin one, but upon its faithful observance the integrity of theology depends. Theological positivism is involved from the first in a commitment to the truth and life-giving power of the referent to which its context points. Such theology confesses what it knows; it does not confess where it does not know. Other forms of positivism derive their integrity from being uncommitted and seek by tentativeness to push back the frontier of ignorance. Non-theological positivism is rooted in a commitment to being uncommitted. Theological positivism is committed to that which *in concreto* elicits its response; that is, it is confessional.

Second, the contextual method for systematic theology exposes the *dialogical* character of theology. It belongs to the dialogical character of theology to express and to explicate the Christian referent to which it is committed, in an openness to and confrontation with other perspectives and referents. There is a confessional theology that is non-dialogical. Such confessionalism seeks to perpetuate the language of theology without sufficient regard to its original context and thus also with insufficient regard to subsequent contexts in which theology must be done. Consequently, the dynamic and dialectical interrelation between the referent and the phenomenology of the Christian community is ignored and the humanizing task of theology is violated. A dialogical confessionalism, however, recognizes that the ultimate test of its humanizing responsibility may well be its hospitality to what it can learn about the genuinely human from other perspectives that do not claim to be what they are not (that is, which do not claim to be theological). The hidden premise of such a dialogical confessionalism is the activity and power of the Holy Spirit.

Third, the contextual method for systematic theology exposes the *catalytic* character of theology. The catalytic character of theology is expressed in its critical function whereby in pressing, in a dialogical way, its own confessional occasion and integrity, it calls into the open the limits of other perspectives in understanding and identifying what is genuinely human, that is, what is the truth and the life. In this way, a catalytic theology becomes the "guardian of the human," to adapt a suggestion of T. S. Eliot, because it refuses either to subordinate the human to its own confession or to exclude from any identification of the human, the self-disclosing initiative of the particular referent which has shaped its own content and setting. Theological criticism and theological self-criticism are thus inseparable. To this extent, a *catalytic* theology is a prophetic theology whose function is and remains that of a *creative iconoclasm.* A creative iconoclasm in the doing of theology is always prepared for the collapse of its own idols as it exhibits the idolatry in other perspectives.

IV

The promise of such a contextual theology may be that as it seeks to be faithful to its confessional, dialogical, and catalytic character, it may become the bearer in our human situation today of the answer to humanity's profoundest need and question. As W. H. Auden has put it, "How can man's knowledge protect his desire for truth from illusion? How can he wait without idols to worship?"[2] A contextual theology may restore theology to its true office, which is to describe and to invite all human beings to share the power by which humanity can "wait without idols," and in this waiting to express genuine humanity. In so doing, a contextual theology exhibits the order by which goodness is the fruit of truth and forges a creative link between confession and responsibility, between the concern for dogma and the concern about ethics.

NOTES

1. First published in *Theology Today* 29, no. 1 (1972), 3–8; reprinted with permission. A previous, shorter version was prepared for the World Presbyterian Alliance at Hoechst/Odenwald, West Germany, July 1965. A more expanded edition appeared as "On Doing Theology: A Contextual Possibility," in *Prospect for Theology: Essays in Honour of H. H. Farmer*, ed. James F. G. Healey (Welwyn: Nisbet, 1966), 119–136; 232–33 (endnotes).

2. W H. Auden, "Advent," *The Collected Poetry of W. H. Auden* (New York: Random House, 1945), 355.

Chapter 3

The Context of Theological Inquiry (1956)[1]

One afternoon last week, I chanced to pass the shop-window of a bookseller across the Yard in Massachusetts Avenue. In the window, a small sign was displayed which bore the legend: "Religion and Philosophy 20% Off." As a seasonal discount, there may be marketable advantages in such an offering. But as a permanent measure of the state of things, a depreciation of this kind can scarcely mark an enduring enterprise.

Philosophy is currently involved in its own "time of troubles." However, without wishing to "pass by on the other side," one trouble at a time is enough. And the present occasion requires that we confine our attention to the discount accompanying the offerings of religion—and specifically to that one among its offerings called, "Theology." At least, as regards the Harvard Divinity School, there seem to have been dissensions and divisions of longer than a week's duration and beyond the bookseller's horizons.

MR. EMERSON'S QUESTION

The records of an early student "Society for Extemporaneous Speaking" (as it was called) contain a March entry in the year 1825. "Subject selected for the next meeting," the minutes note: "'Is it expedient, in consideration of the spirit of the age that a minister should be a profound Theologian?' This question was proposed by Brother Emerson." Of the next meeting, the minutes declare: "Society assembled. Dr. Ware present. Mr. Emerson not being present, Mr. Hill commenced the discussion."[2]

Ralph Waldo Emerson's connections with the Harvard Divinity School appear to have more archeological than theological permanence. But the question which he raised is in search of an answer still. Indeed, it may be said to arise in our time from an even more elemental level. The issue is not so much whether it is expedient, in consideration of the spirit of the age, that a minister should be a *profound* theologian, but whether it is expedient that the minister be a theologian at *all*! Religion being a matter of life not doctrine (as people were wont to say a half-century ago), of existence not dogma (to use a more current way of speaking), theology seems somehow an alien intrusion upon the nearer and more important concern of religion with humanity and meaning in the world. Theology, being a matter of reflective analysis and rational formulation, seems ineluctably to leave the level of simple and direct comprehension of religious experience behind, and to lose itself in a labyrinth of inquiry which mistakes abstraction for profundity, and systematic precision and coherence for the poetic and pragmatic wisdom by which people make their daily choices and ultimately live and die. At least as regards Harvard, it was all foreshadowed a century ago, when we are told that "Harvard Square, still shaded by a fine old elm, was referred to as 'the Village'" and that "the University community was separated from Boston by a long ride in the horse cars."[3] It was then that Francis Greenwood Peabody, recalling his boyhood impressions, compared the faculty to a "monastic order." He praises "their elevation of mind and felicity of thought," and then remarks that "their world was small, but it was high up and the air was pure."[4]

Neither monastic commitments nor monastic tranquility are conspicuous in the university today. The shade of the elm has given way to whatever shade and safety can be frantically and fleetingly gleaned from a transportation shelter. However high up the university world may still be, it is neither geographically nor academically small. Nor is the air either chemically or rhetorically as pure as in an earlier day it may have been. These environmental changes have been immensely salutary for theology, and chiefly because they have made room for a more viable answer to Emerson's question. Let us not enter upon an affirmative declaration that it is expedient, in consideration of the spirit of the age that a minister should be a *profound* theologian. That would be to claim too much. But let us take up the more modest and more elemental consideration of the question and say that it is expedient, precisely in consideration of the spirit of the age, that a minister be a theologian.

It is expedient, not in the opportunistic sense with which the word "expedient" has unhappily come to be burdened. But it is expedient that the minister be a theologian, because without theological discernment and without the discipline of theological knowledge and reflection ministers cannot pursue calling with integrity and meaning. The spirit of the age, whatever else it is, is one in which reason itself is beset, on the one side, by the doctrinaire rigidities of its friends, both secular and religious, and on the other side, by the cultic pretensions of its positivistic, political and psychologistic enemies, with and without the benefit of clergy. "For," as Saint Paul remarked, in a time not unrelated to our own, "as I expect you have heard by now, our fight is not against any physical enemy: it is against organizations and powers that are spiritual. We are up against the unseen powers that control this dark world, and spiritual agents from the very headquarters of evil" (Ephesians 6:12, Phillips translation). It is the office of theology to provide the critical weapons wherewith faith "tests the spirits" (1 John 4:1, RSV) in the warfare which is always at hand and on that line of battle where the peripheral and the central problems of human knowledge, and the proximate and the ultimate questions of human life are discerned and distinguished. "It's terrible what mysteries there are!" says Mitya Karamazov, "I can't endure the thought that a man of lofty mind and heart begins with the ideal of the Madonna and ends with the ideal of Sodom. What's still more awful is that a man with the ideal of Sodom in his soul does not renounce the ideal of the Madonna . . . God and the devil are fighting there, and the battlefield is the heart of man."[5]

It may be hoped that if a minister, in consideration of the spirit of the age, should discern the expediency of being a theologian, ministers would then begin to apprehend the deeper dimensions of theology and of existence which would add profundity to their theological responsibility. Ministers would then be profound theologians not because they had acquired "prophetic powers," and understood "all mysteries and all knowledge" (1 Cor. 13:2, Philips translation), but would be profound theologians in the sense that they would be in all ways open to the dynamic reality that underlies and forges the link between theology and existence. A theological school is, of course, no guarantee of theology with this kind of expediency and depth. But it is worth recalling that this kind of theological concern was, although for times and seasons in abeyance or haltingly pursued, never wholly absent from this university, and that, from time to time, theology in depth and in consideration of the spirit of the age, was eloquently espoused by some of the most eminent leaders of the university's life. Thus, with some prospect of finding what they seek, students of theology who now begin another academic year under the aegis of Andover Hall may be invited to enter, with diligence and discipline, upon a theological inquiry which will lead to the discovery that it is expedient that a minister should be a theologian.

THE CONTEXTUAL CHARACTER OF
THEOLOGICAL INQUIRY

It is the office of theology, we have suggested, to provide the critical weapons wherewith faith "tests the spirits." These weapons, or to use a more irenic metaphor, these "resources" are principally three: (1) a method of reflective analysis and criticism, (2) a doctrinal tradition, and (3) an integrative point of view. These are, of course, intellectual resources. They are the channels through which human reason addresses itself to the opportunity of the world, including the decisive experience of oneself as a personal and social being. Theology shares these resources with other forms of human inquiry, and they define theology as a science, in the original and broadest sense of the word. These resources also define the possibility and the responsibility according to which theology can and must engage in open and critical conversation with all other forms of scientific inquiry. In a word, the scientific character of theology defines the place of theology in the University.

But while theology shares with other forms of scientific inquiry: a method of reflective analysis and criticism, a doctrinal tradition, and an integrative point of view, theological inquiry always also proceeds under a differentiating claim. This claim is expressed, for example, by the New Testament phrase, "to come to the knowledge of the truth" (1 Tim 2:4). A broader New Testament distinction differentiates between the knowledge which one, so to say, in seeking finds, and the knowledge by which, in seeking, one is found.[6] The doctrinal tradition has been wont to take account of this distinction by differentiating between *knowledge* and *saving knowledge*. But the point to be underlined here, in considering the office of theology, is that theology involves both inquiring knowledge and answering knowledge, both critical reason and responding reason. The knowledge of the truth with which theological inquiry deals is a compound both of intellectual knowledge and the knowledge of faith. The composite character of theological inquiry has not infrequently confused the relations between theology and the other sciences and confounded the household of theology to itself. The dissipation of this disarray calls for a more careful consideration of the *contextual character of theological inquiry*.

There have been in the past two main ways of relating intellectual knowledge to the knowledge of faith: the critical to the responding reason in theological inquiry. One way is the way of *synthesis*. Along this route, the claims of reason and the claims of faith were neatly compartmentalized, only then to be connected by a kind of hierarchical superimposition of the knowledge of faith upon the foundations laid by a rational or natural knowledge of God. For the most part this synthetic theological structure was sustained by *vertical* supports, according to which, as in St. Thomas, the knowledge of faith to some extent paralleled rational theological knowledge and to a larger extent reached beyond it. Then, as in Protestant orthodoxy, a kind of circular arrangement of the *loci theologici* [theological doctrines] came to be adopted. On this plan, it was always recognized that the mind could not, *unaided*, reach saving knowledge. But in actual theological analysis, the synthetic relation between the knowledge of reason and the knowledge of faith was accepted, while its application to the corpus of Christian doctrine was not so much *hierarchical* as *symmetrical*. Having laid down the proposition, from a kind of pivotal center, that human reason required the aid of grace, one then treated the *loci* severally as radii of a dogmatic circle. It was scarcely noticed that, having bespoken for human reason the aid of divine grace, theological exposition proceeded with the critical precision and polemical vigor to which the unregenerate reason had long been accustomed.

The other way of relating intellectual knowledge to the knowledge of faith, the critical to the responding reason in theological inquiry, is the way of *system*. The accent here falls—as in Schleiermacher, for example—upon a clear demarcation of the presuppositions of theological inquiry from its doctrinal content, and upon an exposition of the Christian faith according to previously established principles with comprehensiveness and coherence. But to the precise question of the nature of the relation between the knowledge of reason and the knowledge of faith, systematic theology has proposed no unambiguous answer. The tendency has been either to reduce the cognitive factor in faith so considerably as virtually to eliminate it, or to replace the previously adopted hierarchical or symmetrical relation between faith and reason by a dialectical one.

Let me, this afternoon however, venture to pick up a previously suggested but insufficiently considered clue to a further possibility. This possibility would seem to be at once more viable, and more germane, both to what is going on in the act of knowledge and in the particular kind of knowledge with which theology is concerned. The clue is that in theology, rational knowledge, and the knowledge of faith, critical and responding reason, are effectively and fruitfully related when theological inquiry proceeds contextually.

When the Protestant Reformation was getting under way, and its formative thinkers took up the task of theology, they set out from the conviction that theology is not deprived of the fullest resources of the critical reason when the knowledge of faith is recognized as intrinsic to the rational exposition of truth. To be sure, the truth with which the Reformers were chiefly concerned was *Christian* truth. But, despite Luther's polemical diatribes upon the human reason and Calvin's unyielding insistence upon the darkness of the human mind, these Reformers were more deeply and constructively preoccupied with the mystery and the majesty of the context of reality within which the truth in Christ, and the inquiry concerning the truth about humanity and the world, continually and critically occurred. *The Institutes of the Christian Religion* begin with a chapter which bears the superscription: "the knowledge of God and of ourselves is a thing to be conjoined and accordingly internally coherent."[7] Luther sets out the First Article of the Creed in striking allusion to the existential sobriety of the 139th Psalm. Says the Catechism: "This I mean, and believe, that I am God's creature, that is, that He has given me and uninterruptedly sustains body, soul and life and all my members ... Thus we are obligated on this account uninterruptedly to love, praise, and thank

Him."[8] Also, says the Psalm: "I will give thanks unto thee; for I am fearfully and wonderfully made; wonderful are thy works; and that my soul knoweth right well" (Psalm 139:14, RSV). Long before the sociologists of knowledge discerned and drew attention to the ideological factor in all reflective analysis and criticism, the Reformers set theological inquiry upon a contextual course. Along this course, the ways of God with humanity *in* the world, and the ways of humanity with God *and* the world, gave promise of being more fruitful of insight and understanding concerning how things really *are* and *operate*, than preoccupation with the Being of God or the being of humanity or of anything else in the world. Ontology is neither irrelevant nor unimportant. But ontology, like every other factor in theological knowledge, is subject to the steady pressure of a God who acts to create and to redeem, to establish and to renew.

A contextual theology is thus not embarrassed by the ideological factor in its analyses. On the contrary, a contextual theology welcomes its involvement in a dynamic theater of reality and in a point of view. Such an involvement serves on the one hand, as a limitation that prevents theology from oracular pretensions, and on the other hand, as a liberation of theology to take unlimited account both responses of reason to the knowledge of faith and of the critical function of reason in clarifying and correcting the relations between the knowledge of faith and non-theological knowledge about humanity and the world. A contextual theology lacks the neat precision of the hierarchical or symmetrical order of traditional dogmatics. It lacks, also, the orderly coherences of systematic theology. A contextual theology is, however, always prepared to be upset by the jagged edge of some noetic perpendicular by which its analyses are shattered and in consequence of which the pieces and patterns of a theological account of what is going on in the world must be picked up and put together again. This means that theological knowledge, like non-theological knowledge, and like faith itself, is always under the excitement of change and on the threshold of some fresh apprehension of truth.

THE CONTEXTUAL STRUCTURE OF THEOLOGY

If then, theology may be said to be chiefly contextual, rather than dogmatic or systematic, in character, what of the context with which and within which theology works? The lessons from the Scriptures which have been read for us supply the answer to this question, and with characteristic biblical vitality and concreteness:

> Hear, O Israel: the Lord your God is one Lord; and you shall love the Lord your God with all your heart, and with all your soul and with all your might . . . And when the Lord your God brings you into the land which he swore to your

fathers, to Abraham, to Isaac, and to Jacob, to give you . . . then, take heed lest you forget the Lord . . . When your son asks you in time to come, 'What is the meaning of the testimonies and the statutes and the ordinances which the Lord our God has commanded you?' then you shall say to your son, 'We were Pharaoh's slaves in Egypt; and the Lord brought us out of Egypt with a mighty hand . . . and he brought us out from there that he might bring us in and give us the land which he swore to give to our fathers . . . And the Lord commanded us to do all these statutes, to fear the Lord our God, for our good always, that he might preserve us alive, as at this day (Dt. 6: 4, 10, 12, 20, 21, 24, RSV).

Praise be to God for giving us every possible spiritual benefit in Christ! For consider what He has done—before the foundation of the world He chose us to become, in Christ, His holy and blameless children living within His constant care . . . It is through the son, at the cost of His own blood, that we are redeemed, freely forgiven through that full and generous grace which has overflowed into our lives and opened our eyes to the truth. For God has allowed us to know the secret of His plan, and it is this: He purposes in His sovereign will that all human history shall be consummated in Christ, that everything that exists in Heaven or earth shall find its perfection and fulfillment in Him. And here is the staggering thing—that in all which will one day belong to Him we have been promised a share . . . Live life, then, with a due sense of responsibility, not as men who do not know the meaning and purpose of life but as *those who do* (Eph. 1: 3, 4, 7–12; 5: 15, Phillips translation).

Surely these words point to nothing so much as to a contextual account of the divine activity. There is the accent upon the historical self-disclosure of God in revelatory instruction and action, apprehended in and confirmed by the historical destiny of a particular people. There is the accent upon a pivotal center of meaning and fulfillment in an historical person who bears within the self and in action among others and their contemporaries, the secret of personal, community and cosmic existence and fulfillment. Christ, in another New Testament phrase, is "the wisdom of God" and "the power of God" (1 Cor. 1:24, RSV). There is the accent upon the participation of a community of faith in the historical activity of God and in the redemptive disclosure of human and cosmic meaning and consummation. And there is the accent upon the possibility and the power to live responsibly and to make sense out of life until the days of our years shall be filled up with all the fullness of God.

It *is* perhaps possible, then, to understand that the clue to the contextual character of theological inquiry is a single gift of the Reformation to the Christian Church and to the enterprise of human inquiry with which the University is pre-eminently concerned. The Reformers' incisive discernment of the inner structure of biblical experience and faith seems almost naturally to have pointed them towards an intrinsic theological method and structure.

The concreteness, dynamics, and direction of the biblical apprehension of divine activity in the world provide theology with the structural materials for the doing of its work. A contextual theology has, therefore, chiefly to do with the self-disclosure of God to which faith responds and from which human reason fruitfully undertakes its critical task. A contextual theology has to do with an on-going community of faith and life and with the whole compass and corpus of the goings on in heaven and in earth.

It *is*, therefore, expedient in consideration of the spirit of the age that a minister should be a theologian. And we, who are assembled together today to undertake another year of theological responsibility and inquiry are well met in this University if we keep our hearts and minds *fixed upon* and *flexible* in him who is the pivotal center of all learning and life. "For the Time Being," as Mr. W. H. Auden has put it:

> By the event of this birth the true significance of all other events is defined, for of every other occasion it can be said that it could have been different, but of this birth it is the case that it could in no way be other than it is. And by the existence of this Child, the proper value of all other existence is given, for of every other creature it can be said that it has extrinsic importance but of this Child it is the case that He is in no sense a symbol . . . For the Truth is indeed One, without which is no salvation, but the possibilities of real knowledge are as many as are the creatures in the very real and most exciting universe that God creates with and for His love . . . And because of His visitation, we may no longer desire God as if He were lacking: our redemption is no longer a question of pursuit but of surrender to Him who is always and everywhere present. Therefore at every moment we pray that following Him, we may depart from our anxiety into His peace.[9]

NOTES

1. Convocation address delivered at Harvard Divinity School, September 26, 1956. Published in *Harvard Divinity Bulletin* 22 (1957): 61–73; reprinted with permission. Copyright 1957 The President and Fellows of Harvard College.

2. George Williams, ed. *The Harvard Divinity School: Its Place in Harvard University and in American Culture* (Boston: The Beacon Press, 1954), 63–64.

3. Williams, *The Harvard Divinity School*, 84.

4. [Editorial: No citation for Peabody's remarks is provided in the original essay.]

5. Fyodor Dostoevsky, *The Brothers Karamazov* (New York: Grosset and Dunlap, 1957), 114–15.

6. γνωση is, however, also used in the New Testament in the sense of saving knowledge; in Hellenistic Greek, the terms appear to be fluid, and even interchangeable.

7. [Editorial: John Calvin, *Institutes of the Christian Religion*, I.1, ed. John T. McNeil, trans. Ford Lewis Battles, Library of Christian Classics, vol. 20 (Philadelphia: Westminster Press, 1960).]

8. Martin Luther, *Der Große Katechismus*, WA, 30.1.I, 183–84; translation Lehmann's.

9. W H. Auden, "For the Time Being, a Christmas Oratorio," in *The Collected Poetry of W. H. Auden* (New York: Random House, 1945), 451–52, 454.

Chapter 4

The Formative Power of Particularity (1963)[1]

The tasks and opportunities that are about to be entrusted to me are at once solemn and exciting. They are solemn because they are laden with the edifying heritage of this Seminary and with its ever-enlarging involvement in the life and witness of the Christian Church in the world and around the world. The exalted vision of the founders of this institution was, to be sure, not shared by them alone. Yet they combined their dedication to the ideal of "sound learning and true piety" with a resourceful insistence upon a continuing place in the Church and in this city where this ideal could take persuasive shape. I still recall how movingly the paragraph in the Seminary's charter which preserves to posterity this vision and resourcefulness, spoke to my condition of uncertain faith and unripe doubt when I first heard it as a Junior in James Chapel in 1927. I did not know then, of course, how completely my own "pilgrimage of faith" was to be marked and sustained by that vision, then exhibited in this place, and by my teachers. Since then, just as always before, students have come and continue to come, with uncertain faith and unripe doubt into this environment, set aside in the providence of God and the confusion of humanity, for the cultivation of sound learning and true piety. Thus, one can only endeavor to keep faith with one's teachers, one's colleagues, and one's students. This is a solemn endeavor.

But the tasks and opportunities are also exciting. The warmth of the welcome offered by President and Mrs. Van Dusen, Dean and Mrs. Bennett, and the members of the faculty and administration is not only greatly appreciated by my family and me, but also promises a sustaining resource for the doing of theology in this community of faith and learning. Theology, like faith itself, involves risks. And when one can take theological risks in the confidence that if one should go too far or go astray, one is certain to hear about it in a friendly but not uncertain way; one is expectantly, in Pascal's metaphor, "embarked" and free for "the wager" with its infinite range of loss and gain. It is to this excitement of doing theology that I should like to invite your attention on this occasion, an excitement occasioned by the characteristic risk of doing theology at all.

THE RISK OF PARTICULARITY

The excitement of theology is rooted in its functional character. Christian faith and thought were aware long before John Dewey that we learn by doing. "He who does what is true comes to the light," says the Fourth Gospel (3:21). "If we *walk* in the light, as he is in the light, we have fellowship with one another . . . " (1 John 1:7; italics mine). But the excitement of theology is the excitement neither of enthusiasm nor of melodrama. Theology does not arouse the feelings. It exacts the discipline of a claim. Theology does not inflate the pathos and the conflicts of a world of time and space and things and people. It steadfastly adheres to the task of explicating an event that has changed the face of reality, and the bearing of this event upon the human condition, upon humanity in itself and in the social and natural world of which one is a part. "For the same God who said, 'Out of darkness let light shine,' has caused his light to shine within us, to give the light of revelation—the revelation of the glory of God in the face of Jesus Christ . . . When anyone is united to Christ there is a new world; the old order has gone, and a new order has already begun" (2 Cor. 4:6, 5:17; NEB). The excitement of theology is compounded of the embarrassment and the expectation arising from its involvement in this kind of world. Pascal has exposed the risk of this involvement with singular accuracy and force. He saw that the embarrassment and expectation of theology were intrinsic to the peculiar genius of the Christian religion. It is understandable that Pascal's attempt to bring God together with the gaming table, cosmic infinity with the calculus of probabilities, should have relegated the "wager argument" to the periphery of theological reflection. Nevertheless, it has often seemed to me that in perpetuating this peripheral consideration of the wager, theologians have overlooked both a pivotal resource for the doing of theology as well as Pascal's principal concern.

The wager, you will recall, states that when there is the finite to stake in a game of chance, where there are equal risks of gain and of loss, and the infinite to gain—then, the infinite gain is worth the risk, because if you lose you lose nothing, since without the risk you could not have gained infinity anyway. "There is here," Pascal wrote, "an infinity of an infinitely happy life to gain, a chance of gain against a finite number of chances of loss, and what you stake is finite . . . If you gain, you gain all; if you lose, you lose nothing. Wager, then, without hesitation that He [God] is."[2] We need not linger over the mathematics of the matter, even if we could work them out, since

Pascal's real concern lies elsewhere. It lies with what he sometimes calls "the Christian faith," and sometimes, "the Christian religion." This faith, this religion, he says:

> teaches men these two truths; that there is a God whom men can know, and that there is a corruption in their nature which renders them unworthy of Him. It is equally important to men to know God without knowing his own wretchedness, and to know his own wretchedness without knowing the Redeemer who can free him from it. The knowledge of only one of these points gives rise either to the pride of the philosophers, who have known God, and not their own wretchedness, but not the Redeemer.

"And," Pascal continues:

> as it is alike necessary to man to know these two points, so is it alike merciful of God to have made us know them. The Christian religion does this; it is in this that it consists. Let us herein examine the order of the world, and see if all things do not tend to establish these two chief points of this religion: Jesus Christ is the end of all, and the centre to which all tends. Whoever knows Him knows the reason of everything.[3]

The risk of theology is the wager that "Jesus Christ is the end of all, and the centre to which all tends." It is the risk that "Whoever knows Him knows the reason of everything." "When anyone is united to Christ, there is a new world; the old order is gone, and a new order has already begun." Pascal, like Paul and Luther and Calvin before him, and like Kierkegaard after him, understood the doing of theology in terms of the risk of this particularity. Hesitant neither before its embarrassment nor about its expectation—they wagered!

If, then, the excitement of theology is rooted in its functional character, the function of theology may be defined as the expository and critical responsibility for the risk of particularity. Let us try to understand what this risk involves by noting briefly its phenomenological occasion and its formative power.

THEOLOGY IN CONTEXT

Christian theology occurs in a specific setting. This is why—to use a familiar distinction—theology is a *practical* not a *speculative* discipline. But this distinction is misleading. It is misleading partly because doing theology has led to a differentiation within theology itself between practical theology, on the one hand, and biblical, historical, and dogmatic (or systematic, or constructive) theology on the other. These differences used to be clear and precise. But they have been steadily loosening up until in our time what used to be called "theological encyclopedics" has not only disappeared altogether but has left a considerable confusion in its wake. To this point, we shall briefly return.

Meanwhile, let us note another sense in which theology as a practical discipline and theology as a speculative discipline is misleading. This distinction presupposes two uses of human reason—the one oriented toward metaphysics, the other toward ethics. Theology involves the reason as fully as does any other reflective activity; that is, theology is a *science*. But the use of the reason in theology is *responsive* not *reflexive*. Theology is not concerned with reason in the act of thinking about itself, about the structure of the mind, or about the laws of thought. Theology is concerned instead with reason in the act of responding to a limiting condition of a quite particular kind. It is, therefore, more accurate to contrast theology as a *functional* discipline with theology as a *speculative* discipline. Theology goes on in a specific context of occurrences and relationships. Its task is to expound the nature and meaning of this context. Its task is also to criticize its own formulations in the light of this context and to bring its findings critically to bear upon alternative ways of understanding and interpreting; in Pascal's phrase, "the reason of everything."

The theologians of the nineteenth century were not, of course, the first to "do theology" with reference to the context of theology. But theological reflection from Schleiermacher to Ritschl must be credited with the permanent achievement of having discerned the fundamental incompatibility between speculative theology and Christian theology. Speculative theology ignores the fact that Christian theology is by definition a response to, a function of, a concrete context. Christian theology is an analytical and descriptive science, not a deductive and propositional science. This does not mean that theology must avoid propositions and aim at the most adequate systematic arrangement of paragraphs. It means rather that the dogmatic character of theology is not identical with a propositional form and that a systematic theology may also be a dogmatic theology. Whether theology should take a dogmatic-systematic form, or a systematic, non-dogmatic form depends upon the adequacy of either form to the descriptive character of theology. Schleiermacher's *Christian Faith* and Karl Barth's *Church Dogmatics* are not usually regarded as similar. But as regards theological form, they are instructively similar; especially so, when compared to the *Systematic Theology* of Paul Tillich or the recently published, remarkable combination of Christian faith with Christian thought, the Gifford Lectures of 1961–62 by the late Principal of New College, Edinburgh, and my own beloved teacher in this Seminary, John Baillie.[4]

In rejecting speculative theology, the theologians of the nineteenth century were also aware of a response on their part to an authentic impulse of the Reformation that endeavored to create a living bond between theology and faith. "Protestantism as a religious movement," wrote Professor H. Richard Niebuhr, in what has to the loss and sadness of us all become his last published volume, "has not sought to convince a speculative, detached mind of the existence of God, but has begun with actual moral and religious experience, with the practical reasoning of the existing person rather than with the speculative interests of a detached mind."[5] Faith was, indeed, as Luther energetically put it, "a mighty, active, restless, busy thing."[6] It involved the whole person of the believer in what God in Jesus Christ had unmistakably been pleased to do, and was doing. It is this "knowledge of God," in Calvin's phrase, which belongs intrinsically to faith and instrumentally to reason, since reason is the divinely appointed means whereby the knowledge of faith achieves expository clarity and critical power. The distinction between "saving-knowledge," and "scientific knowledge," between "faith-knowledge" and "truth-knowledge," between "value-judgments" and "judgments of fact" is not only a post-Reformation distinction but misses altogether what the Reformers were presupposing when they managed so lively a connection between theology and faith.

Professor John McNeill has pointed out that the Reformers were zealous above all things for the holy, catholic church, for the *congregatio fidelium* [community of faith], for the communion of saints. The church was the context of their believing and their thinking, and thus, of their doing theology. This context protected them against speculation and provided them with a lively sensitivity to the phenomenology of God's activity and of humanity's involvement in what God was and is doing in the world. Harnack rightly warned against the perils of speculation through his epigrammatic characterization of Christian Gnosticism as "the acute secularization of Christianity."[7] But, if we may venture a paraphrase, Harnack was perhaps too careless about leaving the impression that "dogma is the acute Hellenization of Christianity"; that is, that the theological concern for dogma is less intrinsic to the community of faith than it actually is and that this concern cannot be pursued without succumbing to the perils of speculation. In leaving this impression, Harnack was closer to Ritschl than he was to Schleiermacher. But the consequence of this carelessness was that it obscured the nineteenth century accent upon the significance of the Christian community for the doing of theology. In substituting systematic theology for dogmatic theology, the nineteenth century theologians failed to notice that they were merely exchanging philosophical contexts. Consequently, theological energies were drawn off into a critical and apologetic enterprise that lacked sufficient expository substance and power. The vaunted rejection of metaphysics was proper enough. But the "historical Jesus," whose religious self-consciousness and whose consciousness of value were prototypes of the meaning and truth of Christianity, was inadequate to sustain these substitutionary claims. Jesus Christ was, indeed, "the end of all, and the centre to which all tends. Whoever [knew] Him [knew] the reason of everything."[8] But the reason lacked formative power. The risk of particularity had lost its Archimedean force.

Since then, we have learned to put the "reason" in reverse. We have learned that the "historical Jesus" does not carry the Christian community to us but, conversely, the Christian community carries us to the "historical Jesus." More accurately, we arrive at some reasonable facsimile thereof. This is one of the major embarrassments in which the risk of particularity involves us. Before taking up this embarrassment, we must underline the point that the reversal of the sense in which "Jesus Christ is the reason of everything" has made us less sure even than the nineteenth century theologians were that he really is "the end of all, and the centre to which all tends."

THE APOSTOLIC CHARACTER OF THEOLOGY

The way out of the present quagmire of uncertainty is to deal more frankly and more boldly with the risk of particularity than we have been wont to do since the creative impulse came to theology with the Reformation and until the *Kirchliche Dogmatik* [Karl Barth, *Church Dogmatics*] helped us to take note of it once more. The apostolic dimension has dropped out of theology and must be restored to it again. This apostolic dimension informed the earliest theological impulse of Christianity and its earliest impact upon an alien and unavoidable culture. It was never unalloyed, but it was not, on that account, less unmistakable. As Harnack has put it:

> An important part of primitive Christianity was rescued by the conserving force of tradition (faith in the Creator and Redeemer God), but men speculated all the more freely about the world and its wisdom, since they believed that they possessed in the *apostolic* Scriptures, in the *apostolic* creed, in the *apostolic* office, the definite assurance of what is "Christian" . . . In the apologetic theology Christianity is conceived as a religious development brought about by God himself and corresponding to the primitive condition of man and placed in the sharpest contrast with all polytheistic national religions and ceremonial observances . . . The whole positive material of Christianity, however, was transformed into a great *scheme of evidence*; religion did not obtain its content from historical facts—it received it from Divine revelation, which is self-witnessing in the creature-reason and freedom of mankind—but the historical facts serve for the *attestation* of religion, for its *elucidation*, as against its partial obscuration, and for its *universal* spreading.[9]

What is instructive about this account is its stress upon the evidential character of the apostolic substance of Christian faith and thought and life.

Theological exposition and criticism are a function of this apostolic concreteness. Christian theology goes on in this quite phenomenological context.

We are not urging a return to or a reduplication of first and second century theology. This is not only impossible; it is unnecessary. It is unnecessary because the apostolic dimension of theology has formative power as well as phenomenological concreteness. Indeed, this concreteness is the locus of the power. That this is so, is the risk of particularity under which Christian theology properly goes on. Since "phenomenology" is a term currently applied to a philosophical movement, it may be noted in passing that we are not using the word in that sense. What we have in mind is the obvious evidential setting in which Christian theology has always been done, of which theology is an intrinsic, expository, and critical function. This setting consists of a community, a kerygma, a canon, a dogmatic configuration—and above all—a revelatory phenomenon, identified with Jesus of Nazareth, identified as Jesus Christ. In dynamic and dialectical relation with this revelatory action of God, these other concrete phenomena become theologically luminous. Apart from this revelatory action of God, these other concrete phenomena are theologically unimportant. Indeed, apart from this revelatory action of God, Jesus Christ himself is theologically unimportant. He has a tenuous even capricious relation to "the reason of everything," and thus, is really not important at all. "Many argue deeply about Christ," Calvin observed, in commenting upon John 1:45, which records that:

> Philip found Nathanael, and said to him, "We have found him of whom Moses in the law and also the prophets wrote, Jesus of Nazareth, the son of Joseph." . . . many argue deeply about Christ, but they get so subtle and involved that they can never find him. So it is with the papists who refuse to call Christ the son of Joseph. They are particular about his name: but they so empty him of his power, that in Christ's place, they have a ghost. Were it not better to babble crudely with Philip and hold on to the real Christ, rather than with clever and high-sounding talk end up with only a fiction? . . . However, we must seek pure knowledge from the Law and the Prophets, in order that we may not be driven away from Christ by falsehoods invented by men.[10]

THE EMBARRASSMENT OF PARTICULARITY

The formative power of theology in the formative power of Jesus Christ would be a pretentious claim if theology were not on the receiving end. There was a time when theology turned aside from its subservient function and assumed a royal prerogative in determining "the reason of everything." The resumption of this prerogative is happily excluded for good. However, the fear of such a resumption is quiescent rather than extinct. It lurks about sufficiently to deter a widespread hospitality to the formative power of particularity and to conceal the deeper hesitation. The hesitation concerns the embarrassment in which the risk of particularity involves the doing of theology. The expository and critical power available to a theology, which knows in Jesus Christ the reason of everything, seems to put such a theology not so much on the side of the "son of Joseph" but on the side of Joseph, the son of Jacob, whose dreams offended his brethren and brought to them confusion of face. "They hated him yet more for his dreams and for his words" (Gen. 37:8). It did not matter then (at least not before the famine overtook the land) that Joseph was the bearer of the line of blessing whence came Jesus Christ himself. It is hard to see that it matters now. For now, as then, we are embarrassed by the risk of particularity, even when we are prepared to make it.

There are, perhaps, two major factors aggravating the embarrassment of theology today before the risk without which it cannot fulfill its proper function. The one factor is the collapse of literalism in theological interpretation; the other is an insistent historical skepticism about the factual core of the phenomenological context of theology. These are correlative factors, at least as regards their emergence and impact upon the doing of theology today. They are not, however, intrinsically correlative, since the apostolic dimension of theology was not originally as uncompromisingly literal as it afterward became, and since skepticism is not the necessary outcome of evidential historiography. Skepticism is simply the best that we have been able to achieve to date when we apply the tools and the canons of historical investigation to the phenomenological context of theology.

There is an almost paradisiacal wistfulness that overtakes the doing of theology today, a wistfulness for the naive literalism which provided a relatively easy passage to and fro between the early memories and the documentary attestation of the factual core of the apostolic dimension of theology and the language of theological statements. One can observe this easy passage, for example, in the earliest attempts to state the sense in which "Jesus Christ is the end of all, and the centre to which all tends . . . the reason of everything." "The Gentile Christians," says Harnack, "possessed in the full eschatological traditions valuable reminiscences of the original apprehension of the Person of Jesus."[11] These "eschatological traditions" never claimed to exhibit a one-to-one correlation between the empirically verifiable data concerning Jesus of Nazareth and the messianic convictions and associations that clustered about him. Harnack goes so far as to say that "this title given to Jesus ('Christ') became indeed a mere name, since there was no real knowledge of the meaning of 'Messiah.'"[12] Since that was written, New Testament scholarship, especially with Bultmann's help, appears to have filled in the picture somewhat. But the basic skeptical hiatus between Jesus and the title seems to have altered little in half a century. These early Gentile Christians had not learned, of course, to deal mythologically with their "eschatological traditions." In the absence of a way to "demythologize," they cast about among their Old Testament texts and recollections for a link between the "real" Jesus and their apprehension of the Person of Jesus. They moved, if Harnack is correct, in two main directions. They took an adoptionist line which affirmed that Jesus was the one whom God had chosen and in whom the Spirit of God, and later the Godhead itself dwelt. Or they took a pneumatic line which affirmed that Jesus was a heavenly spiritual Being (the highest Being next to God) who became incarnate and after the completion of his work on earth returned to the heavens.[13] But in either case, it was easier then, than now, to keep hold of the fundamental point that Jesus of Nazareth must be *thought* of as ὡς περὶ θεοῦ (as from God), a phrase from II Clement, because he was ὡς περὶ θεοῦ. "In this phrasing of it," says Harnack, "the indirect *theologia Christi, in regard to which there was no wavering* found expression in classical forms."[14] It is the wavering that has increased in the meantime. And this is why one sometimes longs for the earlier conversance with the apostolic dimension of theological exposition and criticism. Without the expository power formed by and derived from the risk of this particularity, it is difficult to see how the critical rejection first of Docetism and later of Gnosticism could have been managed.

A similarly easy passage from the early memories and the documentary attestation of the factual core of the apostolic dimension of theology to the language of theological statements can be observed in the sub-apostolic use of the Old Testament and of the apostolic preaching, and in the subsequent emergence of the *regula fidei* [rule of faith]. The point in each case is that the doing of theology could count upon a naive literalism about the factual core of theological reflection that is simply lost to us today. This *naive* literalism was not completely invulnerable against the distortions of a *crude* literalism. But crude literalism never dominated the formation of Christian theology. As for us, however, crude literalism, both of a biblical and of a dogmatic kind, has so stubbornly and stridently afflicted our immediate theological past as to have deprived us of the courage to take the risk of particularity in spite of our embarrassment.

The displacement of naive literalism by crude literalism, of the knowledge of faith with the knowledge of inerrancy, in the doing of theology has collapsed of its own dead weight. The collapse has been hastened, however, by an insistent historical skepticism. The special importance of this skepticism for the expository and critical task of theology is that it is informed by a concern for the integrity of the knowledge of faith, not poised against that integrity. Whatever the substance and the prospects of a naive literalism may be, they can be neither pursued nor pressed in disregard of the data and the canons of historical evidence. The solemn fact is that the most embarrassing thing about the risk of particularity in the doing of theology today is that there is no evidential certainty about the particularity with reference to which the risk is to be taken. The faith of the community of faith is, perhaps, as full of eschatological traditions as it ever was. But when all the demythologizing has been done, the hard core of fact has eluded us and we find ourselves upon the abyss of historical skepticism. How can we speak of a hard core of fact, if this one fact is ultimately immune to the processes and conclusions of historical investigation and verifiability to which all other facts are subject? On the other hand, how can we avoid the really terrifying dilemma—terrifying both because we are embarked, and because too much has been given us to know about the reasons for everything without conducting us to "the reason of everything"—how can we avoid the terrifying dilemma between the surrender of the hard core of apostolic fact to historical skepticism or surrendering historical integrity to a leap of faith?

With Kierkegaard's melancholy candor, we are compelled to face the question: how can I affirm my existence as an individual? The pathos of this embarrassment emerges when we consider that even when theology draws back from the conclusion that it really would make no difference to Christian faith and life if it should be established historically that Jesus never lived, it seems to possess only the feeblest resources for dealing (with expository and critical power) with the difference it does make that Jesus did live. It does no discredit either to Bultmann or to Kierkegaard to recognize in their efforts to transcend the skepticism to which historical integrity points, the peril of variant existentialist transformations of the apostolic dimension of the particularity which theology must risk. The thesis that Christianity is *philosophy* and *revelation* has been expounded before.[15] Optimum mythological precision about the kerygma or indirect communication, or both—this simply is as far as we can see today through the embarrassment that has overtaken our theological responsibility for the wager that "Jesus Christ is the end of all, and the centre to which all tends . . . the reason of everything."[16]

The Expectation of Particularity

To return to Calvin's reflections upon the fourth gospel, let us hear again what he said to his students about John 6:27 and 10:30. The text says: "Do not labor for the food which perishes, but for the food which endures to eternal life, which the Son of man will give to you; for on him has God the Father set his seal . . . I and the Father are one." "The ancient fathers," says Calvin:

> tortured and misused this verse in order to prove the divine essence of Christ; as though sealed here meant that Christ bore the stamp of the Father. But he speaks

here, not subtly of his eternal essence but of his mandate and mission on our behalf, and of what we are to hope and expect from him. By an apt metaphor, he refers to the ancient custom of sealing with a ring, which made an agreement authoritative and binding. Christ's intention is to declare that . . . it is not for everybody to feed souls with incorruptible food, when Christ comes forth with the promise of so great a blessing . . . He sets out to meet the mockery of the wicked, who claimed that he was in no position to protect his disciples, since he did not possess God's power. He, therefore, testifies that His business and the Father's are one; which means that the Father will not deny his help to him or to his sheep. The ancient fathers misused this verse when they brought it up as proof that Christ is (of one essence) with the Father. Christ is not here arguing that he is one substance with the Father, but that he is of one mind with him; which means that whatever Christ does has behind it the power of God . . . he is our leader not in order to raise us to the sun or to the moon, but to unite us with God the Father.[17]

The risk of particularity that Christian theology must wager is not only confronted by an embarrassment but accompanied by an expectation. The expectation is the promise of the power of God. As Christ bore the stamp of God, so this power is sealed to him, and authoritative and binding upon all who are fed by Christ with incorruptible food. From this expectation, the formative power of particularity is derived. Owing to this expectation, in the formative power of particularity Christian theology receives both expository form and critical power. The risk of particularity in the power of particularity is the mandate of Christ through which the apostolic dimension and apostolic character are restored to theology. Let me conclude with three brief hints of what this restoration involves.

The first concerns the embarrassment that we have just noted. I should like to suggest that the apostolic dimension of doing theology requires a resumption of the *naive* literalism of early Christianity.[18] This does not mean a return to primitivism. It means instead an expository integrity toward the original and originating revelatory phenomenon, not merely *called* Jesus Christ but actual and concrete in him. This phenomenon is not simply a presupposition of theological reflection and interpretation. This phenomenon is the one critical surrender of the neutral to the personal in the arcanum of historical investigation and verification. This phenomenon, a naive literalism may be allowed to insist, is a He who is "the end of all, the center to which all tends . . . the reason of everything." The boundary of skepticism on which Bultmann and Kierkegaard have left us is drawn from their side as they view the other side. The apostolic conviction is that Jesus Christ Himself draws the boundary, in drawing which, He draws us from our side to His. The knowledge of faith at the disposal of theology is not the content of a leap of faith, not the mythological residuum of form-critical inquiry. The knowledge of faith is rather the knowledge received in the power of the Spirit, whereby we cry, "'Abba! Father!' bearing witness . . . that we are children of God" (Rom. 8:15–16). What is naive about this realism is neither its innocence nor its ignorance but its sensitivity to "a new order . . . already begun." Despite the frenzy of the Calvinists, and even Calvin's own sometimes too consistent doing of theology, this sensitivity is really the heart and the point of his doctrine of election. For "what is the end of election," he asks, "but that being adopted as children by our heavenly Father, we may by his favor obtain salvation and immortality? . . . Christ, therefore, is the mirror, in which it behooves us to contemplate our election; and here we may do it with safety."[19] Through this *speculum*, Calvin was able to view the whole *spectrum* of human affairs and demonstrate the sense and the power of Jesus Christ, the reason of everything.

The second hint concerns the role of theology, with its apostolic dimension restored, in the enterprise of theological education. Earlier, we alluded to the misleading character of the distinction between *practical* and *speculative* theology. Under the formative power of particularity, *practical* theology becomes significant once more, not in contrast to *speculative* theology, but in implementing the expository and critical substance of theology in the witness and the structure of the congregation of believers as a concrete and visible church of Jesus Christ. And not only so, I should like also to suggest, that the apostolic dimension of doing theology returns what may be called dogmatic, or systematic, or constructive theology to an integrating position in the theological curriculum. This is a modest, not a manipulative role. But it is also a clear and vocational role. In the present state of theological science, the exercise of this role may well be the firm but unobtrusively prophetic one of reminding the exegetical, historical and practical disciplines of theology that Jesus Christ is the reason of everything and that the time is long overdue for abandoning the giving of hostages to fortune.

And finally, the expository substance of theology, shaped by its restored apostolic character, provides the doing of theology with critical and catalytic power. Theology is not the queen but the servant of the sciences. As the servant of the sciences, however, theology is not their slave but their critic. Not least among the functions that accrue to theology in the formative power of particularity is the one which for his own reasons and in another time, Socrates reserved for philosophy. Theology is the true midwife whose service attends the birth-traumas of the messianic liberation and transformation of the whole enterprise of humanity for the chief end of humanity, the glory of God. The time is also long overdue for theology to assume its servant-critical function through which all the sciences may be summoned once again to their authentic humanistic occasion and promise. The fact is that Jesus Christ has changed the face of reality. He is the reason of everything. "He is our leader, not in order to raise us to the sun or to the moon, but to unite us with God the Father."

As even some of [our] poets have said:

> Jehovah buried, Satan dead,
> do fearers worship Much and Quick;
> badness not being felt as bad,
> itself thinks goodness what is meek;
> obey says toc, submit says tic,
> Eternity's a Five Year Plan:
> if Joy with Pain shall hang in hock
> who dares to call himself a man?
> . . . .
> King Christ, this world is all aleak;
> and life preservers there are none:
> and waves which only He may walk
> Who dares to call Himself a man (Acts 17:28).[20]

NOTES

1. Delivered as Lehmann's inaugural lecture as Auburn Professor of Systematic Theology at Union Theological Seminary in New York. Published in *Union Seminary Quarterly Review* 18, no. 3.2 (1963): 306–19; reprinted with permission.
2. Blaise Pascal, *Pensées*, trans. W. B. Trotter (New York: E. P. Dutton & Co, 1931), Fragment 233.
3. Pascal, *Pensées*, fragment 555.
4. John Baillie, *The Sense of the Presence of God* (New York: Charles Scribner's Sons, 1962).
5. H. Richard Niebuhr, *Radical Monotheism and Christian Faith* (New York: Harper and Brothers, 1960), 116.
6. Martin Luther, "A Sermon on the Manner of Unrighteousness," Lk. 16:1 ff., 17 August 1522. WA, 10.3, 285.
7. Adolf von Harnack, *Outlines of the History of Dogma* (Boston: The Beacon Press, 1957), 58.
8. Pascal, *Pensées*, fragment 555.
9. Harnack, *Outlines*, 81, 118.
10. John Calvin, *Commentaries*, ed. Joseph Haroutunian, trans. Louise Pettibone Smith, The Library of Christian Classics, vol. 23, (London: The Westminster Press, 1958), 159.
11. Harnack, *Outlines*, 50.
12. Harnack, *Outlines*, 50.
13. Harnack, *Outlines*, 50–51.
14. Harnack, *Outlines*, 51. Italics, Harnack's.
15. Harnack, *Outlines*, 120.

16. [Editorial: Blaise Pascal, *Pensées*, Section 8. Available online: https://ccel.org/ccel/pascal/pensees/pensees.ix.html.]

17. Calvin, *Commentaries*, 159–61.

18. Perhaps one could say, *naive realism*. This involves philosophical associations which require clarification, just as *naive literalism* involves literalistic associations from which the present usage must be sharply distinguished. Since we are dealing with the scriptural focus of theological reflection, we shall adopt the phrase, *naive literalism*, without excluding the possible appropriateness of *naive realism*. We wish to stress the self-evidence with which in the New Testament, the revelatory actuality of Jesus Christ was recognized and related to ordinary and ultimate experience in and of the world. It is this self-evidence which is so difficult for us to understand and to employ today. The expository and critical interpretation of this self-evidence is a primary task of systematic theology.

19. John Calvin, *Institutes of the Christian Religion*, book 3, trans. Allen (London: The Westminster Press, 1813), 24–25.

20. Copyright, 1935, by e. e., Cummings. Reprinted from his volume *Poems 1923–1954* by permission of Harcourt, Brace & World, Inc.

Chapter 5

The Dynamics of Reformation Ethics (1950)[1]

The appointment with which I have been formally entrusted today, I accept, in trust, as a privilege and as an opportunity. The privilege is that of living and working in the heritage and fellowship of faith and learning of Princeton Seminary. The opportunity is the task of growing in and applying myself to the heritage and fellowship of this Seminary as to enlarge, enliven, and engrave the impact of Christian faith and truth upon the shape of things to come.

I

The shape of things to come is never the same. The responsibility for and toward the future is determined by the frontiers of the present. This is the unique disclosure and vitality of Christian faith and truth. To believe that God in Christ is Father, Son, and Holy Spirit, and that this faith is at once the key to the meaning of the Bible and the clue to the knowledge of the truth about reality and about society—to believe this is far from accepting a mere theological formula or mouthing an empty creed. The Trinitarian faith of the Church, as the late professor Charles Cochrane has brilliantly shown,[2] provided the terms in which the disintegrating culture and politics of Graeco-Roman society found the basis and the possibility of reconstruction. In that day, the frontiers of the present were barricaded by the nemesis and the nonsense of blind chance. There hung over the shape of things to come the pall of paralyzing disillusionment because the confidence of the past in reason and in virtue had been discredited. In the last analysis, the collapse of Hellenism was due, in Mr. Gilbert Murray's fine and pathetic phrase, to "a failure of nerve." It is this failure of nerve that makes people unable and unwilling to trust the future and to insist, in consequence, upon freezing the status quo and justifying the present in terms of the outworn patterns of the past. Conduct has lost its dynamics, its δύναμις, to use the word that the Greeks had for it. People go on living, to be sure; but without the ethical framework and guidance that enable them to cope with social change.

But Christians are not so—Christians, that is, who have in fact, determined the shape of things to come. They have their own dynamics of conduct. It is the same Greek word, but it carries for Christians the overtones and the undertow of biblical experience. My colleagues in the Old and the New Testament will perhaps allow me to render this biblical δύναμις as *moving strength*. (If not, they will, unfortunately, have to see me outside). But if I am at all within the range of biblical lexicography, the point is that what happens in the world is the work of the *moving strength* of God. It is the moving strength of God that keeps the eyes of God's people fixed upon the future for God's next move. It is the moving strength of God that breaks in upon God's people with one event after another by which they are meant to be redeemed. To be redeemed in this world is to discern and to move across the line between the possibilities that are played out and those that are full of promise. It is the moving strength of God that anchored itself in Jesus Christ in one perpetual present wherein the future meets and fulfills the past by transforming it. Did he not himself declare that "no one who puts a hand to the plow and looks back is fit for the kingdom of God" (Lk. 9:62)? This, he said, to one who wanted to be his disciple without stopping to consider what was involved. And to those who knew only too well what was involved and conspired to put him to death, to them he said—when they tried to trap him between blasphemy and perjury—"ye shall see the Son of man sitting on the right hand of power (τῆς δυνάμεως), and coming in the clouds of heaven" (Mk. 14:62). It was this conviction of the presence and the power of God in Christ that prevented the Christians in the Graeco-Roman world from looking backward for the evidence of God, as though God could be established as an *inference* from reason and experience. Instead, they looked ahead. God was, for them, the *pre-supposition*, not the inference, of all reason and experience. Consequently, they fastened their eyes upon the shape of things to come in dedicated expectation of a fresh and purposeful manifestation of God's moving strength—the Spirit was executor. The doctrine of the Trinity carried the God of the Bible into the formative position in western cultural history. The triune God gave point to the future and politics made sense.

II

Politics is the science of the polis. So, Plato and Aristotle defined it. And while the word has, in modern times, undergone a certain semantic shrinkage, the classical conception and feeling for it still stands. For the polis is the ordered society of humanity. Its problems are still the problems of the terms and the arrangements by which people who, by nature cannot live alone, can live together. In a world of anarchic nation-states, the problems of politics may seem immeasurably more urgent and complex than in a world of rivalrous city-states. More complex, perhaps! But scarcely more urgent:

> They are adventurous beyond their power, and daring beyond their judgment . . . your wont is to attempt less than is justified by your power, to mistrust even what is sanctioned by your judgment . . . Further, there is promptitude on their side against procrastination on yours; they are never at home, you are never from it: for they hope by their absence to extend their acquisitions, you fear by your advance to endanger what you have left behind . . . To describe their character in a word, one might truly say that they were born into the world to take no rest themselves and to give none to others.[3]

Who are *they*? The Russians, according to the congressional record, reporting a major American foreign policy speech? Not at all. *They* are the Athenians, citizens of the paragon of all democracies, according to a speech in the Congress of the Peloponnesian Confederacy at Lacedaemon in 432 B.C., reported by Thucydides.[4] As for ourselves, as Mr. Lionel Trilling sees us, in our time there are only two parties—the party of the Party, whatever its political orientation, and the party of the Imagination: "Unless we insist . . . that politics is imagination and mind, we will learn that imagination and mind are politics, and of a kind that we will not like."[5]

Mr. Trilling's announced aim is borrowed from John Stuart Mill. It is—to "recall liberals to a sense of variousness and possibility."[6] But as though the fortunes of the ancient polis had no profounder lessons to teach, neither Mr. Trilling nor John Stuart Mill have recognized that political liberalism in their discerning and proper sense, is only consonant with Christian orthodoxy in the trinitarian sense. For this omission of theirs, trinitarian Christians must shoulder the lion's share of responsibility. Trinitarian Christians have deserted the ancient achievement of their faith, which was: to make meaningful room in the ordered society of humanity for "a sense of variousness and possibility." They have failed to express in word and in deed the fact that it is in open-ness and change—not in the status quo—that people are to discern the moving strength of God. They have failed to bear witness in faith and in obedience to the fact that the true order of human affairs in the world is a divine order. A divine order in human affairs is the integration of the premises and the institutions of social life so that responsibility for what is going on is continually exercised in the direction of self-criticism. Whenever in human affairs responsibility for what is going on is identified with self-justification, then disorder has become the order of the day.

There is a theological conception of order, which is essential to political life in the broad and basic sense in which we are speaking of it. What this theological conception of order is, I should like to define in terms suggested to me by one of my former students now about to be graduated from the Law School at Yale University. I asked her once, how, on the basis of her studies in theology, and of her studies and reflections upon the nature of law, she would define "order." And this is what she said: "Order is the necessity of so living in one moment, as not to destroy the possibility of the next." If law is the marrow of politics, theology is the breath of politics. And this is why and how Christian orthodoxy in the Trinitarian sense and political liberalism in the sense of order, at the disposal of variousness and possibility, belong together.

III

The disciplined reflection upon theological order: its presuppositions, its character, and its responsibilities—this is Applied Christianity, as a branch of theological learning. The emergence of the discipline, which has been entrusted to me in this Seminary, expresses both the uneasy conscience of the Protestant Reformation and the dynamics of Reformation ethics.

On September 27, 1871, the Reverend Charles Aiken, D.D., was inaugurated as Professor of Christian Ethics and Apologetics in Princeton Seminary. The appointment marked the response of the Board of Directors of the Seminary to a communication from the faculty. In order to underline the conviction of the Directors concerning the basic importance of this new chair, it bore the name of Archibald Alexander who, according to the minutes adopted at the time, "more than any other man, is entitled to be regarded as its (that is, the Seminary's) founder."[7] Professor Alexander's name was not long attached to the chair, nor indeed, was its original scope. By 1880, Apologetics was taken over by Professor Francis Patton under the aegis of the Stuart name and Christian Ethics was left to share Professor Aiken's attention with Oriental and Old Testament Languages and Literature. Princeton Seminary may be pardoned for certain ambivalence in steadying its new chair because at that time theological seminaries were not accustomed to Christian Ethics.

As far as I can discover, the first chair to be expressly named as a chair of Applied Christianity was founded as the Rand Chair at Iowa College in 1892. But Princeton's pioneering position in this matter is marked by the fact that it was the first theological seminary to establish a chair of Christian Ethics and to define the office of that chair in terms which later came to be designated as Applied Christianity. The moving spirit in this theological innovation was Stephen Colwell, Esquire of Philadelphia, and a trustee of the Seminary from 1854–71. The faculty communication declares:

> The design ... was to treat of the Religion of Christ in its bearing upon human society and the welfare of man in general, and, particularly, by developing the gospel law of charity or mutual love, to expound the duties which men owe to their fellow men, not only in their individual capacity, but organized and associated as churches, communities and nations. This subject was to be presented not only didactically but historically, by showing what the gospel has done to change the face of society and ameliorate the condition of man since its first introduction into the world.[8]

Stephen Colwell's writings fairly leap with the passion of this purpose, which was unmistakably the controlling passion of his life. Two things are remarkable about this adventure of Princeton Seminary in honoring his memory. The first is its apologetic setting; the second is its social aim. The initial connection of Christian ethics with apologetics was an unwitting confirmation of Stephen Colwell's judgment upon Protestantism. "Whilst we might dwell upon many triumphs of science, art, and industry, in Protestant countries," he wrote, "we feel bound to say that too great devotion to the pursuit of riches, to the increase of production and the extension of commerce, has been their chief characteristic."[9] Historians of the period are agreed and have further pointed out that Protestantism was becoming increasingly aware of losing its grip both upon the intellectuals, in their pursuit of science and philosophy, and upon the laboring people, increasingly restive under their lot in an industrial society. So, the seminaries set up courses in apologetics and ethics to prove that Christianity was both good for the truth and good for humankind.

But Stephen Colwell's concern was far more fundamental and far-sighted than that! His passion was "to change the face of society." The discernment and forthrightness of his insight has come to me, I frankly admit, with the full force of a discovery. For Colwell grasped the inherent dynamics of Reformation ethics and exposed the failure of the Reformation to be true to its ethical foundations. "The social, political, and commercial institutions of the present day," he declared, "founded upon, and sustained by, a selfishness heretofore unequaled, are the great barriers to the progress of Christianity."[10] And again, "the success of the Reformers ... was remarkable; but they were far from seizing and presenting the whole scope and spirit of Christianity ... It has been the duty of Protestants ever since, not only to vindicate constantly the great truths brought out at the Reformation, but constantly to extend and purify their knowledge; and whilst thus holding up the truth, to aim at a better fulfillment of the duties of Christianity."[11]

IV

To this task, and I pray, with faithfulness to the mind and the imagination of Stephen Colwell's vision, I devoutly dedicate my ministry in the Church of Jesus Christ from the chair in this Seminary, which bears Stephen Colwell's name!

Colwell rightly understood the revolutionary fact that when the Reformers exalted the gospel law of charity as the norm of Christian ethics, the moving strength of the triune God had burst afresh upon the world, requiring new terms of interpretation and action. As the Reformers saw it, the God of the Nicene Creed (the only undisputed ecumenical confession of the Christian Church) was at work in the world in the community of those who are justified by faith alone. Justification is the promise of the forgiveness of sins. The community of the justified is the community of those who, being reconciled to God, are reconciled to one another. Justification means that God is known and obeyed on the frontiers of every present; there, where the new possibilities of life for humanity "not only in their individual capacities but organized and associated as churches, communities, and nations," cut across the outworn patterns of the past.

The Reformers, as Troeltsch's monumental study has shown, were one with their predecessors in the medieval and in the ancient church in assuming the responsibility for a [Christian commonwealth]. They wanted and strove to conform the world to Christ. But the Reformers drew back from the dynamics of their own ethical foundations. Wearied perhaps by their polemics against Rome, they weakened before the threatened anarchy of Anabaptism and of the long-entrenched political and social pressures for a new society. In consequence, they barricaded the dynamics of the community of the justified behind the familiar but cracking bulwarks of an order that the moving strength of God had set aside. They fell back upon the ancient tradition of natural law and of the law and the institutions of Moses.

This retreat has bequeathed to us who are the heirs of the Reformation the great-unfinished task of Reformation ethics. It is the task of reflecting upon and applying the presuppositions, the character, and the responsibilities of theological order. The dynamics of Reformation ethics require an analysis of theological order according to which the moving strength of God is on the side of social change—social change, herald of "things which are not, to bring to nought things that are" (1 Cor. 1:28).

"Very many, it is well known," Stephen Colwell wrote:

> have no faith in moral or social progress; they regard all speculations in reference to social amelioration, as, at the best, mere visionary dreams, if not what is far worse, downright socialism. But let no friend of the human family be

deterred from any research, or inquiry, or speculation, looking to human advantage, by such narrowness of mind. Let him take the Gospels in his hand, and the light of all the other Scriptures, and he may go as far as his intelligence and knowledge of the world will carry him; and if he cannot secure the cooperation or approval of the Christian men of the present day, he will have the full sympathy of those who, having gone before, are observing the world from a point of view where nothing clouds their vision.[12]

NOTES

1. Published in *The Princeton Seminary Bulletin* 43, no. 4 (1950): 17–22; reprinted with permission.
2. Charles Cochrane, *Christianity and Classical Culture* (Oxford: Clarendon Press, 1940).
3. Thucydides, *The Peloponnesian War*, Modern Library Edition (Oxford: Oxford University Press, 1951), 40.
4. Thucydides, *Peloponnesian War*, 40.
5. Lionel Trilling, *The Liberal Imagination: Essays on Literature and Society* (New York: Doubleday Anchor Books, 1950), 100.
6. Trilling, *Liberal Imagination*, xiii.
7. Charles A. Aiken, *Addresses and Essays*, New York, 1871. Inauguration as Professor of Christian Ethics and Apologetics in Princeton Theological Seminary, 4. [Editorial: No additional bibliographic information is included in the original essay.]
8. Aiken, *Addresses and Essays*, 3.
9. Stephen Colwell, *New Themes for the Protestant Clergy* (Philadelphia: Lippincott, Grambo & Co., 1853), 124. [Editorial: For a brief description of Stephen Colwell and his work see Nancy J. Duff, "Steven Colwell," in *American Presbyterians: Journal of Presbyterian History* 66, no. 4 (1988): 254–59. Duff held the Stephen Colwell Chair of Christian Ethics at Princeton Theological Seminary from 2004 until she retired in 2020.]
10. Henry C. Carey, *A Memoir of Stephen Colwell* (Philadelphia: Collins, 1871), 24.
11. Colwell, *New Themes*, 115.
12. Stephen Colwell, *The Position of Christianity in the United States* (Philadelphia: Lippincott, Grambo & Co., 1854), 175.

Chapter 6

Barth and Brunner[1]

The Dilemma of the Protestant Mind (1940)

The current discussion between Karl Barth and Emil Brunner is more than a controversy between two able and conspicuous theologians. It concerns an issue of fundamental importance to Protestantism. Indeed, the polemical urgency of the debate arises from the concern of each of the theologians unless the other return Protestant thinking to a level which has already demonstrably destroyed the integrity of the mind of the Reformation. It is not too much to say that the debate is an exemplification of the historical dilemma of the Protestant mind.

I

The genius of the Reformation theology was its rigorously dialectical appraisal of the relations between God, on the one hand, and humanity and the world, on the other. As far as the world is concerned, this meant the repudiation of the doctrine of the self-evidence of God in the creation, as embodied, for example, in the traditional arguments, and the substitution of the conception of a God who is hidden as well as revealed in the creation. The tension between the *deus absconditus* [the hidden God] and the *deus revelatus* [the revealed God] was resolved by the sovereign witness of the Holy Spirit to the believer. Thus, the relations between God and humanity really governed the thinking of the reformers and, consequently, also their interpretation of God's relation to the world.

The tension between the hidden God and the revealed God appears in the practical experience of the believer in the tension between the law and the gospel. "What does it profit," Luther asks, "that you know that God exists, so long as you do not know how God is minded toward you?"[2] The question carries its own answer. The really significant factor in the relation between God, humanity, and the world is the relation between God and man [humans], and apart from the gospel of the forgiving love of God in Christ, this relation stands under the negative, alienating effect of the law. Every person knows that the question of God's existence is a distinctly secondary question as compared with the question of God's will. And every person knows, too, that one begins to ask seriously about God when one's own existence has lost its self-evident character, that is, when it has been overtaken by the frustration of disobedience. Hence, Luther so often reckons the law along with death and the devil among the instruments of divine wrath, which are abrogated by the disclosure of the divine favor in Christ. The dialectic actually experienced by humans between law and sin, on the one hand, and grace and forgiveness, on the other, leads Luther to the interpretation of God's relation to the world in terms of the dialectic between the *deus absconditus* and the *deus revelatus*. The dynamic character of the God-human relation requires the dialectical analysis of the moments involved in it. The disjunction of these moments by logical deduction or by temporal successiveness makes for static, systematic consistency, to be sure, but oversimplifies the complexity of the actual human situation before God and, therefore, falsifies it.

We shall return later to this distinction between the static, theoretical, essentially Roman Catholic treatment of the problem of natural theology and the dynamic, practical Protestant mind on the matter. But it is important to notice first that the descendants of the reformers have severely compromised the position of the fathers of the sixteenth century.

Two principal lines of interpretation have come down to our day. The so-called literalist or fundamentalist position stems from the Protestant scholasticism of the seventeenth century. Although it has always claimed for itself the privileges of orthodoxy, its degenerative relation to the genius of the Reformation theology makes the term "orthodoxism"[3] more appropriate. The opposite position took shape in the eighteenth-century controversies between the deistic rationalists and the Christian apologists and has found contemporary formulation among the so-called liberal or modernist theologians. The net effect of these two streams of theological influence has been the shift of the basis of the Protestant mind from the dialectical foundation of the reformers to a thoroughly alien one, with the result that Protestant thinking has been in the grip of a fateful dilemma almost from the beginning.

The theological integrity of the reformers had restored the original and paradoxical character of the Christian gospel to the central place in Christian life and thought which it demands and deserves. But the unhappy concomitant of this attempt was the abrogation of the previously existent and acknowledged religious authority. It was, therefore, natural but unfortunate that people should surrender the concern for integrity to that for security in a new authoritarian controversy. Protestant scholasticism undertook to place the architectonic rationalistic methodology of its medieval prototype at the disposal of the Bible and the creed instead of the ecclesiastical institution. The Bible and the creed, however, were less flexible norms for the freedom of inquiry than the institutional sanction of the hierarchical arrangement by which St. Thomas had neatly synthesized the claims of an autonomous reason with those of an equally autonomous faith. The Protestant scholastics were thus in the embarrassing position of insisting upon the supra-rational acceptance of the norms of faith, the articles of belief being rationally consistent once the acceptance had been made. The only defense which this position had against the increasingly rationalistic temper of the times took the form of an obscurantist confusion of the irrational with the supra-rational, which could only bring the religious insights of the Reformation into disrepute. It was a spiritual isolationism for which biblical literalism was an ingenious but ultimately futile support.

Meanwhile, even before the Reformation, the people of the Renaissance were coming into their own. Delivered by the sixteenth century from coming to terms with the medieval institution, they were not hesitant about declaring openly the autonomy of the human reason over all phases of human thought and experience, including what had formerly been reserved for revelation. It was a gradual but persistent declaration of independence. But it could be sustained both because it was more congenial to one's growing at-homeness in the world and because those against whom it was directed were already committed to a rationalistic rather than a dialectical view of the relations between God, humanity, and the world. The articles of the creed of rational religion were less numerous than those of their orthodox opponents, but the debate was held on common ground.

The critical issue was not how to correlate one's natural knowledge of God with the revelation of God in Christ; this formulation of the issue would have been intelligible to St. Thomas and also to Luther and Calvin. But the issue which the age of the Enlightenment debated and committed to the nineteenth century was how the revelation of God in Christ could be justified at the bar of human reason. Such a discussion would have been unthinkable except on the basis of a radically altered theological foundation. The central theological question was no longer that of the relations between God, humanity, and the world but that of the nature of religious truth. The principal interests of the theologian were no longer the dogmatic tradition, logic, and metaphysics, but epistemology, psychology, and ethics. The inner coherence of theological ideas gave place to the general cultural and psychological relevance of theological terms. But all this became possible because the vertical dimension of the relation between God and the world which had characterized the static, theoretical analysis of these relations by Catholicism as well as the dynamic, dialectical analysis by the reformers had been surrendered for the horizontal dimension of polarity in which God and humanity became factors of almost equal value. When the relation was thought of as vertical, God was the factor of incomparable importance; when it came to be thought of as horizontal, humans became the decisive factor. The ascendancy of the principle of polarity brings to light the fateful dilemma of the Protestant mind. The genius of its original appraisal of the theological problem cannot be protected against the Scylla of orthodoxistic spiritism and the Charybdis of liberalistic humanism.

If Karl Barth directs forceful protest against the theology of the nineteenth century, it is because his predecessors there have avoided the orthodoxistic error by a subtle and uncritical perpetuation of the liberalistic one. If recently he has included Emil Brunner in this protest, it is because he suspects Brunner's concern for the problem of natural theology—just because of his own categorical repudiation of the principle of polarity—as the subtlest and ultimate vindication of this principle. And if Emil Brunner has found it necessary to call Barth sharply to account, it is because he suspects in Barth's charge against him, a reaffirmation of the same kind of orthodoxistic isolationism which fostered the enunciation and elaboration of the antithetical principle of polarity. The current debate, then, between these two theologians is significant for the Protestant mind as a whole. The course which it takes and the conclusion toward which it points will have an important bearing on the question of whether Protestantism can be true to its essential genius without repeating ever and again the tortuous hither-and-yon between obscurantism and humanism which has characterized its history to date.

II

Because I can discover in that undertaking[4] only a new promotion of the line Schleiermacher-Ritschl-Herrmann, and because in every conceivable advancement of that line, I can only discover the clear destruction of Protestant Theology and the Protestant Church, because I can no longer see a third alternative . . . between the grandeur and the misery of a natural knowledge of God in the sense of the Vatican and a Protestant Theology which has finally freed itself from the secular misery by nourishing itself from its own source and standing upon its own feet, therefore, I can only say here, "No!"[5]

This passage, which registers Barth's repudiation of the ruling theological tendencies that he had inherited from Herrmann and his predecessors, contains also the definition of his controversy. He accuses his opponents of a methodological commitment to the discussion of the theological problem in analogical as against existential terms. They are "toying with the analogy of being (*analogia entis*)." Nineteenth-century thought is aware of the immense contrast between God and humanity. But this whole sequence of theological writing presupposes an ultimate continuity of being between God and humanity as the basis of their intercourse. There is always something which can be affirmed about humans for which they are not with ultimate practical seriousness dependent upon God but which they themselves bring, as it were, in their own name and by their own right to the relations between them. Some attribute of one's being, if it is only that one is *homo*; some aspect of one's nature, though it be nothing more than one's distinctness from the brutes; some capacity for emotion or cognition or volition—is ultimately presupposed as indispensable to one's communion with God. When one has looked carefully into the premises, the consequences, and the essential spirit of this entire theological tradition, the final word to be said is that one can always "recognize himself and God's revelation in this continuous, already existing (*vorfindlichen*) relation between God and man."[6] The Reformation insight, however, into the relations between God and humanity is thoroughly remote from such a habit of mind. "Not a being (*Sein*), that the creature has in common with the Creator, despite all dissimilarity, but an *act*, that is not contained in any mere theory, the human decision in faith, in spite of every dissimilarity, is analogous to the decision of the grace of God,"[7] by which the promise of the remission of sins through Christ is bestowed.

The idea of an analogy of being is in exact correspondence with the principle of polarity that regulated the religion of the eighteenth century. It is not strange, therefore, that the basic problem in contemporary theological debate should gravitate around this fact. The central question is whether humanity has a natural knowledge of God or not. Is there a constituent element of human nature which makes possible the apprehension of God's existence, and the comprehension of God's will? It has been the special province of a so-called natural theology (*theologia naturalis*) to offer an affirmative answer to this central question and to pursue its implications. Natural theology may be defined as the phase of theological inquiry which concerns itself with the fact that the world is not godless.

On the face of it, this seems obvious. But there are two principal grounds on which the fact of humanity's natural knowledge of God becomes questionable. The one is supplied by the claims of revelation, the other is the phenomenon of human sinfulness. Historical religion has always been characterized by special manifestations of divinity. The inchoate variety of theophanies and oracles of primitive religion anticipate the more orderly and more purposeful visions of prophets and seers that give to the cultural religions their characteristic vitality and content. By far the most difficult and profound expression of humanity's awareness of divine manifestation is the conception of the

Incarnation. Under all the forms which revelation takes, however, there is the common view that regardless of the natural human rapport with God, a special way by which the divine nature and the divine will are to be known has been opened. This fact of the special self-disclosure of God embodies the specific meaning of the term "revelation." And it is the particular province of revealed theology (*theologia revelata*) to concern itself with this fact and its implications. It is really the existence of a theology of revelation that calls the claims of a natural theology into question.

But even apart from revelation's implied attack upon humanity's natural knowledge of God, that knowledge has been subject to question. Whatever direct and original connections there may have been between the human and the divine, they have not been able to put the uneasy conscience at rest. The inescapable conviction of an alienation from God has tended, if not to the complete negation of the natural human theological equipment, at least to its severe limitation. One's natural knowledge of God has never seemed capable of carrying the staggering burden of human sin.

III

The doctrines of revelation and sin require a certain change of emphasis with respect to the principal concern of natural theology. Instead of accepting as a datum of *prima facie* [accepted unless proven otherwise] worth the fact that the world is not God-less, one deals with that fact, from which all natural theology proceeds, as the critical theological question. The God-relatedness of the world is not, so to speak, a mere problem in theological geometry but may become an occasion for serious theological heresy. In light of the doctrines of revelation and sin, one does not affirm that one has a natural knowledge of God. One asks rather: What becomes of one's natural knowledge of God in view of one's corruption? Or, to use the terminology of traditional dogmatics: To what extent has the image of God in humanity been destroyed by the Fall?

It has already been suggested that Roman Catholicism has its own way of dealing with this question. I want to review it briefly, together with the answer suggested by modern Protestantism. Then we shall be prepared to understand the contemporary Protestant theological debate on the problem and to face the immediate theological responsibility of Protestants.

Roman Catholic theology is like a two-story house. The ground floor is based upon and composed of materials derived from the knowledge of God which is immediately available to everyone from the world of nature and the constitution of one's own being. This general revelation corresponds exactly to the biblical doctrines of Creation and Providence. The Creator has left his permanent impress upon all his works and continually manifests his power in them and over them. The Roman Church makes no secret of its indebtedness to the Bible. But the important point is that what the Bible and the church teach is, so far at least, a part of the common rational equipment of humankind, independent of any special biblical instruction. Atheists and believers, can, and indeed must, by taking thought acknowledge their community in a *revelatio generalis* [general revelation]. The unreflective person arrives by faith, under the guidance of the church, at exactly the same point to which the reason must direct a person if it is alert and accurate.

But the house has a second floor. Parlor, dining-room, and kitchen will suffice for the normal routine of living. But life is more than this normal routine. It involves such experiences as receiving a child into the world, of being sick unto death, or of being hounded by anxiety and remorse. Such experiences require a readier access to the heaven of heavens and to him that sitteth on the circle of the earth. Here it is that the person of faith outstrips the natural one in apprehending what belongs to one's peace. For faith has a special knowledge guaranteed by the direct authority of special revelation and enshrined in the bosom of the church—knowledge of an incarnate Christ whose death redeems the wicked and whose resurrection assures life eternal to all the penitent dead.

It must be noted, however, that this *revelatio specialis* [special revelation] is not intended as a compensation for sin. To the question "What becomes of man's natural knowledge of God in view of man's corruption?" Catholic theology replies: "It remains as effectual as before." The *imago dei* [image of God] is the theological analogue of a rational account of the order of things in a contingent world. There is a rational theology, not easily distinguished, except terminologically, from a philosophical metaphysics, and consequently there is a rational ethic or moral philosophy. St. Thomas had no hesitancy about including Aristotle and Jesus in the same theological system. What Luther consistently regarded as irreconcilable functions; Aquinas declared to be merely different functions. For, if one is not to sever God completely from creation and to divide humanity unrecognizably into two, there must be a self-sufficient, uninterrupted, rational *theologia naturalis*, independent of and disconnected from, a *theologia revelata* and solidly undergirding it. To get from the other to the other, one simply goes upstairs. One never accepts or builds a new house. Sin does not count in the ascent. Neither does the Incarnation.

It is on the threshold of the second floor that one runs hard against the barriers of sin. Sin has not touched the *imago dei* at all, but rather the *donum superadditum* [abundantly added gift], the *revelatio originalis* [original revelation], the *perfectio* [perfection]. The graces of an original perfection of knowledge and of virtue cannot be had again. They must be added. And the verb is immensely significant. It is the essentially additive character of Catholic theology that enables it to join together, in perfect unity of thought and life, *theologia naturalis* and *theologia revelata*, revelation and incarnation, sin and grace, creation and redemption. The effects of human defection are overcome in the *visio beatifica dei* [the beatific vision of God], which awaits the believer at the highest reaches of reason and faith.

The theology of modern Protestantism, "the line Schleiermacher-Ritschl-Herrmann," stands in uneasy contrast to its Roman precursor. The truth is that modern Protestantism has simply renovated the dwelling, which the medievals erected. The supposition has been that the ground floor could absorb all the benevolent influences from above without the partitionary ceiling. But since, as it seems, there is no transfer of training, the superior craftsmanship of the Dominican doctor did not reproduce itself. Elementary physics ought to have suggested what theological perspicacity failed to convey, namely, that a ceiling does not vanish but collapses when its supports are tampered with.

Modern Protestantism has tried in its own way to restore order amid the debris. The distinction between a natural theology and a revealed theology has been abandoned as artificially divisive. In its stead the varieties of approach to the problem of the relations between God, humanity, and the world have been brought together into a systematic unity known as theism. This way of speaking has, of course, eliminated the architecture of scholasticism from theological thought and replaced it by a more congenial and, presumably therefore, more promising organic vitality. But it has escaped general notice that the real difference between an architectural and an organic unity does not have to do with the unity at all but rather consists in a different way of arranging various items within the same essential unity. The image of God remains in the same way fundamentally undisturbed by the Fall—whether one talks about the Creator and the Redeemer God or about the creative and the redemptive forces at work in the world; about general and special revelation, or about the correlative intimacy between discovery and revelation; about an omnipotent and providential Deity or about the transcendence and the immanence of God; about the unique Incarnation or about progressive incarnations.

To what extent is the image of God in humanity destroyed by the Fall? The modern Protestant answer is: This is an irrelevant question which can more promisingly be ignored than answered. Since the Enlightenment, people speak of natural religion not natural theology. Consequently, there is no need of speaking about separate spheres of nature and grace or about a lost original perfection or about an incarnate redemption from sin. The *lumen naturale* [natural light] itself has become a revelation, indeed, the only one worth talking about and ultimately the criterion of all others, loosely described by that old theological word. The light of reason, aided only by the objectivity which it sets itself, has brought the age-long fire down from heaven and consumed the distinction between humanity's natural knowledge of God and the knowledge of God in Christ. Sin is exactly what it was for Thomas Aquinas and for Augustine before him and for Plato and Aristotle before them—imperfection.[8] It is not "additively" overcome by going upstairs but gradually rendered inoperative by the ever-widening inclusiveness of the fellowship one seeks with the big happy family in the remodeled one-room mansion one calls home.

IV

This, then, is the reason for Karl Barth's inability to "see a third alternative . . . between the grandeur of the Vatican and a Protestant theology which has finally freed itself from that secular misery by nourishing itself from its own source and standing upon its own feet . . ." But Barth's intense zeal for the integrity of Protestant theology has led him to so rigorous an adherence to its original and paradoxical foundation that he has come dangerously close to undoing his heroic repudiation of the incontrovertibly vicious theological consequences of the principle of polarity. He says, "The possibility of this solution stands or falls by the answer to the question: whether there is a potentiality for divine revelation in existence which is to be understood independently of the actual revelation [that is, in Christ] and which is completed by that revelation. Is there a general human possibility, the actualization of which one must later then attribute to this special revelation?"[9] If one answers affirmatively that there is such a possibility, then one has committed one's self to a natural theology, which can begin, only where Catholic theology begins and end where modern Protestantism ends. But this is an irresponsible repudiation of that strict concern with the revelation of God in Christ that alone guarantees that a theology is orthodox and not heretical.

The ultimate implication of this categorical demand, which Barth has made is the most tragic indication of the dilemma of the Protestant mind. It means that Barth's formidable theological reconstruction is moving securely enough away from the bondage of modern Protestantism to the Enlightenment, but instead of ending in the theology of the reformers it is stopping short in a virulent form of the scholastic theological isolationism of Protestant orthodoxy. The thoroughgoing destruction of the characteristic position of liberalism, God-and-humanity-and-the-world, seems to be driving Barth straight into the characteristic position of orthodoxy, God-against-humanity-and-the-world. The prophetic enthusiasm of the conflict with the heresy of humanism is generating a fanatical espousal of the heresy of spiritism (almost *Schwärmerei* [fanaticism]). The one is synergistic; the other is monergistic. But the astutely dialectical exposition of the Christian faith, which was the genius of the theology of the reformers and which swerved neither to the right nor to the left of the line of orthodox Christocentricity, is not coming into its own. Barth is venturing, in the name of both the Bible and the reformers, upon an entirely new theological emphasis. He is asking for the complete restatement of our leading question about natural theology: We are bidden to ask, not "What becomes of the human's natural knowledge of God in view of one's corruption?" nor "To what extent has the image of God been destroyed by the Fall?" but rather, "Why, in view of the revelation of God in Christ, should one be concerned about humanity's natural knowledge of God at all?" The important theological moments in the relationship between God, humanity, and the world are not creation-fall-reconciliation-redemption but only fall-redemption.

V

It is immensely significant for the present state of Protestant thought that this critical development in Barth's theology should have been most plainly exposed, not by his orthodoxistic and liberal critics, but by his one-time theological colleague, Emil Brunner. The controversy between them shows conclusively that the only egress from the dilemma of the Protestant mind is the correct appraisal of the dialectical relation of anthropology to Christology in the theology of the Bible and the reformers.[10] With the barest hint of Brunner's position over against that of Barth and its bearing upon the possibility of a truly Protestant theology, the present discussion must conclude.

"That man is man and not cat is unimportant."[11] "The difference between man and cat is no trivial and merely secular fact but a matter of the highest theological importance."[12] According to Karl Barth, when one gets too interested in the fact that they are not a cat, one is certain to lose one's interest in Christ. According to Brunner, one must give full weight to the fact that one is not a cat, just because of one's interest in Christ. He agrees with Barth that a natural theology in the outspoken Catholic sense or in the subversive sense of modern Protestantism is a violation of the revelation of God in Christ. But when Barth makes his categorical repudiation of natural theology in the sense of an analogy of being—*analogia entis*—and with it the categorical exclusion of every independent anthropological sentence from theology, Brunner cannot go along.

It is theologically indefensible, as Barth puts it, that "revelation in the narrower and real sense of the word, is preceded by the idea of an already-given revelation of God, given with our created existence as such."[13] Exactly this, according to Brunner, is theologically necessary. He writes:

If we ask ourselves how Barth, with his customary faithfulness to the Bible, and earnest concern for the recovery of the message of the Reformers, comes to such an abrupt and vigorous rejection of a doctrine, which is obviously as biblical as it is a teaching of the Reformation, I believe the answer is to be found in a one-sided conception of revelation. Barth will not admit that where it is a question of revelation and faith, there can be something established, continuing, so to speak, natural. He will have only the act, the event of revelation, but never something already revealed . . . In the assertion of the actual lies the whole strength of the Barthian theology. To be sure, there can only be revelation in the ultimate, complete, sense, as an act, as the speaking of God here and now. But this is only the one side of the biblical conception of revelation. The other is the exact contrary: namely, that God speaks to me here and now, on the basis of what he has spoken . . . The Bible is related to the actual revelation of God as—if I may use this trivial figure—a phonograph record is related to the music which has been engraved upon it and which is replayed. It is a record, an act which has become substantial. The Bible is definite and unalterable, a piece of the world, available to everybody, even though its revelation is not. What is available to everybody is that which—in the solidly established word of the Bible—God uses in order to speak His personal word to me today. He wishes it so; only through this which is definitely established does He will to give me His direct, personal, Word.[14]

Thus, to the question of how far the image of God in humanity has been destroyed by the Fall Brunner will give neither the additive answer of Catholicism nor the gradualist answer of modern Protestantism nor yet the undialectical, spiritistic answer of Karl Barth. Relying on the Reformers' dialectical interpretation of the relation between the *reliquiae imaginis dei* [remains of the image of God] (what Brunner calls the *Imago-Rest* [the residue of the image of God]) and the *restoratio imaginis dei propter Christum* [restoration of the image of God on account of Christ], Brunner believes that the dialectical discipline of a Christian natural theology is permissible and necessary.[15] The formal image of God, Brunner says, has not been destroyed by the Fall. That is, the God-relatedness of humanity and the world, one's humanity, one's sense of responsibility, freedom, *Wortmächtigkeit* [power of speech], that which keeps one forever distinct from the beasts and enables one to stand outside of oneself as well as the world—all this remains in spite of sin. This is the *reliquiae imaginis dei*. But the material image of God—that is, one's knowledge of what God is like, how God is minded toward him, how one is to survive having violated one's responsibility before God, what one's ultimate destiny will be—all this has been irrevocably destroyed by the Fall. It can be restored only by the incarnate and atoning revelation of God in Christ. This is the *restoratio imaginis dei propter Christum*.[16]

The critical bearing of this problem upon the dilemma of the Protestant mind has led Brunner in his anthropological work to go over it all once more with a view to eliminating any misleading terminology. He is willing to abandon the phrase "Christian natural theology," the distinction between the formal and the material image of God, and, as unnecessarily quantitative, even the time-honored, *Imago-Rest* of the reformers. He says:

> My sole concern is with the revival of its [the theology of the Reformers] fundamental conception, which has been lost among the orthodox Lutherans and also in a different way by Barth, namely, the idea that man is to be understood as a totality and in terms of his relation to God, and that on that account the humanity of the sinner is a corrupt humanity, but precisely also on that account, the still-continuing humanity must be understood in terms of the image of God, or the original God-relatedness of man.[17]

The great theological achievement of the Reformers was that they successfully maintained the dialectical relation between the original, continuing humanity, on the one hand, and the sinful, dehumanized humanity, on the other. The inner dialectic of human existence between responsible and irresponsible living, between fulfillment and frustration, hope and despair, godliness and bestiality, is exactly and profoundly comprehended by the dialectic between sin and grace, law and gospel, and, most critical of all, between creation and redemption as found in biblical and Reformation thinking.

The question "What becomes of man's knowledge of God in view of man's corruption?" requires a dialectical, not an additive or a gradualistic or yet an undialectical reply, because the dialectical relation between the Creator and the Redeemer God is at stake. This is a dialectical problem because the contradictory implications of both terms must be resolutely pursued if human existence is not to be falsified and the inner logic of biblical Christianity denied. The satisfactory substantiation of Brunner's analysis of the problem is a matter which lies beyond the province of this discussion. Meanwhile, it must be granted that he has correctly discerned the problem itself and indicated our immediate theological responsibility.

But, as we confront that responsibility, we find ourselves in Protestantism's historic dilemma. If Protestant thought continues in the way for which Barth has sharply reproached it, it can expect only the surrender of its theological integrity to the alien spirit of the religion of polarity. If it goes in the way, which Barth is demanding of it, it can expect only a revival of the very supernaturalistic spiritism against which the Enlightenment quite properly protested. There is a vicious circle of defection from, and direction toward, its own creative genius, which continually threatens to nullify the Protestant attempt to clothe human existence with meaning. And yet in one of the figures employed by the man who more than anyone else has roused our sleeping consciences there lays a clue that points beyond his own failure. Barth says we are like a "bird in flight, *theologi viatores*" [wayfarer theologians]. And if we are willing to be made realistically aware of the chasm of impotence into which we are in danger of falling, it may be given us to use, not one, but both wings, however slipped they may be, as we try to express in terms adequately dialectical the gospel of the Creator and the Redeemer God, by whose sovereign and forgiving word humans are called from their darkness into his marvelous light. *Veni, creator spiritus!*

NOTES

1. Published in *The Journal of Religion* 20, no. 2 (1940): 124–40; reprinted with permission of the University of Chicago Press.

2. Quoted by Theodosius, Harnack, *Luthers Theologie* (Erlangen: T. Blaesing, 1862), 134.

3. So, at any rate, Brunner prefers to speak of it.

4. The reference is to the first edition of Karl Barth's *Die christliche Dogmatik im Entwurf: Die Lehre vom Worte Gottes. Prolegomena zur christlichen Dogmatik* (München: Chr. Kaiser, 1927), v–x. [Editorial: Exact citation cannot be found. The reference includes the entire forward. The work has since been published in the Karl Barth Gesamtausgabe. See Karl Barth, *Die christliche Dogmatik im Entwurf. Die Lehre vom Wort Gottes. Prolegomena zur christlichen Dogmatik 1927*, ed. Gerhard Sauter, GA II.14, (Zürich: TVZ, 1982), 3–9.]

5. Karl Barth, *Die Kirchliche Dogmatik: Prolegomena zur kirchlichen Dogmatik*, I/1 (Zollikon-Zürich: EVZ, 1932), viii.

6. Barth, *KD* I/1, 40.

7. Barth, *KD* I/1, 252.

8. Ritschl called it ignorance, but only because epistemology had replaced logic as a theological method.

9. Barth, *KD* I/1, 37.

10. The most succinct form of the argument appears in Brunner, *Natur und Gnade—zum Gespräch mit Karl Barth* (Tübingen: Mohr, 1935) and in Barth, *Nein!—Antwort an Emil Brunner*. (*Theologische Existenz Heute*, No. 14 (Munich: Kaiser). Brunner's maturest elaboration of the problem is available in his brilliant work on the problem of humanity, *Der Mensch im Widerspruch* (Berlin: Furche, 1937; Eng. trans., *Man in Revolt* (New York: Scribner's, 1939). [Editorial: See *Natural Theology: Comprising Nature and Grace by Professor Dr. Emil Brunner and the reply No! by Dr. Karl Barth*, trans. Peter Fraenkel (Eugene: Wipf and Stock, 2002.)]

11. Barth, "*Nein!*," 25, 27.

12. Brunner, *Der Mensch im Widerspruch*, 85.

13. Barth, "*Nein!*," 133.

14. Brunner, *Natur und Gnade*, 35. [Editorial: See *Natural Theology*, 48–49.]

15. Brunner, *Natur und Gnade*, 17, 52.
16. Brunner, *Natur und Gnade*, 11 ff., 22 ff.
17. Brunner, *Der Mensch im Widerspruch*, 531.

Chapter 7

The Ant and the Emperor (1998)[1]

Two biographers have suggested the title of this incommensurate *coram Deo* [before the face of God] tribute of remembrance and gratitude upon the centenary of the birth of Karl Barth. Eberhard Busch, in his masterly chronicle of Barth's life and thought "from letters and autobiographical texts," refers to the "many visitors [who] found their way up there," that is, to the Bergli, taking no account of Barth's withdrawal to his favorite hideaway due to his feeling "in great need of a rest." They came "like a procession of ants," Barth wrote to his son Christoph on September 21, 1950. Yet they do not seem to have despoiled "the quietist and pleasantest of holidays in living memory."[2] Since my name appears among the ants, the memory is more than a little reassuring.

My own first meeting with Karl Barth had happened in Bonn seventeen years earlier. It occurred in the course of that first fateful week following Hitler's accession to power on January 31, 1933, as then President Paul von Hindenburg invited him to form a government and became Chancellor of the Third Reich. Rumors were rife in Bonn that Barth would be dismissed before the spring semester was over. These rumors were almost confirmed. The door of the Lecture Hall of the university where Barth had been unfolding the story of Protestant Theology in the nineteenth century each weekday at 7:00 a.m. bore a laconic notice that the final lecture of the semester would not be given. Barth, as it turned out, had been summoned to Berlin for a meeting with the Prussian Minister of Cultural Affairs, Bernard Rust, and the newly appointed "Reichsbischof" of the German Evangelical Church, Ludwig Müller.

In Bonn that semester I also learned that the designation *Carolus magnus* [Charles the Great] was no longer to be confined solely to the Imperial Resident of the Palace at nearby Aachen. Another Charlemagne had come upon the human scene whose royal lineage was strangely kindred to his renowned predecessor, not, indeed, by flesh and blood but by baptism and grace. Contemporaries and students of the younger *Carolus magnus* were wont to refer to Karl Barth in this way because of their awe and esteem, their indebtedness and affection that intensified as their own probing of the substance, range, and power of Barth's thought and their experience of his personal human charm developed and deepened. The phrase was a natural and grateful acknowledgement of their discovery through Barth of the excitement of theology and of their own theological formation. It expressed also an unaffected and proleptic sense of a fresh exploration under way of the Augustinian vision of the centrality of Christian faith, thought, and action for the human meaning of human life.

Dei providentia et hominum confusione [God's providence and human confusion] was a favorite phrase of Karl Barth's. Charlemagne's biographer reports that the Emperor was accustomed to being read to at dinner. Serious books were the ordering of the evening ritual and special attention and pleasure was accorded to *The City of God*.[3] But, in Göttingen and Münster, in Bonn and in Basel, the tonalities evoked for those who had ears to hear clearly linked the 4th–5th, 8th–9th, and 19th–20th centuries in "a panorama of the divine economy,"[4] this time under the magisterial perceptions, passions, pertinence, and persuasiveness of the *Carolus magnus* not of Aachen but of Bonn enroute to Basel. At issue were the claims and ambiguities conjoining God with humanity or dividing humanity from God. They are the issues of ultimate loyalties and disloyalties, of ultimate trust (Luther), of the knowledge of God/or ourselves (Calvin), of human community in concord or in conflict (Augustine).

Accordingly, in commemoration of the one hundredth anniversary of the birth of Karl Barth, the ant may be allowed a grateful homage to the Emperor by way of some account of theological formation received *lecti iuvenes, fortissima corda* [from young, strong-hearted people] (Virgil) and, in consequence, of three *notae laudationis* [tokens of praise], briefly but *gravissima atque ornatissima* [weighty and most beautiful] because they are at once central to Barth's perception and practice of Christian theology and to his continuing theological importance; and because they happen also to be insufficiently recognized Augustinian motifs.[5]

OF THEOLOGICAL FORMATION

As for my own theological formation, my first conversation with Barth succinctly gathers it together. I had come to Bonn to learn from Karl Barth what Christian theology was all about, and why. Following the protocol of those days, I sought an appointment for a courtesy call and was received with gracious cordiality into Barth's study. The book-lined shelves looked more like the Reference Room of the library at Union Theological Seminary from whence I had come than the studies of professors I had previously known.

The *Patrologia Graeca et Latina*, the *Corpus Reformatorum*, the *Weimarer Ausgabe*, among others, lined the bookshelves and the small passageways between. I could not suppress a comment upon the conspicuous contrast between what I was then taking in at a glance and what I had previously privileged to note. To this comment *Carolus magnus* replied with unaffected candor, a curiosity and twinkle in his eyes, "*What* do American theologians read, then?" What indeed!

Certainly not Karl Barth! With notable exceptions even to this day, the Karl Barth best known in the United States is the Barth of the second edition of the *Commentary on Romans*, supplemented by a "Reader's Digest" approach to the *Church Dogmatics*. Emil Brunner was the principle "point of contact"—if not with God, at least with "The Strange New World Within the Bible" and with "The Doctrinal Task of the Reformed Churches," breaking in through and breaking up established positions and directions in Continental European theology. The tenacity of this *hauteur de silence* [height of silence] toward Barth is massively evident in James Gustafson's latest exploration of theological ethics, which finds it possible to dismiss the dynamics, range, and complexity of Barth's lifetime of labors with the catchword "theological anthropocentricity."

Careful readers of Barth will recognize, of course, the vast distortion of this reductionism, as also the dubious Edwardian coloration of an almost Islamic account of monotheism and Western culture. "What are American theologians reading, then?" Principally, the architects of American pragmatism, a theological veneer of post-Briggsian higher criticism of the Scriptures, of the optimism and corrective realism of the Social Gospel, of the evangelical liberalism of the best of German and Scottish Ritschlians transplanted to the United States, and of the bewitching "language of Canaan" designed by naturalists and ontologists of "Process Thought." These preoccupations purported to adapt for "the making of the modern mind": the covenantal discourse of mystery and revelation, myth and meaning, suffering and responsibility, history and hope. As things turned out, however, they effected the gradual displacement of the covenantal tradition by the mathematical logic of increasingly quantifiable signs generated by the cybernetic verifiabilities of science and technology. Thus, it is understandable that the heritage, habits, and *foci* of doctrinal and ethical thinking in the United States should *in principio* [in the beginning] have marginalized Karl Barth.

To these quasi-pantheistic, polytheistic, and syncretistic preoccupations Karl Barth alerted me and from them he delivered me. He did so above all else by identifying and exploring the dogmatic center and direction for theology and the church in society, culture, and politics on the move. The move was *from* what Ernst Troeltsch defined as the end of Christian civilization *toward* what Richard Falk has described as a post-Westphalian world, and *for* what Dietrich Bonhoeffer has taught us to recognize as a world come of age. Troeltsch and Falk, between them, strikingly confirm Reinhold Niebuhr's brilliant aphorism that "history, like nature, never buries what it kills." Accordingly, with rare exceptions, the formative voices in American pulpits and theological seminaries—whether conservative or liberal—have nurtured generations of church members and theological students in cultivated ignorance and uncultivated innocence of a formidable dogmatic exposition and analysis of the pertinence of a theology of revelation discerned in Scripture to human believing and hoping, thinking and doing. At stake were and are the foundations and prospects of human freedom and fulfillment amid the rising barbarization of the values, purposes, and commitments that shape and sustain people's lives.

In raising anew and afresh the question of the centrality of dogma for faith and obedience, for the presence and responsibility of the church in the world, and, correlatively, of dogmatics as a theological discipline, Karl Barth has prepared the church for the world of today and the world for the church of today and tomorrow. This is an Augustinian achievement for which the Greeks have, once again, provided the identifying word. The word "*dogma*" was used by Socrates, Plato, and Euripides, among others, to denote a primary responsibility of parents toward their children. In a Greek household, this responsibility was exercised by a person whose primary task was to guide and direct the children. As a steersmen or pilot (*kubernetes*) controls and guides a ship, so by metaphorical appropriation the *kubernetes* were employed to nurture the young in the *dogma*, that is, in all those matters which *one* generation (the parents) was *not* prepared to take responsibility for the next generation (the children) being *without*. Thus, *dogma*—far from identifying an arbitrary limitation imposed upon thought and action—identifies, nourishes, and sustains what it takes foundationally and focally to be and to stay human in the world.[6] Of course, there are notable and irreconcilable differences between Augustine's achievement and Barth's. Indeed, one may say of Barth's relation to Augustine what Barth once said of his own formative theological teacher, Wilhelm Herrmann: "I let Herrmann say to me something so fundamental, that carried through to its consequences, required of me afterwards to say almost everything else differently, and eventually to interpret even that completely differently than he would have done."[7]

The cardinal instance is the Trinitarian center and structure of the *Church Dogmatics*, in spite of—perhaps on account of—the vigorous repudiation of Augustine's recourse to human psychology in expounding the mystery of the Divine Trinity. The Augustinian achievement of *Carolus magnus* neither affirms nor implies a replication of the Bishop of Hippo. But just as Augustine drew upon the authority of Scripture and upon the faith of the church as articulated in the Creeds and Councils, and unfolded a vision of the church as the center and circumference of an earthly and a heavenly human community provisionally commingled mystically and politically, so Barth draws upon Scripture and the Creeds and Councils of the church for a dogmatics-political orchestration of Charlemagne's Augustin-inspired vision of what the community of love, justice, and peace requires of the responsible exercise of power and authority in the world.

NOTAE LAUDATIONIS

In this sense, Barth's dogmatic-political achievement is Augustinian on the grand scale. There are, however, three notable Augustinian accents of his theological endeavors that significantly liberate theology for a world come of age. The first has to do with the relation between dogmatics and language; the second with the relation between dogmatics and humor; the third between dogmatics and political responsibility. These are the *notae laudationis* that signal a saving word for the world of today in and through the church for the world of today and tomorrow. A brief comment upon each must bring these commemorative reflections and reminiscences to a close.

Dogmatics and Language

Carolus magnus delivered theological language and conceptuality from bondage to propositional logic and joined them once again to poetry. This conjunction was not a surreptitious surrender to Platonism, as Bishop Nygren and German, Scottish, English, and American theologians too readily assumed. It was, instead, a dogmatic appropriation of the prophetic and parabolic witness of Scripture to God's unique way of giving Godself to be known and of the responsibility of theology to know and to understand God in this way. Barth's early and too persistent critics were confused by this move, owing to their own conviction that rational coherence buttressed by scientific empirical verifiability was the surest liberation of theology from verbal and textual inerrancy. Thus it was not surprising that Barth's Christocentricity, with its patently obscurantist—and therefore specious—attempt to take the virgin birth of Jesus and his bodily resurrection with utmost theological seriousness again, should be dismissed with habitual disdain and occasional fury. As a young tutor in theology in seminary, I learned through being on the losing end of more than one fierce theological debate how intense and magisterial this repudiation of dialectical dogmatics could be. Much later, I discovered the heretical secret of this knowledgeable and zealous theological attempt to liberate orthodoxy from orthodox literalism. As with Arius before them, the trouble was that these facile repudiations of *Carolus magnus* exhibited nothing so much as the inability of their purveyors to understand a metaphor.[8] What Barth was exploring—without making a theologoumenon of theological method—was the metaphorical content and meaning of language of dogmatics. It is this exploration which informs that epigrammatic injunction to the higher-critical interpreters of Scripture in the Preface to the second edition of the *Commentary on Romans*: "The critical historian needs to be more critical." It is this exploration which takes formal shape in the opening paragraph of the *Church Dogmatics* where the task of dogmatics is described as reflection upon the agreement between the church's language about God and the revelation of God attested in Holy Scripture. Had the recurrent *analogia fide* [analogy of faith], both explicitly and implicitly in Barth's interpretation of Scripture and tradition, *not* been so steadily juxtaposed to *analogia entis* [analogy of being] by those who affirmed and rejected his thought, it might have been noticed and noted that *Carolus magnus* was actually pioneering a metaphorical interpretation of knowledge and obedience of faith. Indeed, he himself seems not to have been fully cognizant of this creative frontier of his thought and writing. The extended sections of "Legend and Story" (*Legende und Sage*) and on "God's Time and Ours," which focused upon "The Miracle of Christmas," "The Divine Perfections," "The Angels," "Election and Ethics" are all cases in point—at least between the lines. His evocative and provocative reappropriation of the Chalcedonian *vere Deus-vere Homo* [very God and very human] would almost certainly have brought to the surface what had been going on all around, clarified his claims, and confused his critics even more, if he had. Nevertheless, without having done so, these dogmatic labors brought him to the transforming edge of the world of today and of the church of today and tomorrow in their need and search for "an essential metaphor."

Among fellow-seekers on the right, the cordial and lively conversations in Basel and in books with Hans Urs von Balthasar over the *analogia entis* and with Hans Küng over grace and faith signaled a dawning Roman Catholic awareness of a lack of metaphorical sensitivity and humor in St. Thomas's view of both truth and conscience, a sensitivity and humor discernible through Barth's similarly structured dogmatic coherence at the service of a high doctrine of the church. As it turned out, Augustine was a partner in these conversations and discernment as he had been of Barth's search for a faithful way to think and speak about God as far back as his early friendship in Göttingen with Erich Przywara, a Jesuit (1927–1928), and with Heinrich Scholz, a philosopher in Münster (1929–1930), both of whom were devoted to Augustine, and continuing with *Ad Limina Apostolorum* after Barth's eightieth birthday in 1966. On this threshold, *Carolus magnus* cheerfully accepted his theological designation as among the *fratres sejuncti* [separated brothers], with the stress upon *fratres*; and there, on the way to a wonderful and memorable visit with Pope Paul IV, he impishly thought of the Proverb: "Who is so smart as not to find his master in the Vatican."[9]

Among fellow-seekers on the left have been those who, having left the faith behind, strangely find themselves in the vestibule of faith and in search of a center of meaning, purpose, and hope for their lives. An unforgettable and moving instance is provided by a conundrum set down in an unpublished paper with which a friend and distinguished colleague in English Letters has favored me. The conundrum identifies exactly what the *vere Deus-vere Homo* turns out to have been and to be all about. The question is: "When is an analogy *not* an analogy?" The answer: "When it is a metaphor."[10] This search for an essential metaphor has proceeded apace and with alacrity—so much so that Hans Frei, one of the ablest interpreters of *Carolus magnus*, has found it rightly appropriate to signal a pause in "the eclipse of the biblical narrative."[11]

Dogmatics and Humor

The search for an essential metaphor goes on, with or without *Carolus magnus*. But just as poetry is not usually associated with Karl Barth's theology, so humor is dissociated from both his theology and his person. Nothing could be more remote from reality. Toward his metaphorically inept critics, Barth's humor easily—and perhaps too readily—bore the bite of satire. But toward himself—which is, after all, the test case of an authentic amalgam of seriousness and humor—Barth unfailingly kept the faith. The Gideon test (Judges 9) of humor is the power and readiness to laugh at oneself. No attentive listener to sermon or lecture, no student or visitor *sans arrière pensées* [without ulterior motives] could miss the twinkle in the eye, the playfulness lurking about the edges of the intensely concentrated gaze, the impish musings turned upon himself as readily as upon his contemporaries. One may add to his account of himself *ad limina apostolorum* [at the threshold of the apostles], already noted, the instant response to the question posed in the winsome BBC film interview toward the end of his life. To the question whether he had ever desired or contemplated being other than a theologian—and if so, what?—he replied: "Not really! But if I had to choose an alternative, I should like most to be a traffic policeman!"[12] As Barth saw it, indicating to people busily engaged in their daily tasks when to wait and when to proceed and which direction safely to take was an engrossing responsibility common in fact to a dogmatic theologian and to a traffic policeman.

Or, there is that charming comment in his "Letter to Mozart." There Barth acknowledges that Mozart has a readier access to the Divine Presence than he does. Hence, he does not know whether God asks the angels to play Mozart or prefers Bach or Beethoven. Nevertheless, *Carolus magnus* ventures to think that when the angels play their chamber music among themselves, *they* play Mozart and God takes special time and pleasure to listen in.[13] I think also of a quiet evening in Barth's study in the Bruderholz Allee, 26, in 1962. He was in a mellow and retrospective mood. At one point, he remarked that sometimes he found himself wondering what the angels think of his *Dogmatics*. This was an opening I found myself unable to pass over. So I said that I, of course, did not know what the angels might think of his *Dogmatics* but he would surely have to agree that the angels are alone among God's creatures in having the time to read it. Barth responded with a gale of spontaneous and hearty laughter—at his reverie and at himself.

3. Dogmatics and Politics

Dogmatics via metaphor and humor to political responsibility—surely this *is* theology in a new key for the church of today and tomorrow and for the world of today in search for tomorrow. It is not accidental that the memory of *der rote Pfarrer* [the red pastor] lingered long in the minds and hearts of some members of his perish in Safenwil. They would have been too responsive to his preaching and teaching to have been beguiled by the Reaganesque Manichaeism in our times or the hypocritical and sentimental talk of reconciliation by Reagan and Kohl in Bitburg Cemetery. Nor is it accidental that Karl Barth should be among the very few theologians in Western Europe, Canada, or the United States who were members of the Socialist parties. In addition to an astonishing number of political essays, the perceptive and proving distinction between the "law-and-order-people" and the "God of things to come" of the *Commentary on Romans*, the answer of *Carolus magnus* to Reinhold Niebuhr's haunting and reproachful *Christian Century* question gathers and focuses it all. "Why is Barth silent on Hungary?" Niebuhr accusingly asked. To which Barth responded in various times and in various ways. The substance of these responses was that as a theologian resident in a capitalist country, the primary responsibility was to note the gulf between biblical and dogmatic insights and claims, bearing upon the relations between authority, power, and justice and the practice of those relations through the structures and by the holders of power in the setting in which he lives and works. The theologian's task is to call into question the structures and practice of authority and power in the light of the scriptural and dogmatic understanding of justice as the love of God in action. The theologian's task is *not* to provide a theological warrant for the self-justification of established power and authority by howling with the wolves the sure and certain identification of the enemy. Accordingly, it is both *beside* the point and a violation of Christian faith and obedience to cry out against Communism from the outside and on behalf of those who live under its domination and know its dehumanization only too well. By the same token, it is very much *to* the point and required of Christian faith and obedience to alert those who live under the dehumanization of capitalism and who seek to justify themselves by anti-communist fanaticism that—since they compound injustice with hypocrisy—they are in a worse case. The mote and the beam, the serpent and the dove, the sheep and the goats have never been more perceptively and politically conjoined with the poetry and politics of the Old Testament prophets, nor more faithfully applied than by Barth's deliberately chosen silence on Hungary.

The Augustinian roots of the Emperor's vision and of *Carolus magnus'* pursuit of theological existence today become concretely—and almost suddenly—contemporary. It seems, as Augustine noted in surveying his own life and time, that the Romans were once defeated in a protracted war because they loved justice for the sake of glory rather than glory for the sake of justice. "Justice, then, being absent," Augustine wrote, "what are kingdoms but great robberies? What are robberies but little kingdoms?"[14] The dialectical relation of dogmatics and politics thus enters upon a metaphorical companionship with the dialectical relation of dogma to language and to humor. Perhaps the greatest legacy of Karl Barth to the present and the future of theological thought and action is his metaphorical interpretation of the *concreteness* of dogmatic analysis and interpretation in a thematic-symphonic statement of the humanity of God for the sake of the humanization of human life in this world and the next. In focusing his search for an essential metaphor upon the Chalcedonian statement, he has provided the need for an essential metaphor with an authentic response and a warrant for a continuing companionship of discernment with wistful unbelievers of the truth of faith and the freedom of obedience that are the gospel of Jesus Christ. In so doing, he has exposed the self-effacing liberation of humor in the grace of which believers may welcome the discernment by unbelievers of the point from which the joy and peace of believing arise; and unbelievers may welcome and bear with their discovery that this is the point that believers, owing to their familiarity with the faith, are liable to miss.

Accordingly, it may be hoped that this commemorative centenary of the birth of *Carolus magnus* may document nothing so truly as the fact that Karl Barth has made it possible once again, in William Butler Yeats's haunting seeing and saying, for "the falcon to hear the falconer," for "the best (who) lack all conviction, while the worst are full of passionate intensity" to celebrate "the ceremony of innocence," and for "centuries of stony sleep" to awaken "towards Bethlehem to be born."[15]

Carole magne! Tibi Deum laudo! Requiescat in pace!
Saint Augustine's Death Day

28 August 1985

NOTES

1. Published in Donald McKim, ed. *How Karl Barth Changed My Mind* (Eugene: Wipf and Stock, 1998), 36–46; reprinted with permission.
2. Eberhard Busch, *Karl Barth: His life from letters and autobiographical texts*, trans. John Bowden (Philadelphia: Fortress Press, 1976), 369–70.
3. Einhard, *Vita Caroli,* 24. The full title is: *Vita et gets Caroli cognomento* Magni, in Reuber Justus, *Verterum Scriptarum* (1619), 1–14. Also, see Einhard, *The Life of Charlemagne*, trans. Samuel E. Turner (Ann Arbor: University of Michigan, 1960; repr. 1972).
4. As Charles Cochrane summarizes Athanasius. See *Christianity and Classical Culture* (Oxford: Oxford University Press, 1957; repr. Magnolia, Mass: Peter Smith, 1984).
5. So, Cicero and Ovid described a witness who bears favorable testimony to character in a court of justice. See *laudatio, laudator,* in Cassell's *New Latin Dictionary*, by D. P. Simpson (New York: Funk and Wagnalls, 1959), 339. For Virgil, see *lego*, 341.
6. See the article on *Dogma* in Gerhard Kittel, *Theological Dictionary of the New Testament*, trans. Geoffrey Bromiley (Grand Rapids: Eerdmans, 1964), 2:230–32.
7. Karl Barth, *Die Theologie und die Kirche* (München: Christian Kaiser Verlag, 1928), 24; translation Lehmann's. See English translation: Karl Barth, *Theology and the Church*, trans. Louise Pettibone Smith (New York: Harper & Row, 1962), 239.
8. A remark about Arius in the article by Gwatkin in the Cambridge Modern History, cited by Charles Cochrane in *Christianity and Classical Culture*.
9. Karl Barth, *Ad Limina Apostolorum*, trans. Keith R. Crim (Richmond: John Knox Press, 1967), 14–15.
10. Edward Leuders, *The Need for an Essential Metaphor*. Professor Leuders is a member of the Department of English in the University of Utah, Salt Lake City. [Editorial: No additional information for this citation was given in the original essay.]
11. Hans Frei, *The Eclipse of Biblical Narrative. A Study in Eighteenth and Nineteenth Century Hermeneutics* (New Haven: Yale University Press, 1974).
12. Interview with Karl Barth by the BBC (London) (October 10, 1963).
13. Karl Barth, "A Letter of Thanks to Mozart" in *Wolfgang Amadeus Mozart*, trans. Clarence K. Pott (Grand Rapids: Eerdmans, 1986), 23.
14. Augustine, *De civitate Dei,* IV. [Editorial: See Augustine, *The City of God*, trans. Marcus Dods, The Modern Library, (Random House, 1950), IV.4, 112.]
15. William Butler Yeats, "The Second Coming," in *The Collected Poems of W. B. Yeats* (New York: Macmillan, 1951), 184–85.

Chapter 8

Theologians Who Have Influenced Me [Reinhold Niebuhr] (1970)[1]

Reinhold Niebuhr arrived on this planet on June 21, 1892, and is now living in retirement and in such serenity as faith distills from suffering in Stockbridge, Massachusetts. To talk about Niebuhr is more difficult for me than to talk about Barth because he has been and still is, a kind of father in God to me, having often been in our home as I was growing up, having preached my ordination, having been and still being, in large measure, one of the principal reasons, if not *the* principal reason that I am in the Christian ministry today and think theology is worth doing. There is another awful embarrassment and that is that in trying to sort out what best we might focus on this morning—I reread a chapter on Niebuhr's Christology, which I had the privilege of trying to write in 1956. I think this was probably a mistake, for it has put me in the bind of deciding between saying what can better be read and boring myself anew or forgetting that I had written it and not saying what I want to say. I still think that if I really wanted to focus on what's up with Niebuhr, I should really just read that chapter—but I won't.

Instead, let me set out, if I may, from a kind of movement from Barth to Niebuhr, which is not a chronological movement but a theological one in terms of my own theological pilgrimage. One might put it like this: While Niebuhr was the occasion and reason for my taking a serious look at theology, Barth was the reason for my taking seriously the theology that I looked at: and Niebuhr continues to be the pressure for and the pressure upon theology to make sense out of one's trying to be human in the world. Thus, it has always seemed to me to be a high privilege of the time in which you and I have been living: if not also something of a predicament, that Karl Barth and Reinhold Niebuhr have been the architects of the sense that being Christian makes in personal life and in social life. To use the metaphors of the Apostle Paul, they have been the architects of the "wisdom of God" and the "power of God" in our times.

In 1955, I think it was, or 1962, I can't quite remember now, I sat in the garden of Karl Barth in Basel, after a quiet and delightful lunch: and he began to catechize me about Niebuhr. Thinking this was probably an arrangement of divine providence, and I took the occasion tactfully, to lecture Karl Barth on what I thought was a theological misfortune in our generation. It seemed to me that he and Niebuhr tended always to talk past each other and never *to* each other or *with* each other. In the course of that hour and a half or so of conversation, I felt that I was making no headway whatsoever. Barth listened and with his, on the one hand gentle, on the other hand terrifying, intensity and he would just poke another question in and then another question in and then another question. So, I went away. Now, it happened also that at that particular time, it was either 3:4 or 4:1, which had just appeared, and the local publisher was out of stock. So, I made an arrangement with a student friend of mine, as soon as the copies were available, to collect one for me and go take it around to Barth, ask Barth if he would inscribe it and then send it on to me. I was then in Vienna or Strasbourg, I forget which. In due course, the book arrived. When I looked over the title page, I read a citation from J. C. Bengel, which said, "In the Kingdom of God there is no neutrality." Well, I was furious! So, I sat down right away and I wrote to Barth and I said I was surprised but not totally unprepared for this superscription. But "had I not learned from you," I wrote, "to shun all theological *Schulmeisterei*, that is to say, all theological contentiousness of schools; had I not learned from you that the doing of theology involved every man in doing his own thing—and now you write in a way that suggests the most unyielding kind of scholasticism?" A reply came by return mail in which Barth said, "My secretary *told* me I shouldn't have written that! But it was too late. What is written has been written. You have my permission, then, to take ink remover and remove it." Obviously, I never took up the permission. But that was very characteristic of Barth. His was a kind of graciousness over a personal embarrassment into which he was surprised to have gotten himself, but in which he always knew he wasn't quite innocent. Here is a kind of parable of the humanity of theology in our times which is scarcely better expressed than in the fact that theologians are also human.

The episode suggests, I think, that you and I, insofar as we take our theological opportunities and responsibilities seriously, have been brought up in a kind of schizophrenia, pulled by and between Barth and Niebuhr. At the same time, I think, that the contentiousness between Niebuhr and Barth has been used to edify the church, as God has his own secret ways of doing. "God," as Calvin remarked, "marvelously preserves his church *quasi ex latebris*, as it were in hiding places." Well, one of these hiding places which is not so inconspicuous is the running controversy between Niebuhr and Barth. It has been a kind of Jacob and Esau deal, really. So, I want to try to say a little bit about what I think the deal is about, and if you want to know what I think Niebuhr is about you can read the chapter on the Christology of Niebuhr in the volume on Reinhold Niebuhr in the *Library of Living Theologians*, which Charles Kegley and Robert Bretal edited over a period of years. This one came out in 1956, I think.

Meanwhile, you can begin to see what's up, if you recall a series of *Christian Century* articles. As I have refreshed my mind about them, it occurred to me that the *Christian Century* sometimes behaves like a gossiping midwife. Anyway, in the years between 1928 and 1959 it really, you know, played the Niebuhr-Barth hassle for all it was worth. Perhaps his Jacob and Esau quarrel made for the edification of the church. But this is a matter for eschatological determination. "Barth, Apostle of the Absolute," says the "Fort Sumter piece" on December 13, 1928. "Barth and political reaction," June 6, 1934. "Barth, Marx and Israel's Prophets," January 30, 1935, "Karl Barth and Democracy," *Radical Religion*, Winter 1938, in the heyday of Niebuhr religious socialist period. "Karl Barth on Politics," *Radical Religion*, Spring 1939. "We are men and not God!" *Christian Century*, October 27, 1948. "An Answer to Karl Barth," February 23, 1949. And the "piece de resistance," WHY IS BARTH SILENT ON HUNGARY?, January 23, 1957, and "Barth on Hungary," April 10, 1957.

Now, D. B. Robertson has collected some of Niebuhr's most valuable pieces in a little book published by Meridian, Inc., called *Essays in Applied Christianity*. The collection reminds us of this Niebuhr-Barth controversy in a kind of capsule form. It goes on to note the point that the distance between Barth and Niebuhr constitutes an important and continual question for the church. Here again the Jacob and Esau tension shows through. There is more Barth in Niebuhr and more Niebuhr in Barth than either of them was prepared to face up to. Thus, Charles West has urged Niebuhr, in his book *Communism and the Theologians*, to be the Barthian he is, which was about as appropriate and fruitful as my attempt to lecture Barth on being a Niebuhrian.[2]

But if we should look first at the Barth, Niebuhr is not; it would look something like this. For Niebuhr—Barth always seemed to insulate the church from the world too much, thus exhibiting what Niebuhr liked to call an insufficient "care of the world." Again, Barth was too eschatological for Niebuhr. The end always seemed to stand above history, obscuring the Biblical idea of the end of history. This is another way of putting criticism of Barth, namely that his two worlds were too Platonic and not sufficiently Biblical and Augustinian. Niebuhr was more Biblical and Augustinian at this point and this is, I think, a pertinent question. Even more, Niebuhr was disturbed, let's say, troubled, let's say angered, by what he calls "an extreme pragmatism" in Barth's thought which seemed to him to disavow all moral principles.[3] Very curious that he should charge Barth at that point, since that was one of the points at which Niebuhr was always being charged by his contemporaries here. There is more of Barth in Niebuhr and more of Niebuhr in Barth than either of them was prepared to face up to.

Further, for Niebuhr, Barth combined "a sophisticated knowledge of all the disciplines of modern culture with a frantic effort to isolate the Christian faith from the allegedly debilitating effects of philosophical and scientific speculation."[4] Niebuhr found it very hard to take when Barth remarked in *Against the Stream* that "the church never thinks, speaks or acts on principle. Rather, it judges spiritually and by individual cases."[5] This seemed to Niebuhr inadmissibly irresponsible.

I never understood quite how to read the small point that Barth was on the whole, the silent partner of the conversation. Niebuhr seemed always to be attacking Barth more vigorously and outspokenly than Barth was attacking Niebuhr. Partly, this may have been Barth's Swiss way of indicating that the Basel aristocracy was still intact even in theology. Or it may be that Barth was so absorbed in the *Dogmatics* and in the fundamental situation that he never really understood what was behind Niebuhr's concern. As you know, he didn't really understand what America was about until he visited at Appomattox and Gettysburg, and until the people in this seminary taught him how to shoot a rifle. This American distance always shadowed this controversy. As far as Barth did really comment on the point, he really thought Niebuhr had "missed the mark," as he said, because he, Barth, and continental theology never were at the point at which Niebuhr thought he found them. On the contrary, Barth thought that the real difference between continental and Anglo-Saxon theology was the irresponsible attitude toward the Bible on the part of Anglo-Saxons, which Niebuhr did not really pause to identify. Perhaps the 1948 Amsterdam Assembly address expresses most succinctly and sharply Barth's real disquiet at Niebuhr's way of doing theology. "No Christian Marshall Plan," he declared, "is the misconception that Niebuhr's criticism of society tended to be an attempt to program society."[6]

Let us turn now from this recurring theological—Jacob and Esau dynamics to comment upon what he believed to be among the central concerns of his work, and try then, tomorrow to indicate the way in which Niebuhr provides certain resources for continuing theological vitality in the life of the church. We can put them in a number of ways. Even putting them down as I have, did not prevent my thinking of putting it all differently again as I was thinking about our conversation on the way to and from breakfast this morning. If I speak for a moment quite autobiographically, what Niebuhr has meant to me, and this may really be the crucial issue between Barth and Niebuhr, has been the insistence upon the relevance of Christian faith. The relevance of Christian faith concerns Niebuhr at two levels: The level of meaning and the level of social responsibilities or ethics. In Niebuhr's preoccupation with the relevance of Christian faith he seemed to obscure for Barth the necessary preoccupation with the truth of Christian faith. Barth, on the other hand, was preoccupied primarily with the question of one truth of the Christian faith and he always seemed to Niebuhr to be insufficiently concerned about the relevance of Christian faith.

Here is a perennial theological tension within which all of us, who are sensitive theologically, find ourselves inescapably involved. This tension erupts with the force of a temptation for those of us who have the frontier responsibilities of doing theology—namely, the preaching of it every Sunday. We are tempted to confuse relevance with being interesting, and to confuse truth with the recognition, which comes from our general presbyters and synodical executives. But one critical problem is: How to preach the truth without being particularly interesting but in such a way as to make the breakthrough of the truth of faith inescapable; then go on to make clear that Christian faith is not a museum piece but a matter of theological contemporaneity. So truth and relevance with the accent on the relevance—this is one major indebtedness of mine to Niebuhr. Related to that is his insistent, incessant preoccupation with justice as the criterion of the integrity of faith and obedience.

There is yet a third major impact of Niebuhr upon my own theological work—about which I will talk particularly tomorrow—namely, the reality and role of power in human affairs. How then do these themes, these motifs work themselves out as Niebuhr worked with them in his own theological pilgrimage? I should like to enumerate and comment briefly upon four accents through which they still come through to us. The first one has to do with a theological understanding of humanity. The second has to do with the relation between idealism and compromise. The third has to do with a relation which is not identified by Niebuhr quite this way, but which has grown on me over the years as the relation between iconoclasm and idolatry; and finally, a relation which, for the most part is not one for which Niebuhr is sufficiently remembered—or even for which he came immediately to the fore, but which I think is as fundamental as any—the relation between piety and criticism. The concern for a theological understanding of humanity, for the relation between idealism and compromise, for the relation between iconoclasm and idolatry, and for the relation between piety and criticism—these seem to me to be somehow at the center of what Niebuhr was up to.

To go back now to the theological understanding of humanity—in the technical language, theological anthropology: I would like to say that in this respect Barth and Niebuhr have made all of us contemporaries of the Reformation. They have made us contemporaries of the Reformation because being contemporaries with them is very much like what it would have been for us to be contemporaries with Luther and Calvin. Calvin's remark, you remember, to which I referred the other day, about the knowledge of God and the knowledge of ourselves and about the possibility in theology of starting with either end of the stick is exactly characteristic of what Barth and Niebuhr were doing. Barth started, following Calvin, with God's end of the stick; Niebuhr started following Calvin also, with humanity's end of the stick. But it was never humanity in a humanistic sense; it was always humanity in a theological perspective. This is really the difference, also between Luther and Calvin as the catechisms make plain. "The chief end of man is to glorify God and enjoy him forever," says the Shorter Catechism. "The chief end of man is the eternal salvation of his soul," says the Lutheran catechism.

So here is a kind of catechetical hassle, at the very gut level of the Reformation, in which, in the providence of God, you and I are being caught up, and which we are being allowed to participate in as contemporaries of these two men—their hassles are our hassles. The difference is that the issues, the tensions of the controversy have gotten more intense, the stakes have gotten higher; so that we are being pushed as it were toward the edge of the seventeenth century, born just in time to be born out of due time. A theology of humanity in contrast to a theology of God, if you like, is evident in Niebuhr's very first book, *Does Civilization Need Religion?* "There are resources in the Christian religion," he wrote in 1927, "which make it the inevitable basis for any spiritual regeneration of Western civilization."[7] This sounds to me in retrospect a little archaic now. But when it was written, it was really the stuff that held things together. And yet, it remained Niebuhr's characteristic concern and remains one of Niebuhr's characteristically formative influences upon Christian theology. "There are resources in the Christian religion which make it the inevitable basis of any spiritual regeneration of Western civilization." Think of that in relation to what I will be saying on Friday about secularized Christianity and the world come of age. How fast things have moved! How problematical it now seems to talk about the spiritual regeneration of Western civilization! Yet if you and I thought we were doing what we were doing without any prospect of regenerating anything, would we be doing it? Our dilemma is that we don't really know whether we are Habakkuk or Jonah, Watchman or Runaway! That's where we are. And we are there because of a nagging loss of confidence that in the Christian religion there is the basis of any spiritual regeneration of Western civilization. "The task of redeeming Western society rests in a peculiar sense upon Christianity," Niebuhr wrote:

> It has reduced the eternal conflict between self-assertion and self-denial to the paradox of self-assertion through self-denial and make the Cross the symbol of life's highest achievement . . . The adoration of Jesus sometimes obscures the real genius of his life but cannot permanently destroy the fruitfulness of his inspiration. If there is any lack of identity between the Jesus of history and the

Christ of religious experience, the Jesus of history is nevertheless more capable of giving historical reality to the necessary Christ ideal than any character in history ... The idea of a potent but yet suffering, divine ideal which is defeated by the world but gains its victory in the defeat must remain basic in any morally creative world view.[8]

Love and justice, truth and relevance, at the level of a pragmatic social criticism; that's where Niebuhr began.

Two years later the pragmatic social criticism became a pragmatic self-criticism in *Leaves from a Notebook of a Tamed Cynic*. "It seems pathetic to me," he wrote:

that liberalism has too little appreciation of the tragedy of life to understand the Cross and orthodoxy insists too much upon the absolute uniqueness of the sacrifice of Christ to make the preaching of the Cross effective ... What makes this tragedy redemptive is that the foolishness of love is revealed as wisdom in the end, and its futility becomes the occasion for new moral striving.[9]

If you haven't read the *Leaves from a Notebook* for a while you might have a go at it again. It will give you a fresh taste of the difference between self-criticism and self-conscious, self-criticism at a level where God and guts are distinguishable, and you can tell the difference: a level where there is no confusion of guts and God as in "T" groups and the like. Niebuhr's theological self-understanding wrestles with the problem of who humans are, beginning with a kind of pragmatic self-criticism, moving then in the Giffords to a full and trenchant statement of the ambiguity of humankind. There, we are reminded that humans are creatures of freedom and creatures of nature. One is involved in sin, on the one hand, and under grace on the other. This single-minded concentration of what once was loosely called Niebuhr's pessimism made everybody nervous. There were those who thought that grace abounds, and that sin had somehow lost its concrete reality—or if you didn't think it had, you had no experience of what it means to be saved. On the other end of the stick were the people who didn't really mind being washed in sin because they couldn't care less about grace. But Niebuhr refused to cop out. He insisted that there was a parallel relation between sin and grace on the one side, and our involvement in freedom and our being deeply rooted in nature, on the other side.

Consonant with this self-critical criticism and critical self-criticism—Niebuhr went on to explore a way of living with ambiguity. The problem is, how to live with ambiguity and at the same time resist the temptation to escape ambiguity by idealist illusions. Niebuhr's consistent, really almost unrelieved criticism of liberalism in theology, liberalism in politics, liberalism in culture—focuses on the point that the liberal estimate of humanity overstated one's freedom, and overlooked one's creature-hood. In some ways, Niebuhr foreshadowed in a more articulate way what Kierkegaard had done in a subtler and precise way, namely, the end of idealism in theology, philosophy, ethics and politics. Idealism in ethics, in its more trivial form, of course, you can always see in the Christian Endeavor view of life; idealism at its serious level is based upon and shaped by the notion that in some way spirit has a kind of indestructible reality about it, no matter how adverse the involvements of life and experience become.

Every time I come down to this seminary, I get reminders of what I keep forgetting, or suppressing—I can't ever quite remember that in your church there is an almost ineradicable idealist conviction, become cliché. It is called the Spirituality of the Church. That was not really an apostolic inspiration, that one. How it could have arisen where there was any sober reading of the Corinthian letters, not to mention the bureaucratic structure of the church, is a little hard to understand. But then I have not been nurtured in the doctrine, so I may not see it rightly, or I may see it with schismatic prejudices.

One lives with ambiguity by resisting idealist oversimplifications and confusion; that's one point. One lives with ambiguity by doing what at that time was a shocking and naughty thing, namely, by recognizing compromise as a sign of grace, not sin. Compromise! Niebuhr's insistence was that compromise was not a way of selling short the ideal. Compromise was a way of being honest about defections from the ideal without surrendering the ideal—that's what it was. The notion, compromise, of course, came from Troeltsch, from whom both Reinhold Niebuhr and his brother Richard really derived their passion for relevance in the fundamental, cultural sense of that word. Troeltsch saw the problem with phenomenal comprehensiveness and clarity which we all in one way or another are aware of, namely, that we have crossed a watershed in our historical and cultural experience so that there is no longer a formative experience of a unifying vision, a unifying vision, a unifying idea, in the language of the absolute, in human and historical experience. Troeltsch was the first to see, and Niebuhr was in one way or another documenting this in his concern for compromise, that there has been—I would ask you to give the utmost serious consideration to this, brethren; I can't spell it out now—but there has been a fundamental alteration of consciousness going on since the eighteenth century that has now come to formative power and is beginning to bear its articulate fruit. This is an alteration of consciousness which has turned humanity's attention from one's relation to eternity, to an ideal world of value, and even from one's relations to nature to oneself.

To use theological jargon, for shorthand purposes—a shift has occurred from an ontological consciousness to an historical consciousness. This shift means that there is a radically different way of being aware of and being related to the reality, whatever it is, which makes sense out of my experience.

We are all children of the epistemological revolution launched by Descartes when he argued that all that humanity is really certain about is that they are really uncertain. The shift from this perspective and perplexity to historical consciousness is the shift from preoccupation with the certainty and uncertainty of knowledge to the question of one's relation in any given present, to one's future and one's past.

Well, this altered consciousness came to the surface for theology and ethics in Niebuhr's insistence upon compromise as a way by which one does not sell the idea short, but is, instead, honest about one's defection from the ideal without abandoning one's purpose to achieve it. That's what compromise is. What Niebuhr is talking about is, in exploring true relations between idealism and compromise is the way one really faces up to the implications of relevance or pragmatic self-criticism. Where he came out was a source at once of Niebuhr's persuasiveness and his puzzlement. I refer to his doctrine of the lesser evil. In a world of evil, one opts for the lesser one. This was Niebuhr's way of making clear that it makes sense still to work at the business of Christian regeneration of civilization by compromise. But it was the doctrine of the lesser evil, which, perhaps more than any other, alienated Niebuhr from the next generation. The doctrine, which fascinated, persuaded, and convinced my generation was the doctrine, which alienated Niebuhr as well as ourselves from the next generation. As things turned out Barth's theological way of doing things was able to bridge that generational gap more effectively than was Niebuhr. Barth, in turn, fell behind at another point. What Niebuhr lost in the field of ethics; Barth lost in the field of the language of faith. But I must turn to the remaining two of Niebuhr's central concerns and then say something about the problem of power.[10]

NOTES

1. Delivered extemporaneously at the Summer School of Theology, Union Theological Seminary in Virginia, July 15, 1970. The transcript of the recorded lecture, can be found in the Lehmann archives in the Wright Library at Princeton Theological Seminary, Box 28:19.

2. [Editorial: Charles C. West, *Communism and the Theologians: Study of an Encounter* (Westminster Press, 1958).]

3. Reinhold Niebuhr, *The Nature and Destiny of Man: A Christian Interpretation II: Human Destiny* (Louisville: Westminster John Knox Press, 1996), 309.

4. Reinhold Niebuhr, *The Self and the Dramas of History* (New York: Scribner, 1955), 108ff.

5. Karl Barth, *Against the Stream*, 114. [Editorial: Karl Barth, *Against the Stream: Shorter Post-War Writings, 1946–52*, ed. Ronald Gregor Smith (New York: Philosophical Library, 1954).]

6. *Christian Century*, 8. December 1948.

7. Niebuhr, *Does Civilization Need Religion?* 235. [Editorial: Reinhold Niebuhr, *Does Civilization Need Religion? A Study in the Social Resources and Limitations of Religion in Modern Life* (Eugene: Wipf & Stock, 2010).]

8. Niebuhr, *Does Civilization Need Religion?*, 235–37.

9. Reinhold Niebuhr, *Leaves from the Notebook of a Tamed Cynic*, 85–86. [Editorial: See Reinhold Niebuhr, *Leaves from the Notebook of a Tamed Cynic* (Louisville: Westminster John Knox Press, 1991).

10. [Editorial: Unfortunately, no recording or transcription of the second lecture has been found either at Union Presbyterian Seminary in Richmond, VA, where the lectures were given, or in the Lehmann archives in Princeton, NJ.]

Chapter 9

Louise Pettibone Smith, Rudolf Bultmann, and Wellesley (1985)[1]

In the Introduction to the English translation of the first volume of Rudolf Bultmann's *Glauben und Verstehen* [faith and understanding], Robert Funk notes that "very little of Bultmann's work had been translated into English at the time the Second World War broke out."[2] To this comment, he adds the following footnote:

> One notable exception is Louise Pettibone Smith's translation (with E. H. Lantero) from the German *Jesus* (Berlin: Deutsche Bibliothek, 1926; 2/1929) as *Jesus and the Word* (New York, Scribner, 1934; paperback edition, 1953). Unlike the vast majority of such cases, the alteration in the title in this instance was an illuminating advance over the German form. Professor Smith remarked in her Preface to the paperback edition that Bultmann was little known in the United States in 1934. It is altogether fitting that she, who led the way in presenting Bultmann originally to English readers, should return after so many years to the unfinished task of providing the wider context for Jesus and the Word.[3]

Accordingly, it is also "altogether fitting," that a centenary commemorative Symposium honoring the birth, life, and work of Rudolf Bultmann should include in its consideration a tribute of respect and admiration, of remembrance and gratitude for the life and work of Louise Pettibone Smith. That Louise Smith should have provided Bultmann with an English title marking an "illuminating advance over the German form," succinctly and simply identifies who she was and is, what she was about, and how she went about it. On Bultmann's behalf, she broke down the "middle wall of partition" (Eph 2:14), dividing the monolingual Anglo-Saxons from their multilingual fellow "travelers through time as they bumble by from birth to death menaced by madness."[4]

Louise Smith was not only a translator of Bultmann. She was also his travel agent in the United States. Consequently, Wellesley College became a kind of center of Bultmannian operations, "not only in Judea and Samaria," in their American counterparts, but "in the uttermost parts of the earth" (Acts 1:8b). As I shall venture to suggest in what follows, the breaking down of the middle wall of partition became for Louise, and for many of us with her, the power of the "chief cornerstone" (Eph 2:20), a bulwark against the time when Bonzo should emerge from Death Valley, and emerge only long enough to leave no stone unturned until all dissenters should be buried there, beyond any prospect of the resurrection of the dead. Thus, when such a symposium convenes at Wellesley College, to the faculty of which belonged this distinguished and stalwart biblical scholar, who happened also to be an Anglo-Saxon of formidable Yankee and Calvinist chromosomes and convictions, it is simply providential wisdom, decency and order—and in the order—that Louise Pettibone Smith should be present to us and with us.

In her youth, Louise had learned the difference between Babel and Pentecost; and she was, though she would cringe at the thought, a Pentecostalist from beginning to end. As far as the heavens are from the earth, so far—it has turned out—is a Pentecostalist in Wellesley from a Pentecostalist Presbyterian in Dallas, who imagines that the second Great Awakening in January 1985 can make Death Valley blossom as a rose.

Louise Pettibone Smith was a professor of Biblical History, Literature and Interpretation at Wellesley from 1915 onward, and until her retirement in 1953. In those days, the *Nephilim* were in this place; and the *Rephaim* too: that is, the fallen ones and the fearsome ones (Gen 6:4; Num 13:33). But in those days, the seed of Abraham and Sarah had not yet been outvoted by the pluralistic, synergistic, Syncretistic fascinations with the *Baalim*, by the Canaanites who were and still are in the land; and who continue to pursue the fantasy that Babel is Pentecost. I believe they call it "religion." In any event, to a young and inexperienced colleague, as ignorant as he was innocent, both of the *Nephilim* and of the *Rephaim,* Louise Smith was in truth "among those who were encountered as giants" (Dt. 2:11, 20).

It is neither accidental nor coincidental that Louise's *Alma Mater*, Bryn Mawr, should have included her among the seventy-five distinguished alumnae to be awarded honorary doctorates upon the occasion of the College's seventy-fifth anniversary. Indeed, among Louise's impressive gifts were a single-minded dedication to scholarship and learning as a fulfilling vocation, to teaching with imagination, precision and conviction, and to a passion and compassion for the "stranger within the gate" (Deut. 5:14; 10:18–19; 26:13); that is, for the outsiders and those to whom the insiders responded with the disregard of alienation and by the subtle and not so subtle preferences of power, so structured as to deny to the different, a meaningful participation in human community.

Let me, then, invite our respect and admiration, remembrance and gratitude for these gifts; and this, more briefly than is their due, and much more inadequately than they require. As an aide-*memoire,* let us, in the tradition of Rudolf Bultmann, engage in what he called *Sachkritik* [criticism of the subject]. This *Sachkritik* has to do with *The Word and the Words,* implied in Louise's imaginative title. *The Word and the Words* in the encounter with her gifts, offers the hope that in remembrance and gratitude Louise Pettibone Smith may come among us again.

When I think of Louise's dedication to scholarship and learning as a vocation, the identifying word that comes to mind is "conscientiousness." When I recall her teaching with imagination and precision, the word "conviction" claims attention. And when the surprise of her retirement activity overtakes my meeting again with her on this occasion, it is the word "conscience" that makes her passion and compassion for the stranger within the gate understandable and unavoidable. Each of these indications of the point and purpose and ethos of her life becomes, when taken together, an invitation that each of us—in welcoming her among us again—to bring commitment and responsibility together, as the point and purpose and ethos of the living of our days.

It was Louise's formidable scholarship and exacting learning that compounded her considerable stature by nature with a yet more considerable stature by grace. She was, indeed, among the giants of the faculty of Wellesley, and in the department of Biblical History, Literature and Interpretation, in the days when I first came to know her here in 1941. There were *Rephaim* and *Nephilim* in the land: the fearsome ones and the fallen ones. Had I known or could I even have guessed that this moving privilege would be mine this evening, I would certainly have tried her patience with my vincible ignorance, by asking her to explain to me the subtleties of Hebrew vocabulary, syntax and folklore, having to do with the *Rephaim* and the *Nephilim.* Having failed to do so, I can only commend my lack of foresight—and even curiosity—to the forbearance of my colleagues in Semitic and Old Testament Studies in this notable gathering; and, in my extremity, venture upon a semantic suspicion of my own, quickened by Louise Pettibone Smith. She had a way of evoking such suspicions, not only in her students, but in her colleagues as well.

My Smithian suspicion is that the difference between the *Rephaim* and the *Nephilim* is a not insignificant one. There are those in whom commitment and responsibility are so *con*joined in competence and excellence as "to fill the mind with never ending wonder and awe," as Kant once said about the stars. These the fearsome ones, the *Rephaim.* On the other hand, there are those in whom commitment are responsibility are so *dis*joined as a center commitment upon themselves and to cultivate responsibility as the sign and measure of self-justifying self-esteem. These are the fallen ones, the *Nephilim.* And they are busy again, on campuses and off, at barricading the "naked public square,"[5] even as they fill it with the corpse of the widows and the orphans and the strangers within the gate: victims of the injustice with which, in our time as in other times, the powerful feed their power. In the first instance, commitment and responsibility are sundered by the terrifying dynamics of self-deceived and deceiving destruction, within and without.

At all events, Louise was one of the fearsome ones, whose scholarship and learning were formidable. She pursued them as a commitment in response to a claim. I used to chide her from time to time, for what seemed to me to be her indifference to the world about her. "How can you," I would ask her, "teach the Old Testament, and especially the Prophets, year after year, and never move beyond this campus?" Her unvarying reply was that she had been appointed by the President and the Board of Trustees of Wellesley College to teach in the Department of Biblical History, Literature and Interpretation. And she could only do one thing at a time—"well!" In that "well!" I always heard a silent judgement upon my misguided youthful attempts to be both a scholar and teacher *and* involved in the world. She would have none of it. It took more than a little while to discover the secret of her conscientiousness.

The secret was the δύναμις (creative power) of her linkage of commitment with responsibility. Perhaps the most notable and memorable sign of her "secret weapon" of conscientiousness was the act of courage expressed in her devotion to Rudolf Bultmann. Her probing of his mind and thought involve little short of a ("radical turning upside down") of the path of scholarship and learning which led her to Bultmann and became the path which she was to continue to pursue. To start all over again—that, I submit, is courage!

In Louise, this *conscientiousness* was companioned by a rare combination of imagination and precision, though her being about whatever she was about, with *conviction*. At this point, the paradoxical identity of Louise Pettibone Smith shows itself in a particularly impressive way. By many of her colleagues and students, she was at once respected and ignored, even disliked. The diffidence that companioned her resoluteness was not readily discernible. As a Yankee and a Calvinist, she found it is impossible to wear her heart on her sleeve as to suggest that coldness of heart was her hidden *élan*. I have found myself speculating about this more than once, during the intervening years. And especially, as I have thought about our coming together here, a number of biographical footnotes in illumination of this point occurred to me.

As I have said, Louise was nurtured as a Yankee and a Calvinist. She used to tell me about her puzzlement as a child over her grandfather. The awesome gentleman never seemed to communicate—not only *not* with children, but not even with adults. As she grew older and wiser, it occurred to her one day, that the secret of her grandfather's inability to communicate was his clear and certain knowledge of the providential grace of God. It seems that, especially on holidays, her immediate family would join with other members of the clan at Grandfather's House and Board. At the festive table Grandfather, to whom nobody would dream of talking unless addressed by him, and from whom nobody would expect to hear very much, used to pray upwards of fifteen to twenty minutes before the ample and tempting meal could be partaken of. Eventually, it dawned upon Louise that her grandfather was not only giving thanks to God as the Giver of all good. He was expressing before God all his deepest feelings and concerns for those whom he loved most, and which he was unable to express to them face to face.

Or there was Uncle Ben, who loved strawberries to the point of an addiction. Every year at strawberry season, the family would gather about Uncle Ben's table upon which he would ceremonially sit down a huge bowl of strawberries and firmly announce, "Doubtless, God could have made a better berry; but obviously, God did not make a better berry!" The reticence and unaffected pleasure natured in her family, Louise brought with her to Wellesley where they found expression through an acute and carefully considered *conviction.*

An incidental instance concerns another of my chidings of Louise. She took particular pleasure in attending worship on Sunday when the sacrament of Baptism was being celebrated. I used to tell her that these services were most diverting and frustrating to me because the infants were always screaming so that one couldn't pay attention to the Word and the words. To this caveat, Louise's reply was: "The screaming of infants at Baptism is always especially meaningful to me because it is a proper protest of nature against grace."

Two further cases in point may be noted in relation to a student event to which the college community looked forward to each year and to an administrative procedure internal to the Department of Biblical History during her tenure as its chairperson. At Wellesley the Junior Class produces and presents each year what is known as "The Junior Show." This spectacle centered upon one or another member of the faculty and came to be regarded as a distinction of favor conferred by the students upon the faculty member chosen as the subject of the evening's frivolity. One year during my time here the choice fell upon Louise. One of the directives most urged upon her was to express her exasperation at whatever it was that was going on, through a punch line that seemed to the juniors to be vintage Louise Pettibone Smith. They wanted her to exclaim in chagrin, "oh, for God's sake!" The producers and Louise were unanimous in the conviction that *that* would not do. And as for the proposed line, Louise resolutely refused. "I will only say what I was brought up to say in such situations, she explained. She finally prevailed; and the line turned out to be. "Shucks and peanut shells!" The line brought down the house, contrary to all directional forebodence; and it made her the star of the show. It was indeed vintage Louise.

As for the biblical department, it happened that during my first year as a member of the faculty, I was reluctant to accept the appointment because of a conviction of my own which was that the better part of wisdom for newcomers in a faculty was to keep eyes and ears open and mouth shut, at least for the first year. One did not, however, refuse Louise Smith on a matter of departmental responsibility, even when she was not the Chairperson. So I reluctantly agreed. Early in the Autumn of 1941, the agenda before the "Small Committee," as it was called, included an item having to do with an appointment to the faculty of the department. On the basis of my brief acquaintance with the candidate under consideration and of the discussion of my colleagues, it seemed to me appropriate to abstain when the vote was called for. It did not seem so to Louise. Apparently, there had recently been a colleague who, as a member of the committee, seemed unable or unwilling to come to a decision and always abstained. Let her identity be cared for by the sign of "X." Upon my abstention, Louise turned directly to me and, with unmistakable impatience and annoyance, emphatically declared: "We won't have any more X's in this department! You vote!" So I did vote, and as a lone minority of one, against the resolution to appoint. It was not the decision which Louise found irresponsible, even though it did not agree with hers. It was indecisiveness which she found inadmissible and inexcusable. Thus did *conscientiousness* combine with *conviction* about who she was and why. The combination spelled integrity to which one could only respond with respect and admiration.

In view of Louise's somewhat aloof disposition, respect for those with whom she disagreed was as remarkable as it was recognizable. But there was one notable precondition. She had great respect for those with whom she disagreed, in whom could be discerned a kindred discipline of scholarship and teaching with imagination, precision, and conviction. We come here upon the basic paradox of her conscientiousness and conviction. This was the conviction that the discipline of responsibility is the gift and practice of freedom. The nexus of this formative paradox is, and was for her, the unashamed acknowledgement and acceptance of the claims of *conscience.*

A notable, even historic, instance of Louise's conscience in action is provided by the surprise of her activities preceding and following upon her retirement.

In the difficult days of the early fifties, to the lasting credit of Wellesley (and perhaps also of Harvard), there were only two professors in the colleges of New England who were summoned before the Senate Internal Security Sub-Committee, headed by Senator Jenner. One of them was Kirtley Mather, a renowned Geologist at Harvard; the other was Louise Pettibone Smith of Wellesley. The Sub-Committee was meeting in Boston, before which Louise was summoned to appear on March 26, 1953. Her testimony has always seemed to me to be an act of courage in conscience, companioning the act of courage in conscientiousness and conviction in her discovery and commitment to Rudolf Bultmann. It must also be gratefully acknowledged that, to the great credit of the Board of Trustees of this College, Louise was assured of the Board's readiness to make available to her its support and such legal assistance as she might have need of in connection with her appearance before the Sub-Committee.

The interrogation went something like this:

"You are Louise Pettibone Smith?"

"Yes."

"You are a Professor of Wellesley College?"

"I was," said Louise; "I am about to retire."

"We have here a note which says you know a certain Mr. Patterson." (Patterson was then a prime target of the Sub-Committee, accused of being a member of the Communist Party.)

"I have debated with Mr. Patterson a number of times," Louise said. "But I do not know him."

"Did you know that he was a member of the Communist party of the United States?"

"No," said Louise. "I have it told that he was, but I don't know it."

"If you did know it, would it make any difference?"

"No," said Louise. "I am sixty-five years of age and have been following my own judgment these many years; and I think I trust my judgment more than Tom Clark's." (Thomas C. Clark was the recent Attorney General of the United States who had prepared the infamous list of subversive organizations)

"Witness dismissed."

Well, in the light of my earlier chidings of Louise's conscience, I was gratified beyond measure. What surprised me still more was that Louise did not let the matter rest there. I had, you see, greatly underestimated the secret power of the integrity which integrated conscientiousness, conviction, and conscience in her being who she was, in what she was about, and how she went about it.

As a Yankee, the rebuke to the Sub-Committee was a natural and self-evident expression of her deeply rooted commitment to the civil liberties, constitutionally safeguarded an indispensable to democratic Society. As a Calvinist, she found it equally natural and self-evident to be aware of and alert to the idolatry of self-righteous self-justification to which all authority and power are vulnerable. In her retirement, these two strains of her heritage were claimed by a providential incongruity for which her teaching of the Bible in this place during all those years had singularly equipped her. She matched her rebuke of one committee by her commitment to the chairing of another. Her rebuke of a committee of overreaching power was followed by the leadership of a committee founded for the sake of human justice, as the foundation and the criterion of the liberties of all people.

Louise accepted the Co-Chair of the American Committee for Protection of Foreign Born in December 1951.[6] This committee had come into existence as far back as 1919, in the wake of the infamous Palmer Raids. These raids exemplified the preference of the U.S. Department of Justice for terror over due process, and for security over justice, in the alleged protection of the freedom and safety of the body politic. The raids split families, denaturalized and deported citizens suspected of syndicalism and of various other activities informed by a commitment to social justice which Republican Administrations, at least since Theodore Roosevelt and William Howard Taft, have more stubbornly disdained than Democrats, and still do. Between the Palmer Raids and the nomination of Edwin Meese III as Attorney General of the United States,[7] the infamous Walter-McCarran Act has presided and prevailed over the slow and subtle erosion of the constitutional guarantees enshrine in the Bill of Rights. It fell to this hitherto little-known Professor of Biblical History, Literature, and Interpretation at Wellesley College, both to confound the House Un-American Activities Committee by her testimony which led to the deletion of the American Committee for Protection of Foreign Born from its list of alleged subversion organizations to write a well-documented history of this Committee entitled, *The Torch of Liberty*.[8]

The principal reason for this retirement commitment, as Louise often explained, was firmly anchored in the Pentateuch; and there, of all places, in the Holiness Code of Leviticus. Therein, it is set down: "You shall have one law for the sojourner and for the native; for I am the Lord your God" (Lev 24:22). "When a stranger sojourns in your land you shall not do him wrong. The stranger who sojourns with you shall be to you as the native among you; and you shall love him as yourself; for you were strangers in the Land of Egypt: I am the Lord your God" (Lev 19:23). Louise was, in truth, among the *Rephaim*, the Hebrew root of which means "heal."[9]

Biblical scholarship and biblical learning find their moment of conscience. When this moment came upon Louise, she naturally and self-evidently seized it. She went in the power of the Word in the words, across the length and breadth of this land. In groups gathered for meeting, and among individuals, she was listened to, heard, and made welcome by labor leaders and labor rank and file, by immigrants, naturalized citizens and native born, many of whom could not have been more distant on the educational spectrum from the student whom Louise had lived and worked at Wellesley College. She talked *to* them and *with* them straight from the Pentateuch and from Jeremiah, about the promise, the hope, and the path of a society of justice and freedom and peace, in which there is one law for the sojourner and for the native. She was received everywhere with respect and admiration and gratitude-and with warm hospitality and friendship, in the wonder of the discovery that she, whom they seemed to have known and trusted always, had been a college professor. How fearfully and wonderfully made (Ps 130:14) it is, that on the occasion of the centenary of the founding of the Society of Biblical Literature in 1980, Louise Pettibone Smith should be among the six members of the Society to have been honored by a special citation and that—*Dei providentia*—upon the centenary of the birth of Rudolf Bultmann, this Symposium should remember her in respect and admiration and gratitude.

Our last meeting happened in November 1980, shortly before she died. All of her capacities of self-discipline and resoluteness, of conscientiousness, conviction, and conscience were then on trial. She had finally to go into the nursing facility of the Retirement Community in Hartford, which had become her home. There, she had to share a room with another person whom she simply could not abide. It was, however, vintage Louise, to bear this also, without a murmur. The American Committee for Protection of Foreign Born, to which she had been so ably devoted, had resolved to help make available to her, a place of her own in the Nursing Facility. But this resolve, too lately made, likewise too lately came to her aid. It succeeded only in transferring her to the waiting list for the next available opening. As we took leave of one another (she was then in her ninety-fourth year) she said, "Paul, one should not live so long." It was an unforgettable sign of her intelligence and her integrity, her diffidence and her forbearance, her faith and her faithfulness that, on the tightrope of faith and doubt, death found her waiting for God's next move.

Louise Pettibone Smith: *Tibi Deum laudamus! Requiescat in pace!* [We praise you, God! Rest in peace!]

NOTES

1. Published in Edward C. Hobbes, ed. *Bultmann: Retrospect and Prospect: The Centenary Symposium at Wellesley* (Philadelphia: Fortress, 1985), 91–101; reprinted with permission.

2. Rudolf Bultmann, *Faith and Understanding I,* ed. Robert W. Funk, trans. Louise Pettibone Smith (New York and Evanston: Harper & Row, 1969), 10.

3. Bultmann, *Faith and Understanding I*, 10n2.

4. W.H. Auden, *The Age of Anxiety* (New York: Random House, 1947), 23.

5. Richard Neuhaus, *Naked Public Square* (Grand Rapids: Eerdmans, 1984).

6. On December 9, 1951, the Committee elected Louise Pettibone Smith and George R. Murphy, Jr., as Co-Chairs, Bishop Arthur Moulton as Honorary Chair, and Abner Green as Executive Secretary.

7. A. Mitchell Palmer was President Woodrow Wilson's third attorney general in 1919. Edwin Meese III awaits confirmation by the Senate as President Ronald Reagan's attorney general. The political kinship between the Palmer Raids and the nomination of Edwin Meese III has been instructively analyzed by Christopher Hitchens, "Minority Report: Why Ed Meese Shouldn't Be Confirmed," in *The Nation* 239, no. 22 (December 29, 1984-January 5, 1985): 697, 701–702.

8. Louise Pettibone Smith, *The Torch of Liberty* (New York: King, 1959), esp. chapters 6, 19, and 20.

9. To this surprising confirmation of my Smithian suspicion, my Union Seminary colleague, Professor George Landes, has called my attention, as this tribute was being prepared for publication.

PART II

The Revolutionary Dimension of the Gospel

In Part II of this volume, we have gathered together a range of essays by Lehmann spanning several decades. Notably, the opening essay from 1944 makes the rather provocative claim that an ethic rooted in a theology of justification consistent with the Protestant Reformation is necessarily a "revolutionary ethic" that is oriented toward a "continuing protest against what has come to be the established order of things in the world." For Lehmann, the resources for an emancipatory and revolutionary theology, which stem from the heart of the Protestant faith, found creative expression in the theology of Karl Barth as a "theologian of permanent revolution," and, perhaps especially for Lehmann, in the theology and ethics of his close friend and colleague, Dietrich Bonhoeffer. Not only did Lehmann contribute to the theological study of Barth and Bonhoeffer in North America, he creatively extended the politically revolutionary potential of their theologies in ways that sought to directly challenge the ideological status quo of white European and North American theologies that so often deployed the Protestant theological tradition to underwrite unjust social orders rather than call them into question at their theological and biblical roots. Toward this end, Lehmann actively opposed the abrogation of civil liberties during the McCarthy era, serving as chair of the Emergency Civil Liberties Committee in 1951, supported the Civil Rights movement in the United States, and defended the revolutionary impulse of the Black Power movement. Constructively critical of certain elements of his Union Seminary colleague, James Cone, Lehmann insisted that the perceived impossibility of a dialogue between white and black theologians "must be faced and overcome, certainly in the United States, and since Fanon, also in the European 'West,' if the truth which alone makes any theology 'Christian' is not to be imprisoned by the unacknowledged rhetoric of a white ideology masking as theology."[1] So, too, Lehmann engaged in conversation with American Indian theologian, Vine Deloria, Jr., among others, wrestling with the question of a Christian theological response to the call for accountability and justice.[2]

In September 1961, Lehmann traveled to Brazil to deliver a series of lectures to a group of Brazilian students who were studying with Richard Shaull, a former Presbyterian missionary and a disciple of Lehmann. The students who attended Lehmann's lectures reflected on his visit: "We remember the commentary of Dr. Paul Lehmann when he said, 'God became human in Jesus Christ in order that all people may be truly human,' and we began to speak in radically different terms regarding humanization and what it signified."[3] Shaull had founded the important organization, Church and Society in Latin America (ISAL), which became a central site for the developing theological conversations oriented around a "theology of revolution" in Latin America throughout the 1960s. In 1968, seven years after Lehmann's visit, Rubem Alves, an exiled Brazilian doctoral candidate studying at Princeton Theological Seminary, defended his dissertation entitled, "Towards a Theology of Liberation," under the direction of Shaull, which would later be published under the slightly modified title, *A Theology of Human Hope*.[4] Regarded by some as the first sustained articulation of the emerging theology of liberation in Latin America, Alves's dissertation was written three years prior to Gustavo Gutierrez's *A Theology of Liberation*. If Alan Neely is right in his claim that no other theologian has "more consistently and directly contributed to the shaping of the thought of the contemporary Protestant theologians of liberation than Richard Shaull," surely too, Lehmann as his former doctoral advisor and his "most important and influential teacher,"[5] should be regarded as among those who directly and indirectly contributed to the distinctively Protestant emergence of liberation theology in Latin America. The work of several other prominent Latin American Protestant theologians, such as José Míguez Bonino and Beatriz Melano Couch, also bear the stamp of Lehmann's direct theological influence.[6]

Lehmann's influence on the emerging theologies of liberation and struggles for justice was not limited to Latin America. An edited volume titled *On Reading Karl Barth in South Africa*, for example, which brought together a range of theological voices wrestling with Barth's theology in relation to the struggle against apartheid in South Africa, is dedicated to Lehmann. In the Foreword, the black South African theologian, Allan Boesak, acknowledged the "profound influence" that Lehmann had on his own theology, noting that *The Transfiguration of Politics*, was one of "the most formative theological studies I have ever read."[7] So, too, Lehmann's influence can be discerned, at least indirectly, in the development of Korean minjung theology, evidenced by the playwright and poet, Kim Chi-ha's reference to Lehmann as a key influence in his writing of the 1975, "A Declaration of Conscience."[8] Lehmann's theological engagement with the revolutionary dimension of the Gospel and the contextual task of theological ethics, informed especially by Barth and Bonhoeffer, led him to embrace local and global struggles for revolution and emancipation as an aspect of "transfiguration" and "humanization," situating him in a unique place in the historical development of liberation theology worldwide.

NOTES

1. Paul Lehmann, "Black Theology and 'Christian' Theology," 200–201.
2. See Paul Lehmann, "The Indian Situation as a Question of Accountability: A Theological Perspective," *Church and Society* 75, no 3 (1985): 179–92.
3. Alan Preston Neely, "Protestant Antecedents of the Latin American Theology of Liberation" (Ph.D. dissertation, The American University, 1977), 164.
4. Rubem Alves, *A Theology of Human Hope* (Washington: Corpus Books, 1969).
5. For Shaull's extended tribute to Lehmann, see Barbara Hall and Richard Shaull, "From Somewhere Along the Road," *Theology Today* 29, no. 1 (1972): 86–101.
6. See Beatriz Melano, "The Influence of Dietrich Bonhoeffer, Paul Lehmann, and Richard Shaull in Latin America," *The Princeton Seminary Bulletin* (2001): 64–84.
7. Allan Boesak and Charles Villa-Vicencio, eds., *On Reading Karl Barth in South America* (Grand Rapids: Eerdmans, 1988), xi. Boesak also dedicated his book to Lehmann, see Allan Boesak, *Comfort and Protest: The Apocalypse from a South African Perspective* (Louisville: Westminster John Knox, 1987).
8. Kim Chi-Ha, "A Declaration of Conscience," in *The Gold-Crowned Jesus* (Maryknoll: Orbis Books, 1979), 26.

Chapter 10

The Shape of Theology for a World in Revolution (1965)[1]

When the question is raised as to what kind of a theological perspective is at our disposal for living with the fact of revolution, the self-evidence of revolution and the possibility of a theology for a world in revolution collide. The collision calls for a confession: since we as human beings and as believers have been drawn more and more into the dynamics of revolution, the church has repeatedly succumbed to silence about the authentic connection between its faith and this tumult. The encounter of theological resources and revolutionary facts, however, shouts its own silence with the remembrance that the self-evidence of revolution in the world is not matched by any such self-evidence about a theology for a world in revolution. It would appear therefore that theology has met its match.

The Christian church, however, has been both brighter and more stupid on this matter than most other structures of society. More stupid because it has tended to escape from revolution and has counseled us against its appropriateness to Christian and theological concerns, brighter because from the beginning of its own life the church has been equipped by mind, imagination, and energy for responding to revolution. The church has perhaps dimly sensed, but not imaginatively explored, its own resources for revolution.

To speak about a "theology for the world in revolution" involves a certain ambiguity in the substance of theological self-understanding. The ambiguity is due to the first preposition in the formulation, "theology for a world in revolution."

For may mean at least two things: for the purpose of dealing with revolution in the world, or "*for the sake of* the world in revolution." The first would mean something like this: you are involved in a certain human condition and then you look around and say to yourself, "Could there possibly be any theology for dealing with this?" This usually passes under the heading of relevance and Christians are always worried about being relevant.

111

But the concern for relevance on its own terms is misleading; it is what always makes Christians fall flat on their faces—because they are out of character. They are not supposed to be relevant; they are supposed to be Christian, which is to be involved in the very center of the dynamics of revolution (much like the eye of a hurricane). The "eye" of revolution erupts with a single fury and a singular inescapability, and Christians tend to be surprised. This is the pathos in which the brightness and the stupidity of the church intersect one another. Christians should have known about revolution all along. It is only the non-Christian who is entitled to be surprised at revolution.

We are concerned about theology "for the sake of the world in revolution." This theology is a description of truth comparing inner and outer meanings of the revolutionary character of human life. This equation illustrates not simply human life in the world but also the world and its life in humanity (because human life is in it). This is what the hurricane is about.

The internal and external connection between a revolution in the world and a theology for the sake of a world in revolution engages us in a description of the context of the meaning and purpose of freedom and responsibility with which the dynamics of revolution and of theology are always concerned. We could say of revolution what Augustine once said of war: "Humanity does not make war for the sake of war; they make war for the sake of peace." Humanity does not make revolution for the sake of revolution; they make revolution for the sake of the world. That is, they do not make revolution at all; they respond to it. Such response makes trivial and pathetic the image of the revolutionary figure as the man with the black mustache and the black satchel. Such a figure is trivial and pathetic because he is the invention of the diseased imaginations of people who are themselves characteristically afraid of the world, because they have defaulted in their responsibility as human beings in the world.

The shape of theology for a world in revolution may be sketched in two formulations. Borrowing a phrase from Pascal, who once said that sickness was the natural state of the Christian,[2] the first suggestion is that revolution is the natural environment of the Christian. The second is that Christian faith is the catalyst of authentic revolution.

THE REVOLUTIONARY ENVIRONMENT OF THE CHRISTIAN

The remarkable thing about Christian faith is that it came into the world with a perspective for responding to the most fundamental perplexities of human life in the world. If we can identify these perplexities as they were identified by the classical Greek culture into which Christianity came, we could put it this way:

Stability and Change: What is it that gives permanence to life? What is it that is dependable? How do we understand the flux, the alteration, the movement of human life in the world, or the world in which humans live?

Decay and Fulfillment: How do we probe the baffling circumstance that we are not only caught up in movement, not only going from a given present toward a given future from a given past, but are also heavily under the shadow of decay? The Greek mind was inescapably oppressed by the fact that this movement ends not in fulfillment but in futility. It is this oppressive sense of decay in responding to change that deprived the Greek mind of any meaningful sense of fulfillment and delivered it over instead to fate.

These fundamental human experiences (which the Greeks labeled, but did not invent) were recognized in like intensity and depth by the Christian mind. But Christian faith enabled human life to make an important alteration in the relations between stability and change and between decay and fulfillment. The alteration is so radical as to amount to a transvaluation. As the Christian mind tried to come to terms with these experiences, it came more and more to regard change as the prelude to authentic stability, and decay as the harbinger of a fulfillment on the way. In this way history was given its fundamental human significance.

In the absence of a creative perspective for relating stability with change and decay with fulfillment, change became the great enemy of stability and decay the great enemy of fulfillment. And there was no integrating word. There was no creative symbol with which humans could make sense out of life and thus achieve the full stature of human freedom. There was no integrating word or creative symbol to help humans connect what was happening to them in the present moment with any fulfilling and compelling purpose.

Christianity moved into this situation with a perspective which completely changed this relationship. From this transformation of the relation between stability and change, decay and fulfillment, history was given its fundamental human significance.

It has sometimes been too loosely said that Christians, or the Old Testament, invented history, as though the Greeks knew nothing about it at all. The late Erich Frank, an eminent Augustinian philosopher, made the intriguing remark that it was Moses who invented history. Although tantalizing and containing much truth, it is not true in the sense that nobody ever used the word history or reflected upon history before Moses. The sense in which Moses invented history is the same sense in which we can say that Christianity invented history: it provided the perspective and the creative word and symbol for giving a human dimension to human life in the world. It provided the resource for humanizing history, for making history the word which designates that aspect of human experience in which the search for meaning and the need for freedom, the quest for purpose and the need of responsibility, are all brought to bear upon the relations between change and stability, decay and fulfillment, so that human beings may confidently take up their lives as *revolutionary* among all the creatures that God has made.

What the Greeks had not been able to see was that change, far from being the enemy of stability or permanence, was the initiator of a stability that was always coming to be. The Greeks could not see that change was itself the inaugurator of a stability that was worth depending upon because one was able to depend upon it. Change did not mean that life was deprived of meaning; indeed, it was precisely the experience of change which meant that the human person was the great pilgrim. The human person was to be in the world as the great pioneer, "a little lower than the angels," a great creator and fulfiller not only of humanity's own destiny but of purposes which were anchored and rooted in the very fabric and structure of the world.

Christians, in spite of this resource and perspective at their disposal, have not always made wise use of it. Their difficulty in seeing this is reflected in another problem which the classical world was unable to resolve adequately: the relation of decay to fulfillment. The Christian perspective declares that decay, far from meaning that there was no fulfillment or that life was hopeless and not worth living, was the prelude to fulfillment and not its negation.

Thus, by putting together change with decay Christian faith created a new connection between fulfillment and stability. It is no accident that Abraham who "went out, not knowing whither he went," is recognized both by the Apostle Paul and by the author of Hebrews as the great model of the Christian life. On the other hand, the Christian is, as Jesus himself insisted, steadily to avoid as though it were the plague the example of Lot's wife, who was not able to live in complete abandonment to the future. She snitched a look at the past and hasn't moved since. Grasping for stability without fulfillment, she was abandoned, not to the future, but to a petrified stability. Her history ended in permanence, not in fulfillment.

This transvaluation of the relations between change and stability and between fulfillment and decay, effected by Christianity, is what gives to human history its human dimension. What the transvaluation means is, in a phrase of Calvin, that "the world is the theater of the glory of God."[3]

There is a hymn upon which I was brought up which is one of the unhappier pieces of theology in the arsenal of Christian education, higher or lower. The hymn is "Abide With Me," a stanza of which is: "Change and decay in all around I see, O Thou who changest not, abide with me." This is as complete a defection from Christian faith and life as anything in Christian hymnody or Christian literature. It is a lapse into the very cultural understanding of the relations between decay and fulfillment and between stability and change which Christian faith and life were designed to transcend and transform. If revised, the hymn should say, "Change and decay in all around I see, O Thou who changest, too, abide with me." The God with whom Christian faith is concerned is not a God who gives the world a shove and stays behind. God is not a God who never got mixed up with the world in the first place, and who is serenely detached in some eternal dimension or area or territory that nobody has ever located. The God with whom the Christian faith is concerned is the God who goes before God's people as a cloud by day and as a pillar of fire by night, who is the end as well as the beginning, and whose beginning is to be understood with reference to God's end. And humans are those creatures whose beginning, like the beginning of God, is to be understood, not with reference to where they came from, but with reference to their end. By virtue of the going forth of God before, after, and along with God's people, the beginning and end of human life is bracketed by the glorification and enjoyment of God by humanity in the theater of the world. For, "the chief end of man," as Calvin said, "is to glorify God and enjoy him forever."[4]

God had better change or we are all in the soup. To say that God changes is to say that God is not, as the church has too long said, chiefly God because God is *impassible*. To say that God changes is to say that God is always "seven light-years" ahead and behind and under us. God is not process, but in the process of being Godself in the dynamics of God's self-identifying self-communication God fashions the integrity of history, holding together the beginning and end of human life within God's own beginning and end. And this was just the point: the Greeks saw, literally, no way of connecting God with change and decay. So they, and God, were imprisoned within the futile world, and found no way to move on to horizons of new stability and fulfillment. The Christian secret of the humanization of history is the transformation which Christian faith effects in human understanding and experience of change *in relation to* stability, and of fulfillment *in its relation* to decay. And that means revolution. For revolution is simply change at an accelerated rate and range. Such revolution is the natural environment of the Christian.

THE FAITHFUL CATALYST OF
AUTHENTIC REVOLUTION

How does Christianity come by this transformation? The answer is that Christians, like their Hebrew predecessors, were brought up on the Bible. And then as now the Bible is a singular resource of mind and imagination for dealing with human experience at its height, depth, length, and breadth, or anywhere where life is really in trouble and really being made over. As a singular resource of understanding, the Bible possesses a particular power of transformation of mind and imagination in a unique way. For this reason the church has never strayed very far from it. For this reason, also, the church is frequently tempted to read the Bible as though it were saying something else than it is. This is why the church has often tried to confuse the Bible with literature or history. This is why the church has sometimes found it embarrassing to bring the resources of its own mind and imagination under the judgment and understanding of this criterion.

But there it is. This is the meaning of the church's ancient decision that the Bible was canon, the rule of faith and practice. Such a decision did not mean that the Bible has no mistakes in it, nor is it to be a text which instructs us in everything under the sun. The decision means that where God and humanity and history are concerned, there the Bible is the fundamentally creative arsenal of mind and imagination for living an historical life.

What Christians know they got from the Bible, and specifically from the Bible's particularly extraordinary way of speaking about God. The Bible doesn't speak about God primarily in terms of conceptions or ideas but of God's activities. And the Bible is singularly astute about this, for when the activity of God is the matter at hand, it understands that what is most appropriate to understanding the activity of God is not an idea but an image. The images of the Bible are very basic. In fact, when looked at very closely, they are political images. And political images are those images which deeply affect human life where human life is lived on the growing edge of social, political, historical change, which is to say, human life in the middle of its revolutionary environment.

Think of the characteristic images of the Bible: God chooses a people. That is God's way of being God. And without any advice from Madison Avenue. No public relations person would ever advise a God to manifest his godness by getting mixed up with people. If one did they should be fired. And this person would be fired because Madison Avenue wants people for commodity purposes, which is not as God wants them. God chooses a people.

And the astonishing thing is that the Bible says that God makes the world because God chose the people. It is perfectly true that Genesis begins with the making of the world, but the point is that it never lets us lose sight of the question of *why* God made the world. Genesis makes it very clear that God made the world for the sake of the humans he decided to put in it. And so God took the risk of getting the world all mixed up. That is how deadly serious God is about people: God made the world for us. We are the why of the world.

Think of other political images: God gave the people for whom God made the world God's law; God gave them a land to dwell in. Then, for reasons that were as dubious to God as to the people, gave them a king to rule over them. When the fortunes of the kingdom turned out to be disappointing, God provided the people with still another possibility: the king who transforms the meaning of kingship because he exercises power with justice; he exercises freedom with mercy; he makes reconciliation the law of historical life.

> For unto us a child is born
> Unto us a Son is given,
> And the government shall be upon his shoulders,
> And his name shall be called
> Wonder counselor, mighty God, everlasting Father,
> Prince of Peace (Isaiah 9:6).

When Jesus came as the Christ, he came preaching: "The kingdom of God is at hand; repent and believe in the gospel" (Mark 1:15). And at the end of the biblical account of God's activity, as at the beginning, "the kingdoms of this world are to become the kingdoms of our God and of his Christ, and he shall reign forever and ever" (Rev. 11:15).

The characteristic mode of God's activity is political. Now, if one is careful enough to understand that, as Aristotle said, "Politics is the art of human community," then we may say that politics is the art of what it takes for one to be a human being in the world.[5] The Bible describes the characteristic way that God has of being God in political images. Political imagery is used in the Bible to proclaim and describe God as the architect of the humanity of human life, to put Christian faith into the middle of the revolutionary environment of human life, and to make Christian faith itself the catalyst of authentic revolution.

MIGRATION AND RESURRECTION

The language of theology, in trying to describe the political images with which the Bible talks about God's humanizing activity in the world, is a code language. And in our time we shall not be able, as human beings and as believers, to face the secular imagination unless we get our code language straight.

Therefore, when theology talks about incarnation, it does not mean many things; it means one thing. It means that in the man, Jesus of Nazareth, God localized God's activity as an architect of human life's humanity in the world.

Therefore, when theology talks about atonement, it does not mean many things; it means only one thing. It means that in this act, wherein Jesus of Nazareth allowed himself to die in obedience to God's way of working in the world, the focus and locus of humanity's secret in the world was exhibited. The secret was that the suffering of humanity in the revolutionary environment in which God has put humanity is the power of redemption.

Reconciliation therefore is the law of historical life because God has localized God's presence in a human person and blazed a trail of suffering through which what humanity is to be, will come to pass "as even some of your poets have said" (Acts 17:28), an unbeliever's question:

> Remember the Word?
> The One from the Manger?
> It means only this—
> You can dance with a Stranger.[6]

So, we have the chance as Christians, now in our time, of sharpening our imagination and nourishing our sensitivity about those frontiers of life where God is breaking in and through to make and to extend the territory of humanization. On these frontiers of time and place God is making humanity all over again.

On the February 13, 1934, the uncommonly gifted Mexican painter, Jose Clemente Orozco, affixed his signature to the last of the panels of the frescoes depicting the epic of America. For two years he had been at work in a large basement room of the Baker Library of Dartmouth. The epic tells in a powerful blending of scenes, colors, and forms the story of America, from the aboriginal culture of the Aztec civilization more than five thousand years ago to the industrial and technological civilization of the twentieth century. The fourteen panels begin with what is labeled migration, the nomadic movements of successive waves of immigrants from the North, motivated by the promised land. The panels end with resurrection: a militant Christ figure, ax in his hand and his cross at his feet astride the wreckage of civilization, symbols of piety and power, of violence and hatred, of aspiration and default. Migration begins in a low key, deep brown on the nearer edge of purple and black. Resurrection breaks across the canvas of the now unmistakably human story in vivid and transforming hues of brilliant yellow on the nearer edge of fiery red and incandescent white. "A world," as the narrator explains, "lies ahead."

Migration and resurrection: from awesome and fearful longing and dying, the human migration probes and presses toward the transfigured freedom of creativity fulfilled and creation consummated, which energies exhibit themselves in inexhaustible possibilities at the very fingertips of seeing and doing.

"The Pilgrim way," in a phrase of W. H. Auden's "has led to the Abyss":

> Was it to meet such grinning evidence
> We left our richly odoured ignorance?
> Was the triumphant answer to be this?
> The Pilgrim way has led to the Abyss.

> We who must die demand a miracle
> How could the Eternal do a temporal act,
> The Infinite become a finite fact?
> Nothing can save us that is possible:
> We who must die demand a miracle.[7]

> Therefore, if anyone is in Christ, he is a new creation. The old has passed away; behold, the new has come. (2 Cor. 5:17)

> For it is the God who said, "Let light shine out of darkness to give the light of the glory of God in the face of Jesus Christ." (2 Cor. 4:6)

Paul of Tarsus, W. H. Auden, Jose Orozco, and imaginative seers across the whole cultural story of humanity are, if not a cloud, certainly a chorus of unclouded witnesses to the changed face of reality hammered out and winnowed away and returned to itself by the power of God's incarnation and Christ's death and resurrection. By this power the Messianic focus of experience and meaning has exploded into an inescapable and irreversible transfiguration of the way things are, of the way things look, and of what now can be done about it. The migration begins at Christmas, the resurrection at Easter. The Messianic transfiguration is the theme of the Christian story of God's humanization of human life through revolutionary social change in whatever form it takes. Such transfiguration and such humanization involve us no less in a change in the way the universe is to be looked at by us, as it does us in the way we feel about the universe and act in it. The political movement of God draws us into its own orbit of connecting fulfillment with decay and change with stability so that we are liberated to see our own true environment as a permanent revolution of mind and heart, and the Christian faith as the catalyst which lays bare the One who holds together the very fabric of human dying and living. Under the power of resurrection, the changed face of reality breaks through to us through a transfigured sensitivity to what has always been going on, to that perspective which we should have been getting all the time but have persisted in missing. It is the perspective and point which Pascal confesses for the sake of the world: "Jesus Christ is the end of all and the center to which all tends. Whoever knows him knows the reason of everything."[8]

NOTES

1. Published in *Motive* 30, no. 7 (1965): 9–13; reprinted with permission.

2. [Editorial: During his final illness, Blaise Pascal was known to say, "Sickness is the natural state of Christians," as he refused the care of his physician.]

3. [Editorial: This phrase is frequently quoted by scholars, but always without citation. For the closest quotation to this one, see Calvin's commentary on Psalm 135:13: "The whole world is a theatre for the display of the divine goodness, wisdom, justice, and power . . . ," John Calvin, *Commentary on Psalms*, vol. 5, copyright in the public domain: https://www.reformedontheweb.com/calvin/16-commentary-on-psalms-volume-5.pdf.]

4. [Editorial: This quotation is from the first question and its answer in the Westminster Shorter Catechism.]

5. [Editorial: No citation provided. Lehmann builds on Aristotle's understanding of politics and community in *Ethics in a Christian Context*, 83–86. Unlike Aristotle, Lehmann never employs the concept of virtue.]

6. Abner Dean, "Grace Note," in *Wake Me When It's Over* (New York: Simon & Schuster, 1955).

7. [Editorial: W.H. Auden, "For the Time Being: A Christmas Oratorio," *W.H. Auden Collected Poems*, ed. Edward Mendelson (New York: Random House, 1976), 274.]

8. Pascal, *Pensees*, Fragment 555.

Chapter 11

Toward a Protestant Analysis of the Ethical Problem (1944)[1]

There is a Protestant analysis of the ethical problem. It is the attempt to deal with the question of the nature and application of "the good" in terms of the Pauline and Reformation conception of justification by faith. The presuppositions and implications of justification offer a more adequate account of ethical motivation, achievement, and failure than alternative philosophical, theological, and religious ethical analyses. In an ethic of justification, all the principal ethical categories and relationships are redefined. The good, for example, is no longer something "in itself" but is rooted and grounded in God, who makes us "perfect in every good thing to do his will, working in us that which is well-pleasing in his sight" (Heb. 13:21). Quite strictly, "No one is good, but God alone" (Mark 10:18). Absolute and relative good are no longer conformed to one another by the varied and complex interrelationships of ends and means. With respect to what is done now, ends and means are technical, not ethical, considerations, since what is to be done now is governed by what God has already done in Christ. Virtues and duties are no longer significant in themselves, that is, as values making for happiness, or as indispensables in the maintenance of existence, or as self-evident norms of action—but they become significant in so far as they express relationships within the dialectic between creation and redemption implied by the conception of justification.

Unfortunately, as Ernst Troeltsch has shown clearly enough, the history of Protestant thought is no proof that a Protestant analysis of the ethical problem is possible. The reason is, according to Troeltsch, that the whole history of Christian ethics has been overshadowed by the Stoic doctrine of the *lex naturae* (the natural law). When the correspondence between the divine reason and human reason is accepted as law and when this correspondence is "Christianized" by grounding it in the biblical doctrines of creation and providence, the way is open for the perpetuation of things as they are over against things as they ought to be. Troeltsch wrote: "Obviously, the continuation of the analogy between the Decalogue, natural law, and Christian law means the infiltration of the infra-worldly ethic into the Christian, as had been the case for the whole patristic and medieval ethics."[2] The Reformation was, according to Troeltsch:

> Not a simple restoration of Biblical . . . Christianity but a re-direction (*Reduktion*) of the . . . dogma . . . Church, and ethics of the Middle Ages toward . . . the Pauline religion of grace through Christ. This is particularly clear from the evaluation of the life of the natural man which the Middle Ages were the first to include within the Christian life, an inclusion which was now (that is, by the Reformation) simply differently motivated and delineated.[3]

Whereas Catholic theology had resolved the tension between the relative *lex naturae* [law of nature] and the ethic of grace by subsuming *lex* under grace, Protestantism resolved the tension by reducing the *lex naturae* to an essentially empty form. It was necessary as the sphere of ethical action, but significant only in so far as it was penetrated by the spirit of love bestowed by grace. The different disposition by Catholicism and Protestantism of the *lex naturae* proves, according to Troeltsch, not that there is anything to choose between them, but rather that the central dilemma of Christian ethics as it tries to work out the duties of humanity before God is the choice between denial of the world and compromise with the world. For Protestantism the compromise is merely less obvious than for Catholicism. It is "imbedded more deeply in the inner life where it is softened in so far as the world is not only accepted as the locus of sin and under dominion of sin but as a direct and positive order of God [*Anordnung Gottes*]."[4] Hence it comes about that "the radical love ethic disappears behind the morality of obedience to authority."[5]

But what Troeltsch does not rightly see is that there is a distinction to be drawn between Protestantism and the Reformation as expressed in the thinking of the Reformers. When Luther, whose work is not merely primary but really decisive in this connection, used the category *lex*, he intended precisely that "simple restoration of Biblical Christianity" that Troeltsch denies to him as well as to his successors. For Luther's whole thought about the ethical problem is dominated by the dialectical relation between law and grace. This means, to be sure, that "the life of the natural human" is "differently motivated and delineated."[6] But the difference arises not from the modification of the Stoic-medieval doctrine of the *lex naturae* but from its rejection altogether. The paradoxical declaration that "the Christian man is a free lord overall and subject to nobody; the Christian man is a servant of all and subject to everybody,"[7] anchors ethical motivation "more deeply in the inner life."[8] But it certainly does not (although this has been the tendency of Lutheranism) obscure "the radical love ethic . . . behind the morality of obedience to authority," in Troeltsch's words. It is the revolutionary character of this ethical motivation, derived by Luther from the Pauline doctrine of justification and made by him the foundation of the ethical thinking of the Reformation, which has never really come into its own. Contemporary Protestantism is greatly indebted to Professor Emil Brunner for reminding it of this omission and for attempting to work out an evangelical ethics on this foundation.[9] The aim of this inquiry is to set down some reflections occasioned by Brunner's discussion and governed by the wider context of the ethical thinking of the principal Reformers.

I

Suppose a person is justified by faith! What does that mean in itself, and what kind of ethical thinking does the conception of justification require? In a word, justification is the forensic judgment of God whereby humanity is predicated with both sin and righteousness. It is the paradoxical declaration: "You are right! You are not right! *Simul iustus et peccator* [simultaneously righteous and sinner]!" Thus, justification includes the ethical problem within the specific relation which it defines between God and humanity in the world. It is a relation of right according to which God has made it possible for humanity to know and to conform to the conditions proper to human life in the world. These conditions are proper to human life in the world because they have themselves been determined by God, in the act of creation. Though not self-evident, they would be evident to humanity had not a darkness overtaken human knowledge and a rebellion overtaken human conformity to the act and the order of creation. That this darkness and rebellion are not the decisive and not the final conditions of human life in the world but are to be transformed in accordance with the order of creation has been determined by God in the act of redemption. The act of redemption is the incarnation of God in the world and the atonement of humanity with God in the life and death of "Jesus of Nazareth . . . whom God has raised up . . . and made both Lord and Messiah" (Acts 2). Thus, human life in the world is a life on the way from the creation, the order of which humans always repudiate but can never avoid, toward the redemption which humans always need but can never acquire. Justification is the act of God whereby humanity's true position in the world—as a pilgrim between creation and redemption—is put within the orbit of human knowledge and behavior in the world. Calvin says:

> The end of regeneration is that the life of believers may exhibit a symmetry and agreement between the righteousness of God and their obedience; and that thus

they may confirm the adoption by which they are accepted as his children . . . As God the Father has reconciled us to himself in Christ, so he has exhibited to us in him a pattern, to which it is his will that we should be conformed. Now, let those who are of the opinion that the philosophers have the only just and orderly systems of moral philosophy, show me, in any of their works, a more excellent economy than that which I have stated. When they intend to exhort us to the sublimest virtue, they advance no argument but that we ought to live agreeably to nature. But the Scripture deduces its exhortation from the true source when it not only enjoins us to refer our life to God the author of it, to whom it belongs, but, having taught us, that we are degenerated from the original state in which we were created, adds, that Christ by whom we have been reconciled to God, is proposed to us as an example, whose character we should exhibit in our lives . . . In order to extricate our minds from every snare, Paul . . . dispels the fascinations which blind us, and . . . at the same time teaches us that we must live as strangers and pilgrims in the world, that we may not lose the heavenly inheritance.[10]

Justification is God's way of dealing with people in the world, not as they are, but as they are in Christ. And justification is the way that people live before God in the world, not as they are, but as they are in Christ. Since it is God's prerogative to act always in conformity with God's will, it is right that God should so deal with people and people should so live before God. Indeed, this rightness is the righteousness of God by which it is necessary and possible for people to live in the world. The righteousness of God is the priority of God's will and the conformity of God's act with God's will with respect to everything that happens in the world. The bestowal of this righteousness upon humanity in the judgment of justification means that humanity is both made right and yet are not right, that they always must live as they never do live, in the world between creation and redemption. The relation between God and humanity in justification is not grounded in a correlation of reason, or will, or desire but in the correspondence of grace and faith: *iustificatio sola gratia sola fide* [justification is by grace alone and faith alone].

This is the positive side of the matter. And the negative side of it is that humans do not have this knowledge of God in themselves, nor does one derive it from the world in which one lives. The nature and the possibility of right action are not open to humanity because of certain unique properties of human being or because right human action is written, as it were, in the stars. Indeed, what human beings can know by self-analysis and by investigation of a reflection upon the world either fails to lead one effectively beyond oneself and one's world or carries one disproportionately beyond the limits of creatureliness and finitude. Human beings dream about a world beyond the one in which they live. But what one can apprehend by sensation and its technical extensions always leaves, as Kant quite decisively pointed out, much of one's world—too much, really, to sustain ethical energy—beyond one's ken. It is the area of right action, the haunting question, to use Kant's words, "What ought I to do?" that so narrowly confines human knowledge that it bears no effective relation to one's hopes. To put the matter within the context of justification, we could say that, even though the pursuit of knowledge and right action should lead humanity beyond self-analysis and beyond reflection upon human experience in the world to God as the author and creator of all things, such a quest could never put the certainty of redemption within humanity's grasp.[11] It could only persuade human beings either that the fullness of knowledge and virtue was within reach or that, since virtue is not attainable, redemption was no problem anyway. These alternatives find no compelling support from history or experience.

If, then, there is no righteousness except as a dream which nourishes in humanity the illusion of moral obligation and achievement, a dream that is ever and again dashed to pieces by the actual course of human history—in short, if an ethic of self-justification is unable to nourish ethical sensitivity amid ethical frustration—it could be that a righteousness based upon divine rather than human initiative, the activity of God rather than the aspirations of humanity, offers a more adequate foundation for and solution of the ethical problem. Such an ethic would, of course, reckon frankly with the redemptive act of the creator God (an act that is not the same as the discovery of redemptive possibilities in the creative process). It would regard such an act as the decisive content of the revelation of the divine will and, on that account, within the orbit of human knowledge and responsibility (a quite different epistemology and ethics than that which presupposes a correspondence or identity between divine and human reason). Such an ethic would commend itself to reason and experience by disclosing the solution of the critical dilemma in which the ethical problem is actually and continually involved. That dilemma is: how, in view of the fact that "the good" when it is applied always turns out to be something other than good, one is to maintain ethical sensitivity amid ethical frustration.

If a person is justified by faith, the ethical problem is the problem of living under and living out the righteousness of God, which judges every human righteousness and overcomes every human unrighteousness. This is a radical alteration of the treatment of the problem in the classical ethical systems—an alteration that conspicuously affects the nature of the good, the nature of moral obligation, and the nature of ethical decision. According to an ethic of justification, (1) nothing is good in itself, but that alone is good which God wills: *the good is act, not principle*; (2) any action is good which can be said to have been called forth by God for the furtherance of God's will for humanity and the world: *duty is not virtue but calling*;[12] (3) what God commands, what God requires, is always single, immediate, and concrete: *the good act is the act of present obedience.*

II

Nothing is good in itself; but that alone is good which God wills. The good is not self-evident and not universal; therefore, it cannot be a matter of principle and is not reducible to law. The good is always bestowed and always specific; therefore, it can only be regarded as willed. Both rationalistic (including the Catholic) and naturalistic delineations of the good are repudiated by this conception of the goal and the norm of ethical life. The distinguishing mark of rationalistic ethics is, in Brunner's phrase, "the hypostatization of the human conception of the good into the 'idea of the Good.'"[13] This is a logical abstraction that rationalism grounds now in the inherent excellence of the soul (Plato), now in the categorical nature of ethical obligation (Kant), and which naturalism finds in the general conformity of human desire. But in each case the dominant concern is with "the good," "the law," as "the principle" of the right ordering of life. That which *is* and that which ought to be are identical in the idea of the good, an identity which can only be conceived but can never become concrete in the world where actual ethical decisions have to be made. The distinguishing mark of naturalistic ethics, on the other hand, is found—not in abstraction from the given world—but in the given world itself. It is not difficult, on this basis of course, to abandon the concern for the good altogether amid the shifting complexity of structure and occurrence which no one can escape who looks at the world in which one lives. The good becomes, then, the useful, that is, the technical, and not the ethical. But this proves only that it is impossible to sustain the ethical sense of the good without universality. And it suggests that the only universality open to naturalism is the universality of impulse or desire or collectivity (depending on whether one is more biologically or sociologically minded). In either case, the good has become transposed from a principle of reason to an inference from a "given," called nature.[14] The distinguishing mark of Catholic ethics is its ingenuous transformation of the plain voluntarism of the gospel so as to conform with the plain ethical demands both of reason and of nature for universality. This is accomplished by the derivation of the *lex naturae* from the structure of the world regarded as created and the extension of the *lex naturae* by the power of grace operative in the world regarded as redeemed. There is a *regnum naturae* [kingdom of nature] and a *regnum gratiae* [kingdom of grace], in each of which the will of God is delivered of caprice by its own laws of operation. *Lex* itself is divine. Hence Thomism categorically rejects the view that "the essential nature of things is ultimately grounded in the free will of God."[15]

Exactly this, however, is the copestone of the ethics of the Reformation. There is no knowledge of good apart from the knowledge of God, and the knowledge of God that is good is that bestowed in the act of justification. Justification means that God wants me—as I am—for Godself; and not only me, but all human beings as they are. The proof of this is that God has become God to me, has given Godself to me in Christ. With this act my life and the life of all humanity is once again included within the self-giving of God. Henceforth I belong to God and know what I have to do. I have to bear witness to the fact that God has given Godself to me and taken me in—as I am—by giving myself to and taking in my neighbor—as God is. God not only gives Godself to me in the act of justification but also expects something from me. God's will, expressed in my justification, is love. This alone is good. God requires that I serve God's love by love. This is the good I have to do.

A rationalistic ethic defines the relation between an ethical norm and an ethical act in a positive way by affirming the universal and axiomatic character of the good. The good is thus never identical with the given because what ought to be done never actually is done as it ought to be. It is, at best, approximated by degrees. But the good is always regulative of the given for this is the law of reason and nature. A naturalistic ethic, on the other hand, defines the relation between an ethical norm and an ethical act in a negative way by confining whatever is universal and axiomatic about the good to what is given. The given is thus identical with the good because what ought to be done is always that which has been and can be done. The good is always immediate and always changing, for this is the "law of nature" which is the distinguishing mark of the given, and the given is always regulative of the good. An ethic of justification, however, defines the relation between the ethical norm and the ethical act in a dialectical way by joining the normative with what is given and distinguishing what is thus "given" from the good. The good is never identical with itself but is always involved in what is given (because what is done, *actually* ought to be done since God created and judges the world). The good is never identical with what is given but is always bestowed from beyond (because what *actually* is done is never what ought to be done, since God has sustained and has redeemed the world). The good is always concretely given in the moment of ethical decision and concretely required. Therefore, every such moment is a moment both of obligation and of frustration, since it is God who bestows and God who requires. The good is, to use the Pauline phrase, the love that is the "fulfillment of the law" (Rom 13:10). An ethic of justification is that ethic that takes seriously the activity of a God who acts.

The good is act. The act of love alone is the good act, for God alone is good and God is love. The concrete form of this divine activity is law.[16] Law is the continuing activity of God in the world which God has created. Law, therefore, defines the context of human activity in conformity with what God does and requires. However, human beings do not act in this context in conformity with what God does and requires. Therefore, the law obscures rather than discloses God's love. That God's love is only hidden behind, and not canceled by, God's law is due to the fact that God has redeemed the world as well as created it. Love and law are neither positively nor negatively but dialectically related. Love can be said to be concretely embodied in law yet never bound by law. Law can be said to give concreteness and direction to love but never define love. Love without law is sentimental or abstract. Law without love is severe or empty. In a word, law is the handmaid of love in the doing of the good between creation and redemption.

According to the ethics of the Reformation, this dialectical relation between love and law delivers the understanding of the good from universalistic enervation and from particularistic disintegration by establishing the actual and concrete character of the will of God as the only good. To regard the order of the world as the gift and requirement of God is to understand that there is no neutral quarter in the world and no extenuating circumstance upon which to rely when the law is not obeyed. And who can—as Luther well enough knew—when confronted by the rigor and the multiformity of the law, escape the judgment that one has not obeyed! Yet, since love is not the denial but the fulfillment of the law, at the moment of the despair of disobedience, the same God from whom the law has been received is seen to stand on the other side of it canceling its rigor and covering the disobedience. This discovery is essentially the discovery that the law is neither the fundamental nor the final will of God, that the legalistic understanding of the will of God with all the pretensions to which it gives rise, is itself the disobedience that is sin.

> Thus, the law is like a mirror, in which we behold, first our impotence; secondly, our iniquity, which proceeds from it; and lastly, the consequence of both, our obnoxiousness to the curse; just as a mirror represents to us the spots on our face.[17]
>
> We say that the law is good and profitable, but in its own proper use: which is, first, to bridle civil transgressions, and then to reveal and to increase spiritual transgressions . . . To what end serveth this humbling, this bruising and beating down by this hammer, the law, I mean? To this end, that we may have entrance into grace . . . When the law so oppresseth thee, that all things seem to be utterly desperate, and thereby driveth thee unto Christ, to seek help and succour at his hands, then is the law in his true use; and through the gospel, it helpeth to justification. And this is the best and most perfect use of the law.[18]

This is the dialectical character of the law: it leads directly to the true knowledge of God only to be discerned at the moment when the threshold has been crossed, as the radical denial of the knowledge of God, as the actual enemy of this knowledge.[19]

III

If the good is that which God wills and bestows, it follows that the obligation to do the good and the achievement of the good are also anchored in the divine will. Any action is good which can be said to have been called forth by God for the furtherance of God's will for humanity and the world. Duty is not virtue but calling. On the face of it, this does not seem to be very different from what any ethically sensitive soul is aware of. Inherent in both rationalistic and naturalistic determinations of the nature of moral obligation is the notion that the one who does the good does not measure one's action wholly with reference to oneself. There is a sense in which one looks beyond oneself and measures one's duty by the obligation which one regards as imposed from without. But what is peculiar to those for whom the will of God is the only good is that they do not see themselves as called upon to contemplate the good or to measure what they have done by that which lies beyond what they have done. They see themselves on the other hand, called to obey. Luther wrote in the Preface to his *Commentary on Romans*:

> Faith is a living, busy, active, mighty thing. It is impossible that it should not always be doing good. It asks not whether good works should be done, but before one asks it does them, and is always doing them . . . Hence, without compulsion, freely, and joyously, everyone will do good, everyone will serve. Thus, a Christian man who lives in this confidence toward God, knows all things, can undertake or abandon all things that are to be done . . . he serves God entirely for nothing, content in this alone that God is pleased. This is the service of God proper to Christians . . . that they know what and why they should believe, are taught also how they should love God and their neighbor.[20]

The duty of the justified person is single: one is to obey. One takes the world as it is and people as they are because God has created both, and one works in the world among people according to what God from time to time requires. But the justified person does not do just one thing. For God has not set them down in that kind of a world. In all things necessary, one thing is needful. There are varieties of duty.

But the relation between the one thing needful and the "all things necessary" is not expressed in Reformation thought by a system of virtues. In such systems virtues are particularizations of the good and are derived from it according to a scale of being (degrees of participation in or manifestation of what is regarded as the essence of the good) or a scale of values (a hierarchic arrangement of approximations of the good at the various levels of experience). This kind of analysis rests upon that universalistic understanding of the good which undoubtedly can be worked out into a system but is, on that account, an abstraction, that is, a self-evident and self-consistent intellectual whole remote from the acute dilemma between sensitivity and frustration in which concrete ethical experience is involved. The Reformers, on the other hand, are at once more personal and more concrete about the nature of moral obligation. The justified are not only called to obey; they are set down—between creation and redemption—in a calling, the right exercise of which is their obedience. The vocation of the justified person is the point at which the singleness of duty and the varieties of duty are joined. The justified do not begin to do their duty by running off in all directions but quite specifically where God has set them down. God has set them down in the world to do a particular work. The work that they are called to do defines the point at which, in the world, they become concretely aware of their own justification and at which their duty becomes concretely ordered. Calvin says:

> A Christian man ought to be so disposed and prepared as to reflect that he has to do with God every moment of his life. Thus, as he will measure all his actions by his will and determination, so he will refer the whole bias of his mind religiously to him . . . How extremely difficult it is for you to discharge your duty in seeking the advantage of your neighbor! . . . the Lord . . . knows with what great inquietude the human mind is inflamed, with what desultory levity it is hurried hither and thither, and how insatiable is its ambition to grasp different things at once. Therefore, to prevent universal confusion being produced by our folly and temerity, he has appointed to all their particular duties in different spheres of life. And that no one might rashly transgress the limits prescribed, he has styled such spheres of life vocations or callings. Every individual's line of life, therefore, is, as it were, a post assigned him by the Lord, that he may not wander about in uncertainty all his days.[21]

In my vocation, I—believing in my justification—am daily reminded that all that I have I have received from God's hand and that I have to work out what God requires. Here I am daily delivered from imagining that I have no duty or that I have done my duty. Indeed, the hardest thing one has to do in the world is to do one's work as God's call and to do it as God calls for it to be done.

But it is just here that one discovers that justification is either a great deception or the only rule of life. If it is the only rule of life, then the criterion of an action is not the general welfare or decency or disinterestedness or efficiency or wisdom or common sense. Certainly, the criterion is not conformity or nonconformity, consistency or inconsistency, the ends which govern the means, or the consequences that follow from the acts. Any act is good that can be said to be one's duty in and through the calling wherewith one is called.

IV

The motive of ethical activity, as we have seen, is quite strictly and quite simply, faithfulness in one's calling. To love God—who is love—with heart and mind and soul and strength is to serve God in those ways that are immediately and specifically determined by one's place in the world. Yet the task of an ethic of justification is not complete when it has defined the norm and the motive of ethical activity. There is still the question of the ethical act itself. Faithfulness in one's calling, in dependence upon the revealed and righteous will of God, tells us where we are to look for guidance and for resources as to what we ought to do and where we are to begin, but it does not without further specification tell us which action to take in any given moment. Indeed, the classical systems of ethics have always seemed to possess a demonstrable cogency and effectiveness precisely at this point. The catalogues of virtue and the schemes of value rest upon a conception of the ethical object and of ethical obligation that is continuous and correlative with human cognition and volition and on this account seem always to place ethical achievement within human reach. Over against these prospects it has always been possible to point out that an ethic based exclusively upon the will of God ultimately undermines ethical responsibility by surrendering human freedom to divine foreordination.[22] The doctrine of vocation has, as the history of Lutheranism amply proves, concretely reinforced this ethical quietism by an ethical conservatism because it never gets beyond things as they are. The freedom of the Christian under the Word of God can readily be identified with or exchanged for a careless indifference toward or a meticulous execution of the daily routine of one's calling. This is, at best, a highly individualistic doctrine of the good life that effectively divorces the salvation of the soul from ethical obligation.

But nobody could have been more emphatic about the fact that faith in one's justification, upon which faithfulness in one's calling is based, issues in good works than was Luther himself, when he writes:

> Christians should be . . . ready to do every good work, not that they may be justified by these things . . . but that in liberty of spirit they may thus be the servants of others . . . Such too, ought to have been the works of all . . . monasteries and priests; every one doing the works of his own profession and state of life, not in order to be justified by them, but in order to bring his body into subjection, as an example to others . . . and also in order to accommodate himself to the will

of others, out of free love . . . We give this rule: the good things which we have from God ought to flow from one to another, and become common to all, so that every one of us may, as it were, put on his neighbor, and so behave toward him as if he himself were in his place . . . We conclude therefore that a Christian man does not live in himself, but in Christ and in his neighbor, or else he is no Christian; in Christ by faith, in his neighbor by love.[23]

Indeed, the relation between faith and works elaborated by the Reformers effectively resolves the tension between freedom and responsibility and between the categorical good and radical evil, which has continually beset and beclouded systematic ethics. The reason is that an ethic of justification derives the concrete ethical act from a concrete understanding of the nature of the good and of moral obligation. It declares not only that the good is act not principle; not only that duty is not virtue but calling; but also, that what God commands and what God requires is always single, immediate, and concrete: the good act is the act of present obedience.

Suppose a person is justified by faith. What is this person called to do in the faithful exercise of his or her calling? Let this one be a cobbler, a mechanic, a physician, or a preacher. What ought this person do? Master the skills of these vocations? Improve them? Pursue them for their own sake or because one must eat in order to live? Attain proficiency in a number of them so that one may relieve the boredom of what has been made necessary by the change and excitement of a hobby? Moralistically, naturalistically, psychologically speaking, perhaps one ought to do all of these things. For all of these things conceivably contribute to the maintenance and enrichment of life. But ethically speaking, that is, after the manner of an ethic of justification, the answer is: None of these things. The justified are to love God where they are set down in the world and exactly *there* are they to love the neighbor as they would love themselves. It is the love of the neighbor which makes the faithfulness in one's calling ethical, and it is the exercise of one's calling that makes the love of one's neighbor concrete. Our Lord's summary of the law and the prophets conjoins the two love commandments in such a way that the love which is commanded toward God and the love commanded toward one's neighbor are not correlative but apposite. It is not that one loves God and also loves one's neighbor. Neither is the love of one's neighbor like the love of God; it is the second commandment that is like unto the first. One loves one's neighbor as one's self because we are first commanded to love God. The love of God requires the love of neighbor and is concretely expressed in that love.

But this is the love which becomes concrete for me in the act of justification. The love of neighbor is not grounded in the creation, so that we have, as it were, our humanity in common; not even our divinely created humanity is the ground of our love toward one another. How frail a foundation for the obligation to love that would be! Those who have not hesitated to rebel against their creator will surely not recognize any decisive limitation of their behavior imposed by any other creature, even a creature like in kind. And human history is surely proof that humanity has not recognized such limitation. Human beings have, indeed, in the name of the Creator and of a common humanity wrought havoc upon their neighbor beyond the capacity of any other creature. But the love of neighbor is derived from the love of God that, in the act of justification, concretely includes humanity within the orbit of God's act and purpose of redemption. Justification bestows upon human beings, who do not and cannot love their neighbor as they ought, the righteousness of God. This is the righteousness which the redemption wrought in Christ has disclosed to be the only good from the beginning. In Christ, human beings can love their neighbor as they ought. Calvin writes:

> There cannot be imagined a more certain rule or a more powerful exhortation to the observance of it, than when we are taught, that all the blessings we enjoy are Divine deposits, committed to our trust on this condition, that they should be dispensed for the benefit of our neighbors . . . The only right dispensation of what has been committed to us, is that which is regulated by the law of love . . . Whoever, therefore, is presented to you that needs your kind offices, you have no reason to refuse him assistance . . . Say that you are obliged to him for no services; but God has made him, as it were his substitute, to whom you acknowledge yourself to be under obligations for numerous and important benefits . . . He has deserved, you will say, very different treatment from me. But what has the Lord deserved? This is the only way of attaining that, which is not only difficult, but utterly repugnant to the nature of man.[24]

Both Calvin and Luther are more strictly biblical on this point than Brunner. All are agreed that justification is the foundation of ethics and that only *sola gratia sola fide* can human beings be what they were created to be. But, if the Reformers did not sufficiently indicate what positive action was to be taken, in view of humanity's justification, Brunner for his part, in considerable dependence upon Martin Buber and Ferdinand Ebner, develops this point by way of an elaborate doctrine of personal relations that actually departs from the ethical foundation of the Reformers.[25] "Every virtue," Brunner says—and by virtue, he means the duty to which one is called—"is a particular way in which the one who is in the love of God takes account of another, 'realizes' him as Thou."[26] Brunner is at great pains to show how the distinguishing mark of the neighbor is this capacity of thou-ness, that is, one who stands over against me as a personal Other. This Other, I can only rightly designate as "thou." I can never rightly identify this Other with myself or regard this Other as a neuter. Every aspect of creation can be subjugated to my self-activity. But my neighbor, the Other, alone breaks the circle of my selfhood. Therefore, my neighbor defines the single, immediate, and concrete will of God for me because the neighbor alone confronts me as I am, where I am. I know what I ought to do with respect to the claims of my neighbor because my neighbor stands over against me as—God (Calvin), Christ (Luther), Other (Brunner). But what difference does this difference make for an ethic of justification? The answer is that it makes a difference when my neighbor's significance is derived, as well as where my own significance is derived; and it is the merit and distinction of biblical and Reformation teaching that both are derived from justification. According to this teaching, it is God's act, a free gift of a righteousness which is neither mine nor that of any person, which defines the significance of my neighbor with respect to my duty and not—*really not*—the capacity of my neighbor to be an Other. The strictest biblical thinking is required to resist the temptation to surrender the ethical act in its immediacy and concreteness to those analyses of the ethical problem which have already been designated as alien.[27]

Nevertheless, Brunner is in line with the strict Reformation view that faithfulness in the exercise of one's calling is ethical in so far as it is governed by the love of neighbor. At the same time, it is in the exercise of one's calling that the love of neighbor is concretely expressed. The conjunction of the personal and the vocational in the ethical act delivers the ethics of the Reformers from the formalism with respect both to the nature of the good and of moral obligation which characterizes the philosophical ethical systems. It separates the ethics of the Reformers from their Protestant successors too. Lutheranism in particular never grasped the fact that the correlation of the love of neighbor with faithfulness in the exercise of one's calling based upon faith in justification is a revolutionary, not a reactionary, ethical position. It is revolutionary because the pursuit of one's vocation in the created world is continually under the judgment and the requirement of the love of neighbor which is based upon the divine act of redemption concretely manifest in justification. Therefore, to love my neighbor—believing in my justification and in theirs—is to exercise my vocation in the world in grateful acknowledgment of the fact that the orders of the world define the areas in which my work is to be done. At the same time, however, I must work in continuing protest against what has come to be the established order of things in the world, for an established order is always the sinful corruption of the created order. Whenever the created order becomes an established order, the freedom of God to act in accordance with God's will is denied in favor of the supposed necessity of some human arrangement, with the result that human beings are separated from one another under an order rather than united with one another under God.

These considerations are sharply focused by Brunner's attempt to work out the practical expression of the love of neighbor in the faithful exercise of one's calling amid what he believes can be established as the fundamental orders of life—family, labor, state, culture, church. Since economic questions are so determinative at the moment of the shape of things to come, it will be instructive to notice how Brunner deals with the duty of the Christian in the economic order.

According to Brunner, the economic order is "the process by which material goods, needed to support life, are produced, distributed, and consumed."[28] This order is an order of creation because the will of God, which has brought the world into being, desires also that this world shall be maintained in accordance with the resources which God has supplied and for the purpose which God has ordained. That purpose is a purpose for humanity. It is human life—that life which has been set down in nature and society for fellowship with God and to which God has come in Christ for its justification. At the same time, this order is a perverted order. "On the one hand, it has been spoiled by its false tendency to become an end in itself, and on the other, by egoistic exploitation by the individual which always works out both as sin and as a curse."[29] The curse of the economic order is evident from the fact that the order itself frustrates every individual's attempt to fulfill the purpose of the economic order. The sinfulness of the individual in relation to the economic order is evident from the persistent attempt to turn the curse of the economic order to one's own advantage. The plain truth about the actual economic order is that "the attempt to bring economic activity under ethical discipline inevitably ruins it, while the man who blindly accepts the whole economic order and its *autonomy* directly undermines his own life, and indirectly also undermines that of the economic community."[30]

> The Christian is, of course, also involved in, and responsible for, the economic order in which he is caught. The Christian must in his own way, and where his lot is cast . . . support all efforts to achieve a better order; and . . . he will be quite clear in his own mind that everyone who does not take part in the opposition movement—of whatever shade of opinion—is simply supporting the existing economic order, and this means that he is supporting economic anarchy.[31]

Thus, what is to be done now—the single, immediate, concrete command and requirement of God—is action against the existing order toward a better order.

Just how concrete this command is, appears from Brunner's analysis of capitalism, which "from the point of view of community [that is, from the point of view of the relations with God and my neighbor which follow from my justification] is an unjust and wicked economic system."[32] The charges which are made against this "wicked system" have by this time found common assent among all those who are working for a "better order," both in the church and out of it. What characterizes Brunner's analysis is the attempt to establish the basis and the direction of action against this order—not upon the rationalistic egalitarianism of the *jus naturale* [natural law], not upon the positivistic egalitarianism of the collective unity of all humankind—but upon the "incomprehensible inequality" of the "creation—quite apart from sin."[33] That God has bestowed upon every human being the gift of individuality and has so ordered the world which God has made that each individual finds oneself, that is, becomes a person, according to the way in which one seeks the other's good as God has commanded—this is the implication of the doctrine of creation for an ethic of justification.

But this also brings us squarely before the striking inconsequence of Brunner's whole position. And it uncovers the critical contemporary issue for a Protestant analysis of the ethical problem. The dialectic between creation and redemption that Brunner regards as the presupposition of justification and that joins him with the Reformers in his delineation both of the nature of the good and of ethical obligation does not define the ethical action itself. What actually takes place is a shift in the dialectic when the act of obedience is considered. Brunner recognizes that Christians act where they are set down: in the family, the state, the economic and cultural community. But what Brunner does not see is that the direction of Christian action toward the "better order" is defined by the tension between that order as created and that order as *corrupt* rather than by the tension between that order as created and that order as *redeemed*. It is not enough to declare that the sinful perversion of the created order is the basis both of my involvement and my frustration in that order. It is not enough to declare that the redemption of that order from the side of God is attested by "the fact that no 'Christian' or even 'just' economic system exists"[34] and that "the point from which we take our bearings differs from a structural principle, so that there is no Christian economic system or program."[35] It is not enough because the point from which Brunner takes his bearings has actually become a structural principle. The structural principle is the principle of the sinful orders of creation in the midst of which the commands of God are to be obeyed. Otherwise, how could Brunner equate "fate" and "calling" with respect to the economic order in which we live?[36] This equation is possible because Brunner's argument departs from its general roots in the doctrine of justification and takes up the doctrine of the orders of creation. Why can there be no "Christian economic system?" Because of sin (Brunner)? No, it is rather that the act of justification is an attack upon the sinful order of creation and as such continually judges that order in the light of the order which is to be. It is not creation but eschatology which aggravates sin.[37] Why must the Christian in the situation in which one is set down nevertheless move against that situation toward the "better order?" Because the world in which one lives has been created and because one has corrupted it? This is really what Brunner says as he traces the insufficiencies in order only to return to the judgment that a Christian can be a Christian in any order. The strict consequence of an ethic of justification, however, would seem rather to be this: That a Christian can be a Christian in any order—not because all orders fall short of the glory of God—but because the Christian has been justified by faith, and therefore not only involved in the sinful perversion of the creation but also in the groaning and the travail of creation until the revealing of the sons and daughters of God. Since Brunner really fails to make use of the redemptive act of God for the justification of the sinner in delineating the concrete ethical act, the rebellion against the sinful order is always qualified at the last by the acceptance of that order—not as it is, to be sure, but, nevertheless, as the decisive "point from which Christian action takes its bearings."

An ethic of justification, however, is a revolutionary ethic. It does not seek the good for its own sake, since nothing is good in itself but that alone is good which God wills. It refers ethical frustration neither to sense, nor to finitude, nor to fate, but to sin. And sin means that human beings cannot do what they ought to do since the order of life and the power to live that are God's gifts of creation are no longer operative as they were intended. Sin means that human beings must do what they cannot do, since God has called humanity to serve God in the order of life that God has established and that God sustains. But justification means the juxtaposition of human impotence with the power of obedience. The power of obedience is the power to do what I am called to do in the situation in which I am located. It is not the power to live with which I was created; otherwise I could live as created, and the quest for ends and means would bring to me the satisfaction of achievement. Justification means the ethical gift of the righteousness of God *and* the power of obedience: the power to live as I have been redeemed. Consequently, I do not accept the situation in which I am located as it is, but I receive it as God's call to me to obey, and move against it—believing in God's redemptive possibility—because it is from that situation that I have been delivered. Justification rests upon the incarnation and the atonement, not upon the creation. Therefore, it is revolutionary. Therefore, the believer in the God who acts and who calls, who creates and who redeems by the power of God's Word, always begins by moving against the focus of power in the existing situation. Such a focus of power is always personal; therefore, the believer moves against oneself—the white person against their whiteness, the black person against their blackness; the strong person against their strength, the weak person against their weakness. Such a focus of power is always also social. Therefore, the believer moves against the political, economic, cultural, and communal concentration of power in any given historical moment—Israelite against Egyptian, and Assyrian against Israelite; mercantilist against monarch; worker against capitalist; democrat against Fascist and imperialist alike. This movement of opposition will not make for chaos, since it will always be related to the organic structure of this world as God's world. And it will not make for utopia, since it will always know that its own assertion of power will need to be judged and opposed at the moment of its coming to power. Such a movement can be only an eschatological movement which lives in the world which God has made by the word of judgment and of mercy which has been made flesh, full of grace and reality. Such a movement is carried by those who wait and struggle and hope for the coming of the Son of God with power to judge both the living and the dead.

NOTES

1. Published in *The Journal of Religion* 24, no. 1 (1944): 1–16; reprinted with permission of the University of Chicago Press.
2. Ernst Troeltsch, *Gesammelte Schriften I* (Tubingen: Mohr Siebeck, 1912), 442.
3. Troeltsch *Gesammelte Schriften I*, 448.
4. Troeltsch, *Gesammelte Schriften I*, 505.
5. Troeltsch *Gesammelte Schriften I*, 504–5.
6. [Editorial: Unattributed citation. Likely Luther.]
7. Martin Luther, *On the Freedom of the Christian Man*, *Luthers Werke* (Weimar ed.), 7, 21.
8. [Editorial: Unattributed citation. Likely Luther.]
9. Emil Brunner, *Das Gebot und die Ordnungen* (Tübingen: Mohr Siebeck, 1933).
10. Calvin, *Institutes*, 3.6.7.
11. This is the real reason why the knowledge of the Creator is beyond humanity's grasp. Reinhold Niebuhr denies this in his Gifford lectures; but significantly, he discusses the same point, namely, the necessary connection between a proper understanding of revelation and humanity's place and duty in the world. It is difficult to see, however, why, if "the assurance of forgiveness and reconciliation . . . is the most distinctive content of special revelation" and "once this character of God is apprehended in special revelation, common human experience can validate it," the knowledge of the Creator should not also be apprehended and validated in this way. Indeed, "the longing for forgiveness" can scarcely be regarded as met, apart from the assurance that the redeemer God is God the creator. This is no less a matter of special revelation than the assurance that the creator God is God the redeemer. Neither assurance seems to me to be given in "common human experience." See Niebuhr, *The Nature and Destiny of Man I*, 143.
12. It is, of course, true that duty is not identical with virtue in the history of ethical thought. Duty is always a kind of middle term between the ethical norm and the ethical act that expresses the mandatory character of ethical obligation. Since this analysis is intended to show that the mandatory character of ethical obligation (and, consequently, the ethical problem as a whole) is significantly different when duty is defined with respect to calling, this somewhat oversimplified formulation of the contrast may, perhaps, be allowed to stand.

13. Brunner, *Das Gebot und die Ordnungen*, 99.

14. Niebuhr has instructively pointed out the ethical ambiguity of naturalistic thought arising from its inability to free itself altogether from rationalistic elements. See Niebuhr, *Nature and Destiny I*, ch. 4.

15. Brunner, *Das Gebot und die Ordnungen*, 579.

16. [Editorial: For Lehmann's further reflections on the difference between law as the form of the gospel vs. law as the norm of the gospel, see Lehmann, *The Decalogue and a Human Future*, 17–19.]

17. Calvin, *Institutes*, 2.7.

18. Martin Luther, *Commentary on Galatians*, *Luthers Werke*, (Weimar ed.), XL, 485–90. Luther and Calvin agree in naming last "the most perfect use of the law." However, they interchange the order of the first two offices of the law.

19. Brunner, *Das Gebot und die Ordnungen*, 130–31. Brunner is simply explicit about the dialectic between the third office of the law and the other two which is implicit in the thought of the Reformers.

20. Quotes drawn variously from Luther, *Werke* (Erlangen ed.), LVIII, 125; Luther, *Sermon on Good Works* in *Werke* (Erlangen ed.), XX, 200; Luther, *Tischreden* in *Werke* (Erlangen ed.), LXI, 126.

21. Calvin, *Institutes*, 3.7.3 and 5; 3.10.6.

22. From the very beginning, the charge was made against Calvinists and Lutherans alike. Yet the more astute among those who witnessed the rise of Protestantism recognized that such a contention was not inherent in the Reformation. Indeed, it was plain enough even for kings. Of the Rev. Dr. Saunderson, eminent Calvinist divine, and his own chaplain, "King Charles I, was wont to say that 'he carried his ears to hear other preachers but his conscience to hear Mr. Saunderson'" (translator's Preface to *Calvin's Institutes* [6th Amer. ed., rev.; Philadelphia, 1928], 9).

23. Luther, *Werke* (Erlangen ed.), XXVII, 197–99.

24. Calvin, *Institutes*, 3.7.5 and 6. See Luther: "Each should become to the other a sort of Christ" in *Werke* [Erlangen ed.], XXVII, 196.

25. Karl Barth has an instructive monograph in which he deals with the same point. After calling attention to the fact that the Reformers "owe us something" in the matter of the positive correlation between justification and law, Barth undertakes to fill "the gap" by adopting, however, "the line which they followed in introducing the Biblical insights (*Gut*) into their confessional symbols." See Barth, "Rechtfertigung und Recht," in *Theologische Studien*, no. 1 (1938): esp. 1–9.

26. Barth, "Rechtfertigung und Recht," 151.

27. Perhaps the most perilous consequence of this surrender is Friedrich Gogarten's use of the "I-Thou" relation to give ethical significance to the authority of the state. Indeed, the dialectic of the law, which in the teaching of the Reformers, turned the believer, despairing of disobedience, toward the gospel becomes in Gogarten's analysis a polar relation between the "myself" and the "other self" (*Mein Selbst und Ich Selbst*), which gives rise to the ethical awareness of radical evil and categorical obligation as the law of personal and social life. The concrete manifestation of this law is the sovereign state that imposes orders of cohesion and duty upon the chaos inherent in the evil involved in the polarity between the self and the other. This is

a curious mixture of Lutheran pessimism, Kantian rationalism, and Romanticist self-transcendence, which not only departs from the ethical presuppositions and implications of justification but ascribes decisive ethical significance to what is diametrically opposed to an ethic of justification. In Gogarten's view, such an ethic would be "that one which, in those inquiries concerning the good which arose for it out of the recognition of the radical evil of men, saw in the state, and in the good which occurred in the state, the only possible good for evil man." Friedrich Gogarten, *Politische Ethik* (Jena: Diederichs, 1932), 57. But one need not turn the ethical possibilities of the "I-Thou" relation into an apologetic for National Socialism. [Editorial: a second paragraph referring to John Baille has been omitted.]

28. Brunner, *Gebot und die Ordnungen*, 396.
29. Brunner, *Gebot und die Ordnungen*, 399.
30. Brunner, *Gebot und die Ordnungen*, 403.
31. Brunner, *Gebot und die Ordnungen*, 431.
32. Brunner, *Gebot und die Ordnungen*, 416.
33. Brunner, *Gebot und die Ordnungen*, 407.
34. Brunner, *Gebot und die Ordnungen*, 426.
35. Brunner, *Gebot und die Ordnungen*, 406.

36. "The economic world in which we live is, to use pagan language, the state 'into which we have been thrust by fate'; from the point of view of faith, it is our 'calling.'" Brunner, *Gebot und die Ordnungen*, 386.

37. "Those self-same orders are somehow suspended from the side of redemption; they are threatened by their end . . . Thus we find in the New Testament a threat to the natural condition of life, which has often been confused with an ascetic repudiation of economic activity, but which is motivated and to be understood in a totally different way, namely, eschatologically." Brunner, *Gebot und die Ordnungen*, 385.

Chapter 12

The Politics of Easter[1]
A Political Celebration of Easter (1980)

Easter has been central in the faith, teaching, and worship of the Christian church since apostolic times. But the celebration of Easter as a *political* feast has come neither easily nor centrally to the fore.

It took some time to fix the precise date of the Feast. The Council of Nicea (325 CE) decided that it should take place upon the first Sunday after the Spring Equinox. The Christological determinations of the same Council chiefly concerned the relations between Jesus and God, and the pivotal consequences of the crucifixion and resurrection of Jesus for human and cosmic redemption. As the Eastern churches tended to be preoccupied with the link between the resurrection and cosmic renewal, so the preoccupation of the western churches with the crucifixion tended to limit the scope of Easter to a vindication of the crucifixion through the resurrection, and thus to confirming the saving efficacy of the death of Christ for humankind. In the Eastern theological tradition, the Incarnation tended to overshadow the Atonement, and in the Western theological tradition, the Atonement tended to overshadow the Incarnation. In either case, and in spite of certain formidable theological concerns with the political matrix of Easter discernible in Scripture, the celebration of the Feast greatly subordinated its political perceptions and implications to cosmic and thus also human and historical renewal in the East, and to human deliverance from sin, death, and the devil, and thus also to history and the cosmos in the West. Instead of a political feast, the celebration of Easter became largely a doxological-sacramental affair in the East, and a largely sacramental-soteriological affair in the West.

These developments facilitated the nurture of a privatized piety, which the festivals of the Christian year tended rather to confirm than to correct. The disregard of the political matrix and thrust of Easter has resulted in a trivialization of the Feast. Cosmic regeneration and consummation have been reduced to symbolizations of the cyclical pattern of nature, most cheerily evident—and with dubious exegetical warrant—in the lilies plucked from the field. Preoccupation with the art of dying rather than with death, as Bonhoeffer's letter of March 27 puts it, has meanwhile become a whole new-old cult of death and dying, a veritable *perturbatio animorum* (Bonhoeffer), as though Easter had never really happened.[2] Redemption has been so persistently and stridently privatized as an individual experience of deliverance from sin, guilt, and death as to make headlines and sidelines all around us. The accent falls upon the moralization of a miracle of personal change. Hustlers leave the purveying of pornography behind and become purveyors of protection.

The political matrix and thrust of Easter, however, cannot be permanently ignored in the obedience of faith. On the contrary, the political implications of the crucifixion and resurrection of Jesus are evident both in Scripture and in the formative thought of the Christian church in the East and in the West. For the present purpose, one instance from each of these traditions of Easter faith may be noted. Athanasius and Augustine are not only among the more Scripturally oriented of the church's theologians, they are also seminally perceptive of the political matrix and thrust of the resurrection. As for Scripture itself, Ezekiel 37 and 1 Peter 3:18–22 are crucial to the perception and experience of resurrection and are political in occasion and thrust.

THE SCRIPTURAL RECORD

The outermost biblical boundaries of resurrection faith and hope are drawn by the experience of exile and persecution. These boundaries are profoundly and forcefully marked by Ezekiel 37 and 1 Peter 3:18–22. It is well known that Israel's reflections upon resurrection are a relatively late emergence in Israel's experience as a covenant people. The pivotal date was the fall of Jerusalem in 586 BCE. Although a doctrine of resurrection from the grave was unknown in the Old Testament before the third century BCE,[3] the stirring vision of Ezekiel concerning the prospects for the restoration to life of the nation after the loss of its capital city, is unmistakably a political adumbration of the resurrection theme.[4] According to the vision:

> The hand of the Lord came upon me, and he carried me out by his spirit and put me down in a plain full of dry bones . . . They covered the plain, countless numbers of them, and they were very dry. He said to me, "Man, can these bones live again?" I answered, "Only Thou knowest that, Lord God!" . . . He said to me, "Man, these bones are the whole people of Israel. They say, 'Our bones are dry, our thread of life is snapped, our web is severed from the loom.' Prophesy, therefore, and say to them, 'These are the words of the Lord God: O my people,

I will open your graves and bring you up from them and restore you to the land of Israel . . . Then I will put my spirit into you and you shall live, and I will settle you on your own soil, and you shall know that I the Lord have spoken and will act." (Ez. 37:1–3; 11–14)

It does not matter that at the time Ezekiel "knows nothing of a revivification of life after death." He saw in the vision of the dry bones "the restoration of 'the whole house of Israel' . . . Ezekiel, living in the time of Israel's humiliation, believed firmly in the future resurrection of [his] nation."[5] The vision echoes loudly in these very days, as anyone who has lived through the Camp David Accords of 1977 must know. The fierce determination of Menachim begins to yield not one inch of "the land of Judaea and Samaria" confirms, however negatively, that resurrection and politics are inseparable in Scriptural perspective and experience.

It took time, of course, but once the political matrix of Israel's resurrection faith and hope emerged in the covenant community of Israel, its application to the life of individuals resurrected from the grave was inevitable. With this development, the Passion narratives of the Gospels, and the Pauline and other Epistles of the New Testament are chiefly concerned. Therefore, only an egregious misreading of this individualization of the political matrix of Easter can underline its privatization and ignore its political context and focus. The context is a covenantal community called into a world created for being human in. This community is destined to be "a signal to the peoples" and a rallying place for the nations (Isaiah 11:10). Its model is the kingdom of David, the image—in remembrance of expectation from that day to this—of a sovereignty that undergirds and means freedom, of laws that indicate the parameters of righteousness and justice, the harbinger of a time when, and a place where, "each man shall dwell under his own vine, under his own fig tree undisturbed" (Micah 4: 4), and "no longer need they teach one another to know the Lord" for "all of them, high and low alike, shall know the Lord" (Jeremiah 31: 34). Surrounded as it is by these political perceptions and hopes, Ezekiel's resurrection vision of the valley of dry bones looks both backward and forward, and concludes with a kind of watershed summation of the political matrix of Easter:

These are the words of the Lord God: I am taking the leaf of Joseph, which belongs to Ephraim and his associate tribes of Israel, and joining it to the leaf of Judah . . . And they shall be one in my hand . . . I am gathering up the Israelites from their places of exile among the nations . . . I will make them one single nation in the land . . . and they shall have one king . . . My servant David shall become king over them, and they shall have one shepherd. They shall conform to my laws and observe and carry out my statutes . . . And my servant David shall forever be their prince. I will make a covenant with them to bring them prosperity; this covenant shall be theirs forever . . . The nations shall know that I the Lord am keeping Israel to myself, because my sanctuary is in the midst of them forever. (Ez. 37:19, 21, 24–26, 28)

The realization of these expectations was destined to come along the road of suffering and humiliation, of rejection and death. The sovereignty that undergirds freedom had to make its way against a power of resistance pervasively masquerading as strength. Under the promise of freedom, it installs tyranny. In the name of righteousness and justice it feeds upon injustice. In the name of law and order it sows discord and division. In the name of national security, it breeds insecurity and distrust. Committed to the madness which celebrates offense as the best defense, it prepares its own destruction by the subversion of humane sensibility in the name of humane values, stealthily harboring despots under the cloak of Hippocrates and international conventions. This sovereignty does not even shrink from messianic mouthings which conceal nothing so much as demonic substitution of the power that shows itself as strength for the power that is made perfect in weakness. "The powers that rule the world have never known it; if they had, they would not have crucified the Lord of glory" (1 Corinthians 2:8).

Meanwhile, the journey from Exodus to Exile has been transfigured by the journey from Exile to Easter. The community which in exile was being shaped through suffering for its passage from despair to hope, was at the same time winnowed by pressures from without and defections from within. The individualism by which Ezekiel attempted to intensify and renew covenantal responsibility, ultimately pushed beyond the polarity between the nation and the person. It culminated in apocalyptic expectation of the coming of a "Son of Man" who would put haughty and hostile principalities and powers to flight, vindicate the righteous faithful, and restore the nation to the fulfillment of its covenantal destiny.[6] With reference to exilic and post-exilic prophecy, and specifically with reference to Ezekiel 37, Gerhard von Rad has pointed out that:

> The confusion of the message of these prophets thus lay in the fact that they spoke of the deep breach in the saving action of God for Israel, a breach in the depths of which lay the death of the people of God. The theological place to which they referred their hearers and contemporaries was precisely that death-zone in which they could no longer be reached by the old ordinances of salvation [*dem Heil der alten Setzungen*], and in which nothing else remained except to cast their total existence upon that future saving action which, even then, was beginning to reveal itself on the horizon of history . . . According to these prophets, the coming new order would come to pass entirely on the model of the old order: as a new Exodus, a new Covenant, a new David, etc . . . The new Covenant would be better, the new Exodus will be more glorious than the

first, and the eschatological servant of God will suffer more deeply, and thus more effectively, than Moses had suffered.[7]

The critical instance of these expectations was the crucifixion and resurrection of Jesus, the Messiah. The second exodus began with the transfiguration, on the near edge of the confrontational entrance into Jerusalem, where before the week was out, a power showdown before Pilate occurred which unveiled the crucial difference between messianic politics and political messianism. In the crucifixion and resurrection of the "Son: on the human level . . . born of David's stock, but on the level of the spirit—the Holy Spirit—declared Son of God by a mighty act in that he rose from dead" (Romans 1:2–4), a line was indelibly drawn between what might be called the "dolorosa politics" of the powers of this world (political messianism) and the politics of Easter (messianic politics) which have already put to flight the *stoixeia tou kosmou* (Galatians 4:9; 5:25).[8] The political matrix of Easter is thus manifest and inescapable. Easter stands exposed as a political feast.

The depth and sweep of an obedient celebration of Easter are signaled by the passage in 1 Peter 3:15–22. Once again, the political thrust has been too little noticed. Nevertheless, together with Ezekiel 37 as the *terminus a quo*, 1 Peter 3:18–22 may be regarded as the *terminus ad quem* of the political matrix of Easter.[9]

The passage, reconstructed as verse, tells us of the crucifixion and resurrection of Christ:

> who suffered once for sins,
> > that he might bring us to God,
> being put to death in the flesh,
> > but made alive in the spirit,
> in which also he preached to the spirits in prison,
> > and having gone into heaven sat down at
> > the right hand
> > of God.
> angels and authorities and powers having been made subject to him.[10]

Read in its prose form, as a single self-contained section of the chapter, the passage seems to be an attempt to encourage Christians under persecution to consider their sufferings in the light of the sufferings of Christ. This encouragement is warranted because between his death and his resurrection, Christ even went to preach to the spirits in prison, a *descensus ad inferos,* and a conquest of the powers of darkness, as a prelude to the light and life of the world to come, already underway in the power of Jesus' resurrection from the dead. "Spirits in prison" (3:19) is echoed in Revelation 20:7, where, at the end of Christ's thousand-year reign, Satan is said to be "loosed from his prison" for the final power showdown. The millennial image measures the ferocity of the persecution as well as the awesomeness of the final battle.

If, however, we follow the verse reconstruction herein proposed, 1 Peter 3:18–22 is greatly clarified. The clarification underlines the political thrust of Easter. The contrasts between "flesh and spirit," an "earthly" and a "heavenly" sphere, between the Redeemer's preexistence and his incarnation,[11] echo a Gnostic hymn in praise of *sophia*. The Petrine passage, however, unlike certain other hymns/passages (for instance, Phil 2, 6–11, Col 1: 15–20, 1 Tim 3: 16) focuses upon the consequences of the atoning death of the Redeemer and upon the cosmic sphere in which the resurrection took place. Indeed, the resurrection is the turning point of the myth. The *descensus ad inferos* [descent into hell] occurs—not between the death and resurrection of the Redeemer—but *after* the resurrection, and is a prelude to the Redeemer's exaltation.[12] "His redemptive work," says Fuller, "is described in terms of the Adam/Christ typology as a victory over the powers."[13] As Bultmann sums it up:

> In a certain sense, "*life*" *is a present thing after all*—present to hoping faith though not as an "experience" in the life of the soul. For . . . participation in Christ's death and resurrection, the important thing is not what takes place in the soul. What it really is is the bestowal of the salvation occurrence and the appropriation of it by the faith of him who in it confesses his faith . . . It is a relationship of concretely living for each other, in which what happens to one cannot but be full of consequence to the other . . . In God, freedom, righteousness, and life have their cause, and it is in them that the glory of God as ultimate meaning and goal comes to its own.[14]

From Ezekiel via the Transfiguration, Passion, and Resurrection, to "the spirits in prison" of 1 Peter, the politics of Easter are the politics of the resurrection. According to these politics, a radical reversal of perspective upon the valuation of the goings-on in heaven and on earth has come to pass. The reversal reads the past and present in the light of an imminent future. The liberation journey towards a new order of human fulfillment in freedom, righteousness, and life moves from Easter to Exodus, not from Exodus to Easter. The God of the oppressed preserves the oppressed from ideological self-destruction through the gift to them of the truth that sets them free. Sovereignties on earth, under the earth, and in heaven, undergo a transfiguration of authority inaugurated by him who, seated at the right hand of God, is the head of all principality and power (Col 2:10); "angels, and authorities and powers having been made subject to him" (1 Peter 3:22).

The self-justifying, self-validations of established orders, institutions, patterns and policies are displaced by the self-validating authority of power that is free from all self-justification and from the vanity of the search for security. Revolutionary passions for new beginnings and a new birth of freedom, justice, and peace are turned aside from self-justifying and self-destructive ideologies, and in the power of a righteousness not their own, are nurtured towards their appointed purposes. Through confidence that the future is not in their hands but on their side, discernment that the violence of their fury need not be converted into policy, and certainty that "there is no hiding place down here" for thrones and powers that "crucify afresh the Lord of glory" (1 Cor 2: 8)—not even for the "spirits in prison"—revolutionary movements signal that through the things that are not, God "has chosen things low and contemptible, mere nothings, to overthrow the existing order" (1 Cor 1: 29).

THE THEOLOGICAL TRADITION

It should be no surprise that the politics of Easter, described and affirmed in Scripture, should have shaped the faith, thoughts, and valuations of two of the formative and more Scripturally oriented theologians of the church. Athanasius in the East and Augustine in the West, each in his own way, make the resurrection central to their reflections upon the significance of the presence of Jesus of Nazareth *in* the human story *to* the human story.

Of Athanasius, Charles Cochrane, with special reference to his treatise on *The Incarnation of the Word*, writes that:

> Athanasius arrives at the central idea of the divine economy, the notion of the redemption of mankind through the assumption of manhood by the Word. For him, the purpose of this event was to serve as a revelation of the invisible through the visible, and thus to indicate the true relationship between life and death . . . Its reality, besides being implied in the very nature of the Word Incarnate, was attested by experience and confirmed by subsequent historical developments. As such . . . he urged, as a reason for accepting the faith, the fact of its salutary influence upon the life of individuals and societies, claiming that it embodied the sole hope of creative peace, since it alone imbued human beings with a really pacific disposition and, by transmuting the strife of man with nature and with his fellows into a conflict against evil, made possible a realization of the promise; *they shall beat their swords into ploughshares and there shall be no more war.*[15]

Similarly, of Augustine it may be said that his *magnum opus* is *The City of God*.[16] Setting out to refute the calumnies falsely leveled against the Christians by the citizens of the Roman Republic, in disarray all around him,

Augustine declares on the basis of Scripture that there are two societies in the world, inhabited by those who belong to "the pilgrim city of King Christ" and those "who shall not eternally dwell in the lot of the saints."[17] These two cities or societies "are entangled together in this world, and intermixed until the last judgment effect their separation."[18]

Meanwhile, these two cities or societies may be distinguished. There is "a city of God, and its Founder [who] has inspired us with a love which makes us covet its citizenship," and "citizens of the earthly city [who] prefer their own gods . . . and so, reduced to a kind of poverty-stricken power, eagerly grasp at their own privileges, and seek divine honors from their deluded subjects."[19] There are those who have loved "glory for the sake of justice" and those who "seemed rather to have loved justice for the sake of glory."[20] There is "the city of the ungodly, which did not obey the command of God that it should offer no sacrifice save to Him alone, and which, therefore, could not give to the soul its proper command over the body, nor to the reason its just authority over the vices, [and] is void of true justice"[21]; and there is "the obedient city . . . where there is . . . this righteousness whereby the one supreme God rules . . . according to His grace, so that it sacrifices to none but Him, and whereby, in all the citizens . . . the soul consequently rules the body and reason and vices in the rightful order, so that, as the individual just man, so also the community and people of the just, live by faith, which works by love, that love whereby man loves God as he ought to be loved, and his neighbor as himself."[22]

Thus, "in order to discover the character of any people we have only to observe what they love."[23] This observation tells us that there are indeed two societies which "have been formed by two loves: the earthly by the love of self, even to the contempt of God; the heavenly by the love of God, even to the contempt of self"[24]; the one, by the love of power, the other by the power of love. From the pivotal point of the resurrection of Christ, the human story is to be read backward to and from the Creation, and forward to and from the Last Judgment.[25] Indeed, we live now—and every now is what happens—between Resurrection and Judgment.

THE VIEW FROM BELOW

The revised and enlarged edition of Bonhoeffer's *Letters and Papers From Prison* includes at the outset a previously unpublished little essay entitled, "The View From Below."[26] Together with the already familiar essay, "After Ten Years," we have at hand a succinct formulation of what the politics of Easter are about. Bonhoeffer has made contemporary what Athanasius and Augustine, each in their own way for their own time, made of the scriptural delineation of the political matrix and thrust of the resurrection from the valley of dry bones to the spirits in prison. There too, the view is hauntingly and decisively, "from below." "There remains," Bonhoeffer wrote, "an experience of incomparable value. We have for once learnt to see the great events of world history from below, from the perspective of the outcast, the suspects, the maltreated, the powerless, the oppressed, the reviled—in short, from the perspective of those who suffer."[27]

It is an almost daily surprise, how easily this perspective can be brushed aside, and how wide the gulf can be which divides the citizens of the earthly city, in their self-justifying self-love, from those who, belonging to "the pilgrim city of King Christ," struggle and pray without ceasing to displace the love of justice for the sake of glory by the love of glory for the sake of justice, who struggle and pray without ceasing without "blindness of perception," against loss of the principle of life and "spiritual wasting away."

Some time ago, there came to my hand, on the initiative of the Ethics and Public Policy Center of Georgetown University,[28] a free paperback copy of a book entitled, *Amsterdam to Nairobi: The World Council of Churches and the Third World*. Its author is Ernest W. Lefever, Director of the Center.[29] It carries a foreword by George F. Will.[30] The author reviews the various pronouncements and resolutions of the World Council of Churches (WCC) from its founding assembly in Amsterdam (1948) to its most recent meeting in Nairobi (1975), including the Geneva Conference on The Church and Society (1966). The text is a not-so-subtle attack on the World Council, chiefly because of its Program to Combat Racism that "from 1970 through 1978 . . . gave $3,063,545.00 to more than a hundred organizations in some two dozen countries. Almost 65 percent of this money went to guerrilla groups seeking to overthrow white regimes . . . in southern Africa and to other organizations supporting political change there."[31] In strong and astonishingly strident tones, George Will declares in part that:

> Professor Lefever is about . . . the question not whether Christians should be politically active, or whether their faith should inform their action. Of course they should, of course it should . . . But it is wrong to believe that this means that Christianity is somehow inherently revolutionary, or that Christians can casually undertake or underwrite political upheavals. Political revolutionaries almost invariably invest in politics a kind of expectation that mature Christians consider not just unrealistic but unseemly . . . Readers of Professor Lefever's essay can decide for themselves the extent to which bad sociology, bad theology, bad faith, and, yes, sin feed on one another and are to blame for what the WCC has been doing . . . The record of the WCC is only in part a record of some people who are well-intentioned but breath-takingly silly. Some of the people involved are more sinister than silly, and even those who are 'only' silly are culpable. Always, but

especially in the high-stakes business of politics, there is a moral obligation to be intelligent.[32]

Having been an appreciative reader of George Will for some time, and an admirer of his acute and informed mind, penetrating analytical powers, and sharp critical judgments, often seasoned with devastating wit, I was unprepared to find him in so exposed a condition of ideological special pleading. Having also tried to be open to the counsel to "beware of Greeks bearing gifts," I found myself puzzled to be receiving a free copy of this bitter indictment of the churches' ecumenical struggles and actions, achievements and failures, skillfully garbed in the time-honored procedures of scholarly research.

The pieces of the puzzle began to fall into place by way of a published list of the "Board of Advisors" of the Ethics and Public Policy Center. It reads like a neo-conservative facsimile of the sometime "Committee for Cultural Freedom" which once gave similarly academic standing to the anti-communist ferocity of Senator Joseph R. McCarthy. A formidable and impeccable group of higher priests and of higher learning had been gathered together to this end.

And then, since I had received the "free gift" as a member of the American Society of Christian Ethics, some of whose more eminent members stared out at me from the list of the "Board of Advisors," I found myself wondering whether there could be a "fiscal angel" lurking somewhere in the wings. Perhaps, under the tutelage of George Will's breath-taking confidence in sorting out the silly from the intelligent, the American Society of Christian Ethics might even be coopted for the "the high-stakes business of politics" where "especially . . . there is a moral obligation to be intelligent." After all, had I not been solicited at about the same time by other "Greeks bearing gifts" in the form of an invitation to participate in the Eighth International Conference on the Unity of the Sciences, to be held at the Century Plaza Hotel in Los Angeles immediately following Thanksgiving? And had I not been rendered speechless by the roster of participants in the exploration of "The Responsibility of the Academic Community in the Search for Absolute Values," among whom I found the names, not only of persons in the highest echelons of the biological, natural, and social sciences, but even those of nearer colleagues in the American Theological Society? It was hard to keep from remembering the remark of a certain hapless boxer, Willie Sullivan by name, who when asked why he submitted himself so unceasingly to one battering after another in the ring, unfeelingly replied: "That's where the money is!"

At least as regards "the Search for Absolute Values," there was no mystery about "fiscal angels." The letterhead said it all. The Founder of the

Conference was none other than the Reverend Sun Myung Moon of the Unification Church.[33] In the case of the Ethics and Public Policy Center, the "angels" were less self-identifying. Taking up George Will's gratuitous allowance that readers of Ernest Lefever's book could decide for themselves the extent to which bad sociology, bad theology, bad faith, and even sin could be feeding on one another in that company of "wise and understanding ones," I was less than totally surprised to come upon more than a hint of a "Dutch Connection." It seems that certain fiscal manipulations might have found their way from South Africa to Georgetown, laundered in the impeccable Calvinist waters of the capitol of the Netherlands. It seems that Professor Lefever himself has recently "completed his 16th trip to Africa where he held interviews with 25 leading churchmen in South Africa and Rhodesia."[34]

Long before Reinhold Niebuhr taught us that reason is corruptible by interest, Calvin that the human mind is a perpetual factory of idols, and Luther that reason is vulnerable to prostitution, Augustine observed that:

> It is very easy for a man to seem to himself to have answered arguments, when he has only been unwilling to keep silent. For what is more loquacious than vanity? And though it be able, if it like, to shout more loudly than the truth, it is not for all that more powerful than the truth. But let men consider diligently all the things that we have said, and if perchance judging without party spirit, they shall clearly perceive that they are such things as may rather be shaken than torn up by their most impudent garrulity, and, as it were, satirical and mimic levity, let them restrain their absurdities, and let them choose rather to be corrected by the wise than to be lauded by the foolish.[35]

One does not need to deny that the theological perceptions of those to whom have been committed the leadership and decisions of the World Council of Churches are, and have been, less than adequately informed by or explained with reference to the politics of Easter. But these regrettable omissions will deprive only those whose progressive blindness of perception already signals a departure from the Word, of the recognition that the actions of the World Council of Churches, so vehemently resented, really do proceed from the view from below. This view has been the sign of the obedience of faith at least since the Lord and Giver of life began to make dry bones come alive, to shatter the stranglehold of death in the power of the resurrection, and to confront the spirits in prison, as a prelude to his own assumption of all authority and power at the right hand of God, angels and authorities and powers having been made subject to him.

The view from below is the view from the perspective of those who suffer. In the light of this perspective, what really matters is "to know Christ, to experience the power of his resurrection, and to share his sufferings, in growing conformity with his death, if only one may finally arrive at the resurrection from the dead" (Phil. 3:10–11). The power of Christ's resurrection is the power to live in this life prepared for death and free from the fear of death. It is the power to live in this life without taking this life for granted or making any of the values and achievements of this life the measure of its meaning and purpose. The power of Christ's resurrection is the power to live in this life with a lively and liberating confidence that God's new world is the warrant for and confirmation of hope and is already under way in all those struggles in which we are called to share Christ's sufferings in conformity with his death. To share Christ's sufferings is to stand with and for all in this life who are without opportunity, without power, and without hope, and to make their cause and claims one's own. This succinct summary of the politics of Easter is apostolically warranted and calls for the celebration of Easter as a political feast.

NOTES

1. Published in *Dialog* 19 (1980): 37–43; reprinted with permission of Wiley.

2. [Editorial: Dietrich Bonhoeffer's letter to Eberhard Bethge, March 27, 1944, *Dietrich Bonhoeffer: Letters and Papers from Prison*, DBW 8 (Minneapolis: Fortress Press, 2010), 333.]

3. See Isaiah 26:19, and later, Daniel 2:12. See Robert Pfeiffer, *Introduction to the Old Testament* (New York: Harper, 1941), 478–79.

4. The thirty-seventh chapter is part of Ezekiel's second volume (1–24; 33–37, possibly, 38–39) and was written in Babylon between 586 and 525 BCE. See Pfeiffer, *Introduction to the Old Testament*, 561.

5. Pfeiffer, *Introduction to the Old Testament*, 497.

6. For an instructive account of the roots, ambiguities, and varieties of meaning surrounding the phrase, "Son of Man," and its appropriation as a Christological title, see Reginald Fuller, *The Foundations of New Testament Christology* (New York: Scribner's, 1965), especially chapters 2–4. These critical clarifications inform the general sense and direction of the interpretation offered here.

7. Gerhard von Rad, *Theologie des Alten Testamentes II. Die Theologie der prophetischen Überlieferungen Israels* (München: Chr. Kaiser, 1965), 280–81; translation Lehmann's.

8. According to Raymond E. Brown, the threshold power significance of the Transfiguration pericope in the Synoptic Gospels is replaced in the Fourth Gospel by the prayer for glory "a visible manifestation of majesty through acts of power," which concludes the last discourse of Jesus before his crucifixion. Raymond E. Brown, *The Gospel According to John*, XIII–XXI, Volume II (New York: Doubleday, 1970), 744–51. Further to the political significance of the Transfiguration pericope, see Paul Lehmann, *The Transfiguration of Politics* (New York: Harper and Row, 1975), chapter 7.

9. Although, if 1:20 is taken account of in relation to 3:18–22, the boundaries become more fluid, and indeed, co-inhere in each other. The *ad quem*, adumbrates a cosmic sweep which includes the preexistence of the Redeemer and the *descensus ad inferos*, as the penultimate act of the resurrected Christ. So also, Ezekiel's resurrection vision is *ad quem* as well as a *quo*. Its roots are in messianism already under way, and it reaches as far as the new covenant inaugurated by the crucifixion and resurrection of Jesus, and the new age already begun with that event.

10. Dr. Fuller, *The Foundations of New Testament Christology*, 218. Fuller's reconstruction follows Bultmann according to whom only verse 18a is relevant to the hymnic origin, poetic structure, and context of the passage. It provides the starting point for the juxtaposition: body spirit; death; life; of v. 19. A typological interpretation of the water of the flood and the water of baptism interrupts the movement of the crucified and risen Christ from the "spirits in prison" (v. 19) to "the submission of angels, authorities, and powers" in heaven where Christ's triumph over all authorities and powers is affirmed by his session "at the right hand of God." See Fuller, *The Foundations of New Testament Christology*, 218–20; and note 38, 238–39. The Bultmann reconstruction appears in an essay, cited by Fuller without its title, and to which my Union New Testament colleague, J. Louis Martyn, had already called my attention. The essay is entitled: Rudolf Bultmann, "Bekenntnis und Liedfragmente im ersten Petrusbrief," in *Coniectana Neotestamentica XI, Festschrift für Anton Fridrichsen* (Lund: Gleerup, 1947), 1–14.

11. Bultmann thinks that 1 Peter 1:20 belongs with 3:18, 19, 21d. 22; 1:20 reads: "who was destined before the foundation of the world, but was made manifest at the end of the times."

12. As in the prose version, and in the Apostles' Creed.

13. Fuller, *The Foundations of New Testament Christology*, 220.

14. Rudolf Bultmann, *Theology of the New Testament I*, trans. Kendrick Grobel (New York: Scribner's, 1951), 348, 350, 352.

15. Charles Cochrane, *Christianity and Classical Culture* (Oxford: Clarendon, 1940), 369–70.

16. Augustine, *The City of God*, trans. Marcus Dods, The Modern Library (New York: Random House, 1950).

17. Augustine, *City of God*, XI, 1.

18. Augustine, *City of God*, I, 35.

19. Augustine, *City of God*, XI, 1.

20. Augustine, *City of God*, V, 22.

21. Augustine, *City of God*, XIX, 24.

22. Augustine, *City of God*, XIX, 23.

23. Augustine, *City of God*, XIX, 24.

24. Augustine, *City of God*, XIV, 28.

25. See Augustine, *City of God*, XVII, 18; XX–XXII.

26. Dietrich Bonhoeffer, *Widerstand und Ergebung* (München: Chr. Kaiser). [Editorial: See Bonhoeffer, *Letters and Papers from Prison*, DBW 8, ed. John W. De Gruchy, trans. Isabel Best, Lisa E. Dahill, Reinhard Krauss, and Nancy Lukens (Minneapolis: Fortress, 2009).]

27. [Editorial: DBW 8, 52.]

28. [Editorial: Founded in 1976, the Ethics and Public Policy Center is a right-wing Washington, D.C.–based think tank founded in 1976. The Center describes itself as "Washington, D.C.'s premier institute working to apply the riches of the Judeo-Christian tradition to contemporary questions of law, culture, and politics, in pursuit of America's continued civic and cultural renewal." https://eppc.org.]

29. [Editorial: Ernest Warren Lefever (1919–2009) was a right-wing political theorist who founded and directed the Ethics and Public Policy Center. In 1981, President Ronald Reagan nominated Lefever for a position at the U.S. State Department. Lefever's nomination was rejected by the Senate Foreign Relations Committee.]

30. [Editorial: George F. Will (b. 1941) is a conservative U.S. political commentator.]

31. Ernest W. Lefever, *Amsterdam to Nairobi: The World Council of Churches and the Third World* (Ethics and Public Policy Center, 1979), 32.

32. George F. Will, "Foreword," in Lefever, *Amsterdam to Nairobi*, vii, ix.

33. [Editorial: Sun Myung Moon (1920–2012) was a controversial Korean religious leader and founder of the Unification Church.]

34. Concerning the Dutch connection, reference may be made to "The Eschel Rhoodie Story," an exclusive interview by the Dutch editor-in-chief of *Elseviers Magazine*, Amsterdam, Dr. Ferry A. Hoogendijk, and published in *Facts and Reports* (31 August 1979). There is also a *Supplementary Report of the Commission of Inquiry into Alleged Irregularities in the Former Department of Information*, Republic of South Africa, chapter XI. Concerning Ernest Lefever's travels, reference may be made to: *To the Point*: News in Depth, World News Published Weekly, 1501 Sandton City, Sandton, Transvaal, South Africa. In the issue of this publication of 31 August 1979, 12, an article appears by Ernest W. Lefever, entitled, *WCC has no Brief to Speak for the Christian Millions*. A perceptive, informed, and critical assessment of *Amsterdam to Nairobi* has appeared, as this article was in preparation, in *Christianity and Crisis* 39, no. 17 (1979): 276–79. Its author is John C. Bennett, president of Union Theological Seminary emeritus.

35. Augustine, *City of God*, V, 25.

Chapter 13

Piety, Power, and Politics[1]

Church and Ministry Between Ratification and Resistance (1982)

Piety, power, and politics are fundamental and formative factors of the human condition. *Piety* refers to the reverence for and response to the transcendent dimension of life in this world. It signals the perennial discovery that as human beings, we live not in one world only but in two worlds at the same time. *Power*—as Bertrand Russell succinctly put it—is to society what energy is to physics.[2] Power is the capacity to initiate and to affect social interaction. *Politics* are the science, art, and practice of human community: of knowing, doing, and achieving what is required for relating and interrelating individuals and groups in the art of giving shape to a society fit for being human in.

The principal institutional forms of the interrelation between piety, power, and politics are religious, governmental, and juridical: in short, church, state, and law. And the principal values upon which the human outcome of these institutional interrelations depend are: authority and freedom; responsibility and limits; justice and concord (or peace). Thus, St. Augustine wrote that "order is the distribution which allots things equal and unequal, each to its own place." And again, that "peace between humanity and God is the well-ordered obedience of faith to eternal law. Peace between human beings is well-ordered concord. Domestic peace is the well-ordered concord between those of the family who rule and those who obey . . . Civil peace is a similar concord among the citizens . . . The peace of all things is the tranquility of order."[3] Thus also—and thirteen centuries later—Rousseau wrote that "the great problem of politics, which I compare to squaring the circle in geometry [is]: How to find a form of government which puts the law above people." And Rousseau goes on to remark that "to put the law above people and thus to establish the validity of laws made by people, *il faudrait des dieux!*" [It would take gods!][4]

With special reference to the significance of these insights and experiences for the beginnings of the interrelations between church, state, and law in the United States, Alexander Hamilton notes in the opening paragraph of *Federalist I* that it has frequently been remarked that "it seems to have been reserved to the people of this country, by their conduct and example to decide the important question, whether human societies really are capable or not of establishing good government from reflection and choice, or whether they are forever destined to depend for their political constitutions on accident and force."[5]

In these days of the strange coalescence of the "New Federalism" and the "New Right" in open and hidden alliance with the "Moral Majority," Hamilton's haunting question has come once again to the top of the agenda of the relations between piety, power, and politics in this country. There is a gathering storm on the horizon of the nearer and the remoter future, touching again the question whether this nation or any nation can long endure half-slave and half-free. The widening chasm between privilege and poverty, between opportunity and deprivation, between trust in the just powers of government, derived from the consent of the governed, and distrust of all authority and power in heaven and in earth, is assuming global proportions in the haunting spectre of world hunger and starvation, of deep and dynamic divisions between developed and developing countries and continents, and of the imminent threat of nuclear catastrophe involving all of humankind, and indeed, of the earth and the stellar spaces on which and under which we live.

In face of these circumstances, church and ministry find themselves—or so it seems, more often than not—caught between ratification and resistance, that is, between the silent or vocal support of those who—in Augustine's words—"love justice for the sake of glory," and faithfulness to the gospel, by which church and ministry are called to call into question all authority and power that do not "love glory for the sake of justice."[6] On the boundary between ratification and resistance—and in the light of the instructive reminders of the struggle of the churches and ministry in Germany between 1933 and 1945 amid "the rise and fall of the Third Reich"—it could be that church and ministry today are being drawn toward a *Declaration of Conscience*.

The place and responsibility of a divinity school in this or any university—particularly a divinity school whose heritage has been shaped by the covenantal story of a people whose destiny is the fulfillment of its messianic focus and faithfulness—are rooted in the vocation so to use this right to teach as "to take every thought captive to the obedience of Christ" (2 Cor 10:5). Since the messianic question is endemic to the human story and neither religious pluralism nor cultural diversity can ultimately render it superfluous, the divinity school has a critical as well as a vocational place and responsibility in the university. Indeed, so critically are divinity school and university linked that the university cannot be a university without a divinity school nor can a divinity school be a divinity school without the university. The fruits of such a vocation and reciprocity are a church and ministry on the frontier of human commitment, expectation, and endeavor. On this frontier, frustration and futility ever and again bring loneliness to the brink of abandonment or despair. In such moments, we all know again—do we not?—what Jeremiah meant when he burst out:

> "Why is my pain unceasing?
> my wound incurable?
> Wilt thou be to me like a deceitful brook,
> like waters that fail?" (Jeremiah 15:18)
> Somehow, when the answer comes, our hearing aids break down:
> "If you have raced with men on foot, and
> they have wearied you,
> how will you compete with horses?
> And if in a safe land you fall down,
> how will you do in the jungle of the Jordan?" (Jer. 12:5)

So—how *will* we do? How *are* we doing?—in the jungle of the Jordan. The footmen and the horses are still with us. But they have been joined by SAM 6s and MX missiles, which threaten to put Utah and the Bekaa Valley into Jeremiah's backyard.[7] Thus, it is a report *from* "the jungle of the Jordan" *about* "the jungle of the Jordan" that I should like to explore with you, and to which I should like to invite your attention.

THE JUNGLE OF THE JORDAN

In Eberhard Bethge's classic biography of Dietrich Bonhoeffer, there is a brief section that bears the title "Colonel Oster."[8] Hans Oster was an officer in the German Wehrmacht whom Bonhoeffer had met during the darkest days of the conspiracy to assassinate Adolf Hitler. That was the period between September 1939 and April 1940. Five Aprils later, on the ninth of that month in 1945, Oster was one of those with whom Bonhoeffer went to his death.

There was a grim issue before those whose loyalty to Germany required them—for the sake of the country to which they belonged and to which they were bound in gratitude, affection, and hope—to enter upon conspiratorial obedience. The grim issue after September 27, 1939, the day that Warsaw surrendered, was "either *with* Hitler from a threatened to an actual world war, or *against* Hitler from a threatened world war to a reasonable peace."[9]

An assault on the West via the "Low Countries" was being planned by Hitler and the German General Staff. The decisive stroke, the removal of Hitler, had to be carried out before that time. In that critical situation, Colonel Oster had decided that he must "inform the Dutch of the date of the coming attack" upon the Low Countries; "and thereby stop Hitler's successes which were bringing disaster on Germany." So, writes Bethge, "the patriot had to perform what in normal times is the action of a scoundrel. 'Treason' had become true patriotism, and what was normally 'patriotism' had become treason." "Anyone," he continues, "who hastily measures the borderline situation of that time by the yardstick of his own principles, or studiously overlooks its peculiar features, distorts its contours and does not see the realities of those months . . . All the world over, 'treason' is normally thought of as a mean attitude, speculation for one's personal advantage, and the intention to injure one's country. The opposite holds good for Oster, Dohnanyi, and Bonhoeffer."[10]

In that same critical situation, Bonhoeffer began to write his *Ethics*. There he wrote, "What is worse than doing evil, is being evil. It is worse for a liar to tell the truth than for a lover of truth to lie."[11] Two years later, in 1942, and as a Christmas present for Oster and Dohnanyi, he set down his reflections in a piece called "After Ten Years."[12] A concluding passage of that piece begins with a question which has surely crossed our minds and thoughts on more than one occasion. "Are we still of any use?" he asked. And then he went on to say:

> We have been silent witnesses of evil deeds; we have been drenched by many storms; we have learnt the arts of equivocation and pretence; experience has made us suspicious of others and kept us from being truthful and open; intolerable conflicts have worn us down and even made us cynical. Are we still of any use? Will our inward power of resistance be strong enough, and our honesty with ourselves remorseless enough, for us to find our way back to simplicity and straightforwardness?[13]

Bonhoeffer himself was already on that "way back to simplicity and straightforwardness." The course, however, was not a return to old values, a restoration of things as they used to be. The way lay ahead of him. It was, as Bethge describes it, an "entering fully into his contemporary world, his place, and his time. That means into a world which his bourgeois class had helped to bring about, rather than prevent. He accepted the weight of that collective responsibility, and began to identify himself with those who were prepared to answer for guilt and try tentatively to shape something new for the future, instead of merely protesting on ideological grounds, as had hitherto been usual on the ecclesiastical plane." According to Bethge, "in 1932 he found his calling;

in 1939 his destiny." The former took him "into the community of brethren which was limited to that ecclesiastical group that protested publicly with him." The latter discovery took him into the conspiracy against Hitler. The former meant the crossing of a boundary from theologian to Christian; the latter meant the crossing of a boundary from Christian to contemporary. After his execution, friends looking back on that journey "discovered in expositions such as, for example, the meditation on Psalm 119, turns of speech that hinted at what was to come."[14]

Since his London days, the psalm had steadily engaged him; and it became for him the most frequently quoted of biblical passages. In Sigurdshof, in Eastern Pomerania, one of the collective pastorates designed to further continuing education for church and ministry between ratification and resistance,[15] Bonhoeffer had gotten as far as Psalm 119:21: "Thou dost rebuke the insolent, accursed ones, who wander from thy commandments."[16] Friends recalled also conversations on his thirty-third birthday (February 4, 1939) "round the tiled stove of the vicarage . . . , when he said that it might be worthwhile, even for a pastor, to risk one's life for political freedom."[17] Among these friends was Oskar Hammelsbeck, gifted student of Karl Jaspers in philosophy, co-worker with Adolf Reichwein, and in the Weimar period, a specialist in adult education. Hammelsbeck had decided late in life that the rest of his life should be given over to the church as it had been shaped by the Barmen and Dahlem Synods. In Bonhoeffer's attic in Berlin, the main subjects of conversation between Hammelsbeck and Bonhoeffer were politics and philosophy. Subsequently, Hammelsbeck recalled in an autobiographical sketch that:

> the question whether my way into the church can be directed back into the world, that worrying question "Church for the World," was exactly what Dietrich Bonhoeffer was asking, and so the conversations with him were the most important for me at that period . . . We endured the time in the *strange schizophrenia of happy thankfulness for the experience of the church, and of suffering through the church's guilt, in a strange mixture of power and weakness*.[18]

Bethge further includes a striking passage from Hammelsbeck's *Diary* because it so strikingly foreshadows the language and thought of *Letters and Papers From Prison*. An entry on January 24, 1941 reads:

> We can make no progress here [in Christ's service in the world] till we radically grasp the idea of our "godless" existence in the world. That means, till we refuse to entertain any illusion of being able to act "with God" from day to day in the world. That illusion repeatedly misleads us into throwing away justification and grace, into artificial piety, into making a legalized ethic, and to becoming unfree in a servitude with all the signs changed.[19]

In the jungle of the Jordan, "'treason' had become true patriotism and what was normally 'patriotism' had become treason." In the jungle of the Jordan, "what is worse than doing evil, is being evil. It is worse for a liar to tell the truth than for a lover of truth to lie."[20] In the jungle of the Jordan, "are we still of any use? . . . Will our inward power of resistance be strong enough, and our honesty with ourselves remorseless enough, for us to find our way back to simplicity and straightforwardness?"[21] In the jungle of the Jordan, "it might be worthwhile, even for a pastor, to risk one's life for political freedom." In the jungle of the Jordan, the question "Church for the World" presses us insistently into "the strange schizophrenia of happy thankfulness for the experience of the church, and of suffering through the church's guilt, in a strange mixture of power and weakness." In the jungle of the Jordan, "we can make no progress . . . till we radically . . . refuse to entertain any illusion of being able to act 'with God' from day to day in the world. That illusion repeatedly misleads us into throwing away justification and grace, into artificial piety, into making a legalized ethic, and to becoming unfree in a servitude with all the signs changed."[22]

For—in the jungle of the Jordan—"insolent and accursed ones who wander from thy commandments" in the name of the old values of family, honesty, the sanctity of life, and prayer in the schools, go—*as yet*—unrebuked. In the jungle of the Jordan, a euphoric shift of power, self-styled their "revolution," equates national security with a defense capability second to none. It identifies a global enemy: on the one hand, as transparently vulnerable to internal economic and moral decay; on the other hand, as propelled by an insatiable conspiratorial appetite to devour the globe. It has invented a logomachy peculiar to its passion for wealth and privilege and power, according to which the exploitation of fears without and fears within, converge upon a new code word. "Terrorism" has replaced "subversion." Red-baiting has been exchanged for the baiting of civil-libertarians. And a distinction of grotesque subtlety—transparent only to those initiated in this revolution backwards—is drawn, on the decisive frontier of human rights, between violators under *totalitarian* and violators under *authoritarian* auspices.

In the jungle of the Jordan, there seem to be no limits to this logomachy of falsehood masquerading as truth. "Winning one for the Gipper" so inebriates the senses that only those empowered to convert perpendiculars into ovals are able to value the rest of us as "Bonzos" in Death Valley, dubiously transposed into the Garden of Joseph of Arimathea. How conventional has the opprobrious become when the President of the United States[23] can find it at once timely and humorous to observe that an automobile worker recently laid off in Detroit could find another job because, "after all, I just got one at the age of 70."[24]

In the jungle of the Jordan, the conversion of the currency of truth into the coinage of falsehood proceeds apace. Perhaps the pièce de résistance of this logomachy of the jungle is the bon mot of Mr. George Will, at once sophisticated and sophomoric, reported in the *New Yorker*. Apparently Mr. Will has discovered "the statistically rich" in tandem with "the truly needy." "Noting that Christ said, 'the poor always ye have with you,'" Will "goes on to make the addition: 'we had better always have the rich.'" In turn, the *New Yorker* goes on to observe that "according to this new, even-handed reading of Scripture, society would balance its compassion for the poor with solicitude for the rich," thus not only reminding us of, but also supplying, a point that was "somehow overlooked by Christ . . . In that arrangement" according to the *New Yorker*, "even the truly needy might be hard put to it to hold their own."[25]

BETWEEN RATIFICATION AND RESISTANCE

In the jungle of the Jordan, church and ministry today are caught between ratification and resistance. And they are shadowed by a double schizophrenia. Except for those blind leaders of the blind who belong explicitly or implicitly to the "Moral Majority," and for whom the question, "Are we still of any use?" never arises, "the strange mixture of power and weakness" and "of happy thankfulness for the church and of suffering through the church's guilt" is compounded by silent acquiescence and the ambiguity of refusal. The blind leaders of the blind have long since succumbed to prophetic amnesia and rejected prophetic obedience. But those who have been and continue to be nurtured in thankfulness for church and ministry may be recognized by their increasing sensitivity to the dilemma between silent acquiescence and the ambiguity of refusal. That haunting line from Tom Stoppard's play, *Rosenkrantz and Guildenstern Are Dead*, brings it all out and wraps it all up. En route to England, bearing letters to the King that, unknown to them, ordered their execution as traitors to the Danish realm, Hamlet's two university friends are musing over their strange odyssey from their calling to their destiny. Says Guildenstern, "There must have been a moment, at the beginning, where we could have said 'No!' but somehow missed it."[26] But "the gate is wide and the way is easy that leads to destruction, and those who enter by it are many. For the gate is narrow and the way is hard, that leads to life, and those who find it are few" (Matt 7:13–14).

Ratification

Ratification, then, is the unreadiness or unwillingness to say "No!" on the part of the church and ministry, deprived of the possibility of being in the world *for the sake of* church and ministry, and called instead to be a church and ministry *in* the world *for the sake of* the world. *Ratification* is the nurture of the obedience of faith in the unrecognized disobedience of taking it for granted that being on the Lord's side is a foolproof guarantee that the Lord is on the side of those who, in Calvin's words, "say or think or meditate or do" as though they were on God's. *Ratification* is the defensive surprise that erupts in the midst of the household of faith when the beliefs and commitments and values and ways of being in church and ministry in the world for the sake of the church are called into question by church and ministry in the world for the world, and not for the sake of the church. *Ratification* is the pattern of thought and life and judgment in church and ministry that basically affirms the prevailing patterns of thought and life and value in the world as congruent with the obedience of faith; which calls the world into question without calling into question the obedience of church and ministry; which nurtures, in and through church and ministry, the pious complacency that practices the tithing of mint and anise and cumin while neglecting the weightier matters of the law, justice and mercy and faith (Matt 23:23; Luke 11:42); which sanctifies the world in sanctifying the church. In short, *ratification* is the cultivation in church and ministry and world of the self-justifying surprise at being called into question by the Lord of the church, as being goats, and not sheep (Matt 25:44).

I venture to think that each of us could readily draw up his or her own list of *ratification items*. Let me, however, note a few such items from my own recent experience in church and ministry.

About three years ago, I was invited to lead a discussion on Dietrich Bonhoeffer for four weeks with an adult class in a Presbyterian church in Connecticut. The person in charge is a brilliant and prominent investment counselor in Manhattan. A former member of the Church Session, he has been a loyal and active member of that congregation. At Yale University, his alma mater, he was a classmate of Dwight Chapin, sentenced to prison for perjury in the case of Daniel Segretti, a member of ex-president Nixon's "Watergate team." Somehow, the investment banker had become especially interested in Bonhoeffer because he thought that there was a parallel between Bonhoeffer's imprisonment and that of Dwight Chapin. Question: How can it happen that so egregious a misunderstanding could take root in so able a mind and so faithful a member of the community of faith? What is the level of nurture in that congregation from which so gross a mis-identification could ever occur? For myself, at any rate, the experience seemed to be a particularly painful, indeed pathetic, instance on the subtlety with which in the church, the ratification of the prevailing patterns of thought and life and value in the social and cultural environment of our time goes on.

Another Presbyterian church in the center of a town which, as I was to learn, is also the bedroom of two-thirds of the corporate power structure of this country, was in some liturgical disarray. The ministers in the church and community had varied the order of worship from time to time by substituting for the time-honored General Confession one or another contemporary form. A murmur arose among the members of the congregation strongly dissenting from these contemporary forms and urging the Session to rule in favor of the General Confession. One reason for this discontent seemed to have been the disinclination to acknowledge the specific determinations of personal and social sinfulness expressed in the variant confessional forms. The acknowledged elegance of the cadences of the General Confession was put forward as a further ground for the alleged inappropriateness of the language in which the concreteness of contemporary departures from the will and the ways of God were described. After all, "All we, like sheep, have gone astray" makes the point without convicting anybody of wife-swapping or of furthering economic and social injustice. How is it that baptized, and even ordained, members of the household of faith have so learned to bring every thought into captivity to the obedience of Christ, as to expect "the Word rightly preached" and "the Sacraments rightly administered" to ratify our ways of being *who* we are, *where* and *as* we are; and evidence surprise that such preaching and administration should call us radically into question? Surely, repentance is a matter—not of rhetoric—but of truth and life!

These instances of ratification point to and point up the world in the church. There are corollaries which indicate the church in the world. If the former are ways of accommodating the church *to* the world, the latter is a way of co-opting the church *by* the world.

In the week of April 5, 1981, the *New York Times* carried a full page ad bearing the banner headline, "Intellectuals and Religious Leaders in Support of the Administration's Foreign Policy of Aid to El Salvador." Among the signers, I found the names of eminent colleagues, and in many other respects, friends of whom I should have expected more. The Committee on Freedom which sponsored the ad seemed to me to be ominously reminiscent of an earlier "American Committee on Cultural Freedom," in which not a few eminent divines joined, thereby furthering the anti-communist hysteria—now emerging again—but then fostered by the lamentable junior senator from Wisconsin, Joseph R. McCarthy.

Quos Deus perdere vult, dementat prius (Those whom God would destroy, God first makes mad).[27] Or, in Dostoevsky's bitterly ironic description of young Richard, twenty-three years of age, condemned to execution for murder:

> in prison he was immediately surrounded by pastors, members of Christian brotherhoods, philanthropic ladies and the like . . . He was converted . . . All Geneva was in excitement about him—all philanthropic and religious Geneva . . . At the scaffold, they call to Richard, "Die, brother, die in the Lord, for even thou hast found grace!" And so, covered with his brothers' kisses, Richard is dragged on to the scaffold, and led to the guillotine. And they chopped off his head in brotherly fashion, because he had found grace. Yes, that's characteristic.[28]

RESISTANCE

So much for the *ratification* factor in the double schizophrenia besetting church and ministry today. So much for the frustrating bind between power and weakness that occasions silent acquiescence before the ambiguity of refusal on the part of church and ministry, called to be *in* the world *for* the world. What about the factor of *resistance*?

In the frustrating bind between power and weakness, the ambiguity of refusal conceals its own warrant for the persistence of silence, as merely the counsel of prudence. As *ratification* tends to detain church and ministry overmuch in happy thankfulness for the church, *resistance* tends, by reason of its very ambiguity, to intensify the suffering through the church's guilt. There must indeed have been a time when we could have said "No!" But this very retrospective discovery is companioned by another, namely, that more often than not, we discover too late what is the "Yes!" that is the bearer of that "No!" *to* the world from a church and ministry *in* the world *for* the world. Except for the "Yes!" that bears the "No!" resistance is vulnerable to the self-righteous negativism that confuses resistance *in* the world with resistance *of* the world. Except for the "Yes!" that bears the "No!" the refusal of the world would be desensitized of ambiguity and thus, vulnerable to ascetic or perfectionist repressions of the schizophrenic reality of that strange mixture of power and weakness, of thankfulness and suffering, of "No!" and "Yes!" that characterize church and ministry *in* the world *for* the world. Except for the "Yes!" which bears the "No!" *ratification* would carry the day *any* day, against *resistance*. "Evil be thou my good!" which Milton said was Satan's self-identifying watchword, would then become the order of *every* day.[29]

The *stoixéia toū kósmoû* (principalities and powers), of which the New Testament variously speaks (for instance, Romans, Ephesians, Colossians), have been winning one for the Gipper on *that* front since long before Bonzo ever set foot in Death Valley.[30] And since worse than *doing* evil is *being* evil, these same *stoixéia* are possessed of an unerring instinct for the jugular which knows when and where their doom has been sealed. Second only to their adroitness in converting evil into good is their adroitness in converting dissent into disloyalty, poverty into irresponsibility, property into privilege, security into weaponry, and justice into power. Thus, the *No-sayers* are identified not by what they affirm but by what they call into question. And *resistance* is called that which endangers the security of the state and goes unrecognized as the state's way of absolutizing itself. A politics of power, second to none in a nuclear age and fueled by a passion for the free market as the safest harbinger of productivity, whereby the good of each is the good of all, inevitably exalts material over human values, private over public liberty, freedom over justice, injustice over compassion, and accelerates its self-destruction. This denouement is inevitable because, as the inscription at the base of the workers' monument in Gdansk, from the Lithuanian-born and Polish Nobel Laureate Czeslaw Milosz, hauntingly puts it, "You who harm a simple human being, do not feel secure. A poet remembers."

Church and ministry *in* the world *for* the world do not, therefore, resist the appointed authorities. The authorities—divinely appointed or otherwise, duly constituted or otherwise—resist the church and its ministry. In the words of *The Theological Declaration of Barmen*:

> In opposition to attempts to establish the unity of the German Evangelical Church by means of false doctrine, by the use of force and insincere practices, the Confessional Synod insists that the unity of the Evangelical Churches in Germany can come only from the Word of God in faith through the Holy Spirit. Thus alone is the Church renewed . . . Be not deceived by loose talk, as if we meant to oppose the unity of the German nation! Do not listen to the seducers who pervert our intentions, as if we wanted to break up the unity of the German Evangelical Church or to forsake the Confessions of the Fathers! Try the Spirits whether they are of God! . . . If you find that we are speaking contrary to Scripture, then do not listen to us! But if you find that we are taking our stand upon Scripture, then let no fear or temptation keep you from treading with us the path of faith and obedience to the Word of God, in order that God's people be of one mind upon earth and that we in faith experience what he himself has said, "I will never leave you, nor forsake you!" Therefore, "Fear not little flock, for it is your Father's good pleasure to give you the kingdom!"[31]

THE RESISTED—YOU SEE—ARE THE RESISTERS!

Church and ministry between ratification and resistance are summoned to break the conspiracy of sound and silence which spells out *ratification*; and to take shape in a congeries of comradeships—within and among congregations, and within and among all judicatories—identified by the resisted as *resistance*! As Bonhoeffer summed it up: "The Church . . . is not there [in the world] in order to try to deprive the world of a piece of its territory, but precisely in order to prove to the world that it is still the world, the world which is loved by God and reconciled with Him."[32]

It could be that in these days of a rising tide of military, moral, and legislative madness, such comradeships of resistance would find themselves drawn together and drawn toward an agenda of "Yes!" and "No!" that would include, at the very least, the following:

- A "Yes!" to the conviction that the global unification of the world requires a reshaping of sovereignties and a redistribution of natural, cultural, and economic resources, so that the security of all peoples may be anchored in the trust of all peoples, is correlative with a "No!" to be said to the passions, policies, and values which exalt military strength and supremacy as the guarantee of security, further the disequilibrium which defense establishments impose upon the livelihood of the peoples, and in so doing, court the risk of a totalitarian imposition of order, in violation of justice, upon the common life.
- A "Yes!" to the primacy of persons over property is correlative with a "No!" to a politics of productivity designed to encourage and reward enterprise above public trust and responsibility.
- A "Yes!" to the conviction that the human good of each depends upon the human good of all is correlative with a "No!" to persuasions and policies that promote the human good of each as the harbinger of the human good of all.
- A "Yes!" to the conviction that the freedom which being human takes is guaranteed and furthered by an unswerving commitment to certain inviolable rights, guaranteeing that the just powers of government shall be drawn from the consent of the governed, is correlative with a "No!" to every legislative and/or executive and/or judicial encroachment upon a *bill of rights* as the charter of the liberties of the people.
- A "Yes!" to the primacy of responsibility for life over the right-to-life is correlative with a "No!" to constitutional or legislative attempts to define when a human life is human, while at the same time exhibiting

a callous indifference to conditions which deny a human prospect to a human life born.
- A "Yes!" to the primacy and priority of human rights over all other considerations in the determination of foreign and domestic policies of states is correlative with a "No!" to governments—whether foreign or domestic—and to those to whom governments entrust the administration of the affairs and the lives of the people, that conceal their commitment to the preeminence of power beneath sophistries seeking to distinguish between totalitarian and authoritarian forms of power.
- A "Yes!" to the conviction that the environment that nature provides for human societies and the resources of the earth belong to all the peoples of the earth, and that their responsible trusteeship *includes* limits and *excludes* private ownership is correlative with a "No!" to values, policies, and warrants that convert availability into development, development into possession, possession into privilege, and privilege into private gain, in disregard of nature's own rhythm of replenishment and of the vulnerability to exploitation intrinsic to technological mastery of and dominion over nature.

From Micah to the Magnificat, church and ministry between *ratification* and *resistance* have been shown what is good. And "what does the Lord require of you but to do justly, to love mercy, and to walk humbly with your God" (Micah 6:8). "He has scattered the proud in the imagination of their hearts, he has put down the mighty from their thrones, and exalted those of low degree; he has filled the hungry with good things and the rich he has sent empty away" (Luke 1:51–52).

A DECLARATION OF CONSCIENCE?

On October 21, 1953, the General Council of the General Assembly of the United Presbyterian Church in the United States of America unanimously adopted a statement entitled: *A Letter to Presbyterians: Concerning the Present Situation in Our Country and in the World.*[33] My recollection is that the statement was also adopted by acclamation when the *Letter* was read to the Assembly in 1954. The *Letter* was a balanced, reasoned plea for a return to sanity and justice in Congressional investigations. It called for a basic defense of human rights and for a positive approach to the problem of Communism. It was a fresh reminder of the historic witness of the Reformed churches to *all* of life. It was hailed here at home as "a new Magna Carta of liberty" and abroad as "the most significant official utterance of any church group in our time."

Among other matters, the *Letter* declared:

Whatever concerns man and his welfare is a concern of the Church and its ministers . . .

Loyalty to truth is the common basis of true religion and true culture . . . The state of strife known as "cold war," in which our own and other nations, as well as groups within nations, are now engaged, is producing startling phenomena and sinister personalities . . . The demagogue who lives by propaganda is coming into his own on a national scale. According to the new philosophy, if what is true "gives aid and comfort" to our enemies, it must be suppressed. Truth is thus a captive in the land of the free. At the same time, and for the same reason, great words like "love," "peace," "justice," and "mercy," and the ideas which underlie them, are becoming suspect . . .

Let us frankly recognize that many of the revolutionary forces of our time are in great part the judgment of God upon human selfishness and complacency, and upon man's forgetfulness of man . . .

While we take all wise precautions for defense both inside and outside our borders, the present situation demands spiritual calm, historical perspective, religious faith, and an adventurous spirit. Loyalty to great principles of truth and justice has made our nation great; such loyalty alone can keep it great and ensure its destiny.

May God give us the wisdom and courage to think and to act in accordance with his will.

Sisters and brothers, in church and ministry between ratification and resistance, we seem to have come full circle. It could be that the time is coming—perhaps even is at hand—for a *Declaration of Conscience*; or at the very least, for a *Second Letter to Presbyterians*. Or, this time around, why shouldn't Methodists, Baptists, or Disciples of Christ take their turn? The flag-draped platform pictured in the 22 February *Time*, showing the President of the United States in the center, proclaiming "A Line Drawn in the Dirt," suggests that for such a declaration of conscience it could be later than we think. Five weeks earlier than the story in *Time*, on January 14, Dr. Martin Niemoeller observed his ninetieth birthday.[34] A press report recalled his memorable remarks frequently made after 1945:

The Nazis came for the communists and I didn't speak up because I was not a communist. Then they came for the Jews and I did not speak up because I was not a Jew. Then they came for the trade unionists and I didn't speak up because I wasn't a trade unionist. Then they came for the Catholics and I was a Protestant, so I didn't speak up. Then they came for me . . . by that time there was no one to speak up for anyone.[35]

In the jungle of the Jordan, let it not be said of us that "by that time, there was no one to speak up for anyone"; or that "there must have been a moment, at the beginning, where we could have said 'No!' but somehow we missed it."

May God grant to us the wisdom and the courage for the living of these days.

NOTES

1. Published in *The Spire* 7, no. 2 (1982); reprinted with permission.

2. [Editorial: Bertrand Russell, *Power*, a new social analysis (1938) can be found online: https://russell-j.com/beginner/POWER1938-TEXT.HTM. This quotation is from Chapter 1.]

3. Augustine, *City of God*, XIX, Chap. 13.

4. In a letter to the Marquis de Mirabeau, July 26, 1767. Cited in Hannah Arendt, *On Revolution* (New York: Viking Press, 1947), 184.

5. The Federalist Papers is a collection of 85 essays written by Alexander Hamilton, James Madison, and John Jay, using the pseudonym "Publius," promoting the ratification of the U.S. Constitution. Originally published as *The Federalist: A Collection of Essays, Written in Favour of the New Constitution, as Agreed upon by the Federal Convention, September 17, 1787* (J. & A. McLean, 1788).

6. Augustine, *City of God*, V, Chap. 22.

7. [Editorial: SAM 6s refer to a Soviet-designed mobile surface-to-air missile system; the MX missile was developed for the US Airforce as a counterattack missile system and tested in eastern Nevada and Utah.]

8. Eberhard Bethge, *Dietrich Bonhoeffer: Theologe, Christ, Zeitgenosse* (München: Chr. Kaiser, 1967); for English translation, see Eberhard Bethge, *Dietrich Bonhoeffer: Man of Vision, Man of Courage*, trans. Edward Robertson (New York: Harper and Row, 1977), 579–80.

9. Bethge, *Dietrich Bonhoeffer*, 575.

10. Bethge, *Dietrich Bonhoeffer*, 579–80.

11. Dietrich Bonhoeffer, *Ethics*, ed. Eberhard Bethge, trans. Neville Horton Smith (New York: Macmillan, 1965), 64–65. [Editorial: Dietrich Bonhoeffer, *Ethics*, DBW 6 (Minneapolis: Fortress Press, 2005), 77.]

12. Dietrich Bonhoeffer, *Letters and Papers from Prison*, rev. ed. Eberhard Bethge, trans. Reginald Fuller from the 12th edition of *Widerstand und Ergebung*, 1964 (New York: Macmillan, 1967), 1–17. [Editorial: Dietrich Bonhoeffer, *Letters and Papers from Prison*, DBW 8, ed. John De Gruchy, trans. Isabel Best et al. (Minneapolis: Fortress, 2010), 37–52.]

13. Bonhoeffer, *Letters and Papers from Prison*, 17. [Editorial: Bonhoeffer, *Letters and Papers from Prison*, DBW 8, 52.

14. Bethge, *Dietrich Bonhoeffer*, 580–82.

15. Bethge, *Dietrich Bonhoeffer*, 494ff.

16. Bethge, *Dietrich Bonhoeffer*, 571.

17. Bethge, *Dietrich Bonhoeffer*, 580.

18. Oskar Hammelsbeck, *Vita* (Wuppertal: 1959); Bethge, *Dietrich Bonhoeffer*, 618–19 (emphasis mine).

19. Bethge, *Dietrich Bonhoeffer*, 619. See also Bonhoeffer, *Letters and Papers from Prison*, especially 186–94. In this context, there is the familiar formulation: "Before God and with God, we live without God" (188). [Editorial: DBW 8, 478–79.

20. [Editorial: Dietrich Bonhoeffer, *Ethics*, DBW 6, ed. Clifford J. Green; trans. Richard Krauss, Charles C. West, and Douglas W. Stott (Minneapolis: Fortress Press, 2005, 77.]

21. [Editorial: DBW 8, 52.]

22. [Editorial: No citations given. Likely from Bonhoeffer.]

23. [Editorial: The reference is to former US President Ronald Reagan (1911–2004), who starred in the movie "Bedtime for Bonzo," directed by Frederick De Cordova, in 1951. Bonzo refers to Ronald Reagan's chimpanzee co-star in the film.]

24. *New York Times*, May 3, 1981, 4, 1.

25. *New Yorker*, March 9, 1981, 31.

26. Tom Stoppard, *Rosenkrantz and Guildenstern Are Dead* (New York: Grove Press, 1967), 125.

27. Regarding the origins of the maxim, see Georg Buechmann, *Gefluegelte Worte* (Berlin: Hande und Spenersche, 1964), 475–76.

28. Fyodor Dostoevsky, *The Brothers Karamazov*, trans. Constance Garnett (New York: Grosset and Dunlap, 1940), 263.

29. John Milton, *Paradise Lost*, IV.1,110.

30. [Editorial: "Win one for the Gipper" refers to a line in the 1940 film *Knute Rockne: All American* with Ronald Reagan playing the coach of the US Notre Dame team in the 1920s. His star player, George Gip, was reported to have told the coach to "Win one for the Gipper," when he was dying. "Death Valley" refers to Ronald Reagan's performance in the television show, *Death Valley Days*, 1952–1970.]

31. *An Appeal to the Evangelical Congregations and Christians in Germany*, 29–31 May 1934. For text of the Barmen Declaration, see *The Proposed Book of Confessions*, Presbyterian Church in the United States, 341 Ponce de Leon Ave., Atlanta, GA 30308 (1976), 145–47.

32. Bonhoeffer, *Ethics*, 202.

33. *Theology Today*, no. 1 (1954): 8–9; 15–21.

34. [Editorial: Martin Niemoeller (1892–1984) was a German theologian and pastor widely known for his opposition to Nazism.]

35. *Lutheran Standard*, a publication of the American Lutheran church, 422 South Fifth St., Minneapolis, MN 55415, 8 Jan. 1982, 20.

Chapter 14

The Christian Faith and Civil Liberties (1952)[1]

The abrogation of civil liberties in the United States continues. A book burning in Oklahoma can be distinguished from the book purge under Soviet auspices in Vienna only by the number of volumes cast into the flames. The battle for free schools erupts in such diverse places as New York and Los Angeles, Phoenix and Bronxville, and afflicts secondary as well as college and university education. The issue of the conflict is the control of the public mind. There are those who believe that the best control of what people think is the free dissemination and discussion of ideas. There are others who believe that ideas and discussion must be controlled by legal or organized social pressure from without.

On this level, American democracy has shown itself healthy and flexible enough to keep a fairly even score between victories and defeats. Meanwhile, an imperceptible and persistent effort of another sort is being made. This is the effort to set the legal stage for the almost instantaneous suspension of the free concourse of ideas should the state of the nation seem to require it. What is going on is particularly perilous because it is almost impossible to keep a vigilant citizenry abreast of it. In July 1951, for instance, James V. Bennett, Federal Director of Prisons, asked, at a hearing before the Senate Appropriations Committee, for a special appropriation "to take over and operate six stand-by camps in connection with the detention of persons who might be picked up as subversives in accordance with the provisions of the McCarran Act."[2]

In January 1952, the press reported the introduction into the Senate of a bill, sponsored by Senator Eastland of Mississippi, which would by concurrent resolution of the Congress declare the existence of an internal security emergency and "place into full effect" the detention provisions of the McCarran Act. Title II of this act (Public Law 831 of the 81st Congress) provides that "whenever there shall be in existence such an emergency, the

President, acting through the Attorney General, is hereby authorized to apprehend and by order detain . . . each person as to whom there is reasonable ground to believe that such person will engage in, or probably will conspire with others to engage in acts of espionage."[3]

A little reflection on these provisions suggests that here is a blueprint for concentration camps, American style. Democratic processes are being used to undermine the very foundations of the American constitutional structure. Happily, the late Adolph J. Sabbath, Congressman from Illinois, had introduced a bill (H.R. 3118), which provides for the repeal of the McCarran Act.

The legislative battle is thus also still open. In the wake of the election, it promises to be waged with renewed and critical urgency. If, as the commentators have been saying, the victory of General Eisenhower was a personal more than a party victory, almost everything depends upon the sincerity and vigor of his determination to implement his campaign commitment against "witch hunts" and "character assassination." The president-elect has carried with him into the Congress, and into the reorganized leadership of the Senate and the House, people whom he not only refused to repudiate during the campaign but who will now be able to reinforce their passion for vilification, distortion, and the turning of every person against their neighbor, by the tremendous power of committee chairmanships.

At this writing, it appears that Representative Harold H. Velde of Illinois is in line for the chairmanship of the House Committee on Un-American Activities. He has already fathered proposals that the Librarian of Congress be required by law to list all books that could be regarded as "subversive," and that a loyalty oath is made a requirement for voting in national elections.

In the Senate, Joseph McCarthy of Wisconsin appears to be in line for the chairmanship of the Committee on Government Operations, until recently called the "Committee on Expenditures in the Executive Department."[4]

Hitherto, the executive branch of the government has refused to surrender its confidential files to the legislative branch. What the newly staffed executive branch will do is not yet clear. But it would be difficult to overestimate its decision as a "straw in the wind."

There can be no doubt what civic action all those who are genuinely committed to the health and survival of American democracy should take. The Bill of Rights is still the crucial test of whether a person is really loyal to the heritage and the foundation of free institutions. And the Bill of Rights is being undermined by the current hysteria of fear and mistrust among us and by those who nourish this hysteria.

What is not so clear is that the responsibility of loyalty to the Bill of Rights is a concrete Christian responsibility. When the clergy of the city of Milwaukee can support Senator McCarthy's campaign by a large majority; when the Synod of New Jersey cannot even bring itself to pass a mild resolution in opposition to Senator McCarthy's tactics and their consequences for fear of being misunderstood; when considerable numbers of Christian people are not only unable to react instinctively against calculated circulation of hatred and untruth but are also able to defend it—the lack of a clear and compelling grasp of the Christian faith and the gulf between the Christian faith and our common life are enormous.

The fear of misunderstanding is certainly no Biblical criterion of the obedience of the Christian Church. Even an elementary understanding of the God of the Bible, of the patriarchs and the prophets, of Jesus Christ and of the apostles can scarcely fail to arouse the conscience of the people of God against those who "bend their tongue, as it were their bow, for falsehood," who "are grown strong in the land, but not for truth: for they proceed from evil to evil, and they know not me, saith the Lord" (Jer 9: 3, ASV). These words are part of a moving description by the prophet Jeremiah of the sorrow and the judgment of God upon the faithlessness and disobedience of the people whom God has singled out for God's favor and service.

It is no accident that when people began to realize that Jesus of Nazareth was God's own gift to humanity for their deliverance, they identified Jesus with Jeremiah. Jeremiah was one of the favorite prophets of Jesus; and the Gospels are emphatic on the point that Jesus is the fulfiller of the Prophets as well as of the Law.

The connection between the Christian faith and the Bill of Rights is derived from this connection between the prophets and Jesus. The connection is, of course, indirect. It is indirect because, according to the Bible, no social or political structures are the unambiguous expression of the will of God. It is indirect also because the Biblical view of God's ways with humanity regards everything in nature and in society as instrumental. "The earth is the Lord's and the fullness thereof, the world and those who dwell therein" (Ps 24: 1, RSV). The decisive question is whether human beings—who are God's chief concern—use the goods of the earth and the institutions of society for obedience or for disobedience.

The criterion of obedience or disobedience is symbolic. Everything depends upon whether the acts and the institutions of humans serve as pointers to the righteousness of God. The righteousness of God is the correspondence between God's will and God's purpose. This means that God is doing definite things in the world to make God's will known and to bring God's purposes to fulfillment. It means too that, in the world as it is, the place to look for what God is doing is at those issues and situations which point up and point to a conflict between the self-righteousness and self-justification of humanity and the patterns of life which God is setting up in order that people may serve one another and acknowledge that God alone is right. At bottom, this is a conflict of power, a conflict between the power of humanity to absolutize ideas and institutions of their own making and the regenerative power of God. In a word it is a conflict between idolatry and praise.

The Bible is thoroughly realistic about this conflict. "For consider your call, brethren; not many of you were wise according to worldly standards, not many were powerful, not many were of noble birth; but God chose what is foolish in the world to shame the wise, God chose what is weak in the world to shame the strong, God chose what is low and despised in the world, even things that are not, to bring to nothing things that are, so that no human being might boast in the presence of God" (1 Cor 1: 26–29, RSV). So, the apostle Paul wrote to the Corinthians. And Paul is in precise agreement with the way Luke saw the conflict caused by the coming of Jesus. Before such a God, humans can only boast or praise.

In so far as the Bill of Rights is a constitutional political instrument for checking the inordinate use of power by nations or by individuals and groups within nations, it may be regarded as symbolic of what Calvin called "a symmetry and agreement between the righteousness of God and obedience in the life of" true believers. Such "symmetry and agreement," Calvin said, is "the end of regeneration."[5] The inordinate use of power breeds self-righteousness and idolatry whenever the structures and the exercise of power are placed beyond effective criticism and control. The Christian faith is faith in a God who acts in the world not only against all self-righteousness and idolatry, but also positively, by transforming the motives and the structures of human life in accordance with the community of the Son of God's love. Therefore, it is of the utmost importance to bring the full weight of the Christian conscience to bear against all who imagine that they can preserve and strengthen democracy in America by weakening the structural guarantees of the liberties of the people.

NOTES

1. Published in *Social Progress* 43, no. 4 (1952): 5–8; reprinted with permission.

2. [Editorial: James V. Bennett (1894–1978) served as the director of the Federal Bureau of Prisons from 1937 to 1964. The McCarran Act, also known as the Internal Security Act of 1950 (Public Law 81–831) or the Subversive Activities Control Act of 1950, was named after its sponsor, the Democratic Senator of Nevada, Pat McCarran. The Act required "Communist organizations," broadly and loosely defined, to register with the US Attorney General and be open to public inspection. It also established a Subversive Activities Control Board to oversee the execution of the Act.]

3. [Editorial: Among other things the original McCarran Act contained this emergency detention statute. In 1952, the McCarran-Walter Act was passed, which included a sweeping immigration ban and permission to deport immigrants and

naturalized citizens involved in Communist organizations or other "subversive activities."]

4. See the dispatch from Washington by John D. Morris in the *New York Times*, November 8, 1952, 30.

5. Calvin, *Institutes*, III.6.1.

Chapter 15

Karl Barth, Theologian of Permanent Revolution (1972)[1]

The conjunction of the name of Karl Barth with the phrase "permanent revolution" seems like a contrivance. The contrivance suggests an expository purpose aimed rather at up-dating a theologian whose work has been overtaken by events than at a serious review of and reflection upon Barth's work and its pertinence for theology in North America in this century. Accordingly, we must note at the outset what sober sense, if any, this conjunction makes.

Actually, the characterization of Barth's work as that of a "theologian of permanent revolution" had not, and probably would not have occurred to me had not my colleague on the Committee planning for this Colloquium, Professor James Smart, dropped the formulation into a discussion about the program. When the Committee adopted Professor Smart's suggestion, it seemed to me to be appropriately collegial as well as democratic, to ponder the suggestion before revising it, or abandoning it altogether. We all know that collegiality and democracy do not unfailingly function in a luminous way. But sometimes they do. And when they do, it belongs to a decent humility, as well as to a decent respect for the fact "that God wonderfully preserves his Church, as it were, in hiding places . . ." as Calvin once remarked, to pay due heed to a gift of grace through the Spirit.[2] Calvin, whom I first learned to understand and to appropriate in this Seminary from William Adams Brown,[3] and in Bonn and Basel from Karl Barth, wrote: "*Deumque mirabiliter ecclesiam suam quasi in latebris servare.*" And while William Adams Brown had as little use for Karl Barth as Karl Barth had for him, they were both rooted in Calvin and grounded *in unam sanctam catholicam . . . ecclesiam* [one holy, catholic church]. It was the *et apostolicam* [and apostolic] that sparked the furies and made them unable to hear and to speak the truth in love.

IN NORTH AMERICA: NO NEW THEOLOGY

Meanwhile, it has become steadily clearer that what was going on "in, with, under" and around that *et apostolicam* was a world in revolution. In retrospect, it is "stranger than fiction" that in North America, where Christianity had been informed and formed, as H. Richard Niebuhr took such impressive pains to show, by a vision of the Kingdom of God;[4] and where theology had been formed and informed by a Social Gospel,[5] Barth should have been initially, persistently, and widely understood and misunderstood as turning theology backwards toward a sterile dogmatics of repristination, thereby effecting a deep and impassable gulf between theology and society, faith and culture, gospel and contemporary humanity. Although Wilhelm Pauck had raised the target question, in his pioneering and bridge-making attempt to get a hearing for Barth in a land exhibiting increasing need for theological irrigation, the answer to Pauck's question was an expulsive, "No!"[6] Pauck had asked, "Karl Barth: Prophet of a New Christianity?" Clearly not where prophets had been working so long and so devotedly at building the Kingdom of God in America that at the outbreak of the First World War, they were taken by surprise, a surprise to which no Christian—at least no prophetically and theologically informed Christian—should have succumbed.

ON BARTH'S HOME GROUND: WHAT IS THEOLOGY?

It was predictable that such a *lapsus mentis theologiae* [theology's mental lapse] should predispose theologians in America toward joining the chorus of Barth's critics on the Continent in dismissing this "new Christianity" as a neo-orthodoxy fleeing behind its dialectical pyrotechnics from the shock, despair, destruction, and suffering of an unprecedented military conflict. Kierkegaard's "infinite qualitative distinction between time and eternity" became the watchword of a theological deprecation of humanity for the glory of God. The total otherness of God was proclaimed from the housetops against all human creativity and possibility. This was indeed a "new Christianity" that carried the worst elements of the theological tradition to their worst extremes. At best, it was psychologically regrettable but understandable. Theologically, however, it was inadmissible. It was Adolf von Harnack, the great teacher of Barth and of many of the formative theologians in North America, who put the matter for them as well as for himself—and with his wonted searching and sobering precision. He wrote to Barth:

> Your concept of *revelation* is totally unintelligible to me . . . Your answers to my questions only show the size of the chasm that separates us, but what

is important is neither my theology nor yours, only that the gospel is taught aright. But if your method should gain the ascendancy, it will not be taught any more at all, but exclusively handed over to revival preachers, who freely create their understanding of the Bible and who set up their own dominance . . . The concept of *revelation* is not a scientific concept . . . I have the impression that Professor Barth [thinks it is] and in so doing calls for assistance on a dialectic which leads us to an invisible point between absolute religious skepticism and naive Biblicism—a most tormenting explanation of Christian experiences and of Christian faith![7]

The concern was indeed that the gospel should be taught aright. And this was indeed a matter of the scientific character of theology, of theology's precise referentiality, and of the faithfulness with which the theologian "does his thing," to borrow a current idiom. If that were all there was at stake, the recent rash of radical theology in this country would have been a remarkable fulfillment of von Harnack's prophecy, and this Barth Colloquium would have become a reminiscence so dubious that the gathering would and should never have been convened. However, the instructive thing about recalling how things looked, in the aftermath of that assent of a dark Church tower during which Barth mistook the bell-rope for the banister, is that very much more was going on.[8] Hindsight is, of course, better than foresight, partly because it is comfortable, if not exemplary, to be wise in one's own conceits (Prov 26:12). Partly, however, wisdom is justified of her children (Luke 7:35), and the way ahead is marked by foresights and hindsights which have corrected and amplified each other.

THE POLITICAL CHARACTER OF BARTH'S THEOLOGY

There is a conjunction between Karl Barth's early and continuing involvement with us and our continuing and gradually surfacing involvement with him. In this conjunction lies the clue to the connection between the name of Karl Barth and the phrase, "permanent revolution." *Quasi ex latebris* [as if from hiding], there came to my desk, as I was setting about this assignment, a timely and intriguing paperback under the colophon of *Les Éditions du Cerf*, Paris. The author's preface bore the date line, *Noël, 1969. Prédication, Acte Politique* was the title; and the editor's Preface began by explaining that for a Catholic theologian to present, in published form, the sermons of a Protestant pastor was no longer an occasion for surprise. He declared:

Catholics, protestants, orthodox, and others manifest different sensibilities . . . toward the social status of the word of God, now with regard to its "situational thrust" *(sa mise en situation)*, now with regard to its incarnation. Some maintain the gospel in its transcendence . . . others immerse that word in actuality . . . It is very easy to eliminate these two extremes of the conscience struggle, the pure idealism which is literally an alienation, as well as the reduction of the gospel to an individual or political morality . . . A political problem cannot be resolved by religious reasons. It makes sense neither to use the gospel as a religious re-enforcement of the established order nor as a sacralisation of revolution. This word, lately received into the language of theologians (it has been long current in other vocabularies) must enter there with its requests (*ses requêtes*) for appropriate political analysis, as rigorous as delicate.[9]

Preaching as Political Act

Georges Casalis, pastor and professor of theology, whose radio-sermons are introduced in this way, makes the same point, with perhaps a sharper edge. He declares:

> The risk of preaching is that of the prophets who liberate historical fatalities and anguish and permit the taking of just decisions in the present which prepare for the future the ways of peace and justice and reconciliation. The preacher has no right to forget for a single instant the risk of an incessant unmasking of all the powers which destroy man. Thus, his message is a political act, debatable and ambiguous as is every clear option in the domain of provisional and relative human situations. But who does not see that this is in any case the fact and that he has the choice *either the objective sacralisation of power, explicitly or implicitly, or confrontation (la contestation).*[10]

It is pertinent but not surprising that M. Casalis should have taken his point of departure from that well known, and well-worn, "Sunday morning situation" of which Barth had spoken in one of his earliest essays.[11] Nor should it be surprising that a key sermon of this collection was preached on May 19, 1968. "We refuse a world in which the certainty of not dying from hunger is exchanged for the risk of dying from boredom. Run, run, the old world is behind you." So ran the slogans on the walls of the old Sorbonne. The text for this political act ran: "Le coeurs des pères sont ramenés vers leurs enfants et les rebelles à la sagesse des justes, pour préparer au Seigneur un peuple bien disposé'" (Luke 1: 17).[12] The preacher said:

> We have well forgotten that God is not the guarantor of our immobilities but the living Lord who calls into question our compromises, our routines, and our comforts, orients our present and projects us toward a future! If it is true that the liberation of today can mount a new oppression, if it is true that all revolution must be constantly purified of the alienations which it engenders, the fact at least remains that we are called to move towards a future, desiring and building a better world, while knowing clearly that nothing in this world will be definite until

the day of the Kingdom. That is why man and the new world will be manifest in their last reality.[13]

THE REVOLUTION IN WHICH WE ARE

Lest it be too quickly objected that the barricades of Paris and Tokyo and Berkeley and the College of the City of New York gave way too quickly to a return to sobriety, tranquility, and study, and that students are in any case a fickle bell-weather of portentous events, let it be recalled that Ernst Troeltsch saw it all coming at least sixty years ago. The accuracy of Troeltsch's assessment is so astonishingly contemporary as to seem to confirm his clairvoyance. He probed the cleavage between old and young with a range and penetration that exposed the cultural and social roots of what we have since learned to call, "the generation gap."

The Trembling Ground: Troeltsch

Troeltsch wrote:

> World war and revolution became teachers of historical perceptiveness (*Anschauungs-unterricht*) of terrifying and shocking effectiveness (*Gewalt*). We no longer theorize and construct under the protection of an order which sustains everything, and can render harmless even the most ingenious and wildest theories. We theorize and construct in the eye of the storm of a new world in the making, where every old word can be tested according to its practical effectiveness or ineffectiveness, where countless matters have become phrases and scraps of paper which formerly seemed to be deadly serious and real. The ground under our feet trembles (*Da schwankt der Boden unter den Füssen*), and the most diverse possibilities for further becoming (*weiteren Werdens*) dance around us . . . It is understandable that a large segment among the youth should keep the problem at arms length and only the intense, dynamic fanatically (*schwärmerischen*) or philosophically arousable should be consumed by these possibilities. Older people . . . do not have to bathe in (*auszubaden*) the new in the same measure as do the youth. Consequently, the young people have ready access to words in these matters, and feel themselves called, if not to the solution of the crisis, at least to stormy demands for new solutions.[14]

So "the initial tremors of eschatology," in Martin Buber's telling phrase (*die ersten Schauer der Eschatologie*), are still signaling the future breaking in upon our present.[15] What is going on is "a revision of the total feeling about life (*eine Umstimmung des ganzen Lebensgefühls*) . . . a pressure towards the complete and the total which is . . . inescapable for us."[16] In a word, a revolution has happened—a revolution of mentality and of life-style—which seems to have marked the twentieth century as "the moment of truth" at which the Constantinian era and the Enlightenment have come to an abrupt and awesome stop. "Remember, if the householder had known at what time of night the burglar was coming, he would have kept awake and not have let his house be broken into. Hold yourselves ready, therefore, because the Son of Man will come at the time you least expect him" (Matt 24:43–44 NEB).

The Gospel is a Hinge, Not a Door: Barth

If our colleagues on the Continent have anticipated us in their theological, cultural, and political wrestling with these matters, they have not preceded us into the *futurum resurrectionis* [future resurrection] which these matters portend. The "tremors of eschatology" have traversed oceans and continents and have exposed the galloping obsolescence of our Monroe Doctrine in more ways than one. The *Camino Réal* has moved to New York without leaving New Orleans, and we all now live and move and have our being in the Plaza called Reality. *The Greening of America*, for example, filled in the distance between Troeltsch and ourselves and exposed deepening and disruptive levels of consciousness—the liberal-bourgeois, the technical-bureaucratic, the human—in search of a liberating vision and a humanizing word.[17] But "in those days the word of the Lord was seldom heard, and no vision was granted" (1 Samuel 3:1 NEB). The *futurum resurrectionis* lacks the power requisite for lift-off. That takes the gospel of salvation. As Barth put it, on the threshold of this revolutionary eruption of the underground:

> The gospel of salvation needs neither to search out nor to flee the conflicts of world religions and world-views. It is there as proclamation of the delimitation of the known world by another, unknown world, a world outside the competition among all the attempts within the known world to discover and to make available relatively unknown higher levels of existence *(Daseinskreise)*. The gospel is not one truth among others; it calls all truths into question. The gospel is a hinge, not a door.[18]

"But how are men to call upon him in whom they have not believed? And how are they to believe in him of whom they have never heard? And how are they to hear without a preacher? And how can men preach unless they are sent?" (Romans 10:14–15 RSV).[19] That was Augustine's perplexity and persuasion too.[20] He also was a theologian of permanent revolution. He was, perhaps, the first theologian outside the Bible for whom the City was a central theological theme.

Theologia urbi et orbi [Theology of the city and the world]

If Barth has concerned himself less explicitly than did Augustine with the City and more explicitly with the charter of its freedom to be *the space for humanization* in the earth,[21] the reason may lie in part in the difference between a collapse in the making and one already too late to do anything about it except to ponder its significance. Be that as it may, Barth is at one with Augustine and with Paul both in perceiving the intimate relation between Christian preaching and Christian theology and in being sensitive to the revolutionary thrust of Christian theology. It is no secret that behind the work of Jacques Ellul is the work of Karl Barth. What has been overlooked is that they are both, though each in his own way, "theological urbanists." Of this, Dr. John Wilkinson has only recently persuaded me, by way of his vigorous and probing "Introduction" to Ellul's hermeneutical exploration of the meaning of the city.[22] There, Dr. Wilkinson remarks that "it is the constant complaint by all or nearly all city planners I have ever met that there is 'no meaning to city planning anywhere' and that the whole enterprise as it presently exists is the greatest of hoaxes."[23] A like integrity may overtake the self-styled "growth scientists," though their "moment of truth" seems yet a great way off. Be that as it may, Dr. Wilkinson goes on to observe, again with specific reference to Ellul and Barth, that "the time may well come again when the existential transparence of the relation of God to man will once more assert itself, as it did during the long ages before 'science' in some unexplained way was supposed to have made it obsolete."[24]

It is one of those non sequiturs, with which the human story is replete, that in "America the Beautiful," where space for humanization spawned visions of "alabaster cities . . . undimmed by human tears," Karl Barth should have been regarded, for most of his theological life, as an alien rather than as an ally. Whatever the reasons may finally turn out to be, it would seem that among them is the conjunction of American optimism with American pragmatism and activism. Consequently, Barth's revolutionary activism and pragmatism passed us by until our own "greening" forced us to abandon the too easy, psychological dismissal of Barth as a despair theology and to face up to him amidst our own revolutionary time of troubles. The fact is that the cultural, social, and political underground of the nineteenth century—Søren Kierkegaard and Nietzsche, Feuerbach and Marx, Dostoevsky and Freud—was in its own way theological, and was companioned by a theological underground as well—Julius Mueller and Hermann Kohlbruegge, the Blumhardts, older and younger, Franz Overbeck and, in a strange way, Adolf Schlatter. Of course, these convulsive currents spilled over into the beginnings of our own century. But the point of intersection between the implicitly theological underground and its explicitly theological counterpart is Ludwig Feuerbach. It is he who makes plain that Schleiermacher's pioneering responses to the seismographic signals of things to come were insufficiently radical. And it is Feuerbach who radicalized the perspective and format which make the *Römerbrief* and the *Kirchliche Dogmatik* a single theological enterprise in which what began as a "dialectical theology" becomes and culminates as a "theology of permanent revolution."

WHERE THEOLOGY AND POLITICS INTERSECT

The extent to which this underground has shaped the times and seasons of our days and shattered our optimism is indicated by the widespread response among us to the theology of Dietrich Bonhoeffer. Bonhoeffer's "theology of secularity" or of "non-religious interpretation," as he would have preferred to say, is both a radical reversal of Feuerbach's reduction of theology to anthropology and a radical attempt to give concreteness to Barth's theology of the Word.[25] The dilemma that Bonhoeffer left unresolved at his untimely death may be a perennial one. It is the "identity-involvement" dilemma, and it engages us in the questions: "How can one maintain one's identity as a Christian while being fully involved in the world? How can one be fully involved in the world without losing one's identity as a Christian?" If we now transpose this dilemma into still more concrete terms, we shall be able to identify the sense in which Barth's theology is not only not yet expendable but is also, in truth, a theology of permanent revolution. Are we not all acutely aware that the doing of theology today is marked by nothing so much as by the sharpening confrontation between the concrete complexities of decision-making to which our activism and pragmatism have brought us *and* a perspective with liberating formative and transforming humanizing power? To supplement Professor Casalis, not only preaching, but theology too is a political act. The choice is "the objective sacralization of power, explicitly or implicitly, or confrontation."[26]

The identical choice informs the dynamics and the purposes of revolutions in human affairs. Children of the French Revolution, as we all are, we have taken the familiar so much for granted as to have lost contact with and interest in the struggle for our birthright. Yet it was the French Revolution which effectively accomplished a semantic shift in the referential context of the word, "revolution," from astronomy to politics.[27] It was that event which provided the concrete context of Hegel's passionate pursuit of a philosophy of Absolute Spirit. And it was that event lurking in the wings, which intensified the struggle between Marx and Hegel over the ultimate and penultimate reading of the human story.[28] If we, today, have been effectively persuaded by Marx that we could not live with Hegel, only lately to discover that we cannot live without him, the reason is fundamentally traceable to a loss of theological nerve. This nerve—Paul would have called it "apostolic boldness" (2 Cor. 3–5)—Karl Barth has recovered for us. The *et apostolicum* is intrinsic—and indispensable—to a *theologia urbi et orbi*. *Quasi ex latebris*, it is on Feuerbachian territory that Hegel and Marx, Barth and Bonhoeffer struggle over the reality and direction of political action, that is, over the relation between truth, power, and fulfillment in human affairs. The second thesis on Feuerbach puts the issue squarely on the confrontation level.

The "This-Sidedness" of Human Thought

Marx wrote:

> The question whether objective (*gegenständliche*) truth can be attributed to human thinking is not a question of theory but is a *practical* question. In practice man must prove the truth, that is, the reality and power, the this-sidedness (*Diesseitigkeit*) of his thinking. The dispute over the reality or non-reality of thinking which is isolated from practice is a purely *scholastic* question.[29]

Truth and practice, the reality and power, that is, the this-sidedness (*Diesseitigkeit*) of one's thinking, led Marx to explore the secret of the holy family in the earthly family, "criticized in theory and revolutionized in practice," as he said.[30] Thus, he could not hear Hegel's lately recovered word directed towards this same this-sidedness: "*Gott als Gemeinde existierend*" [God existing as community].[31] The concrete this-sidedness that Marx found lacking in Hegel, Bonhoeffer, in turn, found lacking in Barth. Yet common to Barth and to Bonhoeffer is a lively sensitivity to the depth and range of Hegel's preoccupation with the this-sidedness of thinking, and a serious search for a more appropriate way than Hegel had found of bringing transcendence and this-sidedness together in the exploration of reality.

Meanwhile, Bonhoeffer's substitution of "Jesus Christ" for "God" in Hegel's aphorism has become a linchpin in the contemporary "theology of secularity." This development, however, would have been unintelligible, if not impossible, apart from Barth's strongly Christocentric movement from reality to possibility in God's relation to humanity and humanity's relation to God and to the world. Actually, this movement is the linchpin of the revolutionary thrust and direction of Barth's theology as a whole, as each succeeding volume of the *Kirchliche Dogmatik* presses the point with ever more inescapable concreteness. This is really why Barth was rather painfully surprised by Bonhoeffer's charge against him of "revelational positivism."[32] Had Bonhoeffer momentarily forgotten the exacting demand upon the theologian for the single-minded "doing of his thing" which arises from the sharpening confrontation between the concrete complexities of decision-making and a perspective with liberating, formative, and transforming power? Had Bonhoeffer momentarily lost sight of the fact that Hegel and Feuerbach and Marx are not so easily disposed of?[33] The degree to which Barth lost sight either of Hegel or of Feuerbach—and on this account, as on every other, where he exhibits an exemplary theological integrity amid our revolutionary time of troubles—emerges from two passages in which Barth notes the importance of Hegel for the doing of theology and the consequences of a weariness with Hegel's concerns.

About Hegel's relation to the theology which preceded him, Barth wrote:

> Who knows but that it is exactly that which was authentically theological in Hegel that has frightened the theology which preceded him? Had the theology understood and received him, many great things would have then received a different outlook in the spiritual life, and perhaps even of the political and economic life of the nineteenth and twentieth centuries. We must content ourselves with looking at him as he was in reality, a great question, a great disillusion and perhaps, nevertheless, a great promise.[34]

About the meaning of Hegel's eclipse for culture and theology since, Barth remarked, in the course of his reflections upon the *History of Protestant Theology in the Nineteenth Century*:

> In the depths of the consciousness of the time a violent shock must have befallen the will common both to Hegel and to it, the attempt to make a key to fit every lock must itself have come under suspicion, a deep resignation must have been born . . . as regards the possibility of such a universal method at all. There is no other way of explaining the retreats which now began in every sector of the front. The natural scientists withdrew into their laboratories. The historians retired to a consideration of the none too subtle question: how was it in those days (*wie es denn gewesen sein möchte*)? The philosophers fell back upon psychology and the theory of knowledge, the theologians upon the historical Jesus and upon the history of religion in general.
>
> There is no other way of accounting for the complete bursting asunder of the *Universitas litterarum* [university of letters] which Hegel had once again saved. It was not only that people had happened to tire of Hegel, but that they had become fundamentally weary of the path which leads to knowledge in general . . . The time was now beginning when the more people talked of method the less they could be content with any method at all, however well founded and worked out it might be. The self-confidence of modern man . . . could only be a broken self-confidence.[35]

The Overcoming of History Within History

Surely this is where we all came in; and this is where we all, with increasingly intense perplexity, are! This is where Barth came in too, and where Barth still is. With steadfast single-mindedness, Barth has challenged our post-Hegelian weariness exactly at that point of no return at which Troeltsch drew the line between failure and hope. In doing so, Barth has made possible a future, not only for the doing of theology, but for involvement in a revolutionary world without loss of Christian identity. Troeltsch's wistful glimpse of the possibility of overcoming history *by* history has begun to happen in the overcoming of history *within* history through the history of the people of God.[36] Barth's unyielding and undeviating preoccupation with the reality of this people—their center, their election, their charter, their mission in the world, and their destiny—makes his theology not a *reaction-theology*, that is, a reaction to cultural, historical, and theological impotence, but an *archimedian theology*, that is, the source and matrix of an unhinging (liberating), forming, and transforming perspective which is concrete for our revolutionary time, concrete for the permanent revolution always going on in human affairs. "The choice is: either the objective sacralization of power, explicitly or implicitly, or confrontation" (Casalis). Barth has seized the confrontation initiative and equipped us for holding that initiative and moving ahead with the building of the City.

PARADIGMS OF PERMANENT REVOLUTION IN BARTH'S THEOLOGY

We are moving ahead—at least, in a halting kind of way. The formative influence of Bonhoeffer's thought upon the doing of theology in North America is still the surest sign that the gap between Barth and ourselves has narrowed. Nevertheless, a certain tentativeness attaches to this indication, owing to the fragmentary and unhappily unfinished character of Bonhoeffer's life and work.

Barth as Executor of Political Theology

The future of the theology of hope is debatable enough to make long-range guesses problematical. Provisionally, however, the instructive thing about Professor Moltmann's thought is the swiftness and range of its impact upon theological attention and reflection, as well as its unmistakable indebtedness to Barth. It could be that the most fruitful factor in Moltmann's thought will be its imaginative and incisive attempt to put Karl Barth and Ernst Bloch together. In that event, the grip of Feuerbach upon Hegelian weariness would have begun to loosen, and Barth's theo-political reversal of establishment and anti-establishment anthropocentricity would have begun to move from a confrontation on the frontier of the future to the liberation, formation, and transformation of that future. The *futurum resurrectionis* of the gospel, in serious engagement with *das Noch-nicht-Seiende* [the not-yet-existing], could be exactly that concrete movement from reality to possibility which frees theology and politics *from* ideological bondage to Right, Left, or Center; and "frees them up" *for* formation and transformation by that *novum ex nihilo* [revolutionary creation out of nothing] through which God "chooses the things that are not to bring to naught the things that are."[37] "God," as Moltmann puts it, "is the power of the future."[38] With this eschatological refinement, Barth's description of God as "*der ganz Andere*" [the Wholly Other], who in Jesus Christ *is* in movement from reality to possibility, from Word to humanity, undergoes a shift of accent. For Moltmann, as for Barth; for Moltmann *because* of Barth, involvement with *this* God is what permanent revolution is all about.

Our colleague, and my respondent this morning, Professor Herzog, has become so involved with this God and with revolution as to propose that "theology in America is on the way towards becoming political theology."[39] The phrase "political theology" is appropriated from Moltmann, and it is used by Herzog to identify both the nature of the revolutionary situation in America and the task of theology, if theology is to avoid the isolation of being concerned with questions which have no discernible relation to what is really happening. At the same time, Professor Herzog worries a little about the radicality of Moltmann's eschatology and thus also of his dialogue with Bloch. Despite Moltmann's strictures against Barth's Christocentric neglect of the biblical category of "promise," and consequently, against the speculative elements, this is, Platonic and Hegelian, in Barth's account of God's self-revelation, Moltmann's stress upon the future is anchored in a past-oriented future, and thus, less open to the radically "*Noch-nicht-Seiende*," about which the debate with Bloch must really go on. "While he (Moltmann) views Christology on the soil of eschatology," Herzog remarks, "he also considers eschatology in the light of Christology. But in the process of developing an eschatological Christology and a Christological eschatology, Jesus Christ seems to appear more as a dogmatic datum than the 'live still point' that he is in God's Word-presence."[40]

At this "still point," I begin to worry a little about Professor Herzog. He may be correct about Moltmann, although the essay on *Das Prinzip Hoffnung* seems to me to exhibit a vigorous leverage with precisely this "dogmatic datum" in the assessment of the insights and limits of Bloch's eschatology.[41] But then, when I read that today, "we yearn not so much for reconciliation as for liberation,"[42] and, in the same essay, I read about Barth's kerygmatic isolation, something significantly non-coincidental is going on. An incipient political theology that rightly begins to focus upon the enormous theological importance of the problem of power seems less sensitive to the Archimedean character of the "still point" than to the insistent pressures of decision-making. So I guess I want to ask my theological comrade to look once again at the paradigms of permanent revolution in Barth's theology, remembering all the while, that one makes haste to go to Bethlehem but not to Barmen.[43] Barmen happens with deliberate speed and only through a continuing struggle with the distinction and the connection between *"das Wort zur Sache"* [the Word on the subject matter] and *"das Wort zur Lage"* [the Word on the situation].[44] Without an Archimedean (liberating) perspective, confrontation can scarcely function formatively and transformingly in the objective desacralization of power.

There Is a Little List

Karl Barth is the executor, not the executioner, of a theology of permanent revolution. There is, therefore, a little list, which never should be missed. We leave the essays and tracts, the open letters and sermons aside, and note only the *Römerbrief* and the *Kirchliche Dogmatik*. The list, we venture to think, is not complete. But among its more impressive components are the following:

1. The analysis of the role of revolution in a Christ-centered history under "the great negative possibility" of submission in the commentary on Romans 12:21–13:7;
2. The freedom of God for humanity and of humanity for God in an experienced movement from reality to possibility, centered in God's human presence in Jesus Christ and forming and transforming history as a predicate of revelation (*KD*, I/2, 14);
3. The priority of election over creation, of people over things, of a chosen people over a random people, whose vocation among all peoples is the overcoming of history within history (*KD*, II/2, 33–34);
4. Co-humanity is the basic form of humanity and people are being formed and fulfilled in their humanity in the reality and power of Jesus' relation to God and to people. In this reality and power, people are able to be *for* one another as well as *with* one another in a shared and fulfilled humanity (*KD*, III/2, 45);
5. God is more certain than anything in creation and all things are instrumental to God's human and humanizing presence in the world (*KD*, III/1, 41);

6. The principalities and powers of this world have no ultimacy. They are radically instrumental to God's human and humanizing presence and activity in the world (*KD*, III/3, 49, 50);
7. The claim of God is the operational reality of God's presence and activity in the world. The Law is the form of the Gospel which means that patterns and structures of human relatedness in the world are never established in themselves and never self-justifying but instrumental to human reality and human fulfillment (*KD*, III/4);
8. The inhumanity of person to person has been shattered, and reconciliation exposed as the humanizing style of human life in the humiliation and exaltation of one human being whose living, dying, and living again is the prototype and prospect of what humanity is to be. He makes the struggle to be human that doing of the will of God on earth as it is in heaven (*KD*, IV/1);
9. There is an experimental community in the world, called and sent as the spearhead of that shaping of all people into the human reality, fulfillment and joy which God in Christ has begun and is carrying through towards that new heaven and new earth in which difference is a thing of beauty and a joy forever, the humanity of humanity is real and complete and God is everything to everyone (*KD*, IV/2, IV/3).

Suppose now we juxtapose this list to the fact of revolution. Where does our exploration of Karl Barth's theology leave us? The answer is: with a perspective and a power to discern the reality of revolution, to accept its permanence as the condition and direction of our involvement in what God is doing in the world for the objective desacralization of power and for the making of room, in space and time, for freedom. In short, Barth's theology leaves us with a perspective and a power for the building of the City. Revolution means, as Professor Moltmann has summarily and precisely put it:

> A transformation in the foundations of a system—whether of economics, of politics, of morality, or of religion. All other changes amount to evolution or reform. But transformation in the foundations of a system becomes a genuine possibility only when previously unsuspected possibilities or powers are at hand. Only then does there emerge a critical consciousness in the present . . . We live today in a world of unrealized but quite realizable humanity. Now that it is possible to eliminate hunger in the world and to control overpopulation, the systems which hinder the realization of these possibilities must be radically changed . . . We experience reality as history, and history as revolutionary conflict between future and past. In the conflict between the "Party of Anxiety" and the "Party of Hope," on which side do we stand? This is the crucial question.[45]

In the last analysis, the paradigmatic statements in which we have ventured to indicate Barth's way of bringing revelation and revolution together describe a double movement: from reality to possibility in God's relation to humanity and the world and humanity's relation to God and the world; and a movement from the self-revelation of God in God's Word to the humanity of God in God's forming and transforming presence in and over human affairs. This double movement bears and exposes the secret and the power by which revolutions are preserved from their fate, which is to devour themselves, and become really permanent; and at the same time by which every establishment is radicalized and cleared away for the enterprise of humanization—God's enterprise and humanity's liberation and fulfillment.

"Around the hero," Nietzsche said somewhere, "everything becomes a tragedy. Around the demi-god, everything becomes a satyr-play. Around God, what?—Perhaps a world?" And Rilke wrote:

> So long as you catch what you yourself have thrown,
> all is skill and justifiable winnings;
> only when you suddenly become the catcher of the
> ball that an eternal playmate
> threw you, dead center, in precisely
> mastered trajectory, in one of those arches
> from God's great bridge-building:
> only then is being able to catch an achievement—
> not your own, a world's.[46]

For Barth, God has scratched the "perhaps" and has placed instead God's indicative presence and activity in a world of God's making for our being and becoming human. Jesus Christ is God's bridge into that world. Of course, the ground trembles under our feet, and God is on the move. But as we move into God's future, there will be a path, for God will be the only path that we could ever want or need. "Theology," as Eberhard Jüngel said in the Commemorative Service in the Basel Münster two years ago, "can only honor Karl Barth by steadfastly 'doing its thing.'"[47]

NOTES

1. Published in *Union Seminary Quarterly Review* 27, no. 1 (1972): 67–81; reprinted with permission.

2. John Calvin, *Institutes of the Christian Religion*, IV.1, 2, ed. John T. McNeill and trans. Ford Battles, *The Library of Christian Classics*, Vols. XX and XXI (Philadelphia: Westminster Press, 1960).

3. [Editorial: Lehmann is referring to Union Theological Seminary of New York City. William Adams Brown (1865–1943) taught Church History and Systematic Theology there from 1892–1936.]

4. H. Richard Niebuhr, *The Kingdom of God in America* (Chicago and New York: Willett Clark and Company, 1937). As is well known, Niebuhr found in Barth's work at once a great liberation and a great peril in the doing of theology. He described the liberation in *The Meaning of Revelation* (New York: Macmillan, 1941), and the peril in *Radical Monotheism and Western Culture* (New York: Harper and Row, 1960). The intensity of Niebuhr's protest against Barth in the latter work is in its own way a sign that Barth had begun to call into question theology and culture in North America, as he had been doing almost everywhere else since the publication of the *Römerbrief* in 1919.

5. Walter Rauschenbusch, *A Theology for the Social Gospel* (New York: Macmillan, 1917). For a fresh look at Rauschenbusch, in the light of his own writings and of developments since, see Robert T. Handy, ed. *The Social Gospel in America* (Oxford: Oxford University Press, 1966), part III.

6. Wilhelm Pauck, *Karl Barth: Prophet of a New Christianity?* (New York: Harper and Brothers, 1931).

7. The correspondence between von Harnack and Barth first appeared in 1923 in *Die Christliche Welt*. For an English translation, see James M. Robinson, ed. *The Beginnings of Dialectical Theology* (Richmond: John Knox Press, 1968), 171, 174, and 186, emphasis in original. The bracketed phrase is mine. It does not, I think, alter von Harnack's meaning, which focused upon what he felt was Barth's rejection of scientific theology and his substitution for it of an objective theology of the Word, in the name of revelation. Similarly, what von Harnack found "totally unintelligible" was Barth's answer to the first of fifteen questions that von Harnack had put to him. This question had to do with the revelatory character of the Bible and its relation to other possible revelations.

8. For Barth's account of this simile of self-description see the Preface to Karl Barth, *Die Christliche Dogmatik* (München: Chr. Kaiser, 1927), IX. [Editorial: Barth, *Die christliche Dogmatik im Entwurf* (1927), 8.]

9. George Casalis, *Predication, Acte Politique* Preface de M D Chenu (Paris: Editions du Cerf, 1970), 9, 11; translation Lehmann's.

10. Casalis, *Predication*, 16–17; translation and italics Lehmann's.

11. The essay was first prepared as an address for a pastoral conference at Schulpforta in July 1922. The theme was "The Need and Promise of Christian Preaching." See Karl Barth, *Das Wort Gottes und die Theologie* (München: Chr. Kaiser, 1924), 99 ff. For English translation see Karl Barth, *The Word of God and the Word of Man*, trans. Douglas Horton (Boston: The Pilgrim Press, 1928), chapter 4.

12. Casalis, *Predication*, 72, 78. The text refers to John the Baptist who, as the *New English Bible* translates "will go before him to reconcile father and child, to convert the rebellious to the ways of the righteous, to prepare a people fit for the Lord." But the French translation seems to convey the dynamics and the concreteness of messianic action more adequately than does the English translation. *Ramener* underlines

that some urgent running is going on, the running akin both to revolution and to reconciliation.

13. Casalis, *Predication*, 75; translation Lehmann's.

14. Ernst Troeltsch, *Der Historismus und Seine Probleme* (Aalen: Scientia-Verlag, 1961), 6; translation Lehmann's.

15. Martin Buber, *Das Königtum Gottes* (Heidelberg: Lamert Schneider, 1956), 118.

16. Ernst Troeltsch, *Der Historismus und Seine Probleme*, 7.

17. Charles Reich, *The Greening of America* (New York: Random House, 1970). Some chapters in this book appeared as essays in *The New Yorker*, in November 1970.

18. Karl Barth, *Der Römerbrief* (München: Chr. Kaiser, 1922), 11; translation Lehmann's. It will be recalled that *futurum resurrectionis* is a recurrent theme of the *der Römerbrief*, especially in chapter 6. [Editorial: Barth's commentary has since been added to the Gesamtausgabe. See Karl Barth, *Der Römerbrief (Zweite Fassung) 1922*, ed. Cornelius van der Kooi and Katja Tolstaja, GA II.47, (Zürich: TVZ, 2010).]

19. The prophet Isaiah reinforced the question and the conviction for the Apostle Paul. Paul refers in the same context to Isaiah 52:1 and 53:1.

20. See Augustine, *The Confessions*, I, 1.

21. The italicized phrase is an adaptation of the suggestion of Hannah Arendt's that the root meaning of the Greek word, *polis*, is "space for freedom." See Hannah Arendt, *On Revolution* (New York: The Viking Press, 1947), 98.

22. Jacques Ellul, *The Meaning of the City* (Grand Rapids: Eerdmans, 1970).

23. Wilkinson, in Ellul, *Meaning of the City*, xii.

24. Wilkinson, in Ellul, *Meaning of the City*, xiv.

25. In another place, we have tried to suggest that Barth and Bonhoeffer are the two theologians of our time who have tried to deal with Feuerbach head-on. Feuerbach pressed upon Christian theology two central questions: a) concerning the truth of theological statements; and b) concerning the relevance of theology to real life. Barth worked mainly at the first question, Bonhoeffer at the second. See, P. L. Lehmann, "Karl Barth and the Future of Theology," in *Religious Studies* 6 (1970): 105–20. The point to be underlined is that Bonhoeffer's theology is a radicalization, not a displacement, of Barth's work, and as such, it illuminates the revolutionary thrust of Barth's theology.

26. [Editorial: Barth, *Die christliche Dogmatik im Entwurf* (1927), 8.]

27. So, at any rate, Arendt, *On Revolution*, 34 ff.]

28. See the account of Marx, Hegel, and the French Revolution in Franz Mehring, *Karl Marx* (New York: Covici-Friede Publishers, 1935), 92–86. See also Marx's "Theses on Feuerbach," especially II, IV, and XI, in Lewis S. Feuer (ed.), *Marx and Engels, Basic Writings in Politics and Philosophy* (New York: Doubleday Anchor Books, 1959).

29. Feuer, *Marx and Engels*, 243. Italics, Marx's. In view of Barth's biblically rooted revolutionary theology and theologically rooted revolutionary biblical interpretation, a passage in Mr. Feuer's "Introduction" seems pertinent to the present interpretation of Barth's work: "The history of the masses . . . has been a history of the most consistently anti-intellectual force in society. The Bible, the book of the masses,

is the supreme anti-intellectual book. It has ... often stirred the people with its revolutionary passages, its demand for justice, its invective against the oppressors ... The Bible begins with curses against Adam for seeking knowledge, and it ends with populist prophets denouncing the culture of cities." Feuer, *Marx and Engels*, xv.

30. Marx, "Theses on Feuerbach," IV.

31. G. F. W. Hegel, *Lectures on the Philosophy of Religion*, trans. E.B. Speirs (New York: Humanities Press, 1962). The recovery has been notably made and corrected by Dietrich Bonhoeffer in *Sanctorum Communio* (Berlin: Trowitsch und Sohn, 1930), 61. [Editorial See, Bonhoeffer, *Sanctorum Communio*, DBW, 1, trans. Joachim von Soosten (Minneapolis: Fortress Press, 1998), 121]. As is well known, Bonhoeffer's correction reads: "Christus als Gemeinde existierend." When Professor Smith translates "Gemeinde" with "church," he is, of course, faithful to the substance of Bonhoeffer's correction of Hegel, although the recovery of Hegel's concern is thereby somewhat obscured. The relation between reality and power implied in Bonhoeffer's recovery and correction has been instructively analyzed by André Dumas, *Une Théologie de la Réalitè: Dietrich Bonhoeffer* (Geneve: Labor et Fides, 1968), esp. ch. 3.

32. Dietrich Bonhoeffer, *Widerstand und Ergebung*, ed. Eberhard Bethge (München: Chr. Kaiser, 1966), 179.

33. I say, "momentarily," because Bonhoeffer's own struggle, from within that prison from which the remark against Barth emanated, focused upon the crucial dilemma between identity and identification which haunts Christian faith, Christian theology, and the Christian life.

34. Karl Barth, *Hegel* (Neuchatel: Delacroix, 1955), 52–53, quoted in André Dumas, *Une Théologie de la Réalitè*, 91.

35. Karl Barth, *Protestant Thought from Rousseau to Ritschl*, trans. Brian Cozens (New York: Harper and Row, 1959), 291–92. See the original, Karl Barth, *Die Protestantische Theologie im 19. Jahrhundert* (Zurich: EVZ, 1947), 365.

36. At the end of *Der Historismus*, Troeltsch wrote: "The task itself, however, which has confronted every epoch, consciously or unconsciously, is particularly urgent for the moment in which we live. The idea of cultural construction means the overcoming of history by history (*Geschichte durch Geschichte ueberwinden*) and planning a platform for new creativity (*die Platform neuen Schaffens ebnen*)." Troeltsch, *Der Historismus und Seine Probleme*, 772; translation Lehmann's.

37. Jürgen Moltmann, *Religion, Revolution and The Future* (New York: Charles Scribner's Sons, 1969), 17. I have joined to Professor Moltmann's phrase, *novum ex nihilo*, the passage from 1 Cor. 1:28, RSV.

38. Moltmann, *Religion, Revolution and The Future*, 5.

39. Frederick Herzog, "Politische Theologie und die christliche Hoffnung," in *Diskussion zur politischen Theologie*, ed. Helmut Peukert (München: Chr. Kaiser, 1969), 125; translation Lehmann's.

40. Frederick Herzog, *The Future of Hope*, (New York: Herder and Herder, 1970), 61. "The still point" is an allusion to T. S. Elliot's *Four Quartets:* "Except for the point, the still point, there would be no dance, and there is only the dance."

41. Jürgen Moltmann, "Anhang," in *Die Theologie der Hoffnung* (München: Chr. Kaiser, 1964), 312 ff.

42. So Frederick Herzog, "Politische Theologie und die christliche Hoffnung," 123, 135. Now also, I begin to see that Barth's virtual absence from Frederick Herzog, *Understanding God* (New York: Charles Scribner's Sons, 1966) was not coincidental, as I had allowed myself to think. This was particularly puzzling in view of Herzog's survey of the theological scene in America without reference to Robert Jenson's *Alpha and Omega* (New York: Thomas Nelson and Sons, 1963), which deals with clarity and care with the dynamics of Barth's thought.

43. I think I should like to ask the same thing of my nearer theological comrade, Professor James Cone. Particularly in his recent book, *A Black Theology of Liberation* (New York: Lippincott, 1970), Barth's kerygmatic confinement seems to me notable and to obscure the revolutionary movement of his theology.

44. See Arthur Cochrane's concise, yet thorough, account of this struggle in Arthur Cochrane, *The Church and the War* (Toronto: Thomas Nelson and Sons, 1940). For more than three decades, first as a preacher and pastor and then steadily as teacher of theology, Professor Cochrane has been the most faithful and single-minded student and interpreter of Karl Barth and his significance for theology in North America.

45. Moltmann, *Religion, Revolution and The Future*, 131–32.

46. Rainer Maria Rilke, *Modern European Poetry*, ed. Willis Barnstone (New York: Bantam, 1966), 118.

47. Eberhard Jüngel, "Karl Barth zu Ehren," in *Karl Barth—1886–1968: Gedenkfeier im Basler Münster* (Zürich: EVZ, 1982), 47–50. "Die Theologie kann Karl Barth nur ehren, indem sie hart an der Sache bleibt." Jüngel, "Karl Barth zu Ehren," 50. [Editorial: Jüngel's lecture was delivered "im Rahmen des Dogmatik-Kollegs an der Universität Zürich vom 11. Dez. 1968" as a tribute to Barth's death, just one day prior on December 10, 1968. The essay was later published in Eberhard Jüngel, *Barth-Studien* (Gütersloh: Gütersloh Verlag, 1982), 15–21 and in English as Eberhard Jüngel, "Karl Barth: A Tribute at His Death," in *Karl Barth: A Theological Legacy*, trans. Garrett E. Paul (Philadelphia: Westminster Press, 1986), 16–21.]

Chapter 16

Black Theology and "Christian" Theology (1975)[1]

It would be presumptuous in the extreme for a theologian, whose formation has been shaped almost exclusively by membership in the white community of the United States, to undertake a *reply* to Professor Cone's trenchant statement of the central reality and significance of black theology. The burden of guilt, which membership in the white community makes at once grievous and inescapable, requires silence and listening before the long overdue claims of the black revolution. Perhaps in retrospect, the textual circumstance that my own discussion of "the politics of God" (to which Professor Cone has referred) sets out from the imaginative remark of a young Muganda woman, may have been a proleptic clue to our present and ongoing conversation with one another. Nevertheless, Cone has rightly brought me up short on the omission of specific attention to black Americans in *Ethics in a Christian Context*.[2] In view of that tiny proleptic clue and our ongoing conversation, as also in view of Professor Cone's invitation to take part in the present symposium, I wish seriously to acknowledge both previous guilt and previous theological deficiency through a *response* that is a footnote, not a reply, to what he has written. Just as Frantz Fanon, whom Cone rightly and approvingly cites, defined the destiny and task of black people in broader terms than those confined to black Americans, so I venture to hope that it may be possible, in assent to Fanon's vision, for Europeans and Americans, including theologians, to break out of their social, cultural, and ideological parochialisms, and join black people in *their* present calling to "work out new concepts, and to try to set afoot a new man."[3] Admittedly, it is easier to show a "willingness to take the risk to create a new humanity"[4] in a verbal exchange than in concrete acts. Since this limitation applies also (though in lesser degree) to Professor Cone, it may, perhaps, be suspended in the interest of the present conversation.

The distinction between black theology and "Christian" theology, under which this response to Professor Cone is being attempted, does not mean that black theology is not Christian theology. Nor does the distinction intend to assert or to suggest that black theology and Christian theology are incompatible. On the contrary! The distinction is intended to affirm with Professor Cone that in the United States today, black theology—in Cone's sense—is the point of departure for exploring "the truth" of "Christian" theology. At the same time, the distinction seeks to take account of the possibility—which Professor Cone does not always seem to do—that "the truth" to which "Christian" theology is open and obedient is not unqualifiedly identical with the concrete reality of blackness or any other concrete reality of the human condition and the human story.

If I understand Professor Cone aright, black theology is an "analysis of the gospel of Jesus, the point of departure [for which is] black liberation."[5] "Liberation" is the word which, in Cone's view, accurately conjoins the biblical account of what is most characteristic of God's way of being God in the world and the realities of black experience in the United States. The distinction, familiar since Harnack, between the "gospel *of* Jesus" and the "gospel *about* Jesus" is obviously neither expressed nor implied in Cone's formulation. On the contrary, Cone is concerned about two conditions fundamental to theological thinking in the light of Christian revelation, faith and experience.

SOCIOLOGICAL CONCRETENESS

The first of these conditions is the human reality and meaning of God's self-disclosing activity in the world as described in the Bible and expressed in the central Christian doctrines of incarnation, atonement, redemption, and reconciliation. The second condition is the insistence upon the *concreteness* of theological conception and analysis. In this insistence, Cone is in line with Irenaeus and Athanasius, with Augustine and Aquinas, with Luther and Calvin, Schleiermacher and Ritschl; and very much on the point at issue between Karl Barth and Dietrich Bonhoeffer. These are the theologians who wrestled in a primary way with the question of the relation between theology and truth, in the biblical sense. Hence, in their thought, the integrity of theology is defined by the congruence of faithfulness with concreteness in dealing with "the great deeds done by God" in such a way as to "express knowledge on our part," in Albrecht Ritschl's phrase.[6] In so doing, Cone is firmly in the tradition which gives priority to the *fides qua creditur* [the faith by which it is believed] over the *fides quae creditur* [the faith that is believed].

It follows from the above, that the concreteness with which Cone's theology is concerned is *sociological*. It is the experience of black people in the

United States, whose history is a movement from slavery to liberation, from powerlessness to power—power being the freedom to be who one is and to participate as one is able, and without dehumanizing restrictions, in the humanization of "the whole human running race" (Sister Corita).[7] The congruence of this sociological reality with the biblical experience of God makes the adjective "black" in Cone's theology a *socio-theological* designation, not an exclusively *chromatic* one. Cone is often misunderstood in this matter, with the result that his theology is simplistically misread as a sanctification of a reverse racist ideology. Of course, there is a color factor in the phrase, "black theology." But the chromatic sense of the phrase is only the point of entry into the primary socio-theological reality of blackness in America required by the concreteness towards which all "Christian theology" must strive. Thus, Cone correctly declares that if God's election of the Israelites

> means anything for our times, it means that God's revelation is found in black liberation. God has chosen what is black in America to shame the whites. In a society where white is equated with good and black is defined as bad, humanity and divinity mean an unqualified identification with blackness. The divine election of the oppressed means that black people are given the power of judgment over the high and mighty whites.[8]

Cone alludes to 1 Corinthians 1:26ff. But one could add also the Magnificat (Luke 1:46ff.).

Nevertheless, although black theology is Christian theology, "Christian" theology is not black theology. The quotation marks around the adjective "Christian" underline the *distance* between any given theology and "the truth" to which every theology is bound. The quotation marks underline also the *tentativeness* with which the self-disclosure of God—in election and incarnation, in crucifixion and resurrection, in a new humanity and a new creation on their way to fulfillment—lends itself to theological description and conceptualization. Just as the God who elects Israel hides God's identity in disclosing God's name; as the child in the manger is the human, yet hidden, presence of the creator and redeemer of the world in the life-time and death-time of Jesus of Nazareth (including his humiliation and exaltation); as the new humanity and the new creation are at once promise and experience, hope and assurance—so the "Christian" character of theology is attested, not by definition, but by the room which such a theology makes for the freedom and priority of "the truth" by which it is claimed over thoughts which take the shape of words.

The signs of this freedom and priority are the "listeningness" and humor with which these words are said. In short, "Christian" theology is a compound of transcendence and humility. The transcendence for which such theology makes room signals the freedom of God in and over every theology. The humility, which breathes in and out of such a theology, signals a due awareness of the ambiguity and frailty of having the truth "as not having it" (2 Cor. 6:8), of holding the truth "in earthen vessels" (2 Cor. 4:7). This is why Calvin urged that the proscription of images set down in the second commandment include also mental images. This is also why the pursuit of "Christian" theology under that proscription preserves for theology the transcendence and humility, the distance and tentativeness which mark the difference between theology and ideology. Professor Cone has made it plain that in the United States today, Christian theology cannot be "Christian" except as black theology. But it must also be made plain that black theology cannot not be "Christian" theology except as the liberation which it proclaims includes also the transcendence and humility which set free black theology, as indeed every theology, from the temptation and practice of ideology and the idolatry implicit in them.

IS DIALOGUE WITH BLACK THEOLOGY POSSIBLE AT ALL?

The foregoing statement, however, itself belongs in quotation marks. That is, the statement can only be set down if at the same time it is suspended. Devoid of quotation marks, the statement would come under Professor Cone's stricture that "no white theologian has taken the oppression of black people as a point of departure for analyzing the meaning of the gospel today."[9] Devoid of quotation marks, the statement is uncomfortably close to—if not another expression of—"the unverbalized white assumption that Christ is white, or that being Christian means that black people ought to turn the other cheek—as if we blacks have no moral right to defend ourselves from the encroachments of white people."[10] As such, Professor Cone could only and rightly reject the statement as "an untruth."[11] Devoid of quotation marks, the statement puts us, with respect to the possibility of theological conversation, in the same corner as are those whom Cone correctly criticizes for thinking and talking about violence and non-violence in total disregard of the question: "Whose violence?"[12] Devoid of quotation marks, conversations between white theologians and black theologians about black theology are *ab initio* excluded. Indeed, so forcefully has Cone put the case for black theology as to raise the question whether conversation between white theologians and black theologians about black theology is possible at all. It is this impossibility which must be faced and overcome, certainly in the United States, and since Fanon, also in the European "West," if the truth which alone makes any theology "Christian" is not to be imprisoned by the unacknowledged rhetoric of a white ideology masking as theology.

The suggestion made above that black theology is the point of departure for apprehending and exploring the "truth" of "Christian" theology does not mean that dogmatics has been transposed from its proper milieu in the community of Word and Sacrament that is the church to a prevailing social milieu which currently is *de facto* black. Jesus Christ is the same yesterday, today and forever (Heb 13:8). For black theology, as for white theology, and for any theology that seeks and finds its "Christian" identity, Jesus Christ is himself the center and the criterion of the "truth" by which theology is claimed. But just as Calvin opened his *Institutio Religionis Christiana* with the admission that the exposition of Christian doctrine could start from either end of the polar relation between God and humanity, so Cone, in contrast to Calvin, insists that the present time requires that theology begin with humanity, specifically with humanity in the concrete reality and matrix of black experience.

One need not proceed at once to the revision of all existing dogmatic efforts in the frenetic attempt at a *Te deum nigrum* [a black God]. But the integrity of dogmatics today requires that at whatsoever point one begins the exploration of Christian doctrine, a "Christian" theology must, from the beginning and throughout, take account, in its talk about Jesus Christ, or about God, or about sin and salvation, of the concrete realities of black experience. Only in this way can black theologians and white theologians be honest about the sociological reality that reminds them at once of their own vulnerability to ideological distortion and of the wisdom of the dogmatic tradition which reserves omniscience for God alone. Only as black theologians and white theologians together take primary account of the concrete realities of black experience, can they reciprocally correct one another in the truth and grace that in Jesus Christ *are* the reality of the human condition. In this way, the commitment to "Christian" theology liberates black theology and white theology for the transcendence and listening which "break down the middle wall of partition" (Eph 2:14) between them and bind both to the "truth that makes us free" (John 8:32). One must agree with Cone's agreement with Moltmann that "truth is revolutionary" and that truth involves "discovering that the world can be changed and that nothing has to remain as it has been."[13]

Professor Cone has identified three factors in such a reciprocally correctional theological dialogue which severely strain its viability. The test by which the possibility of a "Christian" theology beyond black theology and white theology stands or falls is provided by the critical tension between revolution and violence, on the one hand, and reconciliation, on the other. Here I find it most difficult to keep clearly in view the line of demarcation between Cone's proper correction of the ideological taint in my own white theologizing, and a seemingly fierce rejection of the possibility of a

"Christian" theology as open to any theologian whose "white past" virtually excludes him from the "black future" affirmed by the "black revolution."[14] Cone carefully says that the "black revolution involves tension between the actual and the possible, the 'white past,' and the 'black future.'"[15] Yet when he goes on to say that "the black revolution involves . . . the black community accepting the responsibility of defining the world according to its 'open possibilities,'"[16] I find myself troubled. If the "open possibilities" before "the black community" include the transcendence and listening which signal the transformation of black theology and white theology into "Christian" theology, I think it must be recognized that these "open possibilities" at the same time define the boundary between a white theology similarly inclusive of transcendence and listening and a white theology which fails to challenge and thus sanctifies white oppression.

I agree with Professor Cone that it is "incumbent upon us as black people to become 'revolutionaries for blackness,' rebelling against all who enslave us."[17] But the fierce remark of Marcus Garvey, cited by Cone, raises as critical a problem as it is designed to settle. "Any sane man, race or nation that desires freedom must first of all think in terms of blood" will surely strike the ear of Germans, including Christians, with an uncertain, if not dismaying sound.[18] This trumpet blast requires the correction and also the awakening of American memories as well. In Germany as elsewhere, many still remember the bitter struggle for a "Christian" theology against a theology of "blood and soil" in the German experience of National Socialism.

There is another and suppressed memory which Christians in America will need to awaken, both for themselves and for their countrymen. This is the memory that Marcus Garvey was identifying; the memory of a black struggle against white oppression which had closed all open possibilities to the black community save one: "resistance unto blood." When Garvey is read in the light of the Letter to the Hebrews (such as 12:4) rather than in the light of the fanaticism of Adolf Hitler, his dictum does indeed become a test at once of the liberation of white theology from ideological corruption and of the white community for a "Christian" theology through the open possibilities of the black community. However much Cone may be unaware (or seem to be) of the ideological temptations and corruptions of black theology, his case for the revolutionary thrust of black theology cannot on that account be dismissed. Only as a white theology does this kind of listening can it hope to join a black theology in a dialogue of reciprocal correction en route to the freedom and integrity of a "Christian" theology. Such a movement could also mean the liberation of American and European theology from the chauvinistic parochialism which has too frequently and too long alienated and isolated each from the other. And in this event, black theology would have been the catalyst for a genuine theology of the Church for the world, to which European and

American theology for the past two centuries have aspired "in principle" without achieving "in fact."

WHOSE VIOLENCE? – WHOSE RECONCILIATION?

The reality of black experience in the United States and under European colonialism makes it inevitable that the prospect of such a fully church dogmatics is far from a tranquil one. It is the child of the revolutionary travail of a new birth. Not least significant in Professor Cone's forceful and unmasking essay is his readiness to face the ultimate issue of the revolutionary relation between violence and reconciliation which no "Christian" theology can escape. Indeed, the refusal of black theology to circumvent this question may be its major catalytic contribution to the emergence of a "Christian" theology. In his insistence upon the questions "Whose violence?" and "Whose reconciliation?" Cone has rightly unmasked the disobedience which has made "Christians, unfortunately . . . not known for their revolutionary actions."[19] In so doing, he has also exposed the facile self-deception with which Christians are wont to press the distinction between violence and non-violence, with insufficient attention to the sociological reality which by this logic foredooms the victims of oppression both to condemnation and to their oppression.

In pressing the questions: "Whose violence?" and "Whose reconciliation?" Professor Cone has brought that question to a point from which it is possible to make a theological move that regrettably he does not make. The theological move is that the questions: "Whose violence?" and "Whose reconciliation?" lead directly to the recognition of the fundamental human reality of violence as one's radical inhumanity to one which only God's reconciliation can prevent and heal. The gospel is that people can be reconciled with one another only as they are reconciled to God; and when people are thus reconciled to God they give themselves in thought and word and deed to the empowerment of the poor, to the liberation of the oppressed, to the struggle against every dehumanizing dimension of human existence. Cone rightly declares that "reconciliation means that people cannot be human . . . unless the creatures of God are liberated from that which enslaves and is dehumanizing."[20] In this same sentence, Cone writes that "God cannot be God" unless the creature is liberated. But putting it this way involves Cone in an imprecision as regards the gospel which is analogous to the imprecision which Professor Moltmann expresses as regards violence and non-violence. The gospel is that God *refuses* to be God without being reconciled to humanity and in this empowerment one is to be reconciled to one's fellow human. Similarly, Moltmann, whom Cone quotes, rightly declares that "the problem of violence and non-violence is an illusory problem."[21] But one cannot say, as Moltmann then does, that "there is only the question of the justified and unjustified use of force and the question of whether the means are proportionate to the ends."[22] It is because the gospel transposes the question of violence from the ethical to the apocalyptic sphere that it also deprives force of every justification, not least the one that illusorily seeks a proportionate relation of means to ends.

It is understandable that Cone should reject white answers to the questions: "Whose violence?" and "Whose reconciliation?" But there is a dimension of the gospel of special significance for that ultimate confrontation between violence and reconciliation toward which the fallen condition of human affairs inevitably tends. The gospel is the good news of a God who heals as God liberates and liberates as God heals. It is God, therefore, who judges the oppressor and empowers the oppressed; and in so doing, God sustains those whom God condemns with the mercy of hope and restrains those whom God empowers with the mercy of compassion. Meanwhile, under the gospel, oppressors and the victims of oppression can and must continually pray that they may be forgiven as they forgive.

The revolutionary thrust of black theology rightly focuses attention upon the question: "Whose?" and makes black theology the bearer of this ultimate dimension of the gospel in its terrifying and liberating concreteness. But I do not find in Professor Cone's account of black theology an indication of this dimension of the gospel. I do not find an indication of this dimension in white theology either, except as an a-revolutionary avoidance of the question: "Whose?," by addressing the question "to blacks by whites."[23] Thus, in pressing upon Professor Cone the question of the missing dimension of the gospel in black theology, I find myself bound to press the same question upon white theology. In so doing, a risk of faith at another and deeper level than "being completely sure what Jesus did or would do" is involved.[24] At this deeper level, the risk of faith is the risk of obedience to what Jesus *did* and is still doing today. This is to invite men and women, in the power of their humanity for which Jesus has set them free, to engage in the struggle for the liberation of any and all who are oppressed and enslaved; and thereby sharing in the saving risk of creating a new humanity. What Jesus is really about is the possibility and the power of bringing freedom and justice and forgiveness together.

In concluding this response in this way, I venture to join with the risk of faith and the risk of obedience, a risk of hope. This risk is that Professor Cone might find it possible to regard the exploration of the missing dimension of the gospel, common alike to black theology and to white theology, a paradigmatic foretaste of the reciprocal conversation and correction through which black theology and white theology endeavor to make "Christian" theology concrete.[25]

NOTES

1. Published in *Union Seminary Quarterly Review* 31, no. 1 (1975): 31–7; reprinted with permission. It is a response to James H. Cone, "Black Theology on Revolution, Violence, and Reconciliation," published that same journal, 5–14. Lehmann's essay was later reprinted in G.S. Wilmore and J.H. Cone, eds. *Black Theology: A Documentary History, 1966–1979* (Maryknoll: Orbis Books, 1979), 144–51.
2. Lehmann, *Ethics in a Christian Context*, esp. 81ff.
3. Cone, "Black Theology on Revolution," 12.
4. Cone, "Black Theology on Revolution," 12.
5. Cone, "Black Theology on Revolution," 13.
6. Albrecht Ritschl, *Justification and Reconciliation*, vol. 3, trans. Macintosh (Edinburgh: T&T Clark, 1902), 34. The original is in *Rechtfertigung und Versöhnung*, Bd. III (Bonn: Adolf Marcus, 1883), 32.
7. [Editorial: Sister Corita Kent (1918–1986) was a Roman Catholic sister, artist, and educator.]
8. Cone, "Black Theology on Revolution," 13.
9. Cone, "Black Theology on Revolution," 8.
10. Cone, "Black Theology on Revolution," 9.
11. Cone, "Black Theology on Revolution," 9.
12. Cone, "Black Theology on Revolution," 10.
13. Cone, "Black Theology on Revolution," 5.
14. Cone, "Black Theology on Revolution," 5.
15. Cone, "Black Theology on Revolution," 5.
16. Cone, "Black Theology on Revolution," 5.
17. Cone, "Black Theology on Revolution," 5.
18. Cone, "Black Theology on Revolution," 6.
19. Cone, "Black Theology on Revolution," 7.
20. Cone, "Black Theology on Revolution," 13.
21. Cone, "Black Theology on Revolution," 11.
22. See Moltmann, *Religion, Revolution and the Future*, 143.
23. Cone, "Black Theology on Revolution," 13.
24. Cone, "Black Theology on Revolution," 12.
25. [Editorial: For Cone's response to Lehmann's essay and to the other respondents in this special issue (C. Eric Lincoln, Helmut Gollwitzer, Herbert Edwards, and Frederick Herzog), see James H. Cone, "Black Theology and Ideology: A Response to My Respondents," *USQR* 31, no. 1 (1975): 71–86.]

Chapter 17

The Transfiguration of Jesus and Revolutionary Politics (1975)[1]

It must be admitted that "transfiguration" and "politics" are words not usually associated with each other. Even apart from the "transfiguration of Jesus" and "revolutionary politics," the terms seem devoid of a common referent. The Gospel accounts of Jesus' interruption of his confrontation journey toward Jerusalem by ascending "a high mountain . . . where he was transfigured" (Matt 17:1–7, Mark 9:2–8, Luke 9:28–36) have been interpreted in mystical and, in the nineteenth century, in psychological ways—far from the ways of politics. Even the patent messianic facets of the transfiguration accounts were interpreted within rather constricted soteriological limits in disregard of their potent political implications.

These implications begin to emerge when it is noticed that the common referent by which "transfiguration" and "politics" are significantly joined is the fact of *power* in human experience. "Transfiguration" connotes a radicalization of both the responses to power and the uses of power that markedly changes the kind of power used and the purposes to which it is put. The change in the kind of power used may be as marked as the difference between a bullet and a ballot, a strike and a fast. The change in the uses of power may be as marked as the difference between victory and accommodation, tactics and balance, challenge and surrender in a conflict of power. The purposes towards which power is used may differ as markedly as the differences between "a continuation of policy by other means" (von Clausewitz) and a dramatic confrontation when oppression at long last becomes humanly intolerable; between the prevention of a loss of power and the long overdue taking-over of power.[2]

The dynamics of power are such that the rate and range of social change ever and again reach a point of intensity that breaches the limits of tolerance and erupts in a sharp juxtaposition of systemic and revolutionary power, of an established order as against a new order in human affairs. Such a juxtaposition exposes a boundary between a self-justifying perpetuation of power at the service of the established order of things and a revolutionary use of power for the liberation of humanity for human fulfillment.

The radicalization of power connoted by transfiguration is the sign that the operation of power has arrived at its moment of truth. At such a moment the dynamics of power and the human reality and purpose of power correspond. This correspondence is the threshold of transfiguration at which the presence of Jesus of Nazareth in the human story floods both the darkness of the Gospel where revolutions are concerned and the fateful futility of power with which revolutions are concerned with "the light of revelation—the revelation of the glory of God . . ." (2 Cor 4:6), that is, with the panorama and the promise of what God in God's godness is up to with and for humanity in the world.

There is, in short, a politics of transfiguration. Sooner or later, the dynamics of power drive politics across the crucial divide between the futility and the freedom of power where a revolutionary radicalization of power signals transfiguration under way. The transfiguration under way is the confrontation of politics in a more or less familiar sense with the possibility and power of making room for freedom in so unfamiliar a sense as to take nothing less than a totally other foundation for things. "The great problem in politics," wrote Rousseau to the Marquis de Mirabeau in 1767, "which I compare to the problem of squaring the circle in geometry . . . [is]: How to find a form of government which puts the law above man." The trouble was, as Rousseau went on to say, that "to put the law above man and thus to establish the validity of man-made laws, *il faudrait des dieux*!" [it would take gods!].[3] Transfiguration means that Rousseau's circle has been squared.

JESUS TRANSFIGURED

"And in their presence he was transfigured" (Matt 17:2). So runs the pericope. We are confronted here with a breakthrough happening with the seal of reality upon it. In New Testament usage, the force of the phrase "was changed" is apocalyptic. It denotes the radical changes imminent in the world owing to a sudden foretaste of the long-promised and long-expected new world to come. Jesus *was changed* and *in their presence*. Here was no merely subjective experience, an interior vision devoid of external focus. On the contrary, here was a *happening*, pulling past, present and future together; conjoining history and hope, decisions-in-the-making and the making-of-decisions, in the immediate confrontation of a commanding Presence with an inescapable present.

What is going on is the pressure of the end-time upon times rapidly coming to an end. The messianic dynamics of reality—concretely human and humanly concrete in an experienced story of covenant, exodus, advent, crucifixion and parousia—is on the nearer edge of the exposure of its "messianic secret." At stake are the revolutionary character of reality and the reality of the revolutionary response to this reality, in a world once lived and died in by Jesus of Nazareth, the Christ, and over which he still presides.

The accounts of the transfiguration of Jesus occur in the Synoptic Gospels as a kind of dramatic midpoint between the imminent exposure—one might almost say *explosion*—of the messianic secret and the imminence of a messianic exodus. Only the most casual and exterior reading of the Gospel accounts could fail to be drawn into the mounting tension of time running out as the narrative moves from Jesus' scarcely veiled self-identification through conflict and confrontation to crucifixion. The time is indeed at hand!

The question of the Establishment is up for overturn in a radical shift of perspective and direction, and a consequent revision of priorities about "Who's who?" and "What's what?" The question "Whose world is this and by whose and what authority?" is heading for the countdown and a lift-off in a blinding light of shattering presence and power after which the world never can and never will be the same again. A transfiguration—in this case, *the* transfiguration—has happened! And neither history nor nature, society nor culture nor humanity itself, will be experienced as before, for they will not *be* as before. In the transfiguration of Jesus of Nazareth, the Christ, the politics of God has transfigured the politics of persons. "And in their presence he was transfigured; his face shone like the sun, and his clothes were white as light" (Matt 17:2). Or, as Mark with characteristic concreteness observes, "with a whiteness no bleacher on earth could equal" (9:3).

Moses and Elijah are the bearers of this ingression, on that "high mountain" where Jesus was transfigured. The law and the prophets, identified by Moses and Elijah, identify the context and the conditions of Israel's and, through Israel, of all humankind's participation in the humanizing activity of God in the world. This context was and is a pattern of relationships freely offered and freely taken up in election and covenant, in calling and commitment to the foundational, liberating and fulfilling purposes for which the world was purposed.

In this context law expresses the dynamics and the direction of the divine will toward boundaries of freely accepted limits within which the practice of humanness is certain to become "a thing of beauty and a joy forever." In this context the prophets—from Moses to Elijah, from the Law-giver to the Law-fulfiller—were the divinely appointed guardians of the righteousness of God in action. The righteousness of God means "God's presence in the midst of his people as help and salvation."[4]

When the Synoptic Gospel writers tell us that Moses and Elijah are the conversation partners of Jesus on the mountain of transfiguration, they affirm that with Jesus of Nazareth a new Moses has come, that the prophetic guardianship of the humanness of human life has begun to take human shape in human life, that the practice of love is the fulfillment of the law and the prophets, and that the concrete focus of the practice of love is righteousness. With the dynamics and the implications of such a politics of transfiguration, the revolutionary goings-on in these days will have to reckon, as surely as will established principalities and powers. But the critical significance of the confrontation between revolutionary and establishment politics is that revolutions are signs of transfiguration.

REVOLUTIONS AS SIGNS OF TRANSFIGURATION

In the literature of revolution, the word "transfiguration" can scarcely be said to appear with notable frequency. The gap between transfiguration and revolution thus seems as great as the gap between transfiguration and politics. Yet by a curious double coincidence the gap is less formidable than it seems.

On August 6, 1945, a bomb carrying a nuclear warhead was dropped upon the Japanese city of Hiroshima. In a blinding flash of light, "with a whiteness no bleacher on earth could equal," the face of earth and sky were so profoundly and radically changed, not only so as never to be the same again but so as to make the destruction of that city the point of departure for the blazing of a trail either of darkness and death or of light and life for the whole of humankind, perhaps even of the world.

A transfiguration of presence and power, of reality and redemption had happened that signaled that the operation of power in human affairs had reached a point of no return. Its moment of truth had arrived in the imminence, urgency, and inescapability of an ultimate perspective and direction for power, according to which the dynamics of power and the human reality and purpose of power correspond.

Politics in a more or less familiar sense had run headlong into the possibility and power of making room for freedom in so unfamiliar a sense as to take nothing less than a totally other foundation for and style of life. A power revolution had revolutionized the purposes, possibilities and possession of power in the world. No longer could the "principalities and powers," "the authorities and potentates of this dark world," as *The New English Bible* puts it, or even "the superhuman forces of evil in the heavens" (Eph 6:12), prevent or temporize with the breaking out of old and dehumanizing confinements in the direction of new and liberating possibilities for giving human shape to human life.

Phoenix-like, from the ashes of the "age of humanity," the revolution of humanity was rising up to take its place. Yet it may scarcely be gainsaid that no one (or almost no one) in the bodies politic of the world, or even among churchmen of the world, and, least of all, among President Truman and his political and military advisers, was aware that August 6, 1945, was the day of the Feast of Transfiguration. This is the first coincidence.

The second coincidence has to do with coincidental use of the word "transfiguration" in the literature dealing with revolution. Professor Crane Brinton, in the course of his masterful analysis of *The Anatomy of Revolution*, writes:

> Men may revolt partly or even mainly because they are indeed hindered, or . . . *cramped* in their economic activities; but to the world—and, save for a very few hypocrites, also to themselves—they must appear *wronged*. "Cramp" must undergo moral transfiguration before men will revolt. Revolutions cannot do without the word "justice" and the sentiments it arouses.[5]

Brinton does not pause over the phrase "moral transfiguration." His preferred analogy is the medical one of a fever. But the medical and the moral analogies for understanding the phenomenon of revolution become strangely reciprocal and illuminating when the story of revolution as a whole is reviewed as a documentation of transfiguration.

Revolutions happen; they are not made. They happen because sooner or later revolutionary movements cannot do without justice. They cannot do without justice because sooner or later "cramped" is experienced as "wronged"; "wronged" is experienced as "injustice"; and "injustice" is experienced as "dehumanization." Just as a fever signals that the health of the body can no longer be ignored but must be remedied, so revolutions signal that the health of society can no longer be deferred but must be set right.

The "moral transfiguration" that engenders revolution is the conversion of the social and power conditions under which people live to the human and humanizing purposes for which these conditions were designed. The single use of the phrase "moral transfiguration" in Brinton's analysis, with its studied avoidance of philosophical, ethical, and theological evaluations, suggests a kind of "Freudian slip" that brings the phenomenological and the human meaning of revolution together.

The chink in the armor of this resolute pursuit of *"vis medicatrix naturae"* [nature's healing power], with its equally resolute rejection both of God and of Freud, is its inadvertent allusion to the congruence of the dynamics of revolution with a politics of transfiguration. The distance between "cramped" and "wronged"—between economic hindrances because of which "men *may* revolt" and "moral transfiguration" which persons must undergo before "they *will* revolt"—is paralleled by the distance between Hiroshima and the Feast of Transfiguration in the revolutionary ferment of our present "time of troubles" (Toynbee).[6]

The double coincidence that links revolution and transfiguration underlines the conjunction of reality and redemption, of presence and power, of truth and life in the struggle of human beings to be, become, and end up as human beings in the world. The power revolution unveiled in the destruction of Hiroshima on the Feast of Transfiguration is congruent with the moral transfiguration of human affairs unveiled in the revolutionary struggle to humanize the possession, uses, and purposes of power.

The dynamics of Jesus' transfiguration, to which this double coincidence points, unmask not only a providential rejection of the fatalism and futility intrinsic to the self-justifying control and use of Establishment politics. They unmask also the point and destiny of revolutions which, although no less vulnerable to self-justification, are nevertheless bearers of a righteousness not their own and are best and rightly understood as signs of transfiguration.

As *vis medicatrix naturae*, revolutions do not confine social and political reality to the cosmic inscrutability that makes Hobbes's bitter dictum concerning "the war of all against all" inevitable but bearable. On the contrary, as *vis medicatrix naturae*, revolutions herald the profound wisdom of the classical dictum that "whom the gods would destroy, they first make mad."[7] Owing to a providential transfiguration of politics, revolutions make room for a new order of times and of freedom for human affairs in a God-person world.

NOTES

1. Published in *Christianity and Crisis* 35, no. 3 (1975): 44–47; reprinted with permission.

2. [Editorial: Carl von Clausewitz (1780–1831) was a Prussian general and military theorist. The reference here is to his aphorism, "War is merely the continuation of policy by other means."]

3. [Editorial: "Lettre à Victor Riquetti, marquis de Mirabeau 26.07.1767," in *Correspondance compléte de Jean-Jacques Rousseau*, ed. R. A. Leigh (Geneva: Voltaire Foundation, 1979), vol. 33.]

4. [Editorial: Lehmann cites Ludwig Koehler, *Old Testament Theology* without reference to a page number.]

5. [Editorial: Crane Brinton, *The Anatomy of Revolution* (Hoboken: Prentice Hall, 1938), 36.]

6. [Editorial: No reference indicated in the original.]

7. [Editorial: No reference indicated in original.]

PART III

The Future of Theology in a Post-Christian World

In Part III of this volume, we have collected a range of essays from the late 1950s through the 1970s, including one of Paul Lehmann's published sermons, which in various ways take up the question of the future of theology in a "post-Christian world," or in Bonhoeffer's phrase, "a world come of age." One of the challenges of reading Lehmann's theology today comes from the fact that his work is so often driven by a sense of responsibility to address the demands of the moment. Several of these essays reflect Lehmann's concern to respond theologically to the various issues that were emerging in the rapidly changing intellectual, cultural, and political landscape of the time period. On the one hand, this way of doing theology follows naturally from Lehmann's contextual theological method, the particular contours of which Part I of this volume seek to highlight. On the other hand, these essays are shaped by the particular vocational demands of Lehmann's career as a teacher at major U.S. mainline Protestant seminaries and divinity schools.[1] Indeed, Lehmann's theological work is motivated by a keen sensitivity to the changing needs and questions that his students faced, the majority of whom were training to serve as pastors in congregations increasingly shaped by a "post-Christian cultural situation."[2]

Within this changing context, in the first essay Lehmann warns against a Protestantism easily tempted to play "the ostrich game," whether through assimilation into a suburbanized, bureaucratic form of institutional existence or through an ecumenicity that exchanged the "power of faith" for a "faith in power." By contrast, Lehmann insists on the ongoing relevancy of what he calls "the cutting edge of prophecy" characteristic of Protestant faith, one that is "imaginative enough, self-critical enough, sober enough to permeate the culture of the future not from the dominant but the sectarian center of its own life."[3] By retrieving the sectarian center of its life, Lehmann does not mean to suggest that Protestantism should make a "divisive" contribution to an increasingly pluralist society, but rather that Protestantism may serve as a "leaven of dialogue, criticism, and integration," even clarifying the "humanistic foundations" of the university and culture in a time when the threat to freedom of speech and civil liberties had become rampant in U.S. society.

Whether he always intended to be or not, Lehmann was also a *provocateur*. The second essay, "For an Abrahamic People," along with the printed report about the discussion that followed his paper at the Consultation on Church Union in 1974, vividly illustrates some of the strong reactions that his work regularly engendered.[4] In particular, the report highlights the negative reactions of women in the audience to his proposal that the church prioritize the struggle against racism above the problem of sexism, and his suggestion that the feminist movement remained too determined by middle-class interests. According to the attached report, many of the women who attended the meeting "vigorously disagreed" with Lehmann, suggesting that his comments reflected "the way men think." In response, a task force was formed out of which came a resolution concluding that "racism, sexism, and classism" are, in fact, interrelated. However one judges Lehmann's prioritization of racism over sexism and his appeal to Marx to justify such a position, the essay and the disagreement that quickly ensued provide something of a glimpse into the contestations Lehmann's work so often provoked. The essay also reflects the extent to which Lehmann had yet to grapple with the critical insights of Black feminist and womanist thought, which would by the late 70s and early 80s begin to emerge as an important voice in U.S. academic theological spaces, particularly at Union Theological Seminary.

The third essay, "The Changing Course of a Corrective Theology," is an extended reflection on the fresh contributions that Karl Barth and the "theology of crisis" have made on contemporary theological discourse, both in Europe and in America. Lehmann opens the essay with a quote from Barth in which he reflects on the impact his pastoral experience in Safenwil had on the shape of what he calls his "corrective theology" from which his 1919 *Römerbrief* grew. What interests Lehmann is Barth's eminently practical concern that every pastor must face, namely, the need to find a way between "the problem of human life on the one hand, and the content of the Bible on the other."[5] The result, for Lehmann, in both its polemical and constructive content was a "corrective theology" that marked nothing less than a "fundamental re-orientation" of Protestant thought, breaking "fresh ground for theological thinking in the tradition of the Reformation."[6] Beyond the "sterile rigidity" of orthodoxy and a "misleading" liberalism, this corrective theology retrieved the "authentic orthodoxy" of the Reformers, which seeks an exposition of the "the living Word" for a changing contemporary world "in which new possibilities of meaning and behavior are always emerging on the edge of the possibilities which have become old and have played out."[7] For Lehmann, it is precisely the consistently "Christo-centric" character of Barth's theology that not only "changes the nature of theology itself," but has also broken up new ground for vigorous debates about questions related to theological communication, the problem of culture, and hermeneutics.[8]

If one were to read only Lehmann's writings on the theological meaning of revolution, one might be left wondering whether he leaves any room at all for a positive theological account of law. Indeed, Lehmann addresses precisely this question in two essays collected here, "Law as a Function of Forgiveness," originally published in law journal in 1959, and "A Christian Alternative to Natural Law." Lehmann poses the problem this way: "In a world whose creator and redeemer is God, is law a self-evident expression of God's will and purpose or is law instrumental to another and different higher expression of God's will and purpose?"[9] Critical of both the concept of natural law in the Roman Catholic tradition as well as the treatment of law in his own Protestant tradition, which has too often prioritized law over justice and order over freedom, Lehmann seeks to articulate the positive theological significance of law as an instrument of divine activity for the sake of the "humanization of human life."[10] Law can take on a functional significance, according to Lehmann, and become an instrument of forgiveness and reconciliation by concretizing justice and love in human relationships.

Lehmann's concern for the "humanizing" function of law and its instrumental character also opens up space for the critique of laws that oppress human life by becoming a function of state power. Lehmann takes up such a critique in his 1972 essay, "The Stranger Within the Gate," which addresses the perversion of justice that is rightly due to the sojourner, according to the Book of Deuteronomy. In this essay, Lehmann offers a scathing critique of U.S. militarism and power exhibited in his time in the Vietnam war, which had by "indescribable destructiveness" emboldened the nation toward "a politics of death" and had given way to policies oriented against "the stranger within our gates."[11] The same "arrogance of power" evident in U.S. foreign policy, Lehmann sees manifesting itself in U.S. immigration policy, which threatens to turn the American dream into "an American nightmare" through dehumanizing and anti-democratic surveillance programs and deportation strategies rooted in fear, mistrust, and a politics of death. Readers will find in Lehmann's reflections a prescient critique of a dangerous trajectory in U.S. immigration policy that, if anything, has grown in magnitude in recent decades. This essay, along with the other essays included in Part III, provide exemplary cases of Lehmann's investment in doing theology and ethics contextually, demonstrating how the "living Word of God" may, indeed, creatively and prophetically serve the changing needs of the present.

NOTES

1. For schools where Lehmann taught, see footnote 6 in the introduction to this book.
2. Lehmann, "Protestantism in a Post-Christian World," 218.
3. Lehmann, "Protestantism in a Post-Christian World," 222.
4. Lehmann, "For an Abrahamic People."
5. Karl Barth "The Need and Promise of Christian Preaching," in *The Word of God and the Word of Man*, trans. Douglas Horton (London: Hodder & Stoughton, 1928), 100.
6. Lehmann, "The Changing Course of a Corrective Theology," 234.
7. Lehmann, "Changing Course," 235.
8. Lehmann, "Changing Course."
9. Lehmann, "Law," *A Handbook of Christian Theology*, eds. M. Halverston and A.C. Cohen (New York: Living Age Books, 1958), 204.
10. Lehmann, "A Christian Alternative to Natural Law," 294.
11. Lehmann, "The Stranger Within the Gate," 274.

Chapter 18

Protestantism in a Post-Christian World (1962)[1]

If an alliteration may be allowed, the outlook for Protestantism in America today may be characterized with reference to perspective, presupposition, perils, and potential. Yet it would be rash to do even this as an exercise in clairvoyance. One can really only make some remarks that are shaped by a limited angle of vision and by some insistent concerns. The concerns grow out of the Protestant ethos and its creative potential and patent distortion. I propose, however, neither to view with enthusiasm nor to view with alarm, but to try if I can to set out seriously with some irenic irony certain features of the theme. So much for *perspective*.

As the *presupposition* for what comes later, I should like to underline a point fundamental to the proper estimation of our chances. With due regard for Dr. Herberg's analysis, it may be suggested that there is in American society a fourth group—not only Protestants, Catholics and Jews but an even more important group—those who couldn't care less.[2] The outlook for Protestantism is rightly assessed only against the presupposition not just of a *post-Protestant* era but against the presupposition of a *post-Christian* era also.

This is a phrase we hear now on every hand. I suppose it has been given theological currency by Dietrich Bonhoeffer more than by anybody else, particularly in such trenchant phrases as *die Mundigheit der Welt* [the world's coming of age] and *ein religionloses Christentum* [a Christianity that is not religious]. What this means is that our outlook goes a long way back. We are coming now into the fruitage of the breakup of the *Corpus Christianum* of that integration of humanity's cultural life that it took a thousand years to build and has taken about another thousand to undo. The breakup of the *Corpus Christianum* has been displaced by a many-sided pluralism: social, political, religious and also a cultural pluralism that is compounded of images and habits of thought no longer effectively shaped by Christianity.

Chapter 18

GOD IS DEAD

Here is a recent description of this post-Christian cultural situation:

> Western culture is weaning itself from that Christian spirit which has so far nurtured it. The legacy of Christianity includes not only moribund religious phenomena and vestigial if apparently strong ecclesiastical institutions as well as unique museums of the creative imagination and the artistic mind. It includes also science and scientism, technology and the addiction to material and spiritual schedules. Our culture is no longer transcendentalist but immanentist; no longer sacral or sacramental but secularistic or profane. This transition is explained by the fact that the essentially mythological world-view of Christianity has been succeeded by a thorough-going scientific view of reality in terms of which either God is no longer necessary or he is neither necessary or unnecessary, he is irrelevant. He is dead.[3]

Professor Vahanian's thesis is that God dies as soon as he becomes a cultural accessory of the human ideal. And Dr. Herberg's account of American religiosity is a perfect commentary upon the death of God in American society. Nietzsche's prophecy seems on the edge of fulfillment if not already to have been fulfilled. The God with us, this transcendent God to whom Dr. Herberg refers in his conclusion, had to die:

> He looked with eyes which beheld everything. He beheld man's depths and dregs, all his hidden ignominy and ugliness. His pity knew no modesty. He crept into my dirtiest corners. This most prying, over-intrusive, over-pitiful one had to die. The God who beheld everything and also man, that God, had to die. Man cannot endure that such a witness should live.[4]

Now I think we cannot assess our situation as Protestants rightly unless we take with full seriousness the depth and the extent of this post-Christian cultural situation. On the continent of Europe, the situation is already well advanced. It is in an advanced state because it can no longer be so neatly concealed. Here the situation is in an eroded state; that is, it is being hollowed out beneath and meanwhile is still being overlaid by the religious veneer of a transition that Dr. Herberg described.

Globally speaking we might say that the post-Christian era is a particular cultural condition of the West, of the advanced nations. The emerging nations of Asia and Africa are, perhaps, not so much in a post-Christian as in a pre-Christian, or at least in an anti-Christian, situation. These nations do not have to reject an indigenous Christianity but only an imported one.

And if I might be permitted one lapse into clairvoyance, it might be said that there is a certain parallel between the political and the Protestant future of the United States of America. We possibly are headed politically for a destiny as an island of precarious freedom in a world three-quarters Communist. I say "we"—I mean we together with western Europe and the possible inclusion of Latin America, though after what Harvard did in Cuba, Latin America is highly problematic. For the most part it is not inconceivable that we shall have to face and live with the fact that we are an island of hope today owing to a cultural heritage the constructive resources of which are now steadily being undermined by our own misdoings. It is perhaps not too much unlike what happened to Athens when she succumbed to Sparta. Athens continued, though in a position of political isolation rather than domination, to influence the cultural life of western Europe for many centuries.

The Hollowness Beneath

Now about the *perils*. By peril I mean to suggest certain symptoms of diversionary activity in this post-Christian era in which we live as declining Protestants. These symptoms of diversionary activity point to and point up a kind of ostrich game by which the hollowness beneath the surface of our ebbing Christianity is concealed. I would like to note briefly four symptoms.

The first is *suburbia*. I came recently upon some verse, entitled "Society Note," that in my opinion is sociologically and theologically so incisive, painful though it is, that it is only the intensity of its truth that prevents it from being blasphemous.

> A Supper was served yesterday at St. Status' Episcopal at Oak Brook-on-the-N.Y., N.H., & H. There was a tempting cheez-dip with the Body and lovely crystal punch-cups for the Blood and a Women's Guild meeting Afterwards.[5]

The publication of this piece brought, as you can imagine, a storm of protest from the Protestant community roundabout. The piece is clearly not intended for Episcopalians only. Indeed, after reading it, I recalled a traumatic shudder in Princeton some years ago upon being informed that the First Presbyterian Church in the preparation of elements for the Eucharist used grape juice and Pepperidge Farm bread.

Well, here is suburbia. Not all of it to be sure. But something of a glimpse of its inner secularization. Here is the most sophisticated, the most contented, the most protected form of religiosity of which Dr. Herberg has written. And I submit that suburbia is the characteristic mode of Protestantism in America and will continue to be so for a considerable future, unless our political isolation goes on at a more rapid tempo than now appears to be the case. It is suburbia that, more than other manifestations of the Church's life, undermines the confidence of theological students in the parish ministry as a vocation that any person would dare to undertake. Suburbia is one of the symptoms that indicate that the statistical growth of Protestantism in the United States is spurious.

And then there is *bureaucracy*. Wandering about on Morningside Heights in New York City recently, I ruminated about an impressive and not a little terrifying architectural contrast that suggests another symptom of the ostrich game.

Two years ago, I stood speechless before the architectural achievement of Brasilia. Here was an authentic frontier achievement by a people on the move, a people self-conscious about its incipient future role, a people self-conscious about the fact that it has too long labored under the psychological paralysis that nothing it undertook could ever succeed. This people had made visible an architectural creation that put up government buildings, living quarters, and churches in a pattern of authentic experimentation and singular purity of unadulterated line.

I was told that plans for the Roman Church in Brasilia called for a structure most of which was to be below ground. People were to go deep down into the pit, as it were, for their prayers, and then ascend to the light where things were really going on! Terrifyingly secular but matchless in the integrity of a dynamic faith that prevented it from pretending it believed what in fact it did not.

In New York City, on the other hand, I encountered with no little trauma the glory of God inside a massive concrete deformity curiously linked to a papier-mâché replica of a once authentic sensitivity to a God whose transcendence had to be encountered in order to be adored. I never saw that quite so clearly before. When I was a student in New York, Riverside Church seemed to me a little artificial but not un-genuine. Now, exteriorly, at least, and particularly in contrast with Brasilia, it seems to me little short of an architectural travesty upon Christian faith. If it weren't for the papier-mâché and the nearby deformity (the Interchurch Center), one might argue that the beehives of New York are twentieth-century cathedrals.

So I leave it to you whether the limited angle of vision from which I reflect upon the Protestant outlook is merely astigmatic or whether something of an ostrich game is going on. The architectural anonymity of the Interchurch Center says nothing so much to me as that Protestantism is an obstruction in the path of an American society that couldn't care less. It's like the plague of locusts on a desiccated land.

Ecumenicity and Catholicity

And then there is the symptom of *ecumenicity*. Here also there is an ostrich game. I am troubled that the Stated Clerk of the General Assembly of my own denomination could have found it appropriate to join in an attempt to draw American Protestantism into one of the more enervating aspects of ecumenicity that promises, at least for the next decade, to consume its already flagging energies. When one thinks of all of the decisive issues confronting the United States in the world today, what seems to be required is a fresh articulation of the prophetic ethos and of the transcendent sensitivity that once characterized Protestantism.

Let me say as emphatically as possible that I am not opposed to ecumenicity. What I am concerned about is that ecumenicity shows marked traces of being a diversionary activity. The power of faith is thereby exhibited as faith in power. And this, I think, will do us no good in the post-Christian situation that we face.

The fourth symptom of peril has to do with *Catholicity*. Dr. Herberg has reminded us of the transitional situation in which American Protestantism finds itself and of my own situation in Massachusetts, a part of the country that seems to have a good deal of that already behind it. And thus my remarks about Catholicity may be unduly jaundiced by the circumstance of having to "till the soil and eat my bread" in an outpost of the Irish Free State. Nevertheless, let me venture to note that the ostrich game is also being played on that frontier. I live where the battle is joined every day.

The sophisticated, delicate irenicism that emanates from *Christianity and Crisis*, that bi-weekly spiritual affiliate of *Osservatore Romano* [*The Roman Observer*], is no adequate analysis of the power phenomenon with which we have to deal. I think, incidentally, that this organ has not had a very good record on the power issue for the last decade or so. And it has therefore not accidentally widened its cultural horizon in proportion to a waning depth and incisiveness in its account of the impact of the Gospel upon the common life.

We have been told for a long time that the secular version of power in our time was so monolithic in character that we could have no dealings with it. And we are now being told, on the other side, that the religious version of this power is budding with irenic pluralism. Coming as I do from the place where the battle over civil liberties, over education, over the kind of resentments that I think are really post-Protestant is unresting and bitter, I am not quite so certain that the resentments to which Dr. Herberg has referred can be disposed of in that way. I have, of course, to keep my eyes upon *The Pilot* and thus cannot give undivided attention to *Christianity and Crisis*, but let's not underestimate the power issue by a sophisticated, sociological analysis of cultural transition. Protestantism has never done it, and if this is now to be called "paranoia," it may be that the risk of just such a charge will have to be faced if the destiny and the heritage of the Reformation are to be creatively conjoined.

The Cutting Edge of Prophecy

Now a final word about the *potentials*. I do not feel that the ostrich game will do us in. I think there are enormously creative resources of the Protestant faith and ethos. These resources add up to one thing above all others; the subordination of all power—social, political, cultural, religious—to the power of faith. This was a central part of what the Reformers meant when they insisted that people were justified by grace alone, by faith alone.

Theologically, this means that Protestantism is the bearer in the long stream of Christian history and into the modern world of the cutting edge of prophecy. And the cutting edge of prophecy is always there where disruptive usurpation of power in the common life of people over their minds or over their institutions, has raised its head and where a halt must be called.

Politically, this means that Protestant faith and ethos understand power as instrumental. This is why in the body politic civil liberties are the test case. And this is also why in the cultural and social pluralism of our time Protestantism is peculiarly suited to function as a kind of cultural leaven in, with, and under the pluralism and the quest for integration that this culture is pursuing under auspices of a secular kind.

There are two points in the life of the mind of which Protestantism has been particularly the steward and the bearer. The one is that the concrete form of the idea, that the concrete form of human relatedness is always the decisive form, not the general form, not the universal form, not the principal form. And I think the nominalist roots of Protestantism may provide on the frontier of the university, for example, a leaven of dialogue, criticism, and integration that may gradually help to make plain once again that the university and culture with it cannot survive unless its humanistic foundations are secure. And its humanistic foundations cannot be secure on its own terms but only in the light of the dynamic and rejuvenating activity of God.

I look for a Protestantism imaginative enough, self-critical enough, sober enough to permeate the culture of the future not from the dominant but the sectarian center of its own life. By the sectarian center of its own life, I do not mean a center of divisiveness but the kind of center of its own life that understands what our Lord meant by the mustard seed, by the grain that must fall into the ground and die, by the leaven in the lump.

Today it seems that we are not too far removed from what the prophet Samuel described about ancient Israel. "The word of the Lord was rare in those days, and there was no frequent vision" (1 Sam. 3:2). But "if the trumpet gives an uncertain sound, who will prepare himself for the battle" (1 Cor. 14:8)?

DISCUSSION

Herberg

I have two comments I'd like to make. First on the fourth group. This notion of a fourth group in addition to the three groups of Protestant, Catholic, and Jew is developed at length in Martin Marty's book *The New Shape of American Religion*. But what I was trying to say is something very significant and true; this fourth group concept is a misunderstanding of the social structure of America.

You ask Americans what they are—you don't even have to ask what they are religiously—and 95 to 97 percent will classify themselves as Catholics, Protestants, or Jews. These are three vertical columns. Within each column the great mass couldn't care less. This is not a fourth group; this mass, these people who couldn't care less, are in the three groups. They are not a fourth group side by side with the three; they are the great majority of the three. Only the top, a very thin layer, varying in different kinds of places and circumstances, can be regarded as not merely Protestant, Catholic, or Jew by self-identification and social vocation but by their faith and commitment.

Therefore, I would say that the notion of a fourth group is a misunderstanding of the vertical division. The fourth group is really the mass of the three groups, cutting horizontally, in different ways. That, I think, has to be clearly understood. Otherwise the picture will be as though a great mass of Americans identifies themselves non-religiously—nobody does. In a city like New Haven, 97 percent—you know there was practically a house-to-house census there—97.2 percent of the entire population of New Haven identified themselves as Protestants, Catholics, or Jews, and 2.8 percent, as other—like Muslim or Buddhist—or none.

Practically nobody in this country fails to identify himself as Protestant, Catholic, or Jew. These are three vertical columns. But within them there is a horizontal division between those whose Protestantism, Catholicism, or Judaism is a sociological religion of belonging and therefore couldn't care less about the authentic tradition of their faith and those who do care. That's the first point.

The second point, on Romanism, I will merely indicate one aspect of this. We in New York—I used to live in New York—and we in New Jersey—I live in New Jersey now—are also living in places where there is direct encounter with the Roman Catholics. Massachusetts is not the only place in the world. And I won't draw any conclusions on this, I must simply point out one thing.

What Paul Lehmann said about the situation there is certainly well taken. There is this power struggle, there's no doubt about it. But it's wrong to trace it to Roman Catholicism. You must understand the ethnic character of Roman Catholicism.

Let me illustrate one point. In Massachusetts and Connecticut, the Roman Catholic groups have worked steadily to prevent repeal of the birth control laws that Protestants put on the books seventy or eighty years ago. Therefore, it is taken as if it were a Roman Catholic position. But notice, in the one state of the Union in which the Catholics form a great majority—not Massachusetts but Rhode Island—there are now no such laws and nobody ever dreamed of putting them on the statute books. Why? You have to understand the ethnic character of Massachusetts and Rhode Island.

Another point. The propriety of making contraception, which in Roman Catholic moral theology is a sin, a crime of the law has been rejected for fifty or a hundred years by Catholic theologians. And yet the Catholic groups in Massachusetts and Connecticut keep the laws on the books. Why? Because in Massachusetts and Connecticut the dominant Catholic element is Irish. The Irish have piled up an intense fund of resentment. Only a hundred years ago it was different in Boston. There were signs all over, "No Irish need apply." "Irish keep out!" In Cambridge, believe it or not, the Irish have piled up an intense fund of resentment, and as one high-placed Irish Catholic in Massachusetts told me, "They put it on the books, let's see them take it off. We'll show them who's boss here."

Now in Rhode Island, the Catholics are of Polish and Italian background. They've never piled up any big fund of resentment. They don't have any grudge against anybody. They don't have to show anybody who's boss. And you don't have that situation there. You don't have that power struggle in Rhode Island the way you have in Massachusetts and Connecticut. Now this is not a matter of Roman Catholicism. It reflects one of the extremely complex religio-ethnic group struggles in America, which is quite different.

I interviewed a high prelate a few years ago. I said to him, "But look, Father [John Courtney] Murray and others have shown that it is not Catholic doctrine to convert the sin of contraception into crime under the law." He looked at me with his kind of benign, gentle smile and said, "Father Murray, huh? When did Father Murray ever run a diocese?"

Now that's the point I want to make. There's no doubt about a power struggle, but to interpret it as though it were a Protestant-Roman Catholic struggle is quite out of place.

Lehmann

I just want to say with regard to the first point that it could be that the sociology which informs Professor Herberg's stratification is increasingly becoming obsolete. That's to say that I think these three vertical groups or these groups on the vertical basis and the group on the horizontal basis is currently the sociological situation. But what I'm talking about is in the process of formation, and I think it's not inconceivable that in another fifty or a hundred years—things move very fast sociologically—we will either have the fourth group or only one group.

Now on the other situation, as far as I can understand the history and development of the Roman Church, it's always been ethnically conditioned. Indeed, this is one of the great strengths, one of the great geniuses of Roman Catholicism. It has known what the *Corpus Christianum* is about; it has known how to achieve an amalgam of Christian faith and ethnic traditions more effectively than any other group in Christian history. I think this is also, in part, what the Reformation was about.

I think that the question, therefore, of the disposition of the power struggle simply as an ethnic one ignores the history of the development of Roman Catholicism as a system of power. I agree that there is an ethnic factor which makes it unnecessary for the people in Rhode Island to put on the books a matter that is in point of fact already under rather effective implementation. I don't think the circumstance that Protestantism put birth control on the books of the Commonwealth of Massachusetts alters one bit the power enterprise by which Catholicism keeps it there. I don't think it alters it at all.

I think, furthermore, that we have always to keep clearly before us the ethnic diversity and power centrality of the Roman Catholic approach to problems of public life. Even so learned, so irenic, so conversationalist a Roman Catholic scholar as Father [Gustave] Weigel found it appropriate, as we all remember, on the eve of the campaign, to make certain very strange remarks about the obsolescence of the doctrine of temporal power in the Roman tradition. I think your "high prelate" was right—it's the guys who run the dioceses that make the policies.

NOTES

1. Published in *Christianity and Crisis* 22, No. 1 (1962): 7–10, 12; reprinted with permission.
2. [Editorial: William "Will" Herberg (1901–1977), author of *Protestant, Catholic, Jew: An Essay in American Religious Sociology* (Chicago: University of Chicago Press, 1955).]
3. Gabriel Vahanian, *The Death of God* (New York: George Braziller, 1961), xxxii.
4. Friedrich Nietzsche, *Thus Spoke Zarathustra*, pt. 4 (New York: Modern Library, 1995), 264–67.
5. *The Dartmouth*, April 24, 1961.

Chapter 19

For an Abrahamic People (1974)[1]

There are a couple of revivals of ecumenical narcissism that worry me. One of them is bureaucratization. I'm really terribly troubled by the rampant bureaucratization of the church in our time. Maybe it's just since I've gone to Richmond, but what comes through to me is a kind of institutional mentality that supposes that the vitality of the church will one way or another be furthered by what's called the restructuring of the church. Now, even when I was in Morningside Heights (at Union Seminary, New York), I was so close to that phenomenon as to be terrified by the human consequences of restructuring owing to the intensification of the organization, the methodological, the communications mentality which spawn new discommunities. When management consultants become the soothsayers of church renewal—whether in boards and agencies, or in theological faculties, or in local parish, the gulf between human renewal and church renewal threatens the integrity of the obedience of faith by an anemia of Abrahamic faithfulness which crucifies the Lord of glory. Small wonder that "we don't speak any more, we just communicate," as Jean Stafford recently reminded us in the *New York Times*, with regard to the eclipse of language:

"So do dumb beetles," says Miss Stafford, "and jackasses."

WHAT HAPPENS TO LANGUAGE

Sisters and brothers, think what that means for an Abrahamic people who have been formed by and in the mystery, who set language at the vital center of humanness. When we begin to adopt as we are and all around the place, a bureaucratic language, a final sign has come upon us of how intense the bureaucratic preoccupation of the church has become in our time. When we begin to lose sensibility for the fact that verbs and nouns are not the same, adverbs and adjectives are not the same, we show forth nothing so much as

227

a callous disregard of the economy of God, who himself thought it was most indicative of this and our human involvement to shape the world by words, to claim responses from creatures by words. In such a world, under such a God, the language we speak tells almost everything about who we are, at least where I am in theological education. "How to" language, programmatic language, is the order of the day. Meanwhile, where people are really involved over and with their troubles over their humanness, it is not accidental. They have resorted, in their intensity and fury to barnyard language. Barnyard language at least reminds us of our kinship with other creatures. Bureaucratic language reminds us of our de-humanizing fascination with an organizational mentality that celebrates differences by enjoying preferences.

I don't wish to be understood as wishing to do in the bureaucrat. There are diversities of gifts; and among them is the "gift of administration." Hence, bureaucrats are not my enemies. They are creatures who, like the rest of us, sometimes suffer from an excess of enthusiasm for what they are about. But if human renewal is the test case of the renewal of the church, the church in its search for unity in the obedience of faith must draw back from its organizational preoccupation.

"Rampant Montanism"

On the other side of this ecumenical narcissism is the charismatic movement. I think we must take a long, hard look at that, because the charismatic movement is a way of mistaking enthusiasm for renewal, of mistaking who we are for, how we are who we are; of confusing the renewal of the church with a way of bringing human spirit and Holy Spirit so intimately together as to express the effective exclusion of Jesus Christ from the enterprise of human renewal. It is not accidental that in our times both human renewal, of mistaking who we are for how we should be diverted from the Abrahamic reality of both by a rampant bureaucratization on the one hand, and by a rampant montanism on the other.[2] As though the church has had no previous experience about all this, we all begin to get nostalgic or at least we all begin to get envious about why there is no enthusiasm where we are. Now if my thesis is correct, that the vanguard of the renewal of the church is the vanguard of human renewal, then human renewal is not defined by spiritual renewal. Human renewal is defined by involvement where human beings in time and space are prevented from having room for being human in. So the church, as Bonhoeffer nicely remarks, is not in the world to take up a piece of the world's territory and claim it for the church. The church is in the world so that the world may be more truly the world; that is to say, the place created by God and redeemed by Jesus Christ for being human in. This is what I mean when I venture to suggest that human renewal is the test case of the renewal of the church, and why I think the Commission on Institutional Racism is so important an aspect of the church of Christ becoming and a sign that COCU has begun to come in sight of the obedience of faith.

PRIORITY: DISLODGING RACISM

In my view, what the Commission on Institutional Racism means is that racism is the primary matter now on the agenda of the church, on the agenda of history, and if my sisters in Christ will bear with me, not sexism. I am not saying that sexual differentiation and sexist idolatry are not a part of our culture. I'm saying that if the Church of Christ Uniting is to be with and *alongside of*, and *for* fellow human beings in the world, it must move in the struggle for justice in this country to uproot racist behavior in every form and out of that freedom it is promised that we shall be able to move to the next phase of humanization in the human struggle. Otherwise, we shall not easily escape the disquieting circumstances that the feminist movement and the sociology and economics of middle-class existence are not reciprocally critical of one another. They are part of an egalitarian movement which turns out actually to perpetuate what Marx long ago taught us to be aware of—the contradictions in the very society that make for the injustices which have brought the black question to the top of the agenda of the future of this country. So I am suggesting, let us think and re-think, and think again, in a more creative way the relation between inequality and equality in what we are about under the righteousness of God; and let us have a care about an agenda which does not deliver us either to the ant hill or to power domination in the world.

Disagreement Leads to Formation of Task Force

Angered by a remark made by a noted theologian, women involved in the Consultation on Church Union (COCU) went to work here and won new ecumenical ground.

Without audible dissent, the 12th COCU plenary authorized a task force on women that, among other things, will attempt to introduce the churches to what women theologians are doing.

The idea for the task force was born, and grew to maturity, because many of the women at the COCU meeting vigorously disagreed with Paul L. Lehmann, who said the churches should deal with racism before tackling sexism and other injustices. (See next column.)

Cynthia Wedel, an Episcopal leader and former president of the National Council of Churches, said Dr. Lehmann reflected "the way men think."

Men, she said, think in a linear way which allows them to do only one thing at a time. In contrast, women can hold in mind and work on more than one thing at a time, she added.

Alternate Tactic

Instead of verbally attacking or "punishing" the COCU meeting, the women decided to get together to work through the angry feelings they had in response to Dr. Lehmann, who teaches at Union Theological Seminary in Virginia after his retirement last year from Union Seminary, New York.

"As a group, we sorted through our feelings (and) concluded that the insights of women are important to the future of COCU," said Dr. Wedel, explaining that she spoke for "at least a majority" of the women present.

COCU has asked member communions to include as many women as men on plenary delegations. Many churches have not followed that recommendation. Of about 220 delegates at the Cincinnati sessions, some 55 were women.

The resolution on the women's task force said that "racism, sexism and classism" are interrelated.

The new COCU unit, whose members will be appointed by the executive committee, will "draw together the theological and sociological studies done by women relevant to the emerging perspectives on women and to perspectives of women about the church; release resources by and for women in the consultation; and bring its insights into the work of the other (COCU) commissions and to the next plenary."

Delegates concurred with the women in saying "many persons in our nine churches are not aware of work being done by women theologians—lay and clergy—on ministry, the nature of the church, new understandings in biblical translations and interpretation, the theology of liberation and the interaction between racism, sexism and classism."

NOTES

1. Published in *The Presbyterian Outlook*, 1 N. 5th St., Suite 500, Richmond, Va., Vol. 156, No. 44 (December 9, 1974): 5–6; reprinted with permission.

2. Montanism was an apocalyptic movement, traced back to Montanus in Phrygia, in the latter part of the second century. It lived in expectation of the speedy outpouring of the Holy Spirit on the church, of which it saw the first manifestation in its own prophets and prophetesses. It was formally condemned by the Asiatic Synods before 200 CE.

Chapter 20

The Changing Course of a Corrective Theology (1956)[1]

The course of Protestant theology in our time took a sharp turn in the year 1919 with the publication of a commentary on Paul's letter to the Romans. The author was a young and little-known pastor of a village church in Switzerland. Karl Barth is now in his seventy-first year and has just retired from the professorship of theology at the University of Basel. He is feverishly at work, in a race against time, trying to complete a monumental work on the foundations and substance of theology in the tradition of the Reformation. Three volumes in eight large and separate books have already been published. The first two parts of Volume IV have also appeared; and at least two more parts, together with Volume V and its subdivisions are projected. Happily, this continuing work will be done in connection with ongoing lectures in the University for what one can only hope will be an indefinite period. Owing to the range, thoroughness, and penetration of its theological analysis, Barth's *Kirchliche Dogmatik* has been compared to the *Summa Theologica* of Thomas Aquinas. Although Barth has written voluminously, both in books and in articles, it is the *Kirchliche Dogmatik,* and the six editions through which the *Commentary on Romans* has passed, that offer the clearest and most reliable guide to the substance and the development of his thought.

NEO-ORTHODOXY AS A CORRECTIVE THEOLOGY

There are two early passages which provide an illuminating clue to what Barth thought he was doing when he began his theological labors, and why he felt that theology had to turn sharply from its previous course. "May I," Barth asks, "make a brief personal explanation?":

> For twelve years I was a minister . . . I *had* my theology. It was not really mine, to be sure, but that of my unforgotten teacher Wilhelm Herrmann, grafted upon the principles which I had learned . . . in my native home—the principles of those Reformed Churches which today I represent and am honored to represent in an official capacity. Once in the ministry, I found myself growing away from these theological habits of thought and being forced back more and more upon the specific *minister's* problem, the *sermon*. I sought to find my way between the problem of human life on the one hand, and the content of the Bible on the other. As a minister I wanted to speak to the *people* in the infinite contradiction of their life, but to speak the no less infinite message of the Bible, which was as much of a riddle as life . . . I finally went to work upon the Epistle to the Romans, which first was to be only an essay to help me to know my own mind. Naturally and evidently there are many subjects mentioned in the book . . . but you will best understand it when you hear through it all, the minister's question: What is preaching?—not, How *does* one do it? but, How *can* one do it? Contained in it there is a reflection of the light, though not the light itself, toward which I saw that I was pointed and wished to point. And so there grew what threatens now to broaden out somewhat into "my theology" or, let us say, a "corrective theology."[2]

A theology that does not serve the Church by bringing the Bible to life in the midst of human life as it is actually lived is no true theology and must be corrected. Theology serves the Church because the Church is the place where the new and biblical possibility of life occurs. And it is "the need and the promise of Christian preaching," as Barth calls his essay, that this possibility of new life should always be a real possibility and a real event. True to the central rediscovery of the Protestant Reformation, Barth's initial and primary concern was and has been with the living Bible in the living Church. As a result of this concern, and contrary to plan, he found himself the initiator of a corrective theology which he envisaged "as a kind of marginal note, a gloss which . . . loses its meaning the moment it becomes more than a note and takes up space as a new theology next to the others."[3]

The other passage shows that Barth was not unaware of his own exposure to this danger of a new theology. It shows too that although he set out not to write a new theology, and above all, not to found a school, he was, nevertheless, prepared to accept the theological responsibility implicit in his concern for the living Word in the living Church. "May I say, in conclusion," Barth wrote in the Preface to his first and now long supplanted attempt at a systematic elaboration of what he had written in the *Commentary on Romans*:

> one more very unacademic word, a word which . . . seems to me to be necessary for those among my previous friends who have taken and will take it hard that I seem to be on the road towards becoming a theologian . . . ? They will

perhaps remind me of the beginning of my address on "The Need and Promise of Christian Preaching" of 1922, and will reproach me with the charge that in this volume I am obviously going beyond the marginal and corrective theology of that address to a new theology of my own. They will perhaps say that the "peril of orthodoxy" which, as is well known, many have long seen over my head . . . has now transparently overtaken me. They will perhaps complain that the springtime of the "Reformation gospel" which six years ago they found it possible somewhat loudly to celebrate, has been followed all too rapidly by a dubious autumn and that I have certainly become my own enemy. What shall I reply to them? As a look back upon my course, I seem to myself as one who, ascending the dark stair case of a church tower and trying to steady himself, reached for the banister, but got hold of the bell rope instead. To his horror, he had then to listen to what the great bell had sounded over him and not over him alone. He had not wished to do this. Neither can he, nor does he wish to recall it. He has been struck by the event and will continue his ascent as best he may. If my previous labors have here and there had the effect of a marginal note and a corrective, such cannot have been my purpose . . . I do not feel myself . . . justified in taking up the prophet's mantle and to persist as a pioneer, a role in which many momentarily believed me to be cast and would, for their own joy and comfort, like to see me remain. I am an ordinary theologian. Consequently, I must take the unhappy risk which every theologian must take, namely, that he seem "to make a theology" out of the Word of God, out of the truth and reality of God's kingdom. I have, however, never been aware of doing anything else but pursuing theology—is it old? is it new?—whereas the Word of God spoke for itself, or did not speak, according as God willed.

I have since the *Commentary on Romans,* just as before it, gone my own way in the world. That meant for me simply and concretely . . . that I had to study and busy myself with Christian theology without asking myself what might come of it . . . Therefore, I may at least . . . ask whether those who are now shocked . . . ever understood that I did not then, and do not now wish to pull the bell rope; whether they ever understood that I never shared the griping against "orthodoxy" and "scholasticism" (though I did occasionally in this as in other respects howl with the wolves)? Will the bell sound another peal this time? What do I care? Why do I have to ask about that? And why do my readers? I can only ask my friends now as then to busy themselves with the problems, which, now as then, are quite earthly problems.[4]

It must be admitted that the voluminous preoccupation of this "ordinary theologian" with the "quite earthly problems" obscures for the casual, and even careful, reader of the *Römerbrief* and of the *Kirchliche Dogmatik,* the bell-rope and corrective character of this "new theology." Whether or not Barth so desired it, there can be little doubt that since the pealing of the bell, Protestant thought could no longer continue upon its previous way; could not, indeed, avoid a fundamental reorientation. Both in its polemical and in its constructive content, the theology of Karl Barth has broken fresh ground for theological thinking in the tradition of the Reformation. Insofar as the term "neo-orthodoxy" points both to the tradition of the Reformation and to this "fresh ground for theological thinking," it may be said to be correctly applied to what has happened in contemporary Protestant thought as a consequence of the work of Karl Barth and his principal associates. Orthodoxy is the concern for and the formulation of "right" or "sound" doctrine for the sake of the reliable guidance of the Christian mind and the Christian church. This does not mean that departures from orthodoxy, known as heresy, have not been fruitful in the development of theology. Indeed, heresies have been the creative catalysts of orthodoxy. To paraphrase an apt remark of Reinhold Niebuhr's, "every truth has come riding into the field of inquiry upon the back of some error."[5] Nevertheless, every responsible theology aims at orthodoxy; and the "neo-orthodox" theology is no exception to the rule. Even theological liberalism is no exception to the rule. Theological liberalism is a protest against the sterile rigidity of orthodoxy that took the quite necessary and proper form of a liberating and liberal movement for the sake of the reliable guidance of the Christian mind and the Christian church in the "sound" or the "right" way to think about the Christian faith. Liberalism found orthodoxy so heavily burdened with stagnation that it rejected the term. Similarly, Barth and his associates rejected liberalism because they regarded it as misleading of the Christian mind as was the orthodoxy which they joined the liberals in repudiating.

"Neo-orthodoxy" is thus a term which denotes the *historical* position of Barth's reorientation of the course of Protestant theology. The term (in so far as it is not a mere slogan) belongs to historical, rather than to doctrinal or systematic theology. Indeed, from a doctrinal or *systematic* point of view, the phrase "theology of crisis" more appropriately denotes what Barth and his associates are trying to say than does the term "neo-orthodoxy."[6] Nevertheless, from a historical point of view, the theologians of crisis, and all those whose theological thinking has been shaped by their work, may be said to be "neo-orthodox" in the following positive sense. *Neo-orthodoxy is the theological movement in contemporary Protestantism which seeks to correct both liberalism and the orthodoxy against which liberalism rightly protested, by a return to and a contemporary reinterpretation of the fundamental and formative significance of the Bible in the theology of the sixteenth century Reformers, chiefly of Luther and Calvin.* Neo-orthodoxy means that it is impossible rightly to guide the Christian mind and the Christian Church in our day without taking seriously the creative significance of Protestant liberalism; that it is necessary to make the return to the Reformation that liberalism wanted to make, differently than liberalism did; that authentic orthodoxy is always what the Reformers recognized it to be, namely, the exposition of the theology of the Bible in such a way as to give critical and creative meaning to the contemporary situation and to the individual who can only live in *that* and in no other situation. In a word, neo-orthodoxy is the corrective theology required by the living Word in the living church in a world in which new possibilities of meaning and behavior are always emerging on the edge of those possibilities that have become old and have played out. "Therefore, every scribe who has been trained for the kingdom of heaven is like a householder who brings out of his treasure what is new and what is old . . . And no one puts new wine into old wineskins; if he does, the wine will burst the skins, and the wine is lost, and so are the skins" (Mt. 13:52; Mk. 2:22, RSV). It may be objected that the vigorous polemic against liberalism by the theologians of crisis scarcely bears out this mellower interpretation of the relations between these two trends in contemporary Protestant thought. The reply is that one of the marks of the changing course of neo-orthodoxy is its revised regard for the liberal movement, a revision which was explicitly foreshadowed in Barth's early writing. The most moving case in point is Barth's appraisal of his esteemed theological teacher, Wilhelm Herrmann. Barth recalls the panegyric of Gregory Thaumaturgus upon Origen as the model of his own esteem for and departure from his unforgettable theological master. Barth says:

> Herrmann was *the* theological teacher of my student days . . . I came to Marburg already a convinced Marburger. And when, on the day on which I began my first pastoral ministry, five minutes before I was to enter the pulpit, the mail brought me the new fourth edition of the *Ethics* as a gift from the author, I regarded this coincidence as a consecration of the entire future. Was I self-deceived? I cannot deny that through the years I have become a somewhat peculiar Herrmann disciple. But a genuine conversion away from Herrmann, I could never inwardly concede, could not do so even today. What it really means to be the real disciple of a real master, in general, and in theology in particular, finds as yet no unanimity among scholars. As I see it, it means that I received from Herrmann something so fundamental, that thought out to all its consequences, required me afterwards to say almost everything completely differently, and eventually even to interpret differently that fundamental principle itself . . . The last direct contact that I had with Wilhelm Herrmann was in 1918, also a kind of dedication. It carried the laconic remark: "Nevertheless, with kindest regards from W. Herrmann."[7]

Certainly, from the inside—from inside Barth's epoch-making theology, which has shaped the thought of his principal associates and of many more—neo-orthodoxy is the theological elaboration of this *Nevertheless!* Orthodox?—yes!—in the sense in which Herrmann, the theological fountainhead of contemporary liberalism, especially in the United States, wrestled to bring to life the *sola gratia—sola fide* of the *fides salvifica* of the Reformation! *Nevertheless* neo-orthodox!—in the sense that what Herrmann wanted most to say, and indeed, what the Reformers themselves wanted most and most truly to say, had, just on that account, to be said in a new and different way!

The Neo-orthodox movement in Protestant thought is thus committed by its corrective character to a changing course. Despite the polemical vigor and theological bulk of over three decades of accumulating literature, the movement cannot be said to have settled down into a ready-made and rounded-out theology. This is the central thesis of this essay. It is supported, on the one hand, by the developing substance of Barth's own thought, and on the other hand, by the several lines of emphasis and debate among the theologians of crisis themselves and by those whose theological writing has been influenced by the theology of crisis.

THE CHANGING BARTH

Whatever may be the judgment of future historians of Christian thought about the theology of Karl Barth, the present judgment must be this: Barth is the most consistent Christological theologian of the church. This does not mean that his theology is consistent. Nor does it mean that other theologians have not been Christological. What it means is that no other theologian of the church has been as steadily determined to do his theological thinking with a mind single to the fact that Jesus of Nazareth lived, died, was raised from the dead, and, in the words of the Nicene Creed, "sitteth on the right hand of the Father; and he shall come again with glory, to judge both the quick and the dead; whose kingdom shall have no end."[8] The theology of Karl Barth is unique because of the persistence and comprehensiveness with which he has pursued the exploration and the implications of this Christological faith for the mind and the life of the Church. St. Thomas is really the only theologian whose work is comparable in steadfastness and range, and in aim. But the pattern is as different between Barth and St. Thomas as the competence is similar. And the pattern, of course, is decisive. For in theology, as in other disciplines of knowledge and communication, an old and tested maxim of the mind applies: *duo si dicunt idem, non est idem* [if two things say the same thing, they are not the same].[9]

As Barth sees it, the Christological faith of the church requires a christocentric theology. A christocentric theology changes fundamentally what is central and what is peripheral in the relations between God and humanity; changes also the interpretation of humanity's knowledge of God and changes the nature of theology itself. If we look at each of these alterations in turn, we shall acquire both some understanding of the formative conceptions with which Barth works and some understanding of the ways in which his thought has changed in the course of its elaboration.

CHRISTO-CENTRIC THEOLOGY CHANGES WHAT IS CENTRAL AND PERIPHERAL IN GOD'S RELATIONSHIP WITH HUMANITY

In such a theology humanity's search for God becomes peripheral; God's search for humanity becomes central. The peripheral is always fraught with distortion and leads to idolatry. The central is full of reconciliation and leads to the truth that makes humanity free. The "gospel concerning . . . Jesus Christ our Lord" (Rom. 1:3f) whose claims Paul the Apostle pressed upon the Christians in the congregation at Rome, "does not involve . . . the propagation of a personal conviction: the 'Name of the Lord' must come to light, as a sign of the truth, to the people that walk in darkness. The Roman Christians now also stand within the circle cast by the light of this sign of the truth . . . They stand, and they should stand, upon the foundation of a new relation between God and the world, objectively established in Christ; under his grace (6:1 f.) and in his peace (5:1 f.). This is the beginning and the end and the content of the letter to the Romans."[10] And this is really the beginning and the end and the content of Barth's theology. Three years later the meaning of this new relation between God and the world objectively established in Christ came more sharply into focus. "Jesus Christ our Lord," Barth wrote in the greatly revised edition of the *Commentary*:

> this is the Gospel of salvation, this is the meaning of history. In this name, two worlds meet and separate, two levels intersect, a known level, and an unknown one. The known level is the world of the "flesh" created by God but fallen from its original oneness with God, and therefore in need of salvation. This is the world of men, of time, and things; our world. This known level is intersected by another, unknown level; from the world of the Father, the world of the original creation and of ultimate redemption . . . The recognition of the point of intersection is not self-evident. The point at which the intersection is to be and will be recognized is *Jesus,* Jesus of Nazareth, the 'historical' Jesus. Jesus as an historical event *[historische Bestimmung]* means the point of separation between the world which we know and another and unknown world . . . Thus the years 1–30 are at once the time of revelation and the time of discovery.[11]

The reader who pauses long enough at this point of intersection really to take in Barth's meaning will find the main accents of Barth's thought easier to grasp than did many of his early critics. When Barth talked about God as the "wholly Other," he did not—as those who read too quickly were too quick to proclaim—destroy for humanity the possibility of knowing God. On the contrary, the conception of God as the "wholly Other" *(der ganz Andere)* expressed the sovereign freedom of God, first of all to be God in the divine relations with humanity and the world. And then, as the "wholly Other," God's initiative, not only in affecting humanity's salvation, but in any human knowledge of God, could be meaningfully affirmed and sustained. The "wholly Other" God provides, in the *Commentary on Romans,* the foundation for the radical juxtaposition of grace and faith which unhinged the church in the sixteenth century and made the Bible come alive in the recovery by the Reformers of the dynamic thrust and content of the Gospel. In the *Kirchliche Dogmatik,* the "wholly Other" God becomes the God of free and sovereign grace. This grace is "pure act" *(actus purus)*, acted (begotten) and known in the self-communication of the Divine Word.[12] Consequently, and in basic opposition to Roman Catholic thought, God is not known as the First Truth, not as the ground of all being (Being in act), but as the Lord.[13] "God is, who He is, in the act of His revelation . . . What makes God, God: the divine self-hood and discreteness *[Selbstheit und Eigentlichkeit]* the *essentia* or essence of God—will be encountered either there where God deals with us as Lord and Savior, or not at all."[14] Insofar as God, known in this way, can be brought under propositional formulation, the sentence would read: "God is He who freely loves."[15]

Similarly, when Jesus is the "point of intersection" for the knowledge of God and of faith in God, the relations between God and humanity are relations of *crisis*. When Barth talked about *crisis,* he did not mean that humanity lived, and was to go on living, in an uninterrupted dither, at the "fever pitch," as it were, of a diseased and dying existence. Nor did he mean that God's activity in the world of time and space and things was a kind of hit and run game, according to which God had already disappeared to get ready for the next blow, by the time humanity had arrived at the scene of the crash. It is true that in the *Commentary on Romans*, Barth excavates a deep gulf between God and humanity. But the chasm is not unbridged. With Barth, as with Saint Paul, Romans 8 does follow Romans 7, a succession which is not of very great arithmetical but of immense theological significance. The theological significance is that the *crisis* of human existence is not humanity's inability to search and find God. The crisis is due not to humanity's impotence but to God's attack. God's attack upon humanity and the world in Jesus of Nazareth is an act of pursuit in judgment and redemption. Every previous possibility of living and thinking and believing is shut up behind the inexorable barriers of futility and death. But these barriers are inexorable precisely because God has broken through them from the other side. The crisis of human existence is "the crisis of the attempt to live freely" *[Lebensversuch]* between the "great negative possibility" of submission and the great positive possibility of "love."[16] "But because," Barth declares:

> we shall stand before the judgment seat of "God," because this is the critical truth under which we stand, namely that God is He who elects or rejects, therefore, the "strong" (those who are "elect") have not the slightest advantage over the "weak" (those who are rejected). It is as the faithfulness of *God* that faith justifies. It is as the knowledge of *God* that human knowledge is true. It is as *God's* hope that we are saved by hope. It is as the love of *God* that love is the incomprehensible way.[17]

Thus, the *crisis* of human existence is the decision of human beings to look steadily at life from the "point of view" (Kierkegaard) of Jesus Christ and to follow what they see. It is note worthy that in the *Kirchliche Dogmatik*, the conception of *crisis* is conspicuous for its absence.[18] In Barth's systematic theology, the accent falls upon what the church has to say about God's redemptive sovereignty, active and known in the world in and through God's self-revelation in Jesus Christ. There is a striking movement of thought in these volumes away from negation towards affirmation. The most vivid instance is, perhaps, the shift from the rigor of the divine judgment with its implicit particularism to the universalism of the divine favor in and through the divine judgment.[19] But Barth himself is aware of a broader transformation of emphasis. "Nowadays," he says, "there are some who are trying to track down the secret of the alleged or real shift that I have undergone, say, between 1932 and 1938 . . . As I myself see the matter, it is comparatively simple. I have gradually (always, however, still 'eager for debate' *['freudvoll zum Streit']*) come to a deeper and deeper understanding of the affirmations by which and with which a man can live and die."[20]

Christo-centric Theology changes the Interpretation of Humanity's Knowledge of God

The affirmations by which and with which someone can live and die are based upon the knowledge of faith. Christian theology has, in the main, always insisted that faith was a special kind of knowledge. As such, faith could be opposed to other kinds of knowledge, but it never was the antithesis of knowledge itself. From the beginning of systematic reflection upon the world, the governing role in acquiring and organizing knowledge has been assigned to human reason. Consequently, there has been a perennial tension in theology between the claims of faith and the claims of reason to knowledge.

Barth has followed the main line of the theological tradition in insisting that faith is knowledge. But he has broken more sharply with the tradition than any of his predecessors in the way in which he relates the claims of faith to the claims of reason in the determination of what humanity can know and say about the ways of God.

The knowledge of faith is not a direct or immediate knowledge of God and God's ways. According to Barth (and the theologians of crisis), faith is a responding knowledge.[21] *Omnis recta cognition Dei ab obedentia nascitur* [all true knowledge of God is born of obedience], said Calvin.[22] And Barth approvingly quotes this remark in support of his insistence that "faith is a human action determined by . . . Jesus Christ, by God's gracious concern [*Zuwendung*] for man."[23] Here is the thin line which makes all the difference in the world between Barth, following the Reformers, and St. Thomas, following Augustine:

> The togetherness of God and man (that is, in the knowledge of faith) . . . is not a togetherness on the same level . . . It makes no sense to insist upon human self-determination "somehow" and even dialectically . . . over against the determination of man through the action of God. Human self-determination precisely as *determination* is subordinate to *determination by God* . . . In this relation of total subordination to and need of God's determinative action, it is impossible that human self-determination should displace the determinative action of God, as Pelagius wished; or that there should be a co-operative relation between the two, as the Semi-Pelagians wished; or as Augustine desired, that God's determinative action and man's self-determination should be secretly identified.[24]

Barth believes that it is possible and necessary to interpret the knowledge of faith quite strictly with reference to the fact that God communicates God's self in the divine Word. God has so communicated God's self and continues to do so. Obviously, such an interpretation could be expected to raise the cry of *sacrificium intellectus* from the Pelagians, the Semi-Pelagians, and the Augustinians. The objection, however, is beside the point.[25] The epistemological theory developed in the Prolegomena to Barth's theology in KD I states in a scientific and systematic theological way the position taken in the *Commentary on Romans*. In that work Barth is wrestling with the overwhelming reality of God's free and sovereign initiative in determining the human situation. The noetic character of the Word of God is overshadowed by the concern to interpret the actuality of the divine behavior. In the *Kirchliche Dogmatik* the noetic character of the Word of God is in the foreground of attention. But the closest possible connection is maintained between the Word of God as *address* and the Word of God as *deed*. How shall the human reason *not* be operative in the orbit of the divine activity, into which the whole person has been drawn, and totally? The question is not one of the denial of the human reason over against the recognition of it. It is a question of *recta cognitio,* to return to Calvin's phrase, of true knowledge over against blind knowledge, of what Luther would have called, "the bound reason" over against "the fickle and autonomous reason" (in Luther's robust language, "the whoring reason"). The business of the reason is—not to think God according to its lights—but to think God's thoughts after God.

We come now to one of the most controversial aspects of Barth's thought. And on the point at issue, Barth has made one of the major changes in his thinking. Whether the shift is one of position or of emphasis must remain a moot point, at least until the *Kirchliche Dogmatik* has been completed. So much, at any rate, is plain already: there has been a change of emphasis which changes, so to say, the center of gravity of Barth's theology. The point at issue concerns Barth's anthropology and specifically the interpretation of the human side of the knowledge of God. How is the knowledge of God to be understood from the side of the person, the knower?

The answer most consistently given to this question in the theological tradition is the answer of natural theology. Natural theology declares that the possibility of knowing God is inherent in human nature. Humanity's very being requires this possibility, if the knowledge of God is really to be *human* knowledge. There is some human organ, or structure, or capacity, which explains how humanity comes to talk about God, to know anything about God at all. Usually, this possibility of humanity to know God has been ascribed to the human reason, although occasionally the accent has fallen upon human freedom. And the theological doctrine which has usually seemed best fitted to support these claims of natural theology is the doctrine that humanity has been made in the *image of God.*

Barth categorically rejects natural theology. The chief ground for this rejection is that natural theology contradicts the Christological foundation of the Christian faith and the Christian church. Natural theology has no basis in the Bible, and in order to pull the principal peg out from under the claim that it does, Barth offers a remarkably ingenious re-interpretation of the traditional view of the image of God.[26] But the main thrust of Barth's elaborate argument in support of his rejection of natural theology is directed against the conception of the *analogy of being (analogia entis).* The analogy of being, as Barth defines it, is "the fact of a similarity between God and the creature, even in the fallen world, and consequently, of the possibility of applying (in the last analysis also ontologically) to God and to divine things, the presuppositions of profane knowledge and experience."[27] This means that between God and humanity there is continuing relationship previous to and apart from God's self-revelation in God's Word. Besides being un-Christological and un-biblical, this conception is the keystone of Roman Catholic theology, and thus especially inadmissible in any theology that seeks to be faithful to the fundamental insights of the Reformation.[28]

The rejection of an analogy of being is consistent with the sharp confrontation of the "wholly Other" God and humanity in the "crisis" of human existence set out in the *Commentary on Romans*. And on the whole, it is steadily adhered to throughout the *Kirchliche Dogmatik*. Nevertheless, as the latter work has unfolded, certain ambivalences have crept into Barth's theory of knowledge which point, if not to a change in his thought, at least to an impasse that cannot be satisfactorily overcome without a modification of the initial intransigence against natural theology. The clue to these ambivalences is supplied by the relations between Christology and anthropology in Barth's thought. "To understand God 'from the side of man,'" Barth wrote in the *Prolegomena,* "denotes either an essentially impossible procedure or one which can only be followed in the form of a Christology, not, however, in the form of an anthropology . . . There is a way from Christology to anthropology. But there is no way from anthropology to Christology."[29] And in the *Prolegomena*, this theological dictum is strictly, even pragmatically applied.

It will be recalled, that in the *Prolegomena,* Barth sets out both his doctrine of the Word of God and his doctrine of the Trinity. The doctrine of the Word of God is the epistemological result of theological reflection upon a quite pragmatic fact. In the Christian church preaching goes on, on the basis of the Bible. This verbal behavior is either a senseless action or it is the central action of the church. Barth takes the view that the verbal behavior in the Church is central because the words of the sermon and the words of the Bible point to and are based upon the verbal action of God's self-communication in Jesus Christ. "In the beginning was the Word, and the Word was with God, and the Word was God . . . And the Word became flesh and dwelt among us, full of grace and truth" (John 1:1, 14a). Common to all three kinds of speaking are the fact of *communication,* and the fact of communication in and through an *action*. What distinguishes the three kinds of speaking is the time of occurrence and the fact that God's act of self-communication is an act of self-disclosure in a living human and historical person, not in a vocalization of syllables. In the case of the sermon and the Bible, God's self-communication in Jesus Christ is pointed to through the words and signs of living human beings. There is thus a threefold action of divine self-communication which makes the Christian church the church. The several dynamic elements of this action are distinguishable, yet inseparable, and in exact correspondence with the content of what God has made known concerning God's self. "The doctrine of the Word of God in its three-fold form," Barth declares, "is the only analogy to the doctrine which will concern us fundamentally in the exposition of the meaning of revelation, namely, the doctrine of the *tri-unity of God.*"[30] The focal point of the way God makes God's self known and of what God makes known about the divine self is Jesus Christ. And the epistemological consequence is that God can be known, and in fact is known, only through God's Word:

> That the Word of God is heard and received by men can be recognized by themselves and by others only through faith. We say the same thing when we say, through the Holy Spirit . . . Of course, the Word of God is always actual in quite definite human experiences, attitudes, and thoughts, but in its own power and dignity, and not as though these human experiences, attitudes, and thoughts could certify the presence of the Word of God, not as though they were necessarily and unequivocally the signs of its reality.[31]

This may be a tenable theory of knowledge, open to a person on the way from Christology to anthropology. But it does seem to leave one who tries to deal with the knowledge of God from the side of the person, the knower, in a rather exasperating predicament. Now you have it, and now you don't! Now you see it, and now you don't! And it is because of this predicament that the ambivalences in Barth's theory of knowledge emerge.

Consider, for instance, the ambivalence in the treatment of the *analogy of being (analogia entis)*. "We do not," say Barth, "oppose the catholic doctrine of the *analogia entis* by a denial of the conception of analogy as such. What we say is that the analogy in question is not an *analogy of being* but, following Romans 12:6, the *analogy of faith:* the correspondence of the known in the act of knowing, the object of thought in the act of thinking, the Word of God in the conceived and spoken word of man . . . "[32] But in a succeeding volume of the *Kirchliche Dogmatik,* we are told that "we have no analogy on the basis of which the nature and being of God as Lord could be known."[33] It is true, of course, that the denial of analogy refers to its being burdened by association with natural theology. It is true also that the adoption of the term serves to continue the earlier allusion to the Romans passage and to express a certain kind of *relation* between God and humanity, the relation between grace and faith, rather than a correspondence of *being.* Nevertheless, it is difficult to escape the impression that Barth is trying to say more, and indeed must say more, than his presuppositions permit. In the *Prolegomena* Barth is proposing a Christological theory of knowledge which may properly find the analogy of faith more appropriate than the analogy of being. The anthropological elements in this account remain subordinate and implicit. But when the exposition moves out of the *Prolegomena* and into constructive theological formulation, the anthropological elements in the knowledge of God become explicit and press hard against their Christological barrier. As so often in Barth's analyses, everything depends upon the accents. Borrowing from his habit of accenting, we could say that: *the knowledge of God in Christ may well keep the anthropological elements in knowledge within Christological bounds; but where the knowledge of God in Christ is under discussion, the anthropological elements in knowledge have a way of breaking across the Christological barrier in the direction of a more adequate ontological foundation.*

That Barth himself is aware of this "ontological pressure" is indicated by a further ambivalence. The limitation under which human experience, attitudes, and thoughts express real knowledge of God has already been referred to. But once again, when Barth's thought moves out from the *Prolegomena* into constructive theological formulation, the accent changes:

> We can, may, and must be able to speak about the God who awakens us to faith through his revelation. Therefore, this God can, may, and must be recognized *[angeschaut]* and conceived. The limitation within which this occurs must be kept in mind. But now, we must no longer consider only the limitation but the matter itself . . . The proposition *Deus definiri nequit* [God cannot be defined] would cancel itself out if the subject of the proposition could not be understood in spite of its predicate, as knowable; and that means also as recognizable and conceivable.[34]

When Barth turns from the discussion of the doctrine of God to the doctrine of humanity, the same theme appears. The *anthropology* undertakes to be thoroughly Christological and goes so far as to assert that all our knowledge of humanity in general is unsteady and inconclusive, indeed, is without foundation and ultimate sense apart from what theology based upon the revealed Word of God tells us about the relation of Jesus to God, on the one hand, and to humanity, on the other. Weird as it sounds to our ears, accustomed as we are to hearing that Jesus is at best the quintessence of our knowledge of humanity, at worst, irrelevant to it, Barth insists that Jesus Christ is the only basis for understanding and interpreting what he calls "the phenomenology of the human."[35] And yet when Barth comes to state what he calls "the fundamental form of humanity" he proposes, as the "broadest definition," the formulation: "Humanity itself [*schlechthin*], the humanity of each man consists of the determination of his existence by the fact of togetherness with the existence of another human being."[36]

If this is merely a formal statement of theological knowledge, there is no reason in principle why theology cannot state what it knows in terms which have a quite familiar ring in quarters other than theological. Barth himself admits the possibility, although he denies that there is a necessary connection between such theological and non-theological knowledge.[37] But Barth also wants to say more than this. He wants to say not merely what in broadest terms can be known about humanity, but also what humanity actually *is*. And since this is the case, it is a matter of principle whether theology says on the basis of Jesus Christ what Kant (perhaps) and Socrates (certainly) said without him. Barth's constructive position seems here really to have come upon an impasse. Either he has altered the rigorously Christological character of his theory of knowledge, or he cannot give ontological meaning to his doctrine of humanity.[38] In either case, a major shift in Barth's thinking has occurred. In my judgment, it is too much to regard it as a shift of position, since the Christological intention continues with unabated thoroughness. The change is rather to be regarded as a shift of emphasis which changes, so to say, the center of gravity of Barth's theology. When the final volume of the *Kirchliche Dogmatik* is in, the balance may have been redressed.[39] But meanwhile it would seem that Barth's effort to give ontological persuasiveness both to his theory of knowledge and to his anthropology point away from the second, and toward the third person of the Trinity as the pivotal center of his theology.

Christo-centric Theology changes the Nature of Theology Itself

We come now to a change in Barth's thought which is a change, not of emphasis but of position. This has to do with the nature of theology. As is well known, Barth's theological method has been from the first *dialectical*. It is still dialectical. The dialectical way of thinking was first applied in a constructive way by Socrates in his battle against the Sophists. The Sophists had been in the habit of discussing problems by setting statements in opposition to each other, thereby exposing the error in the arguments of their opponents. What Socrates did was to take this method of argument by opposition and use it to expose the truth beyond the opposition, without which the argument itself was pointless. Thus, in all dialectical thinking, there is the method of juxtaposition of opposites. In the theology of Karl Barth, however, dialectical thinking is more than a rhetorical or discursive form. It is a theological form designed to express the actual character of the relations between God and humanity. Owing to the "wholly Otherness" of God and the "crisis" of human existence, the relations between God and humanity are paradoxical. God, for example, is both merciful and just, both eternal and incarnate; human beings, are both forgiven and sinful, both free and bound. These paradoxes cannot be dissolved by arranging their terms in a temporal sequence or by reducing them to a logical and more inclusive statement. One can say, for instance, that God is love, and love includes both mercy and justice; or that humanity is redeemed, and redemption includes both forgiveness and sin. But such statements express neither the exact content of biblical faith, nor the actual situation between God and humanity in the crisis of human existence. "Dialectical Theology," as Brunner succinctly puts it, "is the mode of thinking which defends this paradoxical character, belonging to faith knowledge from the non-paradoxical speculation of reason, and vindicates it as against the other."[40]

In the *Commentary on Romans,* as well as in *Die christliche Dogmatik,* Barth applies this dialectical method as though theology were, so to say, a function of the theologian. Theologians, individuals of their own time and culture, have the task of establishing the independent character of faith-knowledge based upon revelation over against, and in the midst of, other attempts to give meaning to human experience. But how could the *truth* of revelation be made *relevant* to the time and culture of the theologian without weakening the paradoxical character of the truth of *revelation?* On the other hand, if the paradoxical character of the truth of revelation were faithfully expounded, how could theologians avoid the mere repetition of biblical language, and how could theologians make meaningful contact with their own day and generation?

It is characteristic of Barth's theology that he prefers the hammer and tongs to the scissors and paste. Here is the point at which that fundamental principle which he had learned from Wilhelm Herrmann leads him to say everything differently than his revered teacher had done, even the fundamental principle itself. Herrmann wanted nothing so much as to establish the independent character of faith-knowledge. He was the great "auto-pistian," to use Barth's vivid phrase, of nineteenth century theology. But Herrmann, like his great predecessors, Albrecht Ritschl and Friedrich Schleiermacher, did not succeed in finding a platform, in the cultural situation which surrounded him, adequate for launching the rocket-power of God's free and sovereign self-communication in Jesus Christ. The orthodox Christology, to continue the metaphor, had the rocket power, though it was badly in need of improved radar equipment. Or, to take Barth's pre-nuclear metaphor, compared to Herrmann's Christology, the orthodox Christology is like a waterfall of 3,000 meters. Herrmann's Christology, on the other hand, is the hopeless attempt to drive a quiet lagoon to this height with a hand pump.[41] It was obvious to Barth as a preacher in a parish that Herrmann's theological undertaking was unworkable. It became obvious to Barth, after *Die christliche Dogmatik,* that his own efforts at a changed theological course had not gone far enough. He said of *Die christliche Dogmatik*:

> Because I can discover in that undertaking only a new promotion of the line Schleiermacher-Ritschl-Herrmann, and because in every conceivable advancement of that line, I can only discover the clear destruction of Protestant Theology and the Protestant church, because I can no longer see a third alternative . . . between the grandeur and the misery of a natural knowledge of God in the sense of the Vatican and a Protestant theology which has finally freed itself

from that secular misery by nourishing itself from its own source and standing upon its own feet, therefore, I can only say here, "No!"[42]

Theology must be rigorously Christo-centric. This means that it cannot be a function of the theologian in a particular cultural situation. Instead, theology is a function of the church. This is the really ground-breaking change in Barth's theology that appeared in the mere alteration of the title of his revised constructive theology. The theologian is concerned not with *Christian* theology, but with theology in and of the church. Therefore, Barth writes, not *christliche* but *Kirchliche Dogmatik* [not *Christian* but *Church Dogmatics*]. In the church, the theologian reflects upon the central and *church-creating* action of God in God's self-revelation in God's Word. In the church, theology can never be either identical with revelation or the servant of a tradition of revelation which is kept intact by the church for the sake of that revelation. In the church, theology becomes the critical self-reflection and conversation of the church with itself concerning the free, sovereign, and uninterrupted self-communication of God. Such a theology serves Jesus Christ in and over the church and in and for the sake of the church and the world. It is thus always open at one and the same time to the present self-communication of God in God's Word and to the God who in Jesus Christ is "the same, yesterday, and to day, and forever" (Heb 13:8). And in the theology of Barth one does indeed learn to know and to listen to the whole church thinking aloud in every generation the thoughts of God after God.

The categorical rejection both of the Vatican and the line Schleiermacher-Ritschl-Herrmann seemed at first to sever any constructive connection between Barth's theology and the cultural situation in which the theologian works. But there are many evidences that this impression was premature. One of these is Barth's political activity. Another is the importance which he assigns to the artists in the interpretation of the ethical situation with which the theologian must deal. Still a third is the charming, yet highly symbolic, ecstasy over Mozart for whom a foreground position is anticipated, rather than for Bach, when the saints of the Most High gather about the throne of the Lamb in the New Jerusalem.[43]

Perhaps the most impressive evidence of a change in Barth's thought on the question of the relation between theology and culture is indicated by his remarkably positive and articulate regard for Schleiermacher. Barth thinks that those who do not know the excellence of Schleiermacher's personal combination and exemplification of scholar, teacher, author, and preacher, can only be told to go and learn from him what culture really might be, what the theologian's cultural responsibility is. "Ever and again," he declares, "theologians ought to have a very clear picture (of this cultural responsibility) in order not to prattle, if, for example, in contrast to Schleiermacher, they wish to find the secret of Christianity beyond and above all culture."[44] Again he remarks, "no man can say today whether we have actually overcome him, or whether in spite of much loud and fundamental protest against him we are not still in the deepest sense children of his century."[45] Already in an early essay Barth had said that the attack upon Schleiermacher by Emil Brunner and himself was to be regarded as a "war of movement."[46] There can be no doubt that the first campaign of the war for the redirection of theology was a fierce and bitter opposition. But what Barth's revised estimate of Schleiermacher means is that sufficient ground has been won to make possible the extension of the conflict exactly where Schleiermacher himself had taken his stand. Barth writes:

> In the face of a widespread attitude in theological circles today it is necessary to remind ourselves clearly that it is by no means revealed to us that the nineteenth century . . . was a time during which God withdrew his hand from the Church, or that it is permitted us to assume that the nineteenth century theologians were ultimately and decisively concerned about something other than the knowledge and confession of Christian revelation.[47]

This is certainly a change of position. Whether it is an altogether new note in Barth's theology, or merely the explicit elaboration of what had always been implicit, is a minor point. The Schleiermacher episode means that Barth is himself prepared to face and to pursue in principle the responsibility of the theologian for the cultural situation of his day.

A CORRECTIVE THEOLOGY IN TRANSITION

There will, of course, always be people around who will say, "we knew it all along. The theology of crisis had sooner or later to come to its turn of the road. It would have to choose between obscurantism and the way back to culture." These people, who always recognize after the event that they were wise before the event, are what Nietzsche called, "the yesterday people." They never make any social and cultural advances but always move in to hold the gains that others have made and thereby do their best to undo them. The theology of crisis has drawn its share of scorn from "the yesterday people" but happily it has not produced them. On the contrary, the "war of movement" is still going on, and the participants in the changing course of this corrective theology are those who have been creatively indebted to the theology of Karl Barth, while at the same time going their independent ways. Indeed, insofar as movements in culture and in history can be said to have a beginning and an end, the theology of crisis in the strict sense has had a very short life.[48]

The theology which began with the *Commentary on Romans* in 1919 may be said to have ended in 1933 with the displacement of the original periodical series, *Zwischen den Zeiten* (*Between the Times*) by the series, *Theologische Existenz Heute* (*Theological Existence Today*). By this time Gogarten and Brunner had separated from the consistent Christological position adhered to by Barth and Thurneysen, and Rudolf Bultmann's always somewhat remote connection with the original movement was becoming remoter still. The neo-orthodox movement in contemporary theology had itself turned a corner and entered upon a still unsettled way. If we add to those already named, the names of Reinhold and Richard Niebuhr and Paul Tillich, especially because of their connection with the theological situation in the United States, we may note at least some of the problems that confront the theologian of today and tomorrow. It would not be correct to represent Karl Barth as having originated these problems that have since been taken up by the other theologians mentioned. But it can be said that the problems now pressing for theological attention and solution have become the formidable problems that they are because Barth ventured to turn the course of Protestant theology sharply from its previous way. The theologians mentioned belong to the neo-orthodox movement because with Barth they recognize the importance and necessity of the turn given to theology by the *Commentary on Romans* and because they have entered into vigorous debate with Barth over these problems and on a level which presupposes Barth's creative work.

The changing course of Barth's thought has given rise at least to three fundamental problems that are now engaging neo-orthodoxy in transition. One of these problems is the problem of communication; another is the problem of culture; and a third is the problem of hermeneutics. *The problem of communication* is the problem of the possibility and the terms of meaningful thinking and speaking about the God who is revealed in Jesus Christ. It is a form of the problem of the relation between Christology and anthropology and of the problem of the analogy of being so sharply raised by Barth's analysis. As is well known, the break between Brunner and Barth came over Barth's refusal to face the question of a "point of contact" in theological knowledge between God and humanity.[49] And Brunner has since been engaged in trying to draw a sharp distinction between natural theology and the revelation in creation in order to overcome the anthropological and epistemological impasse of Barth's position. Richard Niebuhr has proposed a contextual theory of knowledge which, with Barth, acknowledges the confessional character of theological knowledge, but he draws a less marked distinction between the situation of the believer in the church and the situation of the believer in the world than Barth tends to do.[50] Paul Tillich has frankly begun his systematic theology with an attempt to clarify the terminological ground so that the theologian may say meaningfully whatever said. Like Barth, Tillich is concerned to stress the independent and initiating character of *kerygmatic* theology. But unlike Barth, he thinks that theology must also have an *apologetic* character, chiefly because the theologian uses language which the non-theologian also uses. If theology is not to be reduced to semantics, it must face the ontological problem implicit in all communication.[51]

The problem of culture is the problem of the relevance of the insights of a theology based upon revelation to the total life of humanity, and the ground for this relevance. This has been, of course, the great concern of Reinhold Niebuhr. Niebuhr shares with Barth the conviction that the Biblical revelation does contain primary and independent insights for the interpretation of the total life of humanity. But he thinks that Barth refuses to see that the question of the relevance of theological statement is part of the truth of theological statement, at least to the extent that the truth of theology cannot properly be understood unless its relevance is directly considered while that truth is being thought about and formulated. For Niebuhr the biblical view of Christ as the "wisdom of God" and "the power of God" makes this connection between truth and relevance a Christological necessity.[52] A theology which satisfactorily grasps and states this connection will, in Niebuhr's view, be more relevant to the heights and depths of humanity's cultural existence than alternative attempts to give meaning to human life.

The problem of hermeneutics is the problem of how to understand and to communicate the Bible. Obviously, it is a form of the problem of communication. But it deserves special notice in this connection not only because of the running debate still going on between Barth and Bultmann over biblical interpretation but because the neo-orthodox movement in theology has raised afresh the whole issue of biblical interpretation. Neo-orthodoxy has rejected biblical literalism and transcended biblical criticism in such a way that the problem of a meaningful contemporary interpretation of the Bible has become an urgent one. Bultmann has been particularly concerned about the gulf between the Bible and the modern person, owing to the cosmological outlook of the Bible, particularly of the New Testament. He wants accordingly to "demythologize" the Bible, that is, to show the anthropological rather than the cosmological validity of the Biblical message concerning Jesus Christ. Barth, on the other hand, while agreeing with Bultmann's concern, insists that Bultmann interprets the Bible by means of categories which distort the Christ event and belong more appropriately to existential philosophy (especially to Heidegger) than to the Christological witness of the Bible itself.[53]

It is plain that these are inter-related problems. But their present significance for the ongoing story of contemporary theology is that these problems have acquired fresh and central importance owing to the impact of a corrective theology, and that the work of correction is still going on. Had not Barth himself said at the beginning of his theological work that theology "loses its meaning the moment it becomes more than a note, and takes up space as a new theology next to the others?"[54]

NOTES

1. Published in *Theology Today* 13, no. 3 (1956): 332–57; reprinted with permission.
2. Karl Barth, "The Need and Promise of Christian Preaching," in *The Word of God and the Word of Man,* trans. Douglas Horton (Boston: The Pilgrim Press, 1928), 100, 101, 103.
3. Barth, "Need and Promise of Christian Preaching," 98.
4. Barth, *Die christliche Dogmatik im Entwurf,* Preface, ix, x.
5. [Editorial: No citation given in the original.]
6. Theologians of crisis prefer a different designation: "I have often been asked what 'dialectical theology' is really driving at. The question can be easily answered. It is seeking to declare the *Word* of the Bible to the *world.* If it be further asked why it is called 'dialectical theology' or 'the theology of crisis,' the answer is not so simple. Neither Barth nor I nor any other member of our group has conferred on it this title. Our only possible name for it would be 'the theology of the Bible' or "Christian theology.'" Emil Brunner, *The Word and the World* (New York: Scribner's Sons, 1931), 6.
7. Karl Barth, *Die Theologie und die Kirche* (München: Chr. Kaiser, 1928), 240f.
8. See Philip Schaff, *Creeds of Christendom with a History and Critical Notes II* (New York: Harpers, 1919), 57 ff.
9. Literally translated, "If two say the same, it is not the same." Origin obscure.
10. Barth, *Der Römerbrief* (Bern: G. A. Baeschlin, 1919), 3.
11. Barth, *Der Römerbrief,* 5th ed. (München: Chr. Kaiser, 1922–29), 5.
12. Barth, *KD* I/1, 41ff.
13. Barth, *KD* I/1, 323 ff. See also Barth, *KD* II/1, 306ff.
14. Barth, *KD* II/1, 293
15. Barth, *KD* II/1, 288ff.
16. Barth, *Römerbrief,* 5th ed., 459–510.
17. Barth, *Römerbrief,* 5th ed., 498.
18. This is particularly notable in the anthropology, *KD* III/2, 1948. I believe the word "crisis" does not appear in the *Dogmatik* at all in the sense in which the term is used in the *Commentary on Romans.*
19. Barth, *KD* II/2; for instance, p. 35.
20. Barth, *KD* III/4, ix.
21. Brunner cites Kierkegaard's statement that "the position that God can be known directly is heathenism." Barth, *KD* III/4, 6.
22. John Calvin, *Institutio Religionis Christianae,* I.6.2.
23. Barth, *KD* I/1, 16–17.
24. Barth, *KD* I/1, 208. Parenthesis mine. For Barth's fully developed critique of Augustine on this point, see Barth, "Zur Lehre vom heiligen Geist," *Zwischen den Zeiten,* no. 1 (1930): 39ff.

25. See Barth, *KD* II/1, 7f., where Barth discerningly shows that the charge of a *sacrificium intellectus* really applies to those who wish to interpret the knowledge of God in terms of the knowledge of humanity.

26. Barth, *KD* III/1, 205ff.

27. Barth, *KD* I/1, 40.

28. Barth, *KD* II/1, 274ff.

29. Barth, *KD* I/1, 135.

30. Barth, *KD* I/1, 124–125. See also Barth, *KD* II/1, 73.

31. Barth, *KD* I/1, 190–191.

32. Barth, *KD* I/1, 257. The Romans passage reads: "Having gifts that differ according to the grace given to us, let us use them: if prophecy, in proportion to our faith" (κατὰ τὴν ἀναλογίαν τῆς πίστεως).

33. Barth, *KD* II/1, 82.

34. Barth, *KD* II/1, 254.

35. Barth, *KD* II/1, 220.

36. Barth, *KD* III/2, §44.2.

37. Barth, *KD* III/2, 290.

38. Barth, *KD* III/2, 109–10.

39. Brunner thinks that Barth's doctrine of humanity changes from the position taken in the earlier volumes, which is more than a change of emphasis. He goes too far, however, in supposing that Barth has come around to Brunner's own anthropological view. See Emil Brunner, *Die christliche Lehre von Schöpfung und Erlösung: Dogmatik II* (Zürich: Zwingli, 1950), 93.

40. There are hints of such a redress of balance in a passage *KD* I/1, 190–91, and many others that could be offered.

41. See Barth, *Theologie und Kirche*, 276.

42. Barth, *KD* I/1, viii.

43. Compare, for instance, Barth's political position in *Theologische Existenz Heute*, Heft I, 1933, with that in the little treatise on *Church and State* (London: S.C.M., 1939). On ethics, see Barth, *KD* II/2, 600–603. On Mozart, see Karl Barth, *Die protestantische Theologie im 19. Jahrhundert*, 49ff. There is a charming and characteristically ingenious epigram at the close of "A Letter of Thanks to Mozart," which Barth wrote from Basel on December 23, 1955. "How it is with music, where you now are," Barth remarks, "I can only guess in outline. Once I ventured . . . to put it like this: that I am not absolutely certain whether the angels, when they are engaged in praising God, play Bach—but I am certain that when they are among themselves, they do play Mozart, and that when they do, God also likes especially to listen to them." Karl Barth, *Wolfgang Amadeus Mozart, 1756/1956* (Zollikon: EVZ, 1956), 13.

44. Barth, *Die protestantische Theologie*, 388. Parenthesis mine.

45. Barth, *Die protestantische Theologie*, 380.

46. Barth, *Theologie und Kirche*, 189.

47. Barth, *Die protestantische Theologie*, 13.

48. That is, in the sense of the theology of the small group of those who gathered around Barth at the beginning of his attempt to break new ground in contemporary theology.

49. See Karl Barth and Emil Brunner, *Natural Theology*, trans. P. Fraenckel (London: Centenary Press), 1946.

50. See Richard Niebuhr, *The Meaning of Revelation* (New York: Macmillan, 1941).

51. Paul Tillich, *Systematic Theology,* Vol. 1 (Chicago: The University Press, 1951).

52. See Reinhold Niebuhr, *The Nature and Destiny of Man,* 2 vols. (New York: Charles Scribner's Sons, 1941, 1943), especially Vol. 2, chapter 4.

53. See Werner Bartsch, *Kerygma und Mythos* Vol. II (Hamburg: Volksdorf, 1952), 102- 125. Also and especially, Karl Barth, *Rudolf Bultmann, Ein Versuch ihn zu Verstehen,* Theologische Studien, Heft 34, (Zürich: Zollikon, 1952).

54. Barth, "The Need and Promise of Christian Preaching," 98.

Chapter 21

Law as a Function of Forgiveness (1959)[1]

My remarks are intended as a commentary on the theme "Love for Justice," and the rubric under which I venture to suggest that a commentary might be made is this: *Law, as a function of forgiveness.*

Let me begin by saying some things about the problem before us and the thesis which I should like to try to make sense of. The problem, as I see it, is something like this: Love and justice are words which connote the behavior of Christians in the world. They are not the only words of this kind. Meekness, humility, forbearance, faith, obedience—these are also words which connote the behavior of Christians in the world. But love and justice come into a central position because of the many sidedness and the complexity of the relationships in which Christians are involved in the world and in the midst of which Christians have to behave. This is why it is misleading and even false to suggest, as Emil Brunner does, that love is appropriate to relationships between one person and another, whereas justice is appropriate to relationships involving three or more persons.[2] It is misleading also to say that love has to do with humanity's relation to God and to neighbor, on this one-to-one basis, and justice with humanity in society. It is also misleading to say that love is an impossible possibility with justice as a chastened second best, or that justice is no part of Christian behavior and that the Christian has only one thing to do, and that is to love. Ernst Troeltsch has pointed out that Christians found themselves in a singularly difficult and even regrettable situation when the intimate relationship between Jesus and his initial disciples was broken. On the one hand, Jesus's death deprived his disciples of an immediate love relationship to him and thus to one another; and on the other, the impulse toward the Christian mission turned the attention of the disciples towards the world around them. Consequently, Christians found themselves, as it were, with both the gospel and the world on their hands. What Troeltsch calls the "love individualism and universalism" characteristic of the relations between

Jesus and his disciples became enormously complicated by the problem of continuing to live as Christians in an un-Christian world.[3] One problem at a time would have been more than enough, but to have to deal both with the gospel *and* with the world was more than at the moment it seemed that even God could handle.

It is not strange, therefore, that the early Christians should have cast about for some bridge between the gospel of love and life in the world, and should have attempted to explore the possibilities offered by their cultural environment, chiefly, the Stoic doctrine of a law of nature, the content of which could be defined in terms of justice. Thus love and justice came to take up separate dwelling places, separate centers of activity, separate spheres of operation. Love was the "law" of life as regards human responsibility towards God and towards neighbors individually. Justice was the "law" of life as regards human activities in the world.

It may be that this early Christian predicament has largely shaped the tendency to relate love and justice to each other by means of the conjunction "and." I am, therefore, the more grateful to my colleague on the panel for having insisted that the theme go the other way around. Mr. Berman is right that the proper way to put the matter is "love for justice." Love and justice became the conventional way of putting it owing to the way in which the problem arose, and because of the obvious fact that there was and is a tension between the two. Love and justice are not identical. But love for justice is the correct way to put it because both love and justice have been persistent parts of the Christian's obligation in the world from the beginning, and also because Christianity has never been able to drop the one in favor of the other. Whenever the Christian mind has gotten too exercised about justice, it has been brought up sharply on the side of love, and whenever it has gotten too preoccupied with love, somebody has always stood up in the name of justice. I once heard a distinguished member of the theological faculty of this university say that what this country needs is less prophets and more apostles; and after that gets said for a while, somebody comes along and says that what the world needs is less apostles and more prophets. This shift of emphasis is inevitable because the crucial problem is not *whether* Christians are involved in love and justice, but rather *how* the Christian's love *for* justice is to be expressed in the world.

I

Broadly speaking, the attempt of the Christian mind to explain how the Christian's love for justice is to be expressed in the world has taken the form of some account of the relation between love and law. But today we are in a situation in which both from inside the Christian tradition and from outside, previous and prevailing Christian attempts to state the relation between love and law are under re-examination. They are under re-examination from *inside* the Christian tradition for a number of reasons. There is, first of all, the criticism which the Reformation itself made of the Catholic tradition—polemicized and polarized, but also illuminated by the contrast between faith and works, between biblical law and natural law. There is, moreover, and this is a point not to be overlooked, the criticism of the Catholic tradition by Catholic moralists themselves who are as uneasy as many Protestants are about the formalistic and schematic way in which conventional Catholic thought has stated the relationship between love and law. And thirdly, there is the criticism both of the Catholic tradition and of the Reformed tradition that has emerged in the wake of a renewed biblical scholarship, in the wake of dialectical theology, and in the wake of a new and lively debate over the role of metaphysics in theology anyhow. From outside the Christian tradition, pressure upon the previous and prevailing statement of the relation between love and law has been increasing, owing to the positivist development both in philosophy and in law; owing also to the rise of existentialism, and of the very real and inescapable moral disillusionment overtaking two generations of humanity that had hardly forgotten one world war when another one took its place. And then there is a further reason, namely, the not inconsiderable importance to be attached to the dynamism and the complexity of change in a technological society. Change has always been with us, but I should think not at so great a rate nor with so wide a scope as now.

Now this dissatisfaction with and re-examination of the traditional way of stating the relationship between love and law has brought our problem to a certain impasse. From the side of law, there is an impasse between natural law on the one hand, and positive law on the other; an impasse between the universal and directive principles of order on the one hand, and the particular and changing relationships of human life in communities and states on the other. From the side of Christian thought, there is an impasse between love and justice, between gospel and law, which, if it does not take the form of a clear antithesis between them, takes at least the form of a widespread confusion about them. And from the side of the ordinary but not insignificant simple-minded Christian there is an impasse between what one believes and in consequence believes one ought to do, on the one side; and what one finds oneself able to do and actually doing, on the other. This conference itself is a reassuring sign that lawyers are as vexed, if not more vexed, than are clergy about this impasse between faith and behavior, between belief and practice.

In trying to find a way out of this impasse, I should like to make a very tentative proposal. My hope would be that such a proposal would enable us to arrive at a statement of the relation between love and law that does express, however inadequately, the Christian's love for justice. Such a statement—and this would be a further hope—might also lead us beyond the impasse between natural and positive law. Some years ago, I had an instructive conversation with the President of the Constitutional Court of the West German Republic. He was commenting upon the enormous difficulties that German society in general, and lawyers in particular, were finding in discovering any persuasive basis in terms of which people in their country could be encouraged to take their social responsibility seriously. The moral and legal vacuum in Germany immediately after the war seemed to be complete. Then he said, with some emphasis, "Of course, there is only one basis in terms of which this can be done." And to the question what that basis was, he replied, "The principle that man is made in the image of God and therefore is a creature of reason and responsibility." I did not know what his confessional position was, but I learned afterwards, not to my surprise, that he was a practicing Roman Catholic.

Of course, this is just where the impasse begins. A principle as basic to human nature as the image of God ought to shape behavior so effectively as to prevent the conflict between responsibility and practice. Yet nothing is more obvious than the failure of faith and of reason at precisely this point. A different kind of attempt to express what the Christian's love for justice involves could scarcely fail more conspicuously, and so I submit for your critical examination and reflection the following proposal: *That the Christian's love for justice is authentically expressed in the concern for, and in the implementation of, law as a function of forgiveness.* Expressed in this way, love for justice is faithful to the gospel, that is, this way of looking at law makes sense of the human situation, as that situation is brought about and shaped by what God has done for humanity in Jesus Christ. To put it another way, what gives human reality and meaning to the situation in which human beings finds themselves is that humanity is now always in the same world in which Jesus also has been and is.

All of humanity is involved in the situation defined by the gospel. But those who have been baptized—*they* are in special trouble! For they are not only caught in the human situation wherein humanity stands or falls by coming to terms with Jesus Christ. They are caught in addition with the responsibility for showing in behavior how the living presence of Jesus Christ and human fulfillment go together. "Do you not know that all of us who have been baptized into Christ Jesus were baptized into his death? We were buried therefore with him by baptism into death, so that as Christ was raised from the dead by the glory of the Father, we too might walk in newness of life" (Rom 6:3–4).

Our parents—in so far as they were not merely superstitious—undoubtedly thought they were doing us a favor by bringing us to baptism. And so they were. But what they may not have seen so clearly was that the favor is loaded with risks which we have been having to run ever since. The "nurture and admonition of the Lord," as the baptismal pledge puts it, is quite a training course.

To say that the Christian's love for justice is authentically expressed when law is understood as a function of forgiveness is not only faithful to the gospel, it is also workable. It is workable in the sense that such a statement, or such a view of law, make sense both of what the believer and the lawyer are doing in the world. Law must be viewed as a function of forgiveness because *justice, rightly understood, transmutes love into forgiveness and transmutes law into an instrument of reconciliation.*

Now that requires a bit of commentary, so let me try to explicate what this little thesis is about.

II

It may be helpful to begin by recalling an historical memory or two about the Christian meaning of law. We have already noted that the crucial problem involved in the Christian's love for justice was not *whether*, but *how* this love was to be expressed in the world. There have been at least three formative attempts to express the Christian's love for justice, three Christian meanings of law.

The first proceeds from the relationship between covenant and law. Law is the way in which God's will is expressed for humanity and the world because of a particular relationship between God and the world. This relationship is called a covenant. The covenant is a relationship compounded of God's initiative and human response and involves an agreement to be and to stay on speaking terms with each other. Law expresses both the fact that God expects certain things, indeed commands them (obedience) and the fact that God has made clear God's will to humanity (revelation). Now, unfortunately, this connection between covenant and law has tended to give a certain pre-eminence to the prescriptive character of law. The law is stated in certain propositions. These, when collected together, acquire a certain codified character. Thus, all decent Christians have learned, in one form or another, a kind of catechism of faith and behavior in which the Decalogue has loomed large. (Those Christians who have missed out on the catechism are not indecent, but under-nourished).

But the consequence of this prescriptive character of the law has been that the really *permissive* nature of the law has been obscured. All statements of the law are really meaningful in a particular context. Semitic colleagues tell me that even the "thou shalt," "thou shalt not" form of the Decalogue is not a prescriptive form basically. It is simply a statement of what points to a certain context, and the context is, in broadest terms, a relationship of loyalty and trust between the "Lord of the land" and the "people of the land." In the case of the Hebrew people, the "Lord of the land" was the "God of the people," and the "people of the land" were the "people of the covenant," chosen by this God for a particular destiny in the world. Thus the Decalogue presupposes and points to a relationship of trust in God, and of loyal and willing obedience to the God trusted in. The inner logic of the "thou shalt" and "thou shalt not" runs something like this: since God has permitted you to be in relation with God, and since you have accepted this relationship as the basis of your life, the charter of your freedom and responsibility is as follows. It is not accidental that the whole Decalogue is a commentary upon the first commandment, "I am the Lord thy God; thou shalt have no other gods before me." This "Old Covenant" connection between covenant and law was transformed, then, in the "New Covenant" into the connection between law and gospel. Obviously there was something new in the gospel, so it was not strange that one should have thought of it as a "new law" in contrast to an "old law," and should have regarded this "new law" as the fulfillment of the "old law." But the question that now pressed for an answer was, in what sense the gospel fulfilled the law, in what sense the new law consummated the old. This question still haunts Christian ethical theory. That love is the fulfillment of law is easy enough to affirm, but it is not so easy to know what the affirmation involves.

The second Christian meaning of law may be denoted by the phrase "natural law." In his incredibly instructive account of the development of medieval political theory in the West, A. J. Carlyle remarks that somewhere between Alexander the Great and the Christian era the discovery was made that human beings are homogeneous and rational, or as Cicero put it, that human beings are alike because they are rational and capable of virtue.[4] This discovery eventually took the form of the doctrine that there was a law, at once of reason and of nature, that is human nature. The law was understood as a universal principle of human order and fulfillment, to which all humanity give assent as rational creatures, and the purpose of which was to fashion morals. This was called the "law of nature," or the "law of reason and nature," or "natural law," and in its Latin form *lex naturae*, came to be used as a "technical term" in social and political ethics, both Christian and secular. But what is equally important and interesting is that on the whole this particular universal principle was given a specific content, chiefly the content of justice. In general, a Christian during the Middle Ages would have thought of *love* as the central content of "divine law" and *justice* as the central content of "natural law." And justice, in turn, tended to be specified in the formative terms of Cicero: "Justice is giving every man his due." The principle of the *suum cuique* served as the bond of civil society and could perform this function because of the foundation and framework of natural law upon and within which it was conceived. Law, in this sense, has a Christian meaning not because it originated with Christianity, but because Christianity took it over from Stoicism and allowed it the most persistent and persuasive influence upon the Christian mind of all the meanings of law.

There is, however, a third Christian meaning of law, and this has taken the form of a doctrine of the uses of the law, a doctrine which was developed because even the most generous Christian mind never could quite equate natural law with love, or the fulfillment of the law of love with the keeping of the Ten Commandments. Indeed, Christian thought had to work out some kind of relationship between love and law which took account of natural law, of the Decalogue, and of the Sermon on the Mount. The attempt took the form of a doctrine of the so-called threefold use of the law. The first, or *political*, use of the law was the general recognition that after all the world and society seemed to hang together and not blow apart. It was the political use of the law which explained the structure and order of human life in the world, as well as the restraint of anarchy. The second, or *pedagogical*, use of the law was the recognition that somehow people in the act of behaving required directives to steer by in order to move from a "given" order to a "better" order. These directives were always ultimately supported by the fact that if human beings could not manage order and justice by the "responsible route," they were certain to have to come to terms with order and justice by the "punitive route." But short of so drastic a remedy, humanity could be guided by more salutary and rational (and thus also educative) regulations for living as human beings in the world. The third, or *didactic*, use of the law was reserved for Christians only. Under the gospel of love and motivated by love, Christians were able to accept and implement what the political and pedagogical uses of the law were getting at. Christians did not need the external prodding, gentle or severe, which ordered the behavior of unbelievers, since Christians had moved beyond the temptation to act as though they were a law unto themselves. Being transformed by love, Christians so trusted God and so lived in loyalty to God's will and purpose as to be able to follow Augustine's maxim: "love and do what you will" (*dilige et quod fac vis*).[5]

Indeed, it was the particular wisdom and insight of St. Augustine to make one of the most illuminating and constructive criticisms of the classical tradition of natural law with its conception of justice that has come down to us. Augustine *accepted* the classical conviction that justice was the foundation of civil society, but he felt that Cicero had really not quite got at what justice was about. So long as justice could be interpreted in terms of giving every person his due, Augustine argued, thieves could be regarded also as a civil society because they at least gave each other their due, and thus by that definition there could be a commonwealth of thieves, which Augustine found a contradiction in terms. Accordingly, he re-stated the meaning of justice and its relation both to society and to love. Civil society, Augustine argues, is not based on the principle of giving every person his due, but is based upon the principle of what human beings love. Augustine distinguishes between two kinds of societies, those societies which are informed by the love of power, and those societies which are informed by the power of love, and he works out an incredibly penetrating elaboration of the way human society looks from the point of a view of love as a bond of civil society.[6] Augustine, of course, got the hint from the Bible, and his description of these two societies is heavily informed by biblical imagery and imagination.[7] But the important point is that justice becomes here the form of love which expresses the right ordering of human relations with reference to God's order and purpose, and this is why Augustine could say, "love and do what you will"—not because he was a relativist, not because he was a positivist, but because he recognized that in a context in which love is regarded as the fabric of society, this is how people could, *in fact*, and must, *in fact*, behave in their dealings with one another.

Well, the Reformation picked up this Augustinian lead, and provided a radically revised notion of the social context of the Christian's behavior and of the "rules" by which the Christian behaves. The Reformation doctrines of the communion of saints and of the forgiveness of sins supply the links between our time and the Augustinian insight into society based on and held together by the power of love. Thus for Luther, law, like gospel, is a function of the Holy Spirit which frees one from all prescriptive regulations which get in the way, frees one to be oneself before God, and oneself before one's neighbor; and with Calvin, law is again given its covenantal setting and context. But the Reformers were wiser than they were bright. What they overlooked was that they had really broken with the whole prescriptive way of expressing the Christian's love for justice, and instead of pushing through to the point to which their insight led, they backed away from it and fell back upon the tradition of natural law. They continued the tradition of the three uses of the law, with the result that the ethos of the Reformation was more prescriptive than permissive, more restricting than liberating, more conservative than experimental. When one considers the social attempt of Calvinism in a theocratic context, and the equally unhappy connection between calling and office which informs Lutheran ethics, one begins to understand how fully the Reformation, both in its Calvinist and Lutheran forms, had laid aside the insight into the significance of forgiveness for the community of faith and perhaps also for the human community. The Reformers came down on the side of tyranny, rather than risk anarchy, of order rather than of liberty, or preserving the stability of the *status quo* rather than of exploring the bearing of the forgiveness of sins upon the whole life of humanity. So we must take up the task of finishing what the Reformers started, and this is why I venture to speak of law as a function of forgiveness.

III

When law is a function of forgiveness, justice comes into its rightful relationship with respect to love. I say justice transmutes love into forgiveness. This is the way love really takes on flesh and blood. Those of us who have parental responsibilities know that one can never cut the cake straight—impossible! What happens is that by trial and error the biggest piece gets passed around from time to time so that the same child does not get the biggest piece every time. But the real problem is how to keep the confidence of the child who this time was left out, that the next time injustice will be set right. This is the problem, and if the child takes the parental word for it, this is an act not of justice, but of trust. This is an act of forgiveness which has become a concrete and inescapable thing in a situation in which justice has simply not been done. Or again, there are a good many people who believe in racial equality so long as property contracts are not involved. Restrictive covenants are a concrete instance in which the issue of justice raises acutely the question whether love for the Negro is so much rhetoric or is actually being implemented in relationships between people where they count—not where they are talked about, but where they count. All other talk about love is sentimental or abstract, and law is the critical case in point, because law is the point at which the reconciliation which is the fruit of love becomes concrete.

I happened the other day to be involved in a conversation with a banker. He was telling me about a situation in which he had recently become involved because somebody had signed a rental agreement, and the property, at the time of occupancy, was for reasons of negligence unoccupiable. The rental agreement was unilaterally cancelled. The bank was ordered to stop payment on the check but forgot to stop the payment. Now there was a day when such an error would have so called in question the honor of the bank as to require the bank's assumption of the loss. This was essentially the point of view of the older official in the bank. But what particularly interested me was the difference between the older and the younger bank official in dealing with such a problem. The younger official said, "We have looked over this matter, and find that the order for stopping payment was, in effect, not technically according to the law." The order was not "a legal instrument"—that was the poetic phrase—and thus "since the mistake was partly the fault of the bank and partly the fault of our client, let's split the difference." Meantime, the fellow who owned the house had indicated that the happiest solution would be for himself, as well as the bank's client, to charge it up to experience. Now here was a situation in which everybody stepped gingerly, and held off everybody else at arms length, and finally capitulated to the fact that it was too expensive to get justice. Quite apart from the possible outcome of a trial had one been attempted, the point of the episode in this connection is that it underlines the delicate relation and precarious balance between justice and forgiveness in the most ordinary dealings of people with each other. Outside the context of the link between justice and forgiveness, love is very remote indeed from the operational level of human behavior.

The point I want to make is: the law is the instrumentality which makes reconciliation either a fiction or a human bond. Without that kind of painstaking, detailed, concrete human inter-relatedness, all talk about love is abstract or sentimental. In his little preparatory paper, Professor Jones, you remember, calls attention to the agency of decision which every judge has to make and which every lawyer professionally has to make, a decision which is quite independent of the material circumstances of any given case or any given trial.[8] What Professor Jones wants to know is what light the judge is going to get for such agony of decision, and from whence he is going to get it. Apparently, the judge does not get this kind of light prescriptively. My thesis is that he gets it from his baptism, if he remembers he is baptized into the community of the death and resurrection of Christ, where love is no formula, but a concrete, fact relating God to humanity, and human beings to human beings. In this framework, he is oriented toward the difficult, exasperating, even frustrating, but basically sustaining, task of expressing his love through the practice of justice.

IV

A final word as a kind of vocational epilogue: What this *might* mean is that lawyers have a better chance of being Christians than theologians do. What it *does* mean is that they are no more or no less Christians than are theologians as regards responsibility for law. What differentiates lawyers from the rest of us is that lawyers are the specialists in the instrumentality of law in its relation to reconciliation. *Love functions as forgiveness, and law is the instrumentality through which justice becomes the concrete occasion and context of reconciliation.* This kind of approach to law delivers us from the pride and from the despair which always gather around some perfectionist view of how we ought to love. Love transmuted into forgiveness, and law as the instrumentality of reconciliation, deliver us from the self-justification and futility that always lead us to want to hold on to a certain structure and certain precedents because they have always worked, and to be impervious to the kind of experimental risks on behalf of new precedents and new structures of human relationships. As an old pietistic hymn somewhat sentimentally but profoundly puts it:

> Trust and obey, for there is no other way,
> To be happy in Jesus, but to trust and obey.[9]

Or as Mr. W. H. Auden more robustly and magnificently puts it at the close of his celebration of the Incarnation:

> He is the Way.
> Follow Him through the Land of Unlikeness;
> You will see rare beasts and have unique adventures.
> He is the Truth.
> Seek Him in the Kingdom of Anxiety;
> You will come to a great city that has expected your return for years.
> He is the Life.
> Love Him in the World of the Flesh;
> And at your marriage all its occasions shall dance for joy.[10]

NOTES

1. Published in *Oklahoma Law Review 12*, no.1 (1959): 102–12; reprinted with permission.

2. Emil Brunner, *Justice and the Social Order* (London: Lutterworth Press 1949), 127–28.

3. Ernst Troeltsch, *The Social Teaching of the Christian Churches* (New York: Macmillan, 1931), 58–66.

4. R. W. Carlyle and A. J. Carlyle, *A History of Medieval Political Theory in the West* (Edinburgh: William Blackwood and Sons, 1936), 503ff.

5. Homilies on the first epistle of John, VII, 8 (Nicene and Post-Nicene Fathers ed. 1888).

6. Augustine, *The City of God*, book XIX (Dod's ed. 1876).

7. Augustine, *The City of God*, books XV–XVII.

8. Harry W. Jones, "Christian Ethics and Law in Action" (1953) (distributed to conference participants in mimeographed form).

9. [Editorial: These Lyrics by John Henry Sammis (1846–1919); music by Daniel Brink Towner (1850–1919).]

10. Final chorus in "For the Time Being," *W.H. Auden Collected Poems* (1976), 308.

Chapter 22

No Uncertain Sound! (1973)[1]

> For if the trumpet gives an uncertain sound who shall prepare himself to the battle? (1 Cor 14:8)

Today, gratitude for opportunities and tasks accomplished comingles with a touch of pain at separation. We cross a boundary from a more or less familiar place of focus and fulfillment to a place of strangeness and uncertainty. The future is open enough and evokes from us a certain fascination and even eagerness—which futures are designed to do. The taking of risks is our destiny, as Mr. T. S. Eliot has observed. But just *there* a disquieting option lurks: "whether to put on proper costumes or huddle quickly into new disguises."[2] For if the trumpet give an uncertain sound, who shall prepare himself to the battle?" So—you are to prepare yourselves—or, as the Greek original more vividly expresses it—you are to make ready for the battle towards which you are moving—with no uncertain sound![3]

INAUSPICIOUS TIMES

The times are never as auspicious as the making ready to the battle seems to require. Your ties are no exception. In 1973, an elaborate, logistically staggering conclave of religious curiosity, scholarship, and exploration assembled at the Century Plaza Hotel in Beverly Hills. The gathering was an "International Congress of Learned Societies in the Field of Religion," no less; and its theme was *Religion and the Humanizing of Man*. "How appropriate that the cover artist should symbolize our theme—as a butterfly!," said the Frontispiece of the 125-page Program Brochure. "For the Aztecs," the symbolization continues:

the God of the renewal of the sacred, is pictured as a butterfly. Some northwestern American Indians imagine the authentically human (which is to say, religious) man as embodying a soul visually represented as a butterfly. The butterfly is a family god in Samoa; in German folklore it is the source of babies and new life. Among some African tribes the butterfly is a totem object, . . . in Hawaii and Melanesia . . . the image of life for the death. In sum, the butterfly is the archetypal image of spirit, both in man and man's religions. Perhaps this is the reason Aristotle, Theophrastus, and Plutarch use the Greek word *psyche* (soul) to mean 'butterfly.' Perhaps this is the reason Job's Eliphaz likens God to a moth. Perhaps this is also the reason Jesus, in a cultural context in which the moth is synonymous with destruction, locates the treasure of the kingdom where moths do not corrupt.[4]

There you have it! The diverse ministries, on the threshold of which you stand, may be pursued "under the long forgotten but archetypally generative sign of the spirit's vitality," underwritten by Texas oil and wealth, a not insignificant part of that "cowboy rim of wealth and oil" which, according to a recent analysis in the *New York Review of Books*, links San Clemente with Key Biscayne and marks the southern border of the United States.[5] The butterfly is the badge of your religiousness. Under the sign of the butterfly, you move into a society and culture in which the roots of religious wistfulness are beginning to sprout and to be serviced by a religious pluralism on the nearer edge of syncretism.

This ministration would be other than a "huddle quickly into new disguises," if humanization only involved the horizons of the soul. But there is the not easily expendable factor of the body that insists upon a more than tolerable life in community, so that piety must somehow come to terms with politics. Syncretism becomes a dubious resource of humanization when religious pluralism is compounded with political fragmentation. Indeed, since 1968, which has been called "the year America's ulcer burst"—under the insistent trumpetings of the Black struggle for liberation, the Women's Movement, and at Wounded Knee, political fragmentation has altered the climate of learning and of life in community by a re-ordering of priorities.[6] Power becomes the path to freedom and to truth and bureaucratization becomes the point of entry into power, corrupting both the powerful and the powerless. The pervasiveness and subtlety of these transformations is succinctly indicated by a passing time in the course of the current account in *Newsweek* of what is called: *The Ellsberg "Bag Job."*[7] The context is widely different but a mentality of politicization, like cresting flood waters, has a way of seeping in and through a variety of contexts, and even barricaded ones. Said *Newsweek*, in strangely familiar though quite otherwise directed words: "Then, according to Hunt, Krogh, authorized a trip by Liddy and Hunt to Los Angeles to case the joint [that is, the office of Daniel Ellsberg's psychiatrist]—or, in his bureaucratese, to make 'a preliminary vulnerability and feasibility study for such an operation.'"[8]

Perhaps the nadir of the risks that are your destiny is the deteriorating sensibility to the depth and heights, the delicacy and the delight in the humanness of human things. Consciousness-raising may be a formula for authenticity but it is scarcely a sign of sincerity, as Professor Lionel Trilling has lately been reminding us.[9] And humane sensibility is the immediacy of sincerity in word and deed and style. Forty years ago, Tennessee Williams saw it all coming in that superbly unmasking fugue on vitality and form, brutishness and delicacy in the conflict between Stanley and Blanche at the end of the run of that *Streetcar Named Desire*. Meanwhile, the decline and fall of humane sensibility have followed at a pace almost too furious to take in. So, at least it seems from Mr. Walter Kerr's report on Edward Bond's *Lear*, among the current offerings of the Yale Repertory Theatre. "We were only being invited to watch violence as violence, to accept it as the occasion's sole activity, to endure without explanation Mr. Bond's image of life as a succession of random guttings." But "The Audience Simply Rose and Fled," Mr. Kerr reports:

> I don't think those who left were rudely expressing their displeasure with the play, certainly not with its deliberately savage excesses. I think they were trying to get straight with themselves again, trying to get real responses back in line with real stimuli, refusing to signal by their continued submissive presence that the mayhem on stage was disturbing them. In what may seem a perverse way, they were striking a blow for honesty.[10]

"For if the trumpet gives an uncertain sound, who will prepare himself to the battle?"

CORINTH AND A TRUMPET SOUND

In Corinth, in the mid-first century of our era, a trumpet had sounded. There was consternation and controversy abroad in that once and mighty commercial center on the Isthmus dividing the gulf of Corinth from the gulf of Saronica. A century earlier Caesar had established Corinth anew as the capital of the senatorial province of Achaia. And somewhere in this harbor hubbub, there was an epidemic of butterflies. Jewish and Christian popular, philosophical, and ethical maxims could be read along the streets: "The Wise Man Is King!," "All Belongs to the Wise," "Knowledge is Freedom," they would proclaim.[11] There were cults many and mysteries many, and rituals and ecstasies. There were Apollos-people, and Cephas-people, and Jesus-people; and not least, there were people who spoke in tongues. There was a coterie of spiritual options for the practice of civil religion according to the ups and downs of harbor commerce. Dominating the whole scene was the Statue of Aphrodite.

Well, Paul of Tarsus was a fighter. His use of battle imagery was vivid, vigorous, manifold, and contextual. It resisted sloganization and adroitly asserted Paul's apostolic mandate and purpose, being directed toward a variety of specific human questions and actions involving faith and hope, responsibility and ultimate loyalty. Whether to marry and why? Where is the line between freedom and bondage? How are the strong to deal with the weak those who have left scruples behind with those who seem unable to shake them off? What to make of the curious way that history has of confounding the wise and the mighty and the noble by things low and contemptible, more nothings, to overthrow the exiting order? And to top it all off a poem on love and panegyric on the life after death—the only love that heals and humanizes and overcomes the life that ends in death by the death that ends in life. What else is this but an agenda for searching and for discovering the wisdom and the power of being human in the world? What else but an agenda for the sense and center of our various destinies as ministries and ministries as destiny, whatsoever you may be doing, wheresoever you may be in all your years to come? For Paul, the Apostle, it was Jesus of Nazareth whose death on the cross overcame death by life, made history the avenue of hope, God a secret of human meaning and fulfillment in this world and the next. The trumpet sound said: "Jesus of Nazareth, crucified and risen, is the wisdom of God and the power of God! But—if the trumpet gives an uncertain sound, who shall make ready to the battle?"

Between Butterfly and Full-Calf

You then are called to give no uncertain sound amidst the syncretism, the politicization, and the declining human sensibility in the church and culture and society out of which you have come and into which you now go. And if we, in this community have failed you at any point more than any other it is that we have not helped you make ready to the battle because the trumpets we blow give a most uncertain sound. We have lost confidence in the story line that makes human sense of Jesus of Nazareth and with it the power of the freedom wherewith he has set us free. Our exodus from Egypt has bogged down before the mountain of God, and we share a blurred and hesitant vision of the promised land. You set out from here more aware of a vacuum than of the knowledge of faith. In short, we send you out caught between the butterfly and bull-calf. And where we all are, looks something like this: "As for this fellow Moses, who brought us up from Egypt, we do not know what has become of him." So—our Old Testament reading (Exodus 32:1–14) began to clue us in.

> With the invention and deconstruction and manufacture of the bull, [the people] think they can see and understand in themselves, their redeemer . . . and the hope of their future . . . They know what they want. And what they want is not what they could have expected of Moses . . . He would certainly not have been denied a state burial. But there is obviously no desire to have him back. He and his authority are no longer indispensable. The bull-god and therefore Israel's own knowledge and power will now continue and improve what he has done. Above all, his proclamation of Yahweh, his exposition of the grace and holiness and covenant and commandments of God . . . have become antiquated and redundant, even destructive. It was now necessary that the whole mystery about His persons should be explained clearly and simply as the mystery of the Israelite himself, that the consciousness of God should become a healthy self-consciousness, that the expectation, of help from God should be transformed into a resolution boldly to help oneself, that the holiness of God should be understood as the dignity of Israel's humanity . . . of its national nature and mission and the future development of it . . . The time had come to take seriously the Immanence of God . . . by the setting up of an image which would inspire confidence form the very first because it was its own creation . . . Moses was passé . . . The age of the bull had now dawned and for this epoch Moses had no message.[12]

In our present pre-occupations with experience over tradition, with immediacy over understanding, with immanence over transcendence, self-consciousness over obedience, we are not only in violation of the first and second commandments by which Jesus joined himself to Moses but are risking sending you out upon your several ministries with trumpets ill-equipped for giving no uncertain sound. Caught between the butterfly and bull-calf, how can you make ready to the battle?

The Presence Before, Behind, and In Your Midst

The answer is: in the power of the Presence Before, Behind, and In Your Midst—the Presence of Jesus Crucified and Risen, who meets us as he said he would in the sharing of the bread which is the communion of the body of Christ and in the drinking from the cup, which the communion of the blood of Christ! It is He who dissipates our vacuum and makes us ready to the battle with no uncertain sound!

Marc Chagall has said that "Christ is a poet, one of the greatest—through the incredible, irrational manner of taking pain onto himself." In this act, which transcends human possibilities, Christ seems to him, "the man possessing the most profound comprehension of life, a central figure for the 'mystery of life.'"[13] And a contemporary of ours, in the graduating class at Columbia, has put it like this: "Our responsibility to the world is not to succeed where Christ failed, but to act because Christ ultimately succeeded."[14]

So—"store up treasure in heaven, where there is no moth and no rust to spoil it, no thieves to break in and steal. For where your treasure is, there will your heart be also" (Matt 6:20–21). "For if the trumpet gives an uncertain sound who shall make ready to the battle?"

NOTES

1. This sermon was delivered at Commencement Exercises in May, 1973, at Union Theological Seminary in New York City. Lehmann had just retired from his position as Charles A. Briggs Professor Systematic Theology. It was later published in *Union Seminary Quarterly Review* 29, no. 4 (1974): 273–77; reprinted here with permission.

2. T. S. Eliot, *The Cocktail Party*, in *Complete Poems and Plays: 1909–50* (New York: Harcourt Brace, 1952), Act Two, 376.

3. Archibald Robertson, *First Epistle of Saint Paul to the Corinthians*, ICC, (New York: Charles Scribner's Sons, 1911), 309.

4. *Religion and the Humanizing of Man*, International Congress of Learned Societies in the Field of Religion, September 1–5, 1972, Century Plaza Hotel, Los Angeles.

5. Kirkpatrick Sale, "The World Behind Watergate," *New York Review of Books* 20, no. 7 (1973): 9–16.

6. Richard A. Falk, ed., *The Crimes of War* (New York: Random House, 1971), 447.

7. *Newsweek*, May 14, 1973, 33.

8. *Newsweek*, 33.

9. Lionel Trilling, *Sincerity and Authenticity* (Cambridge: Harvard University Press, 1972). Also, Jean Stafford, "Encounter Groups," *New York Review of Books* 20, no. 5 (1973): 30–33.

10. Walter Kerr, "The Audience Simply Rose and Fled," *New York Times*, Section 2, p. 1, Sunday, May 13, 1973. Italics are Kerr's.

11. Hans Conzelmann, *Erster Korintherbrief* (Göttingen: V&R, 1969), 30.

12. Karl Barth, *Church Dogmatics*, IV/1 (Edinburgh: T&T Clark, 1956), 428–32.

13. Franz Meyer, *Marc Chagall* (New York: Harry W. Abrams, 1970), 16.

14. Robert Minzerheimer, *Bonhoeffer and Action: A Few Thoughts*, an unpublished paper, submitted for a course in Union Theology Seminary, May 10, 1973, 5.

Chapter 23

The Stranger Within the Gate[1]

Two Stories for the American Conscience (1972)

Deeply rooted in the Hebrew-Christian faith is concern for the stranger within the gate. Under the covenant between Yahweh and the people of Israel, care of the poor, the widows and the aliens is a fundamental way of signalizing recognition of Yahweh as sole and righteous God whose continuing presence in the midst of God's people liberates them. Thus, the strongly mandatory Book of Deuteronomy specifies that he is cursed "who perverts the justice due to the sojourner, the fatherless, and the widow" (Deut. 27:19). Concern for the stranger witnesses to the justice intrinsic to God's nature and will and to the integrity of the people's faith.

Jesus of Nazareth was brought up in the piety of the covenant of God with humanity and of people with one another. What Abraham had launched and Moses had given political form in the historical consciousness of the Hebrew people, Jesus affirmed as the secret of human community and fulfillment— a community long awaited and worked for, and suddenly, with his life and teaching, giving present reality to the shape of the future. "The Kingdom of God," Jesus called it; and in the powerful parable summarizing what the kingdom of God was all about, he made it plain that the future belongs to those who welcome the stranger. "I was a stranger," he said, "and you took me in" (Matt. 25:35). With Jesus, an ancient responsibility was brought under the liberating impulse of a community of discipleship. This community was born in the transformation of the babel of languages, which turn strangers into enemies, by a Pentecostal gift through which each understands every other. The people "were amazed and wondered, saying . . . 'how is it that we hear, each of us in his own native language?'" (Acts 2:7–8).

Chapter 23

THE SAVING STORY

If "fantastic" designates a basic and humanizing connection between fantasy and experience, it is fantastic to suggest that the story of civilization is the story of the stranger made to feel at home. Yet it can be said that, from Abraham and Moses to Jesus and the community of his presence and spirit, the good news is that the freedom to be and to stay human in the world is expressed and nurtured by the gift of hospitality to the stranger and that societies gain or lose sense and stability according to how they make room for the stranger within the gate. By the same token, the bad news is that persons and societies who turn out the stranger turn in upon themselves and sooner or later wither and die.

In the United States of America today, however, this saving story and the saving reality it points to are in high disregard. Not least among the devastating consequences of the war in Vietnam is a mounting temptation to convert the stranger among us from a neighbor into a scapegoat. The many urgent and complex problems that beset the nation—poverty, inflation, population explosion, environmental pollution, and the liberation of oppressed groups—are almost all-absorbing, and amid the furious clamor and confusion of attempts to set them right, the voice of the stranger within our gates goes unheard and his plight unnoticed. This default allows the principalities and powers that shape our nation's policies to pursue their subtle violation of the conscience of a people rooted in and nurtured by the saving story.

The choice before us as a people lies between the politics of death—made possible, as Dan Berrigan recently remarked, by an arsenal of indescribable destructiveness produced by "a rotten technology in conjunction with a rotten leadership abetted by a rotten religion"—and a politics of humanity. A politics of humanity would bring an immediate end to the war in Vietnam and turn to redress of the grievances that afflict this nation from within—hatred, mistrust and oppression, poverty and crime, and the arrogance of power which declares, in the words of President Nixon: "no power on earth is stronger than the United States of America today. And none will be stronger in the future . . . for America to continue its role of helping to build a more peaceful world we must keep America No. 1 economically in the world."[2]

It is no accident that the century of unprecedented American power has seen a corrosion of the American dream. The dream grew out of the passion for freedom and the vision of a new beginning and a new order in human affairs to which our founding documents bear witness. The torch of liberty is still held aloft at the entrance to New York harbor, but how long before the flame is quenched? It may well be that the arrogance of power is too far advanced to prevent the corrosion of the American dream to the point at which it becomes an American nightmare. Even so, the saving story records that the regeneration of power begins when and where the powers that be sink to the nadir of degeneration. One such "when and where" is the intersection of the saving story with the story of the stranger in the century of American power.

THE ALIEN IN OUR MIDST

On September 25, 1971, Congress repealed the 1950 Internal Security Act which authorized detention in camps, without charges, hearings or trials, of citizens and aliens alike. The repeal was a response to popular pressure. For two decades liberal forces had been pointing to the detention of 100,000 Japanese in concentration "centers" during World War II. They feared that in the climate of growing opposition to government policies, domestic and foreign, the 1950 law would be used against all dissenters. Repeal of it was correctly seen as a significant civil-liberties victory. But democratic-minded Americans are unaware that another law which provides the basis for large-scale roundups remains in force; namely, the Alien Registration Act, also enacted in 1950, which requires all noncitizens to report annually to the government.

Every December since 1951 the justice department has been giving a Christmas greeting to some 3 million noncitizens lawfully resident in the U.S. On the radio and TV, in the press and through notices in public places, these people are told that, on pain of severe penalties, they must register in January. Like criminals on parole, they are required to present themselves to the authorities for questioning and to give their current address, employment, and other information. The result is that, for those unwilling or unable to become citizens, living under perpetual surveillance has come to seem a natural order of things.

There was a time when immigrants to this country were welcomed. But today many of our government officials and much of our press call them "aliens"—a word implying not only that they are noncitizens but that their way of life is inferior and even hostile to ours.

THE NONCITIZEN AND THE LAW

How does it happen that noncitizens who have committed no crime are treated as outcasts? The story begins with the U.S. entry into World War I. One immediate result of that action was severe wage cuts in the basic industries. At first the workers—many of whom were foreign born—acquiesced. But as they began to realize, along with the rest of the people, that this was a war for plunder and not to "make the world safe for democracy," they started to resist the reduction in pay. The government's response to this situation was reactionary. Instead of affirming the democratic rights of the people, it offered the native a scapegoat: the foreign born, it declared, were largely responsible for the unrest rife in America. The cure it proposed had two parts: foreign-born radicals were to be expelled; and noncitizens, the alleged contaminators of U.S. society, were to be identified as a dangerous group by being forced to register with the police. In 1920, a Democratic attorney general, A. Mitchell Palmer, ordered dragnet raids in which some 10,000 foreign-born persons were arrested for deportation, and the Republican party included in its platform a demand that "all aliens . . . be required to register annually."

As a greater degree of prosperity returned in subsequent years, the pressure in the social boiler abated. But sentiment against the foreign born continued and in 1926 found expression in a bill for alien registration sponsored by a Dixiecrat congressman, James B. Aswell of Louisiana. This bill (HR 5585) was passed by the House of Representatives, but, owing mainly to the opposition of labor and liberal groups, it failed of enactment. At its October 1925 convention the American Federation of Labor had denounced the bill as "dangerous" and "anti-union," and Samuel Gompers, its first president, had declared that "the AFL is opposed to the proposal for registering aliens." Indeed, Gompers warned that requiring aliens to register would lead to citizens' being "compelled to register." His successor in the AFL presidency, William Green, went on record as saying: "No liberty-loving, just-minded citizen of the U.S. will advocate such laws for the U.S."

With the onset of a severe depression in 1929, demands for alien registration were renewed. Forewarned by the defeat of the Aswell bill, Senator Cole Blease presented a bill calling only for "voluntary registration." This passed the Senate, but again powerful resistance prevented its enactment. An "American Committee Opposed to Alien Registration," headed by Alvin Johnson, issued a statement signed by such public figures as Jane Addams, Heywood Broun, Stephen S. Wise, Harry Elmer Barnes, John Haynes Holmes, Arthur Garfield Hays, Amos Pinchot, Suzanne La Follette and George Gordon Battle; and the *New York Times*, the *Nation*, the *New Republic*, *Survey*, *Commonweal* and other periodicals came out against the bill. So did a "National Convention for the Protection of the Foreign Born," which was attended by some 400 delegates from many parts of the country. The Assembly of Hebrew Orthodox Rabbis and the Women's League of the United Synagogues of America joined in the protests. And in the Senate itself the opposition found spokesmen in the persons of Robert F. Wagner, David I. Walsh, and Burton K. Wheeler. Wagner observed that registration bills are "expressions of the prejudice that the immigrant must be received not with sympathy but with suspicion." "Unlawful entry into the United States," he pointed out, "is a crime, and this bill would have millions of people annually go before the authorities to prove that they had not committed that crime . . . It is more important that we build a nation than deport an alien."

In the face of so much opposition, the proponents of alien registration simply dug in and bided their time. By 1939, their protracted campaign bore results; some 70 anti-alien bills tumbled out of the congressional hopper, among them:

- HR 4860—to deport noncitizens who "advocate any change in the government." This passed the House and was favorably reported by the Senate committee on immigration.
- HR 999—to end immigration and deport all noncitizens by the end of the year.
- S 411; HR 279; HR 3051—to deport all noncitizens inimical to the public interest.
- *Plus* eight bills to ensure the national defense by requiring alien registration.

The alien-baiters naturally made Hitlerism serve their purposes. Wrapping themselves in the flag, they even used the legitimate hostility of democratic-minded Americans toward the Quislings and "fifth columnists" to press their campaign. Sentiment in Congress was so much on their side that one of its most powerful members, Representative Howard Smith of Virginia, was emboldened to introduce an anti-alien bill of extreme character. This bill, HR 5138, laid before Congress in March 1939, provided both for alien registration every six months and for imprisonment of citizens advocating, or belonging to organizations advocating, violent change in the government (with deportation of noncitizen members of such organizations). Predictably Smith's bill received the green light while many other bills were gathering dust. Yet the sailing was not altogether smooth.

Struggle in the House of Representatives

Reporting out the bill in June, the House committee on the judiciary eliminated the registration provision, "largely," as it said, "because of the practical difficulties presented by the problem of administration, and the thought that the criminal and more undesirable aliens would pay no attention to these requirements, if enacted into law, while the requirements would seriously inconvenience many perfectly law-abiding residents." The committee thought also that "much of the information sought by the proposed registration could be obtained by the census to be taken next year."

In other words, the committee said that alien registration is a fraud. *If the object of the scrutiny is not the lawful resident, why require him to register? Why not simply a law that unlawful residents must register?* Since such noncitizens were already in defiance of laws directing them to present themselves to the Immigration Service, no one in his right mind actually believed that a law requiring them to register, especially if they were spies or saboteurs, would have any practical effect.

But the anti-alien steamroller was much too strong to be halted at the bar of reason and democratic rights. By mid-1940, congressional resistance to the Smith bill had collapsed. The final tally was 382 for and 4 against. And, though parts of the bill largely curtailed the basic rights of citizens, the legislative package as enacted was labeled "The Alien Registration Act of 1940."

Thus was killed a feature of our democratic Constitution that had for centuries drawn to our shores millions who wanted to escape the police surveillance omnipresent in their native lands. Henceforth newcomers arrived not in the sunshine of liberty but in the shadow of suspicion. Henceforth they were regarded as potential enemies of democratic America and were forced to prove themselves innocent before any evidence of guilt was adduced.

ANNUAL REGISTRATION ENACTED

The Alien Registration Act of 1940 was presented as a limited wartime measure. But resurrection of the bogey of the "alien menace" in the Cold War atmosphere of 1946 paved the way for the passage in 1950 of the Internal Security Act requiring annual registration of noncitizens.

A scant two years later, the Immigration and Nationality Act—aptly named the Walter-McCarran Act after the chairmen of the House and Senate immigration and un-American activities committees—set up further restrictions. Like the pass system traditional in many nondemocratic countries, this act required every noncitizen to carry an identity card to be shown to any police officer on demand. Moreover, in order to make control absolutely current, it required noncitizens to report any change of residence within ten days of the change. The original (1952) registration form contained 11 questions, but in the years since these have been somewhat varied. At present they include the respondent's Social Security number and the name and address of his employer. As erosion of noncitizens' rights continues, who can say how many more questions will be added in the future to make clear to the noncitizen that he has no right to call his soul his own?

THE BILL OF RIGHTS

The Bill of Rights makes no distinction between "persons" and "citizens." It guarantees to all "persons" certain rights, such as freedom of speech and assembly, due process of law and equal protection of the laws. Nevertheless, in being required to register, lawful residents are singled out for exclusion from these constitutional guarantees. If they fail to report regularly to the authorities, they are punishable as criminals. (The penalties provided for willful failure or refusal to register are $1,000 and / or six months of imprisonment; for failure to register annually, $200 fine and / or 30 days; and for failure to carry the registration card on one's person, $100 fine and / or 30 days.)

Invasion of the constitutional rights of noncitizens endangers the constitutional rights of citizens; for as "persons" neither of these has greater stature than the other. There is no way to breach the constitutional wall protecting noncitizens without simultaneously opening the dikes to erosion of the rights of citizens. *The central target is not the "alien," but rather the growing numbers of people alienated from the government.*

Noncitizen annual registration is a stepping stone to universal annual registration. Moreover, if annual registration is constitutional, why not also semiannual or even weekly registration? In fact, weekly reporting is already enforced under a law providing for supervision of noncitizens ordered deported but whose deportation cannot be effected. In view of the multiplying signs of repression evidenced in prosecutions, recently passed laws and pending bills, who can say that citizens will not soon be subject to inquisition? Senator Edward Kennedy recently warned that high officials of the justice department consider the Constitution "a burden [to be] evaded when possible and ignored if necessary."

Alien registration was never a solution for our problems. It is a tool for repression and must be recognized as such by all Americans who want to preserve their democratic rights. At present, alien registration is a sleeper. But when reactionaries are ready to wake it, it will come knocking at the door of the citizen. Let us pay heed to Martin Niemöller's counsel, born of bitter experience as he shared his nation's anti-alien fury and its collapse. Let us be our brother's keeper and seek repeal of alien registration laws now. Today, it is the noncitizen; tomorrow, the rest of us!

A CONTINENT INDISSOLUBLE

It is to the brave that the story of the stranger within the gate speaks, not to the fearful. The brave—those who know that fear generates mistrust, exacerbates isolation, and delivers human beings over to a dehumanizing enslavement to the principalities and powers; in short, to the politics of death. The brave—those who know that "there is no fear in love, but perfect love casts out fear" (1 John 4:18); those who would "let brotherly love continue" and—knowing that "thereby some have entertained angels unawares"—would overcome the "neglect to show hospitality to strangers" (Heb. 13:1–2).

In America today the story of the stranger is one concrete point of entry into the saving story, and conversely, the saving story is the point of entry into the experience and the power which bring memories and hopes together in the liberation of the present. Together, the two stories are a tale of hope for a politics of humanity which those who practice the politics of death among us can neither match nor prevent. Here is a legacy for an America that has neither the need nor the desire to be supreme in the earth because she is in truth a land of promise.

> Come, I will make this continent
> indissoluble,
> I will make the most splendid race
> the sun ever shone upon . . .
> I will plant companionship as thick as trees
> On all the rivers of America
> And all over the prairies.[3]

NOTES

1. Co-written with Ira Gollobin and published in *Christian Century* (1972): 1149–52; reprinted with permission.

2. Quoted in the *New York Times*, June 2, 1972.

3. [Editorial: "For You, O Democracy," in *Poems of Walt Whitman,* The Modern Library of the World's Best Books (New York: Boni and Liveright, 1921), 100.]

Chapter 24

A Christian Alternative to Natural Law (1942)[1]

PRESUPPOSITIONS

Our first presupposition is a notation of the sense in which we use the phrase, "natural law." What is it, to which we are venturing to propose a "Christian alternative?" It may be appropriate to begin with a formulation of Cicero's concerning the natural law. His reflections and writings on the question mark a watershed through which the confluent streams of religious, ethical, and legal probing since Homeric times have nourished the roots of humanity's unceasing preoccupation with the moral foundations and directives of human life in a world of time and space, of people, communities and things. In the *De legibus*, Cicero wrote: "Law is the highest reason, implanted in nature, which commands what things are to be done, and which forbids the contrary."[2] Some measure of the impressive consensus which has both prompted and sustained this view across the centuries may be derived from a formulation, a millennium and a half later, virtually identical in sense, if not in language. "Natural law," wrote Phillip Melanchthon in 1521, "is the common judgment to which all men alike assent, which God has engraved upon the mind of each, and which is designed to fashion morals."[3]

By natural law, then, we understand, the fact that intrinsic to the human reason, and thus, to the nature of humanity, there is the capacity to distinguish between what is right or good, and what is wrong or bad. In this basic sense, the terms "right," or "good," or "bad" are interchangeable. They denote irreducible judgments of value by which human actions are to be adjudged responsible or irresponsible. Accordingly, all people, as human beings, know that there is a fundamental and universal moral (or ethical, the terms are interchangeable) order within which their lives are set. This order claims and limits both the judgements and human actions, both the reason and the will; and in this way, undergirds and guides the responsible life. *The reciprocity between the responsible life and human life is so intrinsic and inviolable that natural law is at once the foundation and the fulcrum of the humanity of human beings.* It does not matter that natural law has functioned more often as a formal than as a material principle of ethics. It does not matter that its content has been minimally and variously defined. "It does not matter," that is, the reciprocity between natural law and the humanity of human beings is not on that account invalidated. Nor can it be urged that the dynamics of the moral life, with its diversity, complexity, and ambiguity effectively nullify natural law. The natural law is a universal principle of ethical discrimination and direction, not a universal principle of ethical or human uniformity. Indeed, uniformity is as foreign to the moral life as conformity is native to it. All this we mean, when we use the phrase, *natural law*. All this—and heaven too!—for despite Cicero's own uncertainty on the point, his predecessors and successors, until Thomas, surnamed not Aquinas but Hobbes, came along, were overwhelmingly persuaded that God was the author and upholder of the natural law. According to it, God's own will went into action; and by it, God determined, as a judgment and in action, the destiny of humanity.

A second presupposition underlying this analysis concerns the sense in which we are venturing to suggest an alternative to natural law. Exponents of the natural law tradition tend to regard such a suggestion as the camel's nose, if not an open door, pointed towards ethical and legal positivism with its concomitants, in varying formulations and degrees, of historicism, subjectivism, and ethical relativism. On this view, those who deviate from the natural law can only end up in moral nihilism. Critics of the natural law tradition, on the other hand, tend to lay such stress upon the dynamics of the moral life, with its diversity, complexity, and ambiguity, as effectively to minimize, or to obscure the substantive importance of the concern for the rational foundations of ethics. The so-called objectivity of moral norms and values is, on this view, reduced at best to agnosticism, at worst to rejection. The focus of ethical attention is given, instead, to such so-called subjective factors as the changing character of moral judgements and values, and functions of these judgements and values, and the more readily verifiable political, psychological, and linguistic roots and functions of these judgments and values. The *ad hominem* [argument against the person] consideration that both exponents and critics of the natural law tradition have sometimes overstated the case may be regarded as an obvious datum of the story of ethical reflection, without pertinence to the present purpose. It is of no little pertinence, however, to pay due heed to the consideration that the critics of natural law are scarcely likely to concede the grim *tertium non datur* [the reconciling third] so movingly formulated, and with astonishing contemporaneity, by Marcus Aurelius[4]:

> Either all things happen, owing to a single, rational source, simultaneously in a single body - and then the part cannot complain about what belongs to the well-being of the whole! Or the world consists of atoms, and there is nothing else but meaningless mixture and separation . . . Say, then, to your soul: you are dead, you are destroyed, you have become an animal, a hypocrite, one of a herd, you live only to eat.[5]

This warning must haunt every attempt at an *alternative* to natural law. Indeed, the sober ultimacy of the Aurelian option exacts an almost forbidding sobriety of the search for a *tertium quid* [unidentified third element] between rational certainty and relativity in ethics and politics.

The search for such a *tertium quid* is not, then, to be regarded as an abandonment of the foundations of ethical certainty. We are insistently concerned about the intrinsic connection between the responsible life and an order of ethical certainty and guidance which has so steadily and unyieldingly marked the adherence to natural law. Conversely, we are fully aware of, and have no wish to court, the perils of thoroughgoing ethical relativism. At the same time, however, we are unable to regard the positivistic protest against ethical absolutism as a nihilistic hybris against the humanity either of God or of human beings. Nor can we regard the decline in the formative power of the natural law tradition as entirely due to a failure of communication. There has been a failure of communication. But there has been something else. This is why neither a return to "the Christian principles of Natural Law" nor a renovation of the role of rationality in ethics can restore vitality and viability to a doctrine of natural law in our time and in the times to come. This "something else" has to do, in a phrase of Karl Barth's, with *die Richtigkeit der Stetigkeiten* (the rectitude, or correctness, or adequacy) in the geometric (not ethical) sense, of the stabilities.[6] There is an internal flaw within the natural law tradition that, together with an external oversight, is the secret of its present "time of troubles" (Toynbee) and which bars the way to a true and lively word about the rectitude of the stabilities.

We shall return to the internal flaw and the external oversight which give rise to the possibility of an alternative to natural law. Meanwhile, we must call attention to a third presupposition of this discussion. This has to do with the adjective "Christian." It is hazardous enough to attempt to identify a third option, beyond absolutism and relativism in ethics, against a swelling tide in both directions and the widening gulf between them. But to attempt to identify this third option as a *Christian* one doubles the difficulty. We all know that the Ciceronian conviction about the natural law was carried into its present position, for attack and counterattack, under the great wisdom and solicitude of the Christian church. As Professor Gilson has put it:

> In whatever way we look at the matter we shall always have to return to Cicero's definition of morality as the habit of acting as reason and nature demand . . . As far as this point is concerned the evolution of ethics may be summed up by saying that the Christian moralists sought first to attach all moral worth to the voluntary act as its root; that at the same time they gathered up the concepts of the beauty and honor of human acts into a concept still more comprehensive, that, namely, of the good; then referred the good to a transcendent principle worthy of all honor in itself and absolutely, more truly even than virtue, which is only honorable on account of this. They regarded . . . virtue itself as honorable only because it leads man to God.[7]

The principal architects of this achievement for the Western church at all events, were undoubtedly Augustine and Aquinas, who may be allowed to speak for themselves on the point with utmost, and most regrettable brevity.

Augustine once addressed himself in a sermon to the question, why the virtues are good? "Why, therefore?" he asks:

> Now let us inquire of these three, Epicurean, Stoic, and Christian, what order lies open to our very eyes? Tell us, Epicurean, what makes a thing blessed? He replies: 'Delight of substance or body.' 'Virtue of soul,' says the Stoic. 'The grace of God,' says the Christian . . . A great and praiseworthy thing: praise, O Stoic, as much as you can; but tell me, whence do you have this possibility? It is not the virtue of your soul that makes you blessed but because he gave you virtue who inspired you to will it and gave you the power.[8]

Saint Thomas, in making the point that since God is the author of reason, to ignore the dictates of reason is to ignore what God prescribes, declares expressly: "whence it accords with the same reason that imperfection and sin are at once contrary to human reason and to eternal law."[9]

This moving and momentous achievement defines the sense in which it is intelligible to speak of a "Christian alternative to natural law." The phrase clearly means that Christian thinkers appropriated the ethical reflections of the classical moralists with the intention of improving upon these reflections by providing them with a more adequate foundation in terms of which their "loud exactitudes of imprecision" might be remedies.[10] But since Christian moralists were trying really to say the same thing as were the classical moralists, but to say it better rather than differently, the alternative is scarcely a real alternative. Some interpreters have preferred therefore, to speak of a "Christian natural law." And in some respects, they are in better case. They take due account of a distinctively Christian way of interpreting natural law without overstating the matter by elevating the distinctiveness to the rank of an alternative.[11] Whether Emil Brunner is correct in asserting that "the Stoic conception of the law of nature is to be found neither in Luther nor in Calvin," and that theirs is "a *genuinely* Christian doctrine of the law of nature," is a moot point.[12] Meanwhile, it is sufficient to observe that there is impressive textual evidence to the contrary;[13] and that in any case, we do not venture to propose a Christian alternative to natural law in quite so apodictic a way. What we hope to be able to find our way toward is a *genuine Christian alternative* to natural law which is neither revisionist, in the Augustinian Thomistic sense; nor correlative, in the sense in which the humanism of the Renaissance and Reformation found it possible to stress the congruence, and even interchangeability between the Ciceronian doctrine of natural law, the Decalogue, and the law of love; nor positivist, in the sense of a relativistically derived disavowal of the importance of objective and normative problems in ethics. A genuine Christian alternative to natural law would be *a descriptive analysis of the intrinsic and inviolable reciprocity between the responsible life and human life, a reciprocity anchored, not in the human reason, with or without divine assistance, but in a perspective upon the foundations and directives for the making of decisions, whether private or public, derived from the insights and sensitivity nourished by Christian faith, Christian thought, and Christian experience.* Such an alternative seeks to overtake the inadequacies of classicism and Roman Catholicism—and no less of positivism by dealing with the human reality and the problems of ethics and politics in a constructive and liberating context.

Fourth, such an alternative seems to us both urgent and viable because Christianity, while intrinsically linked to the reciprocity between ethical and human reality, is not intrinsically bound to the law of nature, as we understand it. But more immediately, it seems to us that the present crisis of natural law is so advanced that neither a return to a "normative" past nor a surrender to the positivist habits of thought that bar the gateway to such a return are really possible. The world has "come of age" in an ethical and political, as well as in a religious sense. The question at issue *is* the question of "*die Richtigkeit der Stetigkeiten.*" The "long minority of humanity," in Comte's phrase, is at an end. If God has no other function than that of chief bailiff, issuing restraining orders and supervising the serving process until the "moral law within" (Kant) catches up with "the moral fuss" (Freud) within and without "until the next attack." Then, God is indeed expendable.[14] God has been effectively displaced by the psycho-dynamics of the behavioral sciences and technocratic social organization which, despite the improvisations of their infancy, are nearer to the *human* equation in ethics than to the ethical equation of the human, anchored in the reason.

Comte, of course, too consistently concluded that a positivistic scientific displacement of the "minority of humanity" by the drawing "maturity of humanity" was as obvious as it was inevitable. But, as we have learned the hard way since Comte, and as many of his predecessors, wiser, if not more knowledgeable than Comte, knew long before, maturity is not so easily come by. Maturity requires not the abandonment of transcendence, but a fresh, meaningful, and integrating connection between transcendence and humanity; in short, an ethic and a politics that are both practical and wise.

This is the "point of no return" at which we seem to have arrived. At the behavioral level, the cultural transition in which we are all involved is terrifyingly evident in the mounting tide of frenzied violence. At the reflective level, hiatus between transcendence and humanity is most critically evident as a methodological impasse. We do not know how to bring what we know and what we observe together, so that our judgments of value and our value judgments can give creative shape to human responsibility and purpose. Since Socrates, Plato, and Aristotle; since Augustine and Aquinas, Luther and Calvin; since Hobbes and Locke, Rousseau and Kant; no one has wrestled with the methodological problem more painstakingly and poignantly than Max Weber. Weber discerned the social, ethical, and methodological impasse of our time with such sensitive and accurate anticipation that he may be allowed to state the case for the urgency of some alternative to natural law and the possibility of a Christian option. In this way, Max Weber may perhaps guide us, as Virgil once conducted Dante, from our "inferno" to the frontier between our "purgatorio" and a "paradiso." Speaking of the transfer of ascetic discipline (that is, of the responsibility which human beings are able to bring upon the work which they do because of the context of meaning and purpose in which they do it) from a monastic to a Puritan context, Weber wrote:

> In as much as the ascetic spirit tried to reconstruct the world and extend itself in the world, external goods acquired an increasing and ultimately inescapable power over man, unique in history. Today, this spirit has eluded its puritan shell (*Gehaüse*). Victorious capitalism, since it rests upon a mechanical foundation has no further need of this support. Even the optimistic mood of its smiling beneficiary, the Enlightenment, seems definitely in decline, and the idea of one's duty in one's vocation circulates as a ghost of former religiously inspired "articles of faith" . . . No one knows as yet who will live in that shell (that is, of capitalism), or whether this momentous development will ultimately produce totally prophets or a mighty rebirth of old ideas and ideals - or, if neither of these, a mechanical petrifaction varnished by a convulsive sense of self-importance. Indeed, the consequence for these "last men" of this cultural development could well be that the prediction could ultimately come true that they are "Specialists without spirit, voluptuaries without heart." This nihilism convinces itself that it has reached a height of human development never before attained.[15]

Whether Weber himself actually assisted this nihilistic prospect is a matter of debate among his supporters and critics. The supporters maintain that he was struggling to transcend the impasse between "objectivity" and "value-judgment" in the social sciences, in the interest of a creative and relevant connection between ethics and policy, for instance, between real values and decision-making, as decisions *actually* are made.[16] The critics maintain that Weber's assessment of what is involved in "historical understanding," and thus, in social science, had already given hostages to fortune, since his attempts to relate value-judgments to historical causality lacked an adequate frame-of-reference.[17]

Be that as it may, Weber's prophecy is instructive for our present purpose for the following reasons: (a) he exposed the crucial dilemma upon which an ethical approach to social and historical change is caught: the dilemma between the objectivity and universality of rationally determined values and the range, rate, and complexity of change; (b) he identified the focal problem in any ethical approach to social change, namely, the operational link between value and policy;[18] and (c) he tried to establish the possibility and actuality of value-judgments by substituting for the untenable gulf between normative and empirical approaches to decision making, the exploration of "frames-of-references" in terms of which social inter-relations, historical traditions, and directional factors (for instance, goals and procedures) in the making of decisions and the shaping of policy could be constructively linked.

For understandable reasons, a biblical Christian frame of reference was not a live option for Weber. But my concern now is to try to show what such an option might involve for understanding and effecting the reciprocity between the responsible life and human life; and then in what sense it may help us beyond the point of no return, beyond the methodological impasse at which the natural law and its tradition have arrived.

PROPOSAL

In his incisive and richly informative discussion of natural law, with reference both to its roots and its present "time of troubles," Professor Leo Strauss has hinted at the possibility of the sort of alternative to natural law which we should like to propose.[19] Unless we have misread him, he does not take up the hint. In doing so, we are indebted to him both for the hint and for helping us to see more clearly than we had done before, what the internal flaw and the external oversight in the analysis and application of natural law involve. Professor Strauss is commenting upon humanity's natural understanding of the natural world, as it happens, also in connection with some discussion of Max Weber. His point is that the origins of the idea of natural right are intimately related to the discovery of nature by the classical philosophers. In this connection, we read: "the information that classical philosophy supplies about its origins suffices,[20] especially if that information is supplemented by consideration of the most elementary premises of the Bible, for reconstructing the essential character of 'the natural world.' By using that information, so supplemented, one would be enabled to understand the origin of the idea of natural rights."[21] The hint, then, which we should like to take up and elaborate upon has to do with the "elementary premises of the Bible" and with the supplemental relation of these ideas to the "information that classical philosophy supplies about its origins."

The point at issue concerns the truth of natural law. If we may borrow a celebrated formulation of St. Thomas, remarkable alike for its precision and its succinctness: "truth is the adequation of the intellect to the thing."[22] By this yardstick, and with all due respect to St. Thomas, natural law is intrinsically false. It can neither properly describe nor creatively resolve the problems with which it purports to deal. In short, it does not and cannot exhibit "the adequation of the intellect to the thing." For natural law attributes to the intellect, either as a divine implantation or as a self-discovery, the intrinsic self-evidence of the reciprocity between the responsible life and human life, and in so doing obscures the persistent and disruptive threats to this reciprocity, both from the side of the ethical claim or norm and from the side of the ethical act or decision. From the side of the ethical norm, the tension between reason and will in human nature calls into question the rational self-evidence of the reciprocity itself. Thus, if the *thing* to which the intellect is *adequate*, is to be understood as the inviolability of the reciprocity between responsibility and humanity in ethics, the intellect is unequal to this assignment. It cannot bear the weight of the burden of truth. On the other hand, if the inviolable reciprocity between responsibility and humanity in ethics and politics is to stand in the court of truth, the intellect requires some other criterion than rational self-evidence. We must look not to *a law of reason* but to a *context for reason*, if the proper ethical, political, and human concerns of natural law are to acquire "the adequation of the intellect to the thing," that is, truth.

The flaw internal to the natural law and its tradition in western ethical thought is that the human reason cannot bear the normative weight assigned to it. The assignment has exhibited an impressive tenacity and resourcefulness in dealing with the chaos and complexity of natural and social circumstance and change, and with the concrete ambiguities and conflicts which beset the goals and motivations of human decision-making. Despite the disproportion between the strength of reason and the claims upon it, the rise and decline of natural law is a moving confirmation of the Marxian dictum that "the beginning of all criticism is the criticism of religion."[23] Conceived in a searching re-examination and eventual rejection of Homeric religion, the natural law from Socrates to Weber was designed to overcome religious arbitrariness and pluralism by subordinating the will to the reason both in human nature and in the nature of the world. Law was conceived and applied as a check upon the capriciousness and superstition of an obscurantist religious matrix for sovereignty and power. So marked was the subordination of the will to the reason that sovereignty was effectively detached from power, and power thereby lost its hold upon order.

But the will was not thereby eradicated. It was sublimated, that is, driven underground. Its continuing tremors were neither unnoticed nor heeded. Neither Stoic resignation, nor ascetic discipline and dualism, nor the Marxian discovery of ideology, nor the Freudian discovery of the unconscious, nor the effective obsolescence of transcendence have been sufficient to turn humanity's attention to the fateful flaw in the truth of natural law occasioned by the transposition of sovereignty from the will to the reason as the dawn of reflection began to demythologize Homeric piety and values. Yet Prometheus and Dionysius are still at war, with ever and again, a short-lived truce. The present "time of troubles" of natural law points to nothing so much as to the absence of an adequate matrix of sovereignty. In such a matrix, the will and the reason can be creatively related as instruments of the power whereby the humanity of human beings is being hammered out and hammered into being. In such a matrix, the self-evidence of the reciprocity between the responsible life and human life lies not in the reason but in the reciprocity itself. This reciprocity is the concrete sign of the order according to which humanity is to be and can become what humanity is meant to be. In the meantime, technology has occupied the vacuum occasioned by the absence of a humanizing "logos of power," in the late professor Charles Cochrane's forceful phrase.[24] Here the "specialists without spirit, the voluptuaries without heart" have made themselves at home, at the price of the humanity of human beings.

It is always possible, of course, that things would have turned out more satisfactorily had the internal flaw in the natural law not been accompanied by an external oversight. The oversight concerns the relation between the "elementary premises of the Bible" and the "information that classical philosophy supplies about its origins." The primary question here is whether that relation is a *supplemental* one or a *catalytic* one. If supplemental, the "elementary premises of the Bible" are fundamentally compatible with the "information that classical philosophy supplies about its origins." They function as marginal correctives or as complementary or consummatory addenda. The most celebrated catchword of this way of regarding the relation is perhaps the Thomistic dictum: "*gratia non tollit naturam sed perficit*" ["Grace does not destroy nature, but perfects it"].[25] Whether Augustine viewed the matter quite in this way is a moot point. It is plain, however, that Thomas understood him in this way, and that this interpretation is compatible with the Neo-Platonist Augustine in particular. Thus, he could write against Faustus a striking supplemental adaptation of the Ciceronian definition of natural law which we have already noted. "*Lex aeterna*," Augustine declared, "*est ratio divina vel voluntas Dei, ordinem naturalem conversari iubens, perturbari vetana*" ["The eternal law is the reason or the will of God, which commands that the natural order is to be preserved and forbids that it be destroyed"].[26] On the other hand, if the relation between the "elementary premises of the Bible" and the "information that classical philosophy supplies about its origins" is a *catalytic* one, then, some fundamental re-arrangements of relations and functions are in order. The most important of these re-arrangements has to do with the relations between will and reason, between sovereignty and order, between power and purpose, between the nature of the world and the nature of humanity. The re-arrangements mean that biblical premises transvalue rather than correct or complete the self-understanding of a culture or of humanity in human culture, whether that culture be primitive, classical, or modern. They mean that a basic shift of contexts has occurred in the light of which old patterns of meaning and action fall apart only to fall into fresh patterns of meaning and possibilities of action. "One does not put new wine into old wineskins; if it is, the skin burst, and wine is spilled, and the skins are destroyed; but new wine is put into fresh wine-skins, and so both are preserved" (Mt. 9:17).

If the internal flaw in natural law is due chiefly to an error of the Socratic criticism of Homeric religion and value, *the external oversight in the tradition of natural law is chiefly due to the way in which the natural law was preserved and perpetuated by the theologians and jurists of the Roman Catholic Church*. According to Luke, at any rate, Jesus "also told them a parable: Can a blind man lead a blind man? Will they not both fall into a pit?" (Luke 6:39, RSV).

The healing gift of sight through Jesus of Nazareth is, of course, one of the elementary premises of the Bible. Indeed, it is a major one. Ernst Troeltsch has cogently argued that there was no way of getting from "the love individualism and universalism" intrinsic to the ethic of Jesus to the ongoing ethical and political decisions and structures of humanity in the world, in which the parousia was delayed, except the way of natural law. On this course, Jesus himself was lost beneath a carefully and powerfully structured sacramental institution. Indeed, this sacramental supplementation of the wisdom of classicism prevailed until the dawn of modern times. Even the Reformation did not successfully depart from it.[27] Although Troeltsch does not say so, it is a fair inference from his account, that along these lines the Bible also was effectively prevented from giving formative shape to the decision-making of them. When, however, the elementary premises of the Bible begin to be taken seriously, the major significance of Jesus begins to emerge from its cultural-sacramental enclave and the possibility of a genuine Christian alternative to natural law begins to come into view.

Reinhold Niebuhr has profoundly observed that "the basic distinction between historical and non-historical religions and cultures may . . . be defined as the difference between those which expect and those which do not expect a Christ. The significance of a Christ is that he is a disclosure of the divine purpose, governing history within history."[28] When the New Testament identifies the Christ with Jesus of Nazareth, it begins to break fresh ground in providing a context within which the reciprocity between the responsible life and human life can effectively shape the way humanity understands what it is called upon to do and do what it has been given to understand. "Jesus Christ," Pascal declared, "is the end of all, and the center to which all tends. Whoever knows Him knows the reason of everything."[29] Taken by itself, this is a debatable proposition which only sharpens the cogency of more evident and more consistent options. But taken in the context of the New Testament in particular, and of the Bible as a whole, Pascal has anticipated the Niebuhrian point and honed its cutting edge.

The context of which Jesus Christ makes sense, and which in turn, makes sense of Jesus Christ, looks something like this. In this occurrence, God's characteristic way of being God disclosed itself as the involvement of an originating and a sovereign will in the enterprise of freeing and enabling humanity to be what, by the same sovereign will and purpose humanity was meant to be, that is, human. By this disclosure, power was brought within the humanizing bounds of will and purpose, and meaningful connection was made between the environment of humanity's life and the living of it, between the world in which humanity found itself and the destiny by which humanity could measure its decisions in the world. Participation in this disclosure and its human prospects was open to "as many as received him" in a community of discernment and commitment whose dynamics and direction pointed towards the inclusion of all humankind. "For as many as received him . . . he gave power to become children of God" (John 1:12).

Here, too, the "beginning of all criticism is the criticism of religion" (Marx). The Socratic criticism of Homeric religion involved the messianic error of shifting the focus of meaning and purpose from history to reason. By contrast, here is a messianic criticism of religion which repudiates arbitrariness in the name of a humanizing transcendence, and subjects religious pluralisms to a humanizing principle of discrimination. The roots of this messianic criticism lie deep in Israel's past. As Martin Buber has put it, "the principal content of Israel's messianic faith is . . . The steady pre-occupation with and expression of the fulfillment of the relation between God and the world in a complete kingly rule of God."[30] But the fruits of this messianic criticism are a perspective and a power to shape the judgments and actions of human beings in the enterprise of humanization, that is, in an authentic reciprocity between the responsible life and human life. In light of such a perspective and power, the natural law has been displaced by an order of providence in which the will of humanity is directed towards the redeeming of the times, the *reason* toward the discernment of the times, and *law* bends the things which have been towards the things which are to come.

Some glimpse of this messianic alternative to natural law tantalized the mind of Augustine and remained for the Reformation to struggle with again. As we should expect, a particularly vivid notice of the line which Augustine was trying to hold firm, concerns his difficulties with Cicero. "We," he declares:

> in order that we may confess the most high and true God Himself, do confess His will, supreme power and prescience. Neither let us be afraid lest, after all, we do not do by will, because He, whose foreknowledge if infallible, foreknew we would do it. It was this which Cicero was afraid of . . . He, therefore like a truly great and wise man, and one who consulted very much and skillfully for the benefit of humanity, of those two chose the freedom of the will, to confirm which he denied the foreknowledge of future things; and thus, wishing to make men free, he makes them sacrilegious. But the religious mind chooses both, confesses both, and maintains both by the faith of piety[31] . . . Therefore, *that* God, the author and giver of felicity, because He alone is the true God, Himself gives earthly kingdoms to good and bad. Neither does He do this rashly, and, as it were fortuitously . . . But according to the order of things times, which is hidden from us, but thoroughly known to Himself; which same order of times, however, He does not serve as subject to it, but Himself rules as lord and appoints as governor[32] . . . If we say that a people is an assemblage of reasonable beings bound together by a common agreement as to the objects of their love, then, in order to discover the character of any people, we have only to observe what they love.[33]

Thus, the way is open for the conjoining of will and reason and law at the disposal of a humanizing sovereignty. Under this sovereignty, love acquires a liberating authority in and over the decision-making of human beings and states. Actually, when the Reformers put their minds to this open way, they dropped a further clue concerning the way ahead. They accepted, as we have said, the natural law, and they tried to anchor it not where Cicero did, but as Brunner has noted, in an order of creation, whence a certain interchangeability between the natural law, the Decalogue, and the law of love could be expatiated upon. But this way of dealing with the tradition only ended where it started: in perpetuating the internal flaw and the external oversight of the natural law tradition. Meanwhile, however, the Reformers kept in mind the side of Augustine which St. Thomas had passed over. When they really faced the question of a *disciplina externa et honestas*, they became absorbed by a variant doctrine of law at their disposal. This bore the identification: *primus usus legis* [first or primary use of the law].

Sometimes they read the *primus usus* as though it meant the "first use of the law." On this reading, they lodged themselves in the familiar confusion. More characteristically, they read the *primus usus* as the "primary" or "principal" use of the law. On this reading, it turned out like this: the law of God is "a divine doctrine in which the just and unalterable will of God *is* revealed as to how man is to be framed in his nature, his thoughts, his words, and his works, so that it may be pleasing and acceptable to God."[34] But this is exactly the Augustinian point. Now, the law is seen as a function of the divine will which operates in an order of governance and love wherein humanity finds a humanizing context for the making of decisions according to an obedience which sets them free in the freedom to obey. A messianic-Augustinian interpretation of the *primus usus legis* is a Christian alternative to natural law which could carry us beyond its present "time of trouble."

AUTHORITY WITH WISDOM: LOVE WITH LAW[35]

How would a messianic-Augustinian interpretation of the *primus usus legis* function as Christian alternative to natural law? To this question, we must now briefly address ourselves. We must do so, *briefly*, partly because the analysis that has brought us in sight of this alternative has already pressed hard upon the outer limits of a testimonial essay. Partly, however, our proposal is a tentative one, and, as of this writing, we see, as in a glass darkly, only some aspects of its implications. We shall try to identify and dispose of a major objection to the alternative to natural law which we have proposed. Perhaps, we shall be able to conclude, then, with a suggestion concerning the relation between the *primus usus legis* and the reversal of the Hobbesian dictum that "authority, not wisdom, makes the law." Our suggestion is that a messianic-Augustinian understanding of the *primus usus legis* opens the way towards an effective congruence between the seat of sovereignty and the dynamic realities of politics.

A Pluralist Objection[36]

Before pursuing this possibility, we must identify and dispose of a major objection to it. We may call it: a *pluralist objection*. The pluralistic objection is that theonomic thinking presupposes the possibility that the cognitive insights of religious faith can affect a creative connection between sovereignty and order. This possibility, however, only compounds the relativism of positive laws with the pluralism of theonomic premises. The result can only be the deepening of the conflict between the sovereignty essential to political order and the realities of the political situation. Many gods are scarcely a persuasive antidote for many lords. And the prospect of a monotheistic unification is, on the face of it, preposterous.

If this were indeed the theonomic option implied by the alternative to natural law here proposed, it could scarcely stand against this pluralistic objection. A messianic-Augustinian understanding of the *primus usus legis*, however, points in a diametrically opposite direction. On this understanding, legal and political positivism and religious pluralism are neither rejected nor subsumed under the inferences drawn by reason form a single confessional or rational faith. On this understanding, legal and political positivism and religious pluralism are functions of a sovereignty in action, fashioning by providential governance and experimentation, the conditions, sustaining and correcting (indeed, for correcting while sustaining and sustaining while correcting) a community requisite for the humanization of human life. These conditions include all things needful for the living and the fulfillment, on journey, of the human sense and point, purposed for humans when the journey began. The discriminating judgments of the reason, the cohesive offices of loyalties, commitments and traditions, which are at once the product and the occasion of the structural arrangements through which the motivational and societal dynamics of human behavior are expressed, acquire in this context a guiding sovereignty and a liberating order.

In a world, in which Jesus of Nazareth has restored, by the full dimensions of his presence and activity, all created things to their proper subsistence and centered all created things upon the priority and possibilities of human fulfillment, there is an order of things and ties which sustains and effects a continuing reciprocity between responsible life and human life. This order bears the secret of a sovereignty which, as Augustine observed, is "hidden from us, but thoroughly known to Himself; which same order of times, however, He does not serve as subject to it, but Himself rules as lord and appoints as governor."[37] In such a world, *law,* understood, not as *lex naturae,* but as *primus usus legis,* means the primary order in which humanity's behavior is set, and by which one's behavior is corrected and sustained. A messianic-Augustinian understanding of law changes the meaning and significance of law. Law is a *function*, not a *principle* of order. In a world, which God has made, and in which God is at work giving human shape to human life, *law is the behavioural function of providence.*

Thus, the *primus usus legis* denotes a political reality. Its recognition is a datum of the knowledge of faith. Its functional reality, however, is independent of such recognition. A refusal to entertain the possibility that faith can supply what reason cannot arrive at, is itself the expression of a faith, indifferent or blind to political reality. The dynamics of the *primus usus legis*, however embrace both positivism and pluralism as penultimate instruments of a sovereignty whose unifying action is the point and the purpose of politics.

The Reversal of the Hobbesian Dictum

It now remains for us to note the effective congruence between the dynamic realities of politics and the seat or source of sovereignty. The messianic-Augustinian option which we have been exploring identifies its congruence as love. Love, as Jesus embodied and taught it, is the particular presence of God in human decision-making. By this presence, human behavior, *where* they are and *as* they are, is steadily drawn into the orbit of that humanizing direction and purpose which characterize the realities of politics. By this presence, the reciprocity between responsible life and human life is steadily corrected while being sustained and sustained while being corrected. Love, as Augustine discerned and proposed it, is the secret according to which the priorities and viabilities of "the order of things and time," of politics, are creatively established and creatively function. Perspective and policy, sovereignty and structure, law and order, in *that* order of priority and viability, acquire through love, a congruence which functions as the sign of the effective congruence between love and law in human affairs. This congruence means that love is the immediate occasion of every decision and the ultimate meaning of providence. The stakes are the humanisation of life for the sake of the humanity of humans.

Thus, intrinsic to the *primus usus legis* is that combination of authority with wisdom which, in reversal of Hobbes, makes law a function of sovereignty, order a function of freedom, power a function of purpose, and community a function of humanity. Under such a perspective and power, human *will* is directed toward the redeeming of the times, the *reason* toward the discernment of the times, and *law* bends the things that have been toward the things that are to come. The *primus usus legis* combines perspective, discriminating judgment and social experimentation in a creative congruence between love and the dynamics of politics. This congruence convicts the nation-state of obsolescence and provides a world in process of unification with the prospect of an integrating and a liberating sovereignty. The congruence between love and law continually returns politics to its humanizing task and opens up before politics a humane and humanizing way.

NOTES

1. Published in Karl Dietrich Bracher, ed., *Die Moderne Demokratie und Ihr Recht: Festschrift für Gerhard Leibholz* (Tübingen: Mohr Siebeck, 1966), 517–542; reprinted with permission. Pages 517–20 of the original essay, which give tribute to Gerhard Leibholz on his sixty-fifth birthday and explain Liebholz's concept of natural law, are omitted here.

2. Cicero, Deleg., 1, 6, 18.

3. Phillip Melanchthon, *Loci communes*. See the translated and edited text by Clyde Manschrek in the Library of Protestant Thought XXIX (New York, 1965).

4. [Editorial: "the law of excluded middle" states that for every proposition, either this proposition or its negation is true.]

5. Marcus Aurelius, *Meditations*, IX, 39.

6. Barth, *KD* II/2, 569.

7. Etienne Gilson, *The Spirit of Medieval Philosophy* (New York: Charles Scribner's Sons, 1936), 327, 325.

8. Augustine, *Sermo*, 150, 7, 8–8, 9.

9. [Editorial: Thomas Aquinas, *Summa Theologica*, Parts I–II, Question 71, Article 2.]

10. A phrase of E. E. Cummings describing the self-confident self-containment of a scientific culture (our culture) that has so vigorously called the tradition of natural law into question. See Cummings, *Xaipe* (New York: Oxford University Press, 1950), 61.

11. See Ernst Troeltsch, for example, in *Social Teachings of the Christian Church* (Philadelphia: Westminster John Knox Press, 1992).

12. Emil Brunner, *Die Gerechtigkeit*, 269/270.

13. See John T. McNeill, "Natural Law in the Teaching of the Reformers," *The Journal of Religion* 26, no. 3 (July 1946).

14. Sigmund Freud, *New Introductory Lectures on Psychoanalysis* (New York: Norton, 1938), 88.

15. Max Weber, *Gesammelte Aufsätze zur Religionssoziologie*, Bd. I, (Tübingen 1920), 204; translation and parentheses Lehmann's.

16. Edward A. Shils, *The Methodology of the Social Sciences* (Glencore: Free Press, 1949), ix ff.

17. Leo Strauss, *Natural Right and History* (Chicago: University of Chicago Press, 1953), 42 ff.

18. See Max Weber, "The Meaning of Ethical Neutrality," in *Methodology of the Social Sciences*, ed., trans. Edward A Shills and Henry A. Finch (New York: Free Press, 1949), 10.

19. Leo Strauss, *Natural Right and History*. I may have misunderstood the argument of this exciting book by assuming that "natural right" and "natural law" are equivalent terms for identifying what Cicero later defined as the *summa ratio, insita in natura*. If a distinction may be made between these two phrases, the meaning would be that "natural right" is the *fons et origo*.

20. I take it that this means the origin of the idea of nature and *pari passu* of natural right.

21. Leo Strauss, *Natural Right and History*, 79, 80.

22. Thomas Aquinas, *Quaest. Disp. De Veritate*, qu. 1, art. 1 and 2. See also, Anselm, *De Veritate*, Cap. X111.

23. [Editorial: Karl Marx, "A Contribution to the Critique of Hegel's Philosophy of Right: Introduction (1983–4)," in *Early Writings*, trans. Rodney Livingstone and Gregor Benton (London, Penguin Books, 1975), 243.]

24. Charles Cochrane, *Christianity and Classical Cultural: A Study of Thought and Action from Augustus to Augustine* (New York: Oxford University Press, 1957).

25. [Editorial: Thomas Aquinas, *Summa Theologica*, Part 1, Question 1, Article 8, Response to Objection 2.]

26. Augustine, *Contra Faustum*, XXII, 27. The "reason or the will of God"—this is a classic instance of the marginality of the elementary premises of the Bible to classicism; no less of the subordination of the will to the reason in the natural law tradition.

27. Ernst Troeltsch, *Die Soziallehren der christlichen Kirchen und Gruppen*, Gesammelte Schriften, Bd. 1 (Mohr Siebeck: Tübingen, 1923), Pt. I.

28. Reinhold Niebuhr, *The Nature and Destiny of Man II* (New York 1932), 4, 5.

29. Pascal, *Pensées*, Fr. 555.

30. Martin Buber, *Das Königtum Gottes* (Heidelberg: L. Schneider, 1956), LXIV.

31. Augustine, *De civitate Dei*, 5.9.

32. Augustine, *De civitate Dei*, 4.33; emphasis mine.

33. Augustine, *De civitate Dei*, 19.24.

34. *Solida Declaratio*, the Second part of the Formula of Consensus, V, 17.

35. [Editorial: Pages 537–39 in the original, describing Leibholz's ideas regarding sovereignty, are omitted.]

36. [Editorial: portion of the paragraph on pages 539–40 has been omitted.]

37. Augustine, *De civitate Dei*, 4.33.

PART IV

Dietrich Bonhoeffer
A Theological Friendship

Paul Lehmann first met Dietrich Bonhoeffer when Bonhoeffer spent the academic year 1930–31 as a Sloan Fellow at Union Theological Seminary in New York City, where Lehmann was a student in the Ph.D. program. Because Lehmann's first language was German, and because he shared an interest in the work of Karl Barth, a close friendship was forged, and Bonhoeffer became a frequent visitor in Paul and Marion's home.[1] According to Eberhard Bethge:

> Paul and Marion Lehmann's house in New York became a kind of American home for Bonhoeffer; he celebrated his twenty-fifth birthday there. With Lehmann he could talk and argue; Lehmann understood the nuances of European culture and theology. Lehmann came from the Evangelical and Reformed Church, but later joined the Presbyterians; he was working on his dissertation at Union Theological Seminary, where he was also a tutor in systematic theology. He could understand why the theological statements of professors and students at the seminary could make Bonhoeffer's hair stand on end.[2]

After Bonhoeffer left Union Seminary in May 1931, Lehmann saw him again when he and Marion traveled to Berlin in April 1933. According to Bethge, while visiting Bonhoeffer's family home, "it struck Lehmann that Klaus Bonhoeffer would occasionally get up—in the course of conversations that, admittedly, were not wholly innocuous—to see if anyone was listening outside the door."[3] Among their topics of conversation was how to send information to Lehmann about the events in Germany and to "the right circles in America, including Rabbi Stephen Wise, whom Bonhoeffer had met during his 1930–31 visit."[4] After that visit to Berlin, Lehmann only saw Bonhoeffer one more time. On July 6, 1939, he traveled from Columbus, Ohio, where he and Marion were spending the summer, to meet Bonhoeffer in New York, hoping to talk Bonhoeffer out of returning to Germany.

Prior to Bonhoeffer's trip to New York, Lehmann, along with Reinhold Niebuhr and Rabbi Steven Wise, had secured work to keep Bonhoeffer in the United States during the crisis in Germany. For his part, Lehmann had written to thirty or forty colleges, securing invitations for Bonhoeffer to teach and give lectures. But, according to Bethge, when Lehmann realized that Bonhoeffer had changed his mind about staying in the U.S., he "accepted it with the greatest understanding" and was, Bethge says, "Bonhoeffer's companion and loyal helper at the most important turning point in his life."[5]

Some decades after Bonhoeffer's execution, Lehmann contributed to the preservation of Bonhoeffer's work by securing a place at Harvard Divinity School in 1976 for Eberhard Bethge to begin editing Bonhoeffer's writings and to begin work on the biography, having already published Bonhoeffer's manuscripts of the *Ethics*. According to Bethge, "Paul Lehmann—apart from his own further theological development of the groundwork laid by Bonhoeffer—took part, with the strongest initiative, in the history of Bonhoeffer's influence on the ecumenical world."[6] The essays in this section reflect three ways Lehmann's work relates to Dietrich Bonhoeffer by offering (1) his impressions of Bonhoeffer as a person, (2) his interpretation of Bonhoeffer's theology, especially the provocative ideas and phrases he wrote from prison, and (3) suggestions of Bonhoeffer's influence on his own work.

First, there are essays that give Lehmann's account of his personal impressions of Bonhoeffer. In several essays Lehmann describes Bonhoeffer as "the most un-German of Germans," mentioning his education and erudition, but also his openness to new things, including his increased awareness of racism in the United Sates through his friendship with the African American student, Franklin Fisher. These essays also describe Lehmann's memories of Bonhoeffer's time in New York City several years later in 1939, and Bonhoeffer's decision to return to Germany rather than live out the war in safety. Correspondence between Bonhoeffer and Lehmann provides additional information regarding Bonhoeffer's decision not to remain in the U.S. in 1939.

Second, some of these essays provide Lehmann's interpretation of Bonhoeffer's theology, including what Bonhoeffer meant by "world come of age," "worldliness," "mandates," "religionless Christianity," and "arcane discipline," expressing Lehmann's sharp criticism of those who used Bonhoeffer's ideas to serve their own agendas. Lehmann was interested then, as many are now, in both the enthusiasm for Bonhoeffer's work and the distortions, which are sometimes one and the same. In terms of enthusiasm, he refers positively to the popularity of Bonhoeffer among college students, who could relate Bonhoeffer's struggle with faith and doubt to their own experience. On the other hand, while he appreciated Bonhoeffer's positive reception in Marxist countries, he did not agree that Bonhoeffer himself could be claimed as a disciple of Marxism. Lehmann is particularly critical of the death of God theologians in the United States who claimed Bonhoeffer as their inspiration. Turning his attention especially to the work of William Hamilton, he argues that only a misunderstanding of Bonhoeffer's phrase "world come of age," could lead to the belief that Bonhoeffer had given up on Christianity or, worse, had given up belief in God altogether. Instead, Lehmann claims a dialectical relationship between faith and worldliness in Bonhoeffer's thought: there is no worldliness without faith and no faith without worldliness. Furthermore, he argues, as many do today, that the key to understanding what Bonhoeffer meant by "world come of age," is found in Bonhoeffer's Christology.

Finally, there are essays that show how Lehmann's own work was influenced by Bonhoeffer. While it is impossible to know which features of Lehmann's theology and ethics were his alone, only coincidentally sharing similarities with Bonhoeffer, and which are grounded in Bonhoeffer's work, the similarities are definitely there. In "Logos in a World come of Age," Lehmann not only reflects on Bonhoeffer's meaning of terms but presents his own theological perspective. Here one finds the distinctive apocalyptic character of the Gospel as he understands it. In Jesus of Nazareth, the very "face of reality" has changed. Christ has a "transforming impact upon the world of people, principalities, and powers, and of time and space and things," making history and nature "new." Likewise, Lehmann rejects the interpretation of the *Logos* as connecting the Gospel with "the intelligible structure and order of the world" and prefers the more apocalyptic understanding that *Logos* "functions as the principal mode of God's self-disclosing action of making all things new." These reflections overlap with Bonhoeffer's understanding of "reality" as created in God's reconciliation of the world in Christ. The two scholars also share a dismissal of the absolute character of moral law and principles, emphasizing instead the contextual character of revelation and an emphasis on relationality in ethics.

This section begins with Eberhard Bethge's description of Lehmann's contribution to his own work on Bonhoeffer in "Paul Lehmann's Initiative." Three of the essays that include Lehmann's reflections on Bonhoeffer as a person have never been published before, including Lehmann's manuscript for a special BBC broadcast on March 13, 1960; his remarks at the dedication of the Bonhoeffer room at Union Seminary in 1984 ("Dietrich Bonhoeffer: Some Vignettes of Remembrance and Interpretation"); and remarks he made at a lecture series at Union Theology Seminary in New York in January 1968 ("Dietrich Bonhoeffer: Four Theological Giants Influence Our Faith"). The exchange of letters with Bonhoeffer in "Correspondence between Bonhoeffer and Paul Lehmann, 1938–39," previously published in volume 15 of the Dietrich Bonhoeffer Works, gives additional information about Reinhold Niebuhr's and Lehmann's efforts to bring Bonhoeffer to New York in 1939 and Bonhoeffer's decision to return to Germany. Finally, Lehmann's interpretation of some key ideas in Bonhoeffer's work as well as a presentation of his own theological perspective can be found in "Faith and Worldliness in Bonhoeffer's Thought," "Logos in a World Come of Age," and "Bonhoeffer—Real or Counterfeit." This section concludes this book of Lehmann's work with a sermon he delivered at the University of North Carolina on June 8, 1947, drawing on some ideas of Bonhoeffer to address Gal. 5:1, 13 in "Called for Freedom."

NOTES

1. Paul and Marion Lehmann are interviewed about their time with Bonhoeffer in the documentary, *Memories and Perspectives*. Trinity Films Incorporated, directed by Bain Boehlke, 1983. This documentary is available on DVD or can be viewed online: (https://www.youtube.com/watch?v=IfygwFwUsIc).
2. Eberhard Bethge, *Dietrich Bonhoeffer: A Biography* (Minneapolis: Fortress Press, 2000), 155.
3. Bethge, *Dietrich Bonhoeffer*, 264.
4. Bethge, *Dietrich Bonhoeffer*, 267.
5. Bethge, *Dietrich Bonhoeffer*, 156.
6. Eberhard Bethge, "Paul Lehmann's Initiative," 304.

Chapter 25

Paul Lehmann's Initiative (1974)

Eberhard Bethge[1]

It must have been in the summer of 1955. Paul Lehmann sat in my dark study of the tumbledown German parsonage in Forest Hill, London. I was the minister of a German congregation in London, the same one which Dietrich Bonhoeffer served as minister twenty years before. We sat in the same room in which Dietrich had once worked. Paul was on his way home from a conference of the Reformed World Federation in Europe.

There Paul posed the question to me, which until then I had neither asked myself nor at that moment was able to answer. He asked, "Who in the German church or in a theological faculty at home could really give you the means and time to organize, preserve, and make accessible Dietrich's legacy down there on your bookshelves?" I answered "No one." I had actually not yet come to think that my ecclesiastical superiors in Germany or Dietrich's former theological faculty could have perhaps considered it and allowed me to be free of my duties as a parish minister for a while. Paul seemed to find that hard to understand. He had already evaluated very well—better than I—what lay hidden there, as yet unedited and exposed to the danger of definite loss. But, then, he also came from a country in which one knows how to handle skillfully, generously and with a sense for systematic scholarship the legacies of important people, and where one does not shy away from the cost. Where else is there a greater number of such archives and libraries?

Paul did not add much more to that; surely he said, characteristically, "That's unthinkable!" How he managed it, then, I am not certain. But in any case, two years later I found myself at Harvard Divinity School freed for a year on sabbatical in order to undertake the first work toward editing Bonhoeffer's collected writings and also to venture the first steps toward the biography. And Paul, who had made me a kind of temporary colleague of his at Harvard, accompanied these steps with advice and necessary encouragement. Perhaps his friendship to Bonhoeffer, which had been unable to prevent Bonhoeffer's return in 1939 to the German catastrophe, compelled him all the more to reveal Dietrich's impact through his works.

At first, I compiled the ecumenical documents of Bonhoeffer's legacy. Contained in them was that work which was of special concern to Paul: Dietrich's diary of that decisive summer of 1939 in New York.[2] I had brought it along with me in 1949, when I met Paul for the first time in Princeton. At that time, I belonged to a group of Germans who were permitted to travel three months in the States, at the expense of American taxpayers and organized by the U.S. military regime in Berlin, "to be re-educated democratically." I took it for granted that now I had to tell Paul of Dietrich's last years. Thereby I discovered how he had sealed his friendship with Dietrich in 1930 at Union Theological Seminary, renewed it in 1933 in Berlin, and had confirmed it in 1939 in New York; that friendship was now transferred unconditionally and immediately to me. I gave him that diary that so deeply involved Paul himself. He supplied me with the correspondence which had occurred in that summer of 1939 with him, with Reinhold Niebuhr, and with Henry Leiper, which I had not seen until then. I also showed him pieces from my prison letters from Dietrich, which in 1949 I had not yet ventured to think of publishing. The *Ethics* had only just been published. (This publication, too, was made possible with the help from the English-speaking world: George Bell had repeatedly pressed my Bishop, Otto Dibelius, whose Adlatus I was after my release from prison, "How far along is Bethge with the *Ethics*? Does he have time enough?")

Thus, Paul Lehmann—apart from his own further theological development of the groundwork laid by Bonhoeffer—took part, with the strongest initiative, in the history of Bonhoeffer's influence on the ecumenical world.

NOTES

1. Published in *Union Seminary Quarterly Review* 29, no. 3 and 4 (1974): 151–52; reprinted with permission.
2. [Editorial: See "American Diary, New York, June–July 1939," in Dietrich Bonhoeffer, *Theological Education Underground: 1937–1940*, DBW 15 (Minneapolis: Fortress Press, 2012), 217–38.]

Chapter 26

Invitation and Contribution of Lehmann for a BBC Broadcast about Dietrich Bonhoeffer (1960)

The British Broadcasting Corporation
630 Fifth Avenue
New York, N.Y.

WASHINGTON, D.C. NEWS OFFICE   NEW YORK OFFICES
NATIONAL PRESS BUILDING   TELEPHONE CIRCLE 7-0656
TELEPHONE EXECUTIVE 3-1465   CABLES: BROADCASTS, N.Y.
CABLES: NEWSCASTS, WASHINGTON

January 20, 1960

Dr. Paul Lehmann
Harvard University
Divinity School
Cambridge, Massachusetts

Dear Dr. Lehmann:

Dr. Colin C.W. James of BBC's Religious Department is preparing a program on the life of Dietrich Bonhoeffer. The program is to be scheduled by BBC on March 13th. We are hoping to include in the program several recordings by some of the eminent people in Britain, the United States and Germany who knew Dr. Bonhoeffer. Dr. Reinhold Niebuhr has already recorded his contribution in New York and I am writing to ask if you would also be willing to contribute a three to four minute recording. This would consist of your recollections of Dr. Bonhoeffer as a fellow-student during his first visit to the

United States, reminiscences of his 1939 visit and the reasons for his coming to this country and his return to Germany.

If you are willing to accept our invitation to take part in the program, I would welcome a reply from you at the earliest possible date. The recording should reach London by early February. Perhaps you could telephone me collect. As far as the actual recording is concerned, I believe it can be made with the cooperation of station WGBH in Cambridge unless you prefer to record at the Divinity School if the necessary technical facilities are available there.

Sincerely yours,
Lillian Lange
Program Director

It was late in September of the year 1930 that I first met Dietrich Bonhoeffer in the Hastings Residence Hall of the Union Theological Seminary in New York. That he had come from abroad and had barely arrived in the United States was not difficult to discern. Except for the blond, wavy hair and the cut of the shoe, one would not at once have guessed that he had come to the Seminary as an exchange student from Germany. This slight external hint at a basic and formative paradox has lodged in my memory because it pointed to the most important characteristic of the Bonhoeffer whom I knew as a student. *Bonhoeffer was the most un-German of Germans.* He was German as regards the furnishings of his mind and spirit. This meant a conspicuously thorough schooling in language and letters, in philosophy and theology, and an uncommon competence at the piano. He was German, too, in the intensity and methodical precision with which he tackled every fresh problem whether in the academic world, with which he was familiar, or the new world of the United States, with which he was to become astonishingly familiar in an uncommon minimum of time. He was German in his passion for perfection, whether of manners, or performance, or of all that is connoted by the word *Kultur*. Here, in short, was an aristocracy of the spirit at its best.

But at the same time Bonhoeffer was the most un-German of Germans. His aristocracy was unmistakable yet not obtrusive, chiefly, I think, owing to his boundless curiosity about every new environment in which he found himself and to his irresistible and unfailing sense of humor. Thus, he could suggest without offense that we should not play tennis together since he commanded a certain expertness at the game which I could not claim.[1] And on the other hand, he could insist that I accompany him half way across the country in a second-hand car, offered him by a German family whom he had met on his voyage to the United States, in order to supervise his driving competence for which the instructions he had taken did not seem to him sufficient. The car, in fact, broke down at various points along the route but Bonhoeffer pressed ahead; his goal was Mexico and he did, indeed, complete the journey and could return the car in tolerable condition to its owner.[2] This curiosity about the new and different, this unfailing humor (even when he was himself directly involved) always turned the incongruity between human aspiration and human failing away from human hurt to the enrichment of comradeship. Here was the un-German side of Bonhoeffer as one knew him. What the paradox comes to is that Bonhoeffer was unique among his countrymen in achieving what the German spirit at its best seeks but does not in like measure succeed in, namely, the capacity to see oneself and the world from a perspective other than one's own. This paradox of birth and nationality in Bonhoeffer has seemed to me increasingly during the years since, to have made him an exciting and conspicuous example of the triumph over parochialism of every kind.

One secret, of course, of this triumph over parochialism was Bonhoeffer's transparent humanity. He was a living embodiment of the dictum of the classical Roman poet, "I am a man; nothing human is foreign to me."[3] During the student year in New York this passionate humanity became particularly apparent in two widely different ways. The one was an intense curiosity about every form of church life in the United States. To many of us at the time this seemed so inconsequential as to be a waste of time. But Bonhoeffer was interested not merely in the institutional forms of American Protestantism. He was trying restlessly to understand whether and in how far the Protestant church in the United States, disparaged in Europe for its disinterest in theology and for its activism, could really be said to find and to meet people where they are in the whole range of their lives as human beings. The church of Jesus Christ as the potentially fulfilling human community—*this* was his concern and drive! The other conspicuous evidence of Bonhoeffer's passionate humanity was his restless curiosity about the Negro problem in the United States. Of course, he had known enough before he came, to know that it was a particularly acute social problem in this country. But what was so impressive was the way in which he pursued the understanding of the problem to its minutest detail through books and countless visits to Harlem, through participation in Negro youth work, but even more through a remarkable kind of identity with the Negro community so that he was received there as though he had never been an outsider at all.

The true secret of Bonhoeffer's life, however, was neither his triumph over parochialism nor his passionate humanity, but his companionship with Jesus Christ. The notable thing about this was that he never wore his Christianity on his sleeve. His theological articulateness and wide human interests were evident on every hand. But that participation in the life of the church, the regular devotional reading of the Bible, the self-evident living of one's life as though Jesus Christ himself were the real and intimate comrade along the way, that these convictions had become habits, and that these habits had become the inconspicuous but vital springs of his way of looking at life and of living it—all this remained to be discovered much, much later.

My last meeting with Dietrich Bonhoeffer was on July 9, 1939.[4] After an interval of almost nine years he had returned, ostensibly for another extended stay. The critical struggles of his brethren in the German church, the steadily deteriorating international situation, and the imminence of war, however, compelled his return. He was resolute against every persuasion to wait out the crisis in the United States. We parted just before midnight, never to meet in this life again. But on that ship, he confided to his diary that "the inner turmoil about the future has ceased. I can look back upon an abbreviated time in America without reproach. My prayerbook contains for this day one of my fondest words from my favorite Psalm: 'I thank thee that thou hast chastened me and taught me thy commands.'"[5] Long before that night, when an unspeakable Nazi despotism robbed him and us of his life, what Bonhoeffer meanwhile had described as "the hiddenness of the devout life" had been lived among us in New York.

NOTES

1. [Editorial: According to Lehmann, when Bonhoeffer asked him whether he played tennis, he replied, "a little." Bonhoeffer responded by saying, "If you only play a little, why play at all?" Lehmann told this story in good humor, making it far different than the fictional account offered by Denise Giardina in her "historical" novel, *Saints and Villains* (New York: Fawcett Books, Ballantine Publishing, 1998), 36.]

2. [Editorial: Jean Lasserre, who accompanied Bonhoeffer to Mexico, gives an account of this car trip in the documentary, "Dietrich Bonhoeffer: Memories and Perspectives," Trinity Films Incorporated, directed by Bain Boehlke, 1983. The interview with Paul and Marion Lehmann also describes preparations for the trip.

3. [Editorial: Publius Terentisu Afer, commonly referred to as Terence, was a playwright in the Roman Republic, whose plays were performed between 170–160 BCE. This well-known quotation is from *The Self-Tormentor*, Act I, scene 1, line 25.]

4. [Editorial: Lehmann came to New York from Columbus, Ohio (where he and his wife, Marion, were spending the summer) to meet with Bonhoeffer on July 6 at Union Theological Seminary, hoping to persuade him to stay in the United States. According to Bonhoeffer's diary, it was July 7 (not the 9th as Lehmann says here) that Lehmann accompanied Bonhoeffer to the ship that returned him to Germany. See Dietrich Bonhoeffer, "American Diary," in Dietrich Bonhoeffer, *Theological Education Underground: 1937–1940*, eds. Victoria J. Barnett and Claudia D. Bergmann, DBW, vol. 15, 237.]

5. [Editorial: Psalm 119:71. For Bonhoeffer's diary entry see, Bonhoeffer, "July 9, 1939," *Theological Education Underground*, 238.]

Chapter 27

Dietrich Bonhoeffer[1]

Some Vignettes of Remembrance and Interpretation (1984)

Let me try ever so briefly, on this moving commemorative occasion, to share with you some recollections of Dietrich Bonhoeffer, whose name, life, work, martyrdom—and presence through his enviable vantage-point in the Church Triumphant—are henceforward to be specifically identified *by* and gratefully remembered *in* this room.

It was here, on Thursday, July 6, 1939, that I was granted the privilege and joy of renewing a friendship which had begun as fellow-students in 1930. According to Dietrich's *Diary of the American Journey*, he had arrived in New York on Monday, June 12; and according to an entry of the following day, the Seminary had allocated to him, what he called "the Prophecy Chamber." Within four days, however, he had overcome the language adjustment and wrote to me on June 17: "Now . . . I am here again . . . I am living in Union, Prophets' Chamber."[2] The present space and its promising purposes bear a notably contrasting resemblance to the surroundings in which our two days of intense conversations took place. But Dietrich recalled "the lovely view of the Quadrangle. I had forgotten much," he told his Diary; "but everything quickly returned, including the aroma of the house."[3] Memory, as we all know, does play tricks on us. So that the archivists and investigative reporters may still plague us with their doubts about whether the name, however spelled, and this place really belong together. Nevertheless, as we also know, administrators have a way of keeping their own counsel, so that those of us who were students in 1930–31, were never asked nor ever told exactly why the guest facilities of the Seminary had been assigned to the space immediately over the Seminary's Gateway Arch, at Broadway and 121st Street. An eyewitness may, accordingly, be allowed to report that the "Prophets' Chamber" was, indeed, this space, between the present entrance to it and the windows overlooking the Quadrangle. Never mind the absence of bathing facilities and cross-ventilation. After all, there was Hastings Hall, less than a stone's throw away; and guests were not normally to need to inhale the increasingly polluted air of the city indefinitely. So, let it be noted for the record, on this commemorative occasion that the nucleus of what is now this room was indeed, the Prophets' Chamber, where Dietrich Bonhoeffer lived as a guest of the Seminary, from June 13 until his departure on July 7, 1939.

One indication of this contrast has been noted in Eberhard Bethge's superb biography of Dietrich.[4] There we may read that Professor John T. McNeill, later to become a member of the Union Faculty in the Historical Field, followed Dietrich into the "Prophets' Chamber," since McNeill was a guest of the Seminary lecturing in the summer session, and since Dietrich had just vacated the premises. McNeill was more than a little surprised by "the masses of illegible sheets of paper of his (to him) unknown predecessor, and at the quantities of cigarettes that he had smoked," that he found in the room when he arrived. "It was not till later," Bethge remarks, "that it dawned on him who had lived there before him and there made the most difficult of all his decisions."[5]

Startling as that contrast may be, it is companioned by another that concerns not so much the room itself as the ethos of the Seminary of which this room was then, and still is to be a part. From that same letter of Erwin Sutz, to which President Shriver has referred, I cull a passage which I could not forego sharing on this occasion. Following up on the now historic "clue line," which has identified Bonhoeffer's room in Hastings Hall during 1930–31: "That famous one—who knows!—in 510," Sutz continued:

> And now there must be other boys in all these rooms, other boys listening to Fosdick's triumphant and easy gospel—full of tears and laughing hearts—to Ward's fear for hard winters to Niebuhr's despite of personal morality, to Lyman's touching curiosity for insignificant things and Baillie's logical God— other European boys enjoying roundtableness with Americans and playing Laval-Hoover with ideas of Page and Eddy near homey fires.[6]

How different it all is now: theologically, socio-politically, and architecturally—in the Seminary and beyond! As different as the residential occupancy of Hastings Hall *then* and *now*. As different as the Second World War, *then* imminent and inevitable: and the Third World War, *now* all but inevitable, not yet but almost imminent, and linked by the awesome ambiguity, bordering on irresponsibility, of American power. *Then*, Dietrich found it possible and faithful to pray for deliverance *through* that power. *Now*, he would find himself belonging to a widening company who find it faithful and urgent to pray for deliverance *from* that power.

Let me, then—and in the light of that *then*—venture to suggest for our *now*, and for the days to come, a thematic focus of these vignettes of remembrance and interpretation of Dietrich Bonhoeffer. This focus could be appropriately identified by the dedication and commitment of this room to the pursuit of excellence, openness, and destiny that centrally marked Dietrich's life and death, in "the power of Christ's resurrection" (Phil. 3:10), and thus, marks this room as an eminently fitting place in this Seminary community in remembrance of him.

I think, first of all, of the discipline of excellence under which Dietrich committed the gifts of body, mind, and spirit; of culture, privilege and opportunity; of faith and humor to the single-minded sensitivity to all things genuinely human; to learning and thinking, scholarship and interpretation, meditation and prayer, the needs of others and the needs of the self, for which the vocation to which he felt called, had claimed him. He was not one to wear his heart on his sleeve, or to impose upon others the way from which he could not turn aside and be at peace and free. He found it necessary to redeem the time, for the time prepared from before the foundation of the world, rather than to waste it with and among those who preferred to cut corners and to masquerade. But for the meditation and prayer—which none of us knew about who were here in the Seminary with him in 1930–31, and which only gradually began to show through the pages of the American Diary of 1939, and afterwards in Finkenwalde—this commitment to excellence could have become a subtle self-justification of snobbery. But never were those founding commitments of this Seminary to "sound learning and enlightened piety" more creatively and un-self-consciously joined than in Dietrich Bonhoeffer. To be sure, Dietrich did not suffer fools gladly. But, at the core, he was a "no-nonsense person," more rigorous with himself than with those whom he preferred rather not to be with than to censure.

This discipline of excellence, Dietrich directed towards himself as well as towards his fellow-students and his eminent theological teachers. Dietrich was himself no unaccomplished pianist. During the years, 1930–31, he would sometimes play the piano in the Social Hall for his own pleasure, whether or not anybody else was there to listen. One late afternoon, as I assume, he came to play again. But Erwin Sutz had preceded him; and Sutz played with such perfection that Dietrich thereafter would never play in the Social Hall again. Sutz was not only too good; but so much better than he, that he freely acknowledged and accepted superior excellence.

As for his teachers, not even Karl Barth escaped. Reinhold Niebuhr, who in 1930–31, could find no trace of a political streak in Bonhoeffer, recalled an incident from the spring of 1939, when he expressed appreciation of Bonhoeffer just after the war. As Eberhard Bethge records it, Reinie said:

> I still remember a discussion of theological and political matters I had with him in London in 1939, when he assured me that Barth was right in becoming more political; but he criticized Barth for defining his position in a little pamphlet. "If," he declared in rather typical German fashion, "one states an original position in many big volumes, one ought to define the change in one's original position in an equally impressive volume and not in a little pamphlet."[7]

So, as you see, Dietrich's commitment to excellence, both less than German, and too German, is directed toward "the little ones"—Sutz's charming self-designation—and toward "the famous ones," with unfailing but liberating integrity.

In tandem, with the discipline of excellence, there was a discipline of self. Two remembrances come here to mind. The first has to do with Dietrich's passion to go to India. In the spring of 1931, we patrolled the New York Harbor Front in search of a ship's captain who might be willing to take us aboard a freighter to the sub-continent of Asia because of Dietrich's eagerness to meet and to learn about Gandhi. We failed, of course, to persuade any ship's captain that we knew what we were about. The puzzling factor in this futile enterprise to me was that Dietrich had at his disposal through his father, a deposit of $2500.00 in the Wall Street Branch of the Chase-Manhattan Bank. With a friend like that, who needs to go begging along the New York waterfront? The answer is: Dietrich Bonhoeffer! And the reason is an ineradicable memory of his own. We talked about it once, and he told me that he had never been able to forget the day, between the First and the Second World Wars, at the height (or depth) of the German inflation, when his father came home from the market with a quart of strawberries. Placing them upon the kitchen table, he explained to the family that he had just cashed in a life-term insurance policy in order to make available to the family a bit of joy and hope which for so long they had been denied. Dietrich simply could not take that risk again, especially for his own personal preference and probable advantage.

Whenever I recall this instance of self-discipline, I think almost simultaneously of another. By 1939, the "Greasy Spoon" had disappeared. But during that year between September 1930 and June 1931, there was in the vicinity of the Seminary, along Broadway just beyond the Manhattan School of Music (in those days, Juilliard was there), a dubious eating establishment, one of a chain. I found the place so uninviting as to put any alimentary system in mortal peril. Not so, Dietrich. He used often to take breakfast there and occasionally a quick lunch or dinner. The legal name of the place has escaped me. But it was known to the students as "the Greasy Spoon." Dietrich found my adamant refusal to enter the place insufferably rigid and snobbish. His was a larger purpose designed for wider horizons. The "Greasy Spoon" greatly aided him in at least three ways. It kept both the delights of dining and hunger at a safe distance. It kept his father's account at Chase from predatory dispersal. And it contributed to his travel budget for India.

Looking back upon these vignettes of Dietrich's practice of the self-discipline of self-denial during the intervening years, I have found myself wondering from time to time—and again this afternoon—whether a larger and more sustaining Providence than he could possibly have been aware of, was already preparing him for the self-disciplined denial which was later to be his portion: in his prison cell in Tegel after his arrest on April 5, 1943; in the Gestapo Cellars of Prinz-Albrechtstrasse, to which he was removed on October 8, 1944; in Buchenwald, to which he was removed on 7 February 1945; and in Flossenbuerg, where he was executed on April 9, 1945.

At all events, as Bethge has noted, that prison cell in Tegel, during Bonhoeffer's eighteen months there, gave us "more writings ... than we have from any other period of his life: notes, letters, scholarly and literary writings."[8] The discipline of excellence, it seems, combined with the discipline of self to give form to a remarkable and memorable freedom of the self in openness to the different, to the other, and to the world. Indeed, hidden in this movement and direction of freedom, there was the secret of Dietrich's witness as a Christian to what it means to be a Christian, of the power of his faith to express in life what the freedom and faithfulness in Jesus Christ *really are*. Only a providential way of looking at life and of living it, can explain as it illuminates and illuminate as it explains, the curious replication of the joy and intensity, the struggle and the probing that dominated the fleeting conversations and hours in this room on that Thursday and Friday, July 6 and 7, 1939, only to surface again under time fore-shortened and destiny inescapably imminent, in that cell in Tegel prison. The conversation partner then, in July 1944, was Eberhard Bethge who had been allowed to visit Bonhoeffer there. Writing to Dietrich about that visit afterward, Eberhard identified the secret of Dietrich's learning and scholarship, discipline and openness, and let the secret out. "Emotion was not our first concern," he wrote to Dietrich, "because we went gaily, concentratedly and as quickly as possible *medias in res*. This is because you have no self-pity and do not seek for any acknowledgement of what you are doing." To be sure there was "suffering and anger, but never self-pity or scruples concerning what he was doing."[9]

One vignette of Dietrich's openness to the different and to the Other in Otherness must content us here this afternoon. As for his openness to the different, I now understand what was at once baffling and vexing in 1930–31. I refer to Dietrich's interest in and concentrated study under the direction of Professor Eugene W. Lyman. Lyman was a gentle, kindly, unassuming person whom, as such, one could not help admiring and respecting. In the classroom, his command of the literature of American philosophy and philosophy of religion was prodigious and enviable. But the lectures were tedious, more often boring than captivating, and defenseless against the subtle intrusions of Morpheus. Coupled as these lectures frequently were, with an inexhaustible patience with the stupidity of a student's question, and with the endeavor to transform stupidity into a "learning experience," as the Teachers' College jargon of the time was wont to require, Professor Lyman's conscientious labors were more than enough to try the patience of the saints, which none of us thought we were, or thought of being. But Dietrich was captivated and engrossed. His openness to the different led him to discern in Eugene Lyman's mastery of "The Meaning and Truth of Religion,"[10] through his authoritative interpretation of the creators of American Pragmatism, an invitation to an exciting and enlarging adventure of "faith seeking understanding." Bonhoeffer notes in his report of the year 1930–31 in the Seminary, that he "read almost the entire philosophical work of William James . . . of John Dewey, Perry, Russell, and finally also J. B. Watson and the literature of behavioral psychology. At the time, the study of Whitehead, Knudson, Santayana was not so illuminating for me as these radical empirical thinkers."[11] William James, he wrote, "captivated me to an unusual degree."[12] Bonhoeffer was on the trail of a principal root of what in August 1939, he was to identify and to probe as "Protestantism Without Reformation."[13]

So much for openness to the different on the level of the attempt to understand and to think about a radically different mode and manner of theological interpretation. A companion vignette on openness to the different may be drawn on the level of Bonhoeffer's personal involvement with difference as Otherness on the boundary on which the neighbor and the enemy meet. On this boundary, the distant Other is brought near in the discovery of the enemy as the neighbor and the neighbor as the enemy. The essay on "Protestantism Without Reformation" contains a brief but penetrating section on "The Black Church" which begins with a brilliantly astute and succinct assessment of "the race question" as a critical problem for American Christianity.[14] It is widely known that Dietrich's involvement with that question was direct and personal through his participation in the worshipping life of the Abyssinian Baptist Church on 138th Street in Harlem. Our fellow-student, Franklin Fisher, was on the staff of that church during the year 1930–31, and greatly contributed to Dietrich's welcome in that parish and to his probing grasp of the complex and painful problem posed by the race question for the churches in the United States. Under Fischer's perceptive and knowledgeable tutelage, Dietrich's openness to Otherness took on human and faith dimensions which otherwise could scarcely have come to him in so short a time. Those Sabbath celebrations in that congregation of Black fellow-Christians not only made Dietrich a lover of the Spirituals but made the Spirituals an inseparable part of his subsequent life and work as a theologian and as a Christian.

A particularly bitter experience of the boundary which keeps neighbors and enemies apart because it makes enemies of neighbors, was occasioned by Fisher's birthday. Dietrich wanted to celebrate by way of a dinner in mid-town and invited Marion and me to join Franklin and him. I was delegated by Dietrich to make the appropriate inquiries and reservations. At this remove in time and circumstance, it would not occur to any member of the Union community to telephone a restaurant to inquire whether black members of any party would be served. But back there, then—a half century and a half decade ago—it seemed the best way to avoid embarrassing encounters. So, I telephoned two or three restaurants, and I was informed by each in turn, that blacks were not welcome and no party for whatever reason, of which blacks were a part, would be admitted. Dietrich was at once consternated, furious, and resolute. He would not submit to *that* intolerability. The dinner party was transferred instead to Marion's and my students' apartment on the first floor of what is now known as "McGiffert Hall" but was then called, "99."

Dietrich's martyrdom must surely forbid any complacent self-satisfaction in the distance we have come during the half-century between then and now, even as it deepens our thankfulness for that distance. But that martyrdom tells us even more about that "amazing grace" in and through which discipline, openness, and destiny are joined. A providential mystery and pressure already *then*—in Harlem and in mid-Manhattan—were breaking down "the dividing wall of hostility" (Eph. 2:14) and shattering the precarious hold on privilege and power of those who prefer enmity to neighborhood so that enemies may become neighbors in freedom and in truth. *Now*—in this room, and henceforward from this afternoon—this same providential mystery and pressure have prepared a place and sign of a new and human future already come upon us which will not be denied. For Dietrich that meant and means the thankful acceptance and practice of the gift of a remarkable kind of identity with the black community. He was received there as though he had been no outsider at all. For this room, its providential context and occasion meant a place and time for the acceptance and nurture of Dietrich's special gift, which Eberhard has sensitively and movingly described as "a gift of restoring the pride and self-confidence of the vulnerable and the sensitive."[15]

Already, "the view from below," of looking at life and of living it "from the perspective of those who suffer,"[16] was being anticipated and tested. Already here, in 1930–31, prudential discipleship was giving way to discipleship as deputyship. Already, the "more resolute Christ-centeredness" conjoined with "a more realistic openness to the world"[17] into which Dietrich was being irreversibly drawn was taking him from Berlin via Union to Harlem; and from Harlem to Finkenwalde, Tegel, and Flossenburg. Let, then, this room in which that momentous decision to live at the risk of death was taken, be set apart for the discovery and the nurture of Dietrich's discovery and exploration of what it means to be a Christian. "Jesus Christ is our life," we read, listen and hear, in the *Ethics*:

> And so now, from the standpoint of Jesus Christ we may say that our (fellow human being) is our life and that God is our life . . . We "live" when, in our encounter with (our human companions) and with God, the "yes" and the "no" are combined in a unity of contradictions, in self-less self-assertion, in self-assertion in the sacrifice of ourselves to God and to (humanity) . . . The life which confronts us in Jesus Christ, as a "yes" and a "no" to our life, requires the response of a life which assimilates and unites this "yes" and this "no."[18]

In conclusion, let it be reported that on Friday, July 7th, 1939, Dietrich and I set out from this room, as it then was and was used, for the North German Lloyd Line Pier on 12th Avenue at 48th or 49th Street. I could not accompany him aboard; nor even to the Pier itself because of the Gestapo and the S.S. Security Police. Dietrich had already learned at firsthand what life in a totalitarian state is like. We parted at 11:30 p.m. and beneath the cover of darkness and the cover of the corner, I watched him from across the Avenue, board the ship and disappear. That was, as I have said, in 1939. This afternoon, we gather in this room, now reconstructed and otherwise purposed, in grateful tribute and remembrance—39 years and two days after Dietrich's execution on 9 April 1945.

NOTES

1. "Remarks upon the occasion of the inauguration of the Dietrich Bonhoeffer Room in Union Theological Seminary, New York on Wednesday, 11 April 1984 at 4:00 p.m." The transcript of Lehmann's remarks was sent to Nancy Duff on May 25, 1984, requesting her to type it. This presentation has not been previously published and is not presently in the Lehmann archives.

2. So, Dietrich Bonhoeffer, "Tagebuch der Amerikareise (1939)," in *Gesammelte Schriften. Oikumene Briefe, Aufsätze, Dokumente, 1928–42*, Bd. I, ed. Eberhard Bethge (München: Chr. Kaiser, 1965), 291–315; the entries of 12. and 13. June are on 295–96. Translation, Lehmann's. The letter to Lehmann is in the Bonhoeffer Archive in Berlin; a copy is in Lehmann's files. See further, Bethge, *Dietrich Bonhoeffer*, esp. 54–62. [Editorial: For Dietrich Bonhoeffer's diary entries in English translation from his time in New York, June 8, 1939-July 9, 1939, see Bonhoeffer, *Theological Education Underground: 1937–1940*, DBW 15, 217–38].

3. Bethge, *Dietrich Bonhoeffer*, 296; translation, Lehmann's. [Editorial: See Bonhoeffer, "American Diary," 220.]

4. [Editorial: see Eberhard Bethge, *Dietrich Bonhoeffer: A Biography*, ed. Victoria J. Barnett, revised edition, (Minneapolis: Fortress Press, 2000), 655.]

5. Bethge, *Dietrich Bonhoeffer*, 559. [Editorial: Bethge, *Dietrich Bonhoeffer*, revised edition, 655.]

6. From an unpublished letter to me from his Parish in Pratteln, Switzerland. The letter was dated, 25 October 1931. Herbert Hoover was then President of the United States and Pierre Laval, the Prime Minister of France. Sherwood Eddy was a widely known Secretary of the National Student Y.M.C.A. and a close friend of Reinhold Niebuhr. Kirby Page, a minister of the Disciples of Christ, was a frequent speaker on college campuses and was an eloquent exponent of the American Social Gospel.

7. See, Bethge, *Dietrich Bonhoeffer*, 525–26. [Editorial: Bethge, *Dietrich Bonhoeffer*, revised edition, 621.] For the original report of this conversation, see *Christianity and Crisis* 5, no. 11, 6. The pamphlet at issue was Barth's pamphlet called, *Rechtfertigung und Recht* (Justification and Law), and his letter to Hromadka. [Editorial: No date is given for this volume of *Christianity and Crisis*.]

8. Bethge, *Dietrich Bonhoeffer*, 732. [Editorial: See Bethge, *Dietrich Bonhoeffer*, revised edition, 829.]

9. Bethge, *Bonhoeffer*, 732. [Editorial: See Bethge, *Dietrich Bonhoeffer*, revised edition, 829.]

10. Eugene Lyman, *The Meaning and Truth of Religion* (New York: C. Scribner's Sons, 1933).

11. Bonhoeffer, *Gesammelte Schriften*, 84–103; and especially, 88, 91. Translation Lehmann's. [Editorial: For a translation of Bonhoeffer's "Report on My Year of Study at Union Theological Seminary in New York, 1930/31," see Dietrich Bonhoeffer, *Barcelona, Berlin, New York, 1928–31*, ed. Clifford J. Green, trans. Douglas W. Stott, DBW 10 (Minneapolis: Fortress Press, 2008), 305–320, esp. 310.]

12. Bonhoeffer, *Gesammelte Schriften*, 91. [Editorial: Bonhoeffer, *Barcelona, Berlin, New York, 1928–31*, DBW 10, 310.]

13. Bonhoeffer, *Gesammelte Schriften*, 323–54. This essay on "Protestantism Without Reformation" was intended as a report on his stay in the United States, in June-July 1939. [Editorial: The essay, "Protestantism Without Reformation" is published in Bonhoeffer, *Theological Education Underground: 1937–1940*, DBW 15, 438–462.]

14. Bonhoeffer, *Gesammelte Schriften*, 347–49. [Editorial: See Bonhoeffer, *Theological Education Underground: 1937–1940*, DBW 15, 456–458.]

15. Bethge, *Dietrich Bonhoeffer*, 114. [Editorial: Bethge, *Dietrich Bonhoeffer*, revised edition, 155.]

16. Dietrich Bonhoeffer, *Letters and Papers From Prison* ed. Eberhard Bethge, (New York, The Macmillan Company, 1978), 17. [Editorial: See "A View from Below," at the end of "An Account at the Turn of the Year 1942–43," in *Dietrich Bonhoeffer: Letters and Papers from Prison*, DBW 8, 1–52.]

17. Bethge, *Dietrich Bonhoeffer*, 625.

18. Dietrich Bonhoeffer, *Ethics*, ed. Eberhard Bethge, based on the sixth German edition, 1963, (New York: The Macmillan Company, 1965); 1965, 221–22. Parentheses indicate where I have altered the translation but not Bonhoeffer's meaning, in the interest of inclusive language. [Editorial: See Dietrich Bonhoeffer, *Ethics*, DBW 6, 254.]

Chapter 28

Faith and Worldliness in Bonhoeffer's Thought (1967)[1]

The response to Dietrich Bonhoeffer's fertile and fragmentary theological ideas has been, in the main, twofold. On the continent where he lived and wrote, suffered and died, he has been alternately hailed and ignored. The response has been shaped by the Oder-Neisse line.[2] On the eastern side of that boundary, Bonhoeffer has been accepted, and even celebrated, as "the prophet of a new Christianity," a phrase once used by Professor Pauck to put a question to American theology about Karl Barth.[3] To Christians living in a Marxist society, the insights, style, and images that erupt from the Bonhoeffer fragments nourish both the conversation of the church with itself, in its preaching and teaching, and the dialogue with Marxist unbelief and secularism. The most perceptive interpretation of Bonhoeffer's thought to date makes him all but a Marxist, or at least, the great Christian apostle to the Marxists.[4] As Paul of Tarsus once went westward to the Gentiles, so Bonhoeffer has reversed the direction and gone eastward to the Gentiles of a world come of age.

On the western side of the Oder-Neisse line, Bonhoeffer's thought has been both seriously probed and widely ignored. He has continued to speak to an inner company of his former students and companions in the struggle of the church against Hitler. This company has been joined by a larger circle in a series of annual conferences devoted to the clarification of Bonhoeffer's ideas and the assessment of their implications. This group has been responsible for a periodical which bears the title of this colloquium. *Die Mündige Welt* (*World Come of Age*) has appeared in four volumes between 1955 and 1963.[5] For the most part, however, it must be noted that Bonhoeffer has not seriously shifted the focus of attention of German theology from its concerns, on the one hand, with hermeneutics from Bultmann to Herbert Braun and, on the other hand, with neo-confessionalism in which the mentalities of the Barmen Declaration and of Lutheran creedalism continue a debate on which fewer and fewer people listen in.

Meanwhile, in the United States the response to Bonhoeffer exhibits both enthusiasm and distortion. The enthusiasm is widespread among college students and the segment among them that finds its way into theological seminaries. The reasons for the enthusiasm are varied, and they do not relate mainly to his martyrdom. They relate rather to the candor and contemporaneity with which the language, ideas, and concerns of Bonhoeffer give life to the theological tradition and point to radical new formulations which risk abandonment of tradition rather than subject the reality and power of faith to its deadening weight. Bonhoeffer seems to be concretely involved in the critical struggle of faith with doubt that characterizes serious theological curiosity today. The curiosity may be coming alive or coming of age. The response to Bonhoeffer is at least one important measure of its sensitivity. Insofar as theological faculties have lagged behind their students in this response, they seem precariously prey to the dilemma between obsolescence and an *odium theologicum* [literally, theological hatred].

DISTORTING THE WORLD COME OF AGE

We are more concerned, however, with the distortion which afflicts the response to Bonhoeffer in this country. It is not strange that the distortion should have focused upon the phrase "the world come of age," since even Bonhoeffer's closest students and friends have been puzzled by it and are still pursuing its implications. What *is* strange is the expropriation of the phrase for purposes alien to the intimate connection between Bonhoeffer's own faith and spirit as a Christian and his theological concerns. The phrase has, accordingly, functioned as a misleading half-truth, carelessly and sometimes capriciously disseminated. As such a half-truth, "the world come of age" has supported the sloganizing of "the death of God," of "holy worldliness," and of "religion-less Christianity." Consequently, Bonhoeffer has been caricatured as the apostle of Christian atheism, the troubadour of the new optimism, the St. George of the post-Christian era whose sword of the secular spirit has decapitated the two-headed dragon of tradition and transcendence. As Sigmund Freud calmly addressed an imaginary believer, so Bonhoeffer is said to have crusadingly addressed a Christianity which he was passing up and passing beyond. "I think," said Freud, "you are defending a lost cause . . . My illusions are not like religious ones, incapable of correction."[6]

Subtle Carelessness

Perhaps the most extreme form of this distortion has found its way into the *New York Review of Books*.[7] There William Bartley III, whose own odyssey has carried him beyond God to enlightenment, writes about Bonhoeffer as follows:

> It becomes rather urgent for a person holding a view like Bonhoeffer's—that there is literally no need for Christianity or for God in an adult world—to explain what if anything does distinguish a Christian from others, and why, indeed, anyone should in such circumstances remain a Christian. It is precisely at this point that Bonhoeffer, who is rarely profound but usually clear, becomes as vague as any conventional German theologian. The role of the Christian is conceived now as a fundamentally ethical one of total engagement in social and personal life in full collaboration with likeminded liberal secularists.[8]

Bartley also wonders whether Bonhoeffer, had he not been executed, might not have quite simply "forsaken Protestant theology."

Paul Tillich and Reinhold Niebuhr are even more condescendingly assessed. Bartley charges them with "shallow and wooly eclectic thinking" and with "occasional downright incompetence and self-deception." How Bartley can conclude so firmly that "the role of the Christian is conceived now as a fundamentally ethical one of total engagement in social and personal life in full collaboration with like-minded liberal secularists" is uncertain. More serious is the fallacy which enables Bartley to insist that, since for Bonhoeffer "there is literally no need for Christianity or for God in an adult world," he is required "to explain what if anything does distinguish a Christian from others, and why, indeed, anyone should in such circumstances remain a Christian." Only a little less ignorance of Bonhoeffer would tell an honest reader that this is exactly Bonhoeffer's point. The difference that being a Christian makes is not the need for Christianity or for God at all—in an adult world or some other world. According to Bonhoeffer, this has always been a grievous error of Christian preaching and teaching. The difference which being a Christian makes is simply faithfulness to the life of God in the world as this life takes shape in Jesus Christ and in human life. But then, as Michael Novak has remarked, Bartley has "registered a characteristic Anglo-American philosophical complaint."[9] To this complaint, Alasdair MacIntyre has replied with a not altogether dissimilar impertinence: "The creed of the English is that there is no God and that it is wise to pray to him from time to time."[10]

If William Bartley's expropriation of the phrase "the world come of age" is a capricious dissemination of a half-truth, the expropriation of the phrase by the so-called radical theologians is, at the least, a careless dissemination of a half-truth. The carelessness is at once difficult to deal with and difficult to ignore because of the subtlety with which it makes "confusion worse confounded." Perhaps Professor William Hamilton is the most deliberate and strident disseminator of this subtle carelessness. His various attempts at it have been gathered together in a readily accessible paperback, *Radical Theology and the Death of God*.[11] Professor Hamilton's acknowledged indebtedness to Bonhoeffer is candid and explicit.[12] At the same time, he recognizes that Bonhoeffer may not always be correctly understood as going as far as he is himself willing to go in the world come of age.[13] The carelessness and the confusion, however, arise in this way. On the one hand, Hamilton writes: "We really don't know what Bonhoeffer meant by religion, and our modern study of the problem of religionlessness must be carried on quite independent of the task, probably fruitless, of establishing just what Bonhoeffer meant."[14] On the other hand, he writes: "Technically, what Bonhoeffer is saying is that in the modern world that can do without God, the idea of the innate religiousness of man, the religious a priori must be rejected . . . Put more clearly, Bonhoeffer states that in the world come of age, we can no longer be religious, if religion is defined as that system that treats God or the gods as need-fulfillers and problem-solvers."[15] If we really don't know what Bonhoeffer meant by religion, how can we say "technically, what Bonhoeffer is saying?" Nor is it easy to understand why Professor Hamilton would state clearly what Bonhoeffer says about religion in an essay admittedly written for "an audience that had no special background information about the current theological influence exercised by Bonhoeffer,"[16] having said already two years earlier, in a self-styled "programmatic essay"[17] that we probably could never establish what Bonhoeffer meant.

Fortunately, in this colloquium, Dr. Eberhard Bethge, holder of the 1966–67 Fosdick Professorship in Union Seminary, has happily agreed to address himself to the very question Dr. Hamilton says we don't really know anything about. Thus, the record is in imminent prospect of being set straight, supported, beyond Dr. Bethge's address to come, by the recent publication of Dr. Bethge's long-awaited, full-length biography, with which Bonhoeffer himself at last has a chance of coming of age in a world come of age.[18] "Those who do not believe in God," the President Emeritus of Princeton Seminary was wont to remark, "are not prepared to take account of undesigned coincidence." At least by charter, Union Seminary still does believe in God. To the Seminary's own archival recollections of one of its notable alumni may thus be added, both as a *coincidentia oppositorum* [coincidence of opposites] and as a *coincidentia providentiae* [coincidence of providence], the notation that Dr. Bethge's impressive biographical achievement and his incumbency in the Foskick Chair happened together.

Meanwhile, we shall venture to risk the opinion that Dr. Hamilton's distortion of the phrase "the world come of age" will be, like Freud's illusions, capable of correction by the record. Hamilton's careless subtlety will then stand exposed by the careful subtlety of Bonhoeffer himself. The critical instance of the exposure takes us to the center of our present task.

APPLYING DIALECTICAL ANALYSIS

The relation between faith and worldliness in Bonhoeffer's thought is a dialectical one. Like the relation between God and the world come of age, between Christology and religionless Christianity, between church and humanity, theology and ethics, forgiveness and love, hiddenness and openness in the life of discipleship—or any other combination among the characteristic Bonhoeffer themes—and not least, Bonhoeffer himself in a world come of age—there is a single focus of a many-faceted preoccupation that functions as the clue to a correct assessment of Bonhoeffer's thought and of his contribution to the theological unrest and adventure of the present time. I owe to Dr. Bethge the proper language for Bonhoeffer's consuming theological concern and for his dialectical analysis and application of it. The concern is with Jesus Christ: with who Jesus Christ is for us today and with what it means today to be a Christian. Today is the world come of age. The relation of Jesus Christ to this "today," to the world come of age, is the dialectical one of "identity and identification" (Bethge). How can a Christian discover and respond to one's identity as a Christian without weakening or surrendering one's identification with the world? How can a Christian identify with the world without losing or abandoning one's identity as a Christian?

Professor Hamilton clearly and correctly sees the central importance of these questions to Bonhoeffer's thought. He wrestles with them himself with such earnestness, fascination and candor as to confess that, as a theologian, he does not know whether "we discovered this (that is, his own role as a theologian) in him, and then in ourselves; or in ourselves, and then rejoiced to find it in him."[19] He struggles to maintain the depth, range, and persistence of Bonhoeffer's subtlety in probing the problem of identity and identification. "The Christian life," he declares:

> as the discernment of Jesus beneath the worldly masks can be called work or interpretation or criticism; while the Christian life as becoming Jesus looks a little different. At this point the Christian is the sucker, the fall guy, the jester, the fool for Christ, the one who stands before Pilate and is silent, the one who stands before power and power-structures and laughs. Whichever of the paths one takes to find or define Jesus in the world . . . the worldliness of the Protestant can never . . . have an utterly humanistic form. I may be proposing . . . a too narrowly ethical approach to Christological problems, but it should at least be

noted that however acute the experience of the death of God may be for us . . . a form of obedience remains to us in our time of deprivation.[20]

But then Hamilton seems to waver in the dialectical subtlety of his concern to keep identity and identification together. "We are the not-havers, whose un-dialectical 'yes' to the world is balanced by a 'no' to God," he declares in his enthusiastic optimism.[21] "The combination of a certain kind of God-rejection with a certain kind of world-affirmation is the point where I join the death of God movement," he goes on:

> This faith is more like a place, a being with or standing beside the neighbor. Faith has almost collapsed into love, and the Protestant is no longer defined as the forgiven sinner . . . but as the one beside the neighbor, beside the enemy, at the disposal of man in need . . . Really to travel along this road means that we trust the world, not God, to be our fulfiller and problem-solver, and God, if he is to be for us at all, must come in some other role.[22]

But for Professor Hamilton, God does not come; at least, not yet. There is only un-dialectical waiting, only the possibility of a presence, only the place beside the neighbor, as the place "where Jesus is to be found and served."[23]

Professor Hamilton's treatment of Bonhoeffer, and of his own relation to him, is significant for the present attempt to explore the relation between faith and worldliness in Bonhoeffer's thought because it shows not only what can happen to Bonhoeffer in a world come of age, but also what can happen to a world come of age when Bonhoeffer's subtle probing of the dialectic between identity and identification is abandoned. Faith does indeed collapse into love; and love collapses into the neighbor; and the neighbor into Christ; and Christ into humanity; and humanity into the optimistic worldliness by which, in a marked inversion of Mr. Auden's not-of-tragedy-but-of-anxiety, one knows how to place every "what" in one's world, including why he is both God and good.[24] We do not wish to extol Bonhoeffer either as the architect or the patron theologian of a world come of age. We do raise the question, however, whether it is theologically admissible to play games with Bonhoeffer's language and ideas; and especially, whether a closer attention to Bonhoeffer's own dialectic might point to more creative relations between faith and worldliness than that proposed by a self-styled radical theology, namely, the death of God in a world come of age. This is not an occasion of gamesmanship, even if there were time. It is, however, time and occasion to note some aspects of Bonhoeffer's analysis of the dialectical relation between faith and worldliness with particular reference to their bearing upon the difficult task of being a Christian today without losing either one's identity or one's identification.

Conceptualizing Reality

The dialectic between faith and worldliness is the ethical mode of the basic and inescapable dialectic of a Christian between identity and identification. The relation between faith and worldliness characterizes the behavior of a Christian in the world. As Bonhoeffer sees it, there is not true worldliness without faith; and contrariwise, there is no true faith without worldliness. Ultimately, for Bonhoeffer, there is only one proper adjective for worldliness. It is the adjective "Christian." For semantic and cultural reasons, however, it is impossible to speak of "Christian worldliness." The Christological reading of reality that underlies this phrase is a biblical option that can only function as an option in a pluralistic world of rival idolatries and competing ideologies. Freud and his disciples and correctors are but the latest documenters of the fact that the "reality principle" has always had hard going in a world in which illusions are hard to break and fulfilling loyalties hard to come by. On the reality question the Church has done no better than the world; the world is now trying once again to do better than the Church. Bonhoeffer's own odyssey, which Dr. Bethge has brilliantly described and documented as a movement from theologian to Christian and from Christian to contemporary, is the best commentary upon his relentless responsiveness to this reality, however radically its language and structures in church and world might have to be revised. Thus, he declares in his *Ethics*:

> There are not two realities but only one reality. This is the reality of God in the reality of the world, revealed in Christ. Participating in Christ, we stand at one and the same time, in the reality of God and in the reality of the world. The reality of Christ includes within itself the reality of the world . . . It is a denial of the revelation of God in Jesus Christ to wish to be "Christian," without seeing and recognizing the world in Christ.[25]

The risk of faulty seeing is so great that Bonhoeffer will not speak of "Christian worldliness" but rather of "true worldliness" (*echte Weltlichkeit*).

In a world come of age, it is particularly important to bear this in mind. Otherwise, we shall have to live down the radical theology needlessly. The Christological leverage for Bonhoeffer's view of reality I shall leave to Dr. Bethge's subsequent discussion. Meanwhile, let us content ourselves with his reminder:

> Bonhoeffer often expressed the view that the *Ethics* was to be his life's task . . . The concept of "reality," already intimated in *Act and Being* . . . is developed [in the *Ethics*] in new ways and appears as tightly anchored in Christology . . . In this way Bonhoeffer tries to avoid both the positivistic and the idealistic understanding of reality. He regarded both as abstractions . . . He wished [also]

to circumnavigate the reefs and rocks [*Klippen*] of a merely actualistic situation ethic, and yet retain its proper concern. He wished also to overcome the pale remoteness of a normative ethic, and yet take up its concern about continuity. Thus, again, he wished to mediate between two contradictory positions.[26]

In *The Cost of Discipleship*, Bonhoeffer was almost monastically scornful of the world.[27] In the light of his concentration upon the glorification of Christ, the world appears to be under the heavy shadow of negation. A kind of ultra-Lutheranism seems to lurk beneath the surface of his description of discipleship and threatens to exchange an Augustinian Luther for a Franciscan one. As Dr. Bethge's biography now helps us to see more clearly, however, what was really going on—on the way from *The Cost of Discipleship* to the *Ethics*, that is, from 1937 to 1945—was a steady and dynamic preoccupation with the dialectic between faith and worldliness.[28] The movement was a shift of attention from the response to the lordship of Christ in the Church to the response to the lordship of Christ in and over the world. The terms of the shift concerned the relation between the command of God, as *primus usus legis*, and the mandates under which and through which the Christian lives in the world—more strongly even, through which the world is structured or conformed to the world-reality of Christ.

The Thrust Towards Worldliness

As Bethge has put it: "The Church had claimed Bonhoeffer's attention for such a long time that the world in its creatureliness and historicality (*Geschöpflichkeit und Geschichtlichkeit*) had—with good reason—gone unnoticed. Now, the world claimed fresh attention as the sphere of the *regnum Christi*."[29] The mandates carry the formative behavioral load of this thrust towards worldliness. The term "mandates" was first used explicitly in relation to the conception of the *regnum Christi* [kingdom of Christ] and especially as a substitute for the dangerous notion of the "orders of creation" which had characterized Protestant theology and ethics since the Reformation. Even the notion of "orders of providence," which had appeared in the first try at the *Ethics*, was abandoned in favor of mandates. The mandates function for Bonhoeffer as the guidelines of "true worldliness." They do this partly because they express the relation of humanity to the world as the sphere of Christ's rule, partly because they indicate the concreteness of the claim of Christ in every identification with and task in the world, and partly because in this way whoever takes responsibility in the world for the world is given freedom of action and real history takes place (Bethge).

The list and explanation of the mandates raise the question whether the English translation, "divine decree" for *göttliches Mandat*, says exactly what

Bonhoeffer wished to express. For Bonhoeffer, "mandate" refers to a human structure in the world that functions in a basic way to express and to order God's purpose for the world. God's purpose is that the world shall be the place of the humanization of human beings, as Jesus Christ gives form and freedom and fulfillment to all that one is and does, is intended to become and can become. Bonhoeffer arrives at these structures through a reading of the Bible in the context of human history, sociology, and politics. He finds these structures confirmed through a reading of human history, sociology, and politics in the context of the Bible. Here too the dialectic of faith and worldliness is operative in his thought. In Bonhoeffer's own words, "we understand by 'mandate,' a concrete, divine task, grounded in the revelation in Christ and attested in the Scriptures. Furthermore, a 'mandate' is the power and authorization for carrying out a specific divine command, the bestowal (*Verleihung*) of divine authority upon an earthly situation."[30] The mandates are four in number. They are operational structures particularly appropriate to doing the will of God in a world come of age. Bonhoeffer's word is *Gestalten*. The structures or *Gestalten* of "Christian worldliness," therefore, are: church, marriage and family, culture, and authority (*Obrigkeit*).

Our purpose here is not to follow through on Bonhoeffer's account of these mandates in operation. We are concerned with emphasizing that they provide the structures of true worldliness through which the dialectic between faith and worldliness shows itself in behavior. Two letters to Bethge must suffice in support of our suggestion that faith and worldliness belong together; and that when seen in their interchangeability, Bonhoeffer's contribution to a world come of age is his restless and open-ended search for ever new language and ever more concrete ways of keeping the identity of a Christian in the world and the identification of a Christian with the world together.

On June 25, 1942, he wrote:

> My strong activity along the worldly sector in recent days ever and again gives me pause. I am astonished at myself that I live and can live for days without reading the Bible. (Were I to force myself to it, I should find that autosuggestion.) I understand that such autosuggestion can be a great help and is; but I am afraid that along this route, a genuine experience could be falsified and not lead to genuine help after all. When, then, I turn to the Bible again, the book becomes new for me and a joy as never before, and I have the urge once again to preach . . . I sense how the opposition to everything "religious" grows in me . . . But of God and of Christ, I must continually think. My great concern is with integrity, freedom, compassion . . . In this sense, I understand my present doings on the worldly sector.[31]

Two years later, on January 23, 1944, he wrote with special reference to friendship:

It is not easy to give a sociological account of friendship. Friendship probably belongs under the conception, culture . . . and education . . . Marriage, work, state, and Church have their concrete divine command. But what about culture and education? . . . They do not belong to the sphere of obedience but to the sphere of freedom which surrounds all three mandates. He who does not know about this sphere (*Spielraum*) of freedom, can be a good father, citizen, and worker, and even a good Christian. But I question whether he can be a complete human being (and to this extent cannot really be a Christian in the full sense). Perhaps—so it almost seems today—it is the conception of the Church which alone offers an understanding of the sphere of freedom (art, learning, friendship, play)? Thus, the "aesthetic existence" [Kierkegaard] would be not alien to the Church but really be newly established within it. Who, for example, can nourish without difficulty in our time, music or friendship or play or joy? Certainly not the "ethical man" but only the Christian . . . I think that within the realm of freedom, understood in this way . . . friendship is the rarest and most expensive good.[32]

This is the subtle dialectic of faith and worldliness which arrests the so-called radical theology's distortion of the world come of age and makes Bonhoeffer a more profound resource for celebration of and in the secular city.

The Secret Discipline of Faith

There is, however, an aspect of the dialectic between faith and worldliness which calls for some attention before we suspend the present consideration. It has to do with one of the more obscure and problematical of Bonhoeffer's thoughts about the dialectic of identity and identification. Perhaps also for this reason it has been insufficiently noticed. I am referring to what I describe as "the secret discipline of faith." Bonhoeffer's own word for it is *Arkandisziplin*. In the course of a long letter to Bethge, April 30, 1944, Bonhoeffer came to the question of the biblical message and the modern person. "Are not righteousness and the kingdom of God on earth the center of everything?" he asked. "The real concern is not with the Beyond but with this world, how it was created, how it will be sustained, held in order, reconciled, and renewed. What goes beyond the world, and is according to the Gospel, must be for the world." And then, following his strictures against Karl Barth's revelational positivism, he declares: "There must be a restoration of an arcane discipline, through which the mysteries of Christian faith may be preserved from profanation."[33] What is this arcane discipline? And what is its relation to "true worldliness" in a world come of age?[34]

The phrase seems to refer to an earlier experience of the Church in a world come of age. This time the Church has come into the world. In our time, the world is leaving the Church behind. But in both instances, the dialectic between identity and identification takes similar forms. In the post-Constantinian era, as Lietzmann has noted, "the Church became an essential element of public life; she became an indispensable part of the world which she had hitherto passionately fought against."[35] As a defense both against the confusion of Christian mysteries with secular ones, as well as against the mere externalizing of Christianity in the world, the Church laid great stress upon the painstaking ordering of its own life in worship and catechesis. When the post-Christian era began to dawn, well before anybody suspected what was going on, the Church, this time also in the context of the Reformation, gave special concern to the distinction between the baptized and the unbaptized, between those prepared to receive the Eucharist and those excluded from it. The theologians of the seventeenth century called this practice of special stress upon worship and catechesis, "arcane discipline."

Bonhoeffer seems to have returned to this tradition. "What is the meaning of worship and prayer in a religion-less time?" he asks. Does an arcane discipline now acquire . . . new significance?"[36] And so, in our turn, we might ask, how Bonhoeffer could post these questions without drawing back from a world come of age and into a revival of the Constantinian spirit: of a *corpus Christi* [body of Christ] within a *corpus Christianum* [Christian commonwealth or society]? Doesn't the secret discipline of faith cut the Gordian knot of the dialectic between faith and worldliness so necessary to keep identity and identification together?

That Bonhoeffer did explore, and even propose such an arcane discipline can scarcely be denied. Already in the *Sanctorum Communio*, he lays great stress upon the visible Church, upon the world and sacrament, upon Bible study and prayer as marks of the sociological reality of the Church as a community of faith in relation to the communities of the world. In *The Cost of Discipleship*, he seems to stress even more strongly the separation of the Christian from the world and the hiddenness of the devout life. And even in the *Ethics*, the mandate of the Church penetrates all the other mandates, even as it penetrates the whole of humankind.

Inconclusive as they must remain, there are perhaps two things to be said in conclusion about the secret discipline of faith. For the first time the arcane discipline is radically instrumental to the *regnum Christi* in the world. For Bonhoeffer, then, the discipline of faith is necessary to keep identification of the Christian with the world from swallowing up his identity. If one recalls Professor Hamilton's readiness to wait for the possible arrival of a God whose presence can now at best be expected, Bonhoeffer's waiting is neither empty of activity, nor completely filled with neighbor identification. He knows something about the relation of prayer and fasting to the casting out of demons. Secondly, Bonhoeffer pursued the traditional forms of the secret discipline of faith in a pragmatic and functional way. He did not find it necessary to say an un-dialectical "no" to God in order to say an un-dialectical "yes" to the world. Thus, he ventured to risk something concrete on behalf of the identity of the Christian in the hope that thereby his identification with the world might bring its true identity to the world itself. In his own life, it worked. He died as a theologian and a Christian who had become a contemporary. If, in a world come of age, we wish to pursue the dialectic between faith and worldliness without surrendering our identity as Christians to identification with the world, and thus betraying the world, we must ask ourselves how we propose to nourish identity so that identification may be protected against idolatry and ideology and thus bless the world and all people therein with freedom, fulfillment, and joy.

NOTES

1. Published in *Union Seminary Quarterly Review* 23, no. 1 (1967): 31–44. It was later reprinted in P. Vorkink, ed., *Bonhoeffer in a World Come of Age* (Philadelphia: Fortress Press, 1968); reprinted here with permission.

2. [Editorial: The "Oder-Neisse line" refers to the boundary between Germany and Poland defined by the Oder and Neisse rivers.]

3. Wilhelm Pauck, *Karl Barth, Prophet of a New Christianity?* (New York: Harper & Bros., 1931).

4. Hanfried Müller, *Von der Kirche zur Welt* (Leipzig: Koehler & Amelang, 1961).

5. Eberhard Bethge, et. al., *Die Mündige Welt*, vols. I–IV, (München: Chr. Kaiser, 1955–1963). Certain of the essays from these volumes have been published in English; R. Gregor Smith, ed. *World Come of Age* (Philadelphia: Fortress Press, 1967).

6. Sigmund Freud, *The Future of an Illusion* (New York, 1964), 86–87. See also Michael Novak, "Christianity: Renewed or Slowly Abandoned?" *Daedalus*, XCVI (1967).

7. W. W. Bartley III, "The Bonhoeffer Revival," *The New York Review of Books* 2, (1965). Quoted in Michael Novak, "Christianity: Renewed or Slowly Abandoned?," 239.

8. Novak, "Christianity: Renewed or Slowly Abandoned?," 239.

9. Novak, "Christianity: Renewed or Slowly Abandoned?," 239.

10. Alasdair MacIntyre, "God and the Theologians," *Encounter* 21, no. 3; reprinted in part in David L. Edwards, ed., *The Honest to God Debate* (Philadelphia: Westminster, 1963), 225–28.

11. Thomas J. Altizer and William Hamilton, *Radical Theology and the Death of God* (New York: Bobbs-Merrill Co., 1966).

12. Hamilton's essays, in *Radical Theology and the Death of God*, which underlie this interpretation are: "The Death of God Theologies Today" (1963); "Thursday's Child" (1964); "Dietrich Bonhoeffer" (1965); and "The New Optimism" (1966).

13. Hamilton, "Death of God Theologies Today," *Radical Theology*, 39.

14. Hamilton, "Death of God Theologies Today," *Radical Theology*, 39.

15. Hamilton, "Dietrich Bonhoeffer," *Radical Theology*, 117 and 116.
16. Hamilton, "Dietrich Bonhoeffer," *Radical Theology*, 112.
17. Hamilton, "Death of God Theologies Today," *Radical Theology*, 22.
18. Eberhard Bethge, *Dietrich Bonhoeffer: Theologe-Christ-Zeitgenosse* (München: Chr. Kaiser, 1967).
19. Hamilton, "Thursday's Child," *Radical Theology*, 93.
20. Hamilton, "Death of God Theologians Today," *Radical Theology*, 50.
21. Hamilton, "New Optimism," *Radical Theology*, 169.
22. Hamilton, "Death of God Theologians Today," *Radical Theology*, 36, 37, 40.
23. Hamilton, "The Death of God Theologians Today," *Radical Theology*, 50.
24. W. H. Auden, *The Age of Anxiety* (New York: Random House, 1947), 24.
25. Bonhoeffer, *Ethik* (München: Chr. Kaiser Verlag, 1949), 62. [Editorial: See Bonhoeffer, *Ethics,* trans. Ilks Tödt, Heinz Eduard Tödt, Ernst Feil, and Clifford Green, DBW 6, 58.]
26. Bethge, *Dietrich Bonhoeffer: Theologe-Christ-Zeitgenosse*, 804–5; brackets and translation Lehmann's.
27. [Editorial: When Bonhoeffer's book *Nachfolge* was first translated into English, his one word-title, "Discipleship," was changed to "The Cost of Discipleship." The newest translation uses the original title. Dietrich Bonhoeffer, *Discipleship*, eds. Geffrey B. Kelly and John D. Godsey, trans. Barbara Green and Reinhard Krauss, DBW 4 (Minneapolis: Fortress Press, 2001).]
28. Bethge, *Dietrich Bonhoeffer: Theologe-Christ-Zeitgenosse*, 805ff.
29. Bethge, *Dietrich Bonhoeffer: Theologe-Christ-Zeitgenosse*, 805–6; translation Lehmann's.
30. Bonhoeffer, *Ethik*, 222; translation Lehmann's. [Editorial: Bonhoeffer, *Ethics*, DBW 6, 389.]
31. Bethge, *Dietrich Bonhoeffer: Theologe-Christ-Zeitgenosse*, 810–11; translation Lehmann's. [Editorial: Dietrich Bonhoeffer, *Conspiracy and Imprisonment: 1940–45*, ed. Mark S. Brocker, trans. Lisa E. Dahill, DBW 16, (Minneapolis: Fortress Press, 2006), 329.]
32. Bonhoeffer, *Ethik*, 222–23; translation Lehmann's. [Editorial: Bonhoeffer, *Letters and Papers from Prison*, DBW 8, 268.]
33. Dietrich Bonhoeffer, *Widerstand und Ergebung* (München: Chr. Kaiser Verlag, 1952), 184–85.
34. For an instructive discussion of this problem, see Gisale Meuss, "Arkandisziplin und Weltlichkeit bei Dietrich Bonhoeffer," in *Die Mündige Welt III* (München: Chr. Kaiser Verlag, 1960), 68–115.
35. Meuss, "Arkandisziplin und Weltlichkeit," 72.
36. Meuss, "Arkandisziplin und Weltlichkeit," 71.

Chapter 29

Logos in a World Come of Age (1964)[1]

The difference between a world come of age and a world initially surprised by the advent of the logos is that in a world come of age the logos must create new conditions for the experience and apprehension of transcendence, not merely correct conditions already at hand. This is a new experience for the logos which does not make the logos any less a new experience for the world.

The relation between gospel and *logos* has been a perennial theme of Christian theology. In view of the infrequent connection between the two terms within the New Testament itself, this persistence requires some explanation. Although the word *"logos"* occurs in the Greek New Testament more than three hundred times, its use as a Christological title is confined to the Johannine writings and even there to but a few passages.[2] This would seem to mean that as a vehicle for the interpretation of the gospel, in so far as gospel involved an intimate connection with Jesus of Nazareth, the New Testament was neither limited to nor dominated by the use of the term *"logos."* Yet, the relation between gospel and *logos* has been a major preoccupation of Christian thought. In this preoccupation, the Christian mind appears to be not only unaware of a departure from a central concern of the New Testament but also aware of a connection indispensable to the content and meaning of the life and message of Jesus himself.

If the relative silence of Scripture concerning the relation between gospel and *logos* did not prevent the ancient church from a dominance of its Christology by the term *"logos,"* the relative prominence of the word *"logos"* in the culture into which the gospel initially spread may not be regarded as a sufficient explanation of the connection between gospel and *logos*.

Indeed, as regards this connection, the development of the Christological dogma exhibits more than a casual oversight. Theology seems not only to have overborne the Scriptures but the creedal shape of Christian faith as well. If, in the New Testament, the use of *logos* in relation to gospel is infrequent, the use of *logos* in the ecumenical symbols of the faith is missing altogether. If the creeds are to be taken at their word, the word "*logos*" admittedly ranks very low in the divine vocabulary. It may be, of course, that God has not so much overlooked the semantic power of *logos* as that the church and, in particular her theologians, have never rightly grasped what God has been trying to say. While always keeping open to this possibility, we venture, nevertheless, to take up its contrary. The relative silence of Scripture and creed about the relation between gospel and *logos* and the relative articulateness of classical theology about this relation point, each in turn, beyond linguistic and cultural coincidences to a fundamental and far-reaching theological problem. The question of the relation between gospel and *logos* is not merely a perennial theme of Christian theology but is a continually recurring critical question by which theological exposition and interpretation may be assessed.

I

The relation between gospel and *logos* brings sharply into focus the critical question by which Christian theology is at once haunted and measured. This is the question: what is involved in giving the shape of words to the gospel? Gospel, like *logos*, is, of course, also a word. But even "in, with and under" the semantic preoccupations of a world "come of age," it may surely be allowed that whatever else the word "gospel" may also mean, it has functioned in Christian theological reflection and discourse in every age as a pointer to Jesus of Nazareth and to his transforming impact upon the world of people, principalities, and powers, and of time and space and things. Gospel denotes the "good news" that history and nature are *new* in Jesus of Nazareth and in consequence of him. In Jesus of Nazareth, the face of reality has changed and with this change, the experience of reality, the perspectives, terms, signs, and symbols by which the new reality is apprehended and interpreted have changed also. Gospel denotes and thus means that God "is the source of your life in Christ Jesus, whom God made our wisdom, our righteousness and sanctification and redemption" (1 Cor. 1:30).

If this be gospel, what, then, is *logos*? When we move to this side of the relation between gospel and *logos*, our theological troubles increase. The denotation of gospel and its significance may count upon a readier theological consensus than that available to a denotation of *logos* and its significance. Broadly speaking, Christian theology has tried to relate the term "*logos*" to the gospel concerning Jesus of Nazareth along two principal lines of interpretation. On the one hand, a dominantly Hellenic connotation has been appropriated, according to which *logos* connected gospel with the intelligible structure and order of the world. The relation between gospel and *logos* was understood and explicated primarily as a relation of *intelligibility*. Indeed, *logos* functions in this enterprise as the possibility and the principle of intelligibility of gospel. On the other hand, Christian theology has taken up a dominantly Hebraic connotation of *logos*. According to this connotation, *logos* connects the gospel concerning Jesus of Nazareth with the self-communication of God as a personal and concrete action. As Professor C. H. Dodd has noted:

> In so far as the Greek term *logos* means reasonable or considered *speech* it approaches the meaning of the Hebrew term *dabhar*, "word," and is fittingly used to translate it. Beyond this common area of meaning, however, the denotation of the Hebrew term expands in a different direction from the Greek . . . No such concrete meaning ever attaches to *logos* in a properly Greek context; but this concreteness is integral to the Hebrew term.[3]

In this enterprise, the relation between gospel and *logos* was understood and explicated primarily as a *revelatory* relation. *Logos* functions as the principal mode of God's self-disclosing action of making all things new. As the New English Bible has put it:

> and what God was, the Word was. The Word, then, was with God at the beginning, and through him all things came to be; no single thing was created without him. All that came to be was alive with his life, and that life was the light of men . . . He was in the world; but the world, though it owed its being to him, did not recognize him . . . But to all who did receive him . . . he gave the right to become children of God . . . the offspring of God himself. So the Word became flesh; he came to dwell among us, and we saw his glory . . . full of grace and truth (John 1: 1–4, 10–14).

It cannot be too strongly stressed that both these lines of interpretation of the relation of *logos* to gospel are Christological in character. The aim was to explicate—not God's relation to the world—but the place and role of Jesus of Nazareth in relation to God, on the one hand, and to humanity on the other. *Soteriology* rather than *intelligibility* was the focus of reflective attention. Apparently, the formative factor in this theological preoccupation was the Prologue to the Fourth gospel. Its eloquence and force were such as to have overcome the curious reticence of Scripture and creed in relating *logos* to gospel and to have lifted the term *logos* to primary and even indispensable appropriateness in giving the shape of words to the gospel.

As is well known, Antioch and Alexandria never arrived at a meeting of minds about the primacy of *logos* in relation to gospel. Geographically and culturally nearer to the scene of Jesus's life and death, Antioch husbanded a livelier sense of the humanity of Jesus with its suffering and crucifixion. But the Antiochene attempt to bring this sensitivity together with the *logos* could not overcome the obstacle of the divine impassability without which it seemed impossible to take proper account of the relation of Jesus to God. At Alexandria, theologians encountered the opposite difficulty. Convinced as they were of the divinity of the *logos* they were unable to take due account of the humanity of Jesus, involving as it did his suffering and death. Thus, as Grillmeier has reminded us, the inconclusiveness of Chalcedon was not only unavoidable but the better part of its wisdom.[4]

We are not, however, concerned in this discussion with these Christological difficulties in the narrower sense, important as they are. The mystery of the God-humanness of Jesus with which the struggles over the hypostatic union were once concerned may well require other language, especially in a "world come of age." Curiously enough, in such a world, the Christological focus of the problem of *logos* and gospel has been blurred not so much by the remoteness of the Chalcedonian impasse and its language but by an articulate rejection of the problem which for the early church was a concomitant problem. The question of the place and role of Jesus of Nazareth in relation to God, on the one hand, and to humanity, on the other, took the center of the theological stage because this problem was and still is pivotal in any theology which takes seriously the revelatory action of God in Christ. Nevertheless, the problem of the bearing of the *logos* Christology upon the question of the relation between God and the world was not only not dispensed with but functioned as concomitant problem precisely because of a long-standing apperceptive consensus about God and the world. There was a God and there was a world. There was much to be known about both and much that remained mysterious. But however diverse the transmutations of language and varied the interpretations, there was a consensus that in some sense the world was God's handiwork and that the most impressive features about God's relation to the world were the order of the world's motions (causality) and the accessibility of this order to the human reason owing to its kinship with the divine reason (intelligibility). Thus, the Apostolic Fathers and particularly the Apologists were free to give major attention to the question of the relation between Jesus and *logos* in their attempt to give the shape of words to the gospel. They could then take their time about explicating the implications of this Christological intrusion for the apperceptive and conceptual consensus into which this intrusion had wondrously and bewilderingly occurred.

II

In a "world come of age" much, if not all, of this apperceptive context of the relation of gospel and *logos* has fallen into disrepair. It still lingers widely and unpersuasively about as tradition. But the laboriously forged link between *soteriology* and *intelligibility* that once, and for a long, long time, gave the shape of words to the gospel has been shattered in and by a world from which God is effectively absent.

The fragmentary character of Dietrich Bonhoeffer's legacy to contemporary theology should not obscure the significance of the phrase, "a world come of age," to which he has given such wide currency. Critics of Bonhoeffer appear to have found it easier to stress the inconclusiveness and vagueness of the phrase than to pause over the theological seriousness of its clear and simple meaning. As an attempt to chasten the popular excesses of an incipient theological slogan, a critical caveat is in order. But the basic theological issue cannot in this way be ignored. Actually, Bonhoeffer was not really coining a phrase. Instead, he was trying to take seriously the point made long before by Auguste Comte. Comte's point was that the religion of humanity would displace all previous forms of religion, including Christianity, when "the long minority of humanity" shall have been superseded by the "majority" which Comte imminently and confidently expected. Bonhoeffer may have erred in accepting the Comtian dream as having come true. But it was this Comtian understanding of the "majority of humanity" which Bonhoeffer recognized as the decisive context within which Christian theology in our time must be pursued, if at all. This does not mean that Bonhoeffer has espoused the "religion of humanity." On the contrary, religion itself is expendable, including the "religion of humanity," because the vision and passion of the Enlightenment have achieved sufficient cultural form and force as to have exposed the un-tenability of a God, or a Christ, or a cult which are answers to one's problems, fulfillers of one's needs. In so far as Christian faith and thought have lapsed into expectations concerning God, into ways of thinking and speaking about God, which exhibit the intrinsic bond between religion and such a *Deus ex machina* [God as machine], Christianity must follow the way of all religion into the limbo of rejection by a world in which humans dominantly believe and think and act in terms of the prospects and the achievements of human creativity and power. In a world come of age, the gulf between soteriology and intelligibility is complete. Immanence has displaced transcendence; and "God" has joined words like Gospel and *logos* as waning functions of religious language, itself under the shadow of increasing obsolescence. In so far as such obsolescence is not yet apparent, the reason is—at least as regards Christian theology—that the referential substance of Christian words has disintegrated to such a degree as to make possible the dispensing of other words as distinctions without a difference.

It may be objected that Bonhoeffer has overstated his case, that the world is not as mature as that, or that its own coming of age, if true, does not exhibit so marked a moratorium upon the time-honored concerns of religion. The gulf between soteriology and intelligibility may be complete. But soteriological symptoms appear to be as conspicuous as ever, and the problem of their intelligibility only adds a grim urgency to the problem of life's meaning as such. Theology and philosophy may have been caught short by a world come of age; but clearly not politics and art which are permeated with soteriological passion.

Our present concern is not to make the case for or against the question whether the world has or has not come of age; and certainly not for or against Bonhoeffer's indictment of Christianity and religion. Our concern, however, is with one fundamental feature of the present cultural situation which is more readily identifiable if we assume that the world has come of age in Bonhoeffer's sense. This fundamental feature has to do with the question of transcendence. The effective absence of God from the world in which we live and labor is due not to God's actual absence but to the effective breakdown of the language and the sense for transcendence, that is, for that adequate distance from the world across which God's relation to the world and his active presence in the world can be discerned and understood. This means that the original question of the relation between Gospel and *logos* is still lurking about somewhere in the wings waiting upon a promising occasion to "zero in." The difference between a world come of age and a world initially surprised by the advent of the *logos* is that in a world come of age the *logos* must create new conditions for the experience and apprehension of transcendence, not merely correct conditions already at hand. This is a new experience for the *logos* that does not make the *logos* any less a new experience for the world.

Unlike the church's theologians, the *logos* is a specialist in surprises and prepared in advance to deal with them. *C'est son métier* ["It's his job"]. It could be, therefore, that the critical significance of the problem of transcendence for theology in a world come of age is itself the work of the *logos*, active in the church and in the world. It is not necessary to censure the Fathers of the church for having tried to deal with a problem in one way which we must now deal with differently. The task of giving the shape of words to the Gospel is a continuing task of theology in the church. This is a task of finding words suitable both to convey the reality of God's self-communication in Jesus Christ and to fashion the apperceptive conditions for a continuing and meaningful response to this divine revelation. The juxtaposition of Gospel and *logos*, which the church has handed down to us from the second century onwards, underlines the central problem of theology in the performance of its task: the problem of describing and sustaining a creative relation between soteriology and intelligibility. Christian thought has always been clear that the incarnation and the atonement required a movement from soteriology towards intelligibility. That is to say, the crucifixion of the Word made flesh radically altered the shape of things so that God and humanity and the world were apprehendable in a new and different way that altered the possibilities and terms of reflection and interpretation. The error of pre-Chalcedonian theology was not its failure to recognize the importance of this movement but that it took a wrong turn in making the move. The Apostolic Fathers and the Apologists after them attempted to give the shape of words to the Gospel by means of the *logos*. But the apperceptive power of the link between the divine impassability and the rational character of the divine self-communication was so strong as to obscure the fateful theological shift that was in fact going on. God's personal act of self-communication and of human and cosmic transformation through this self-identification with Jesus of Nazareth came to be explicated as a self-communication of the divine reason which, through the incarnation of the *logos* in Jesus of Nazareth, set up a rational order and structure of inter-communication and intelligibility between God and humanity and the world.

"We have been taught," wrote Justin in the *First Apology*:

that Christ is the First-Begotten of God and have previously testified that he is the Reason of which every race of man partakes. Those who lived in accordance with Reason are Christians, even though they were called godless . . . So also those who lived without Reason were ungracious and enemies to Christ, and murderers of those who lived by Reason. But those who lived by Reason, and those who so live now, are Christians, fearless and unperturbed. For what cause a man was conceived of a virgin by the power of the Word of God according to the will of God, the Father and Master of all, and was named Jesus, and after being crucified and dying rose again and ascended into heaven, an intelligent man will be able to comprehend from the words that were spoken in various ways.[5]

And, in similar vein, Clement declares:

But the good Instructor, the Wisdom, the Word of the Father, who made man, cares for the whole nature of His creature; the all-sufficient Physician of humanity the Saviour, heals both body and soul . . . We, however, as soon as He conceived the thought became his children, having had assigned us the best and most secure rank by His orderly arrangement, which first circles about the world, the heavens, and the sun's circuits, and occupies itself with the motions of the rest of the stars for man's behoof, and then busies itself with man himself, on whom all care is concentrated; and regarding him as its greatest work, regulated his soul by wisdom and temperance, and tempered the body with beauty and proportion. And whatever in human actins is right and regular, is the result of the inspiration of its rectitude and order.[6]

Here a theological shift seems to be going on according to which the soteriological function and meaning of *logos* is being overtaken by its significance and function as a principle of intelligibility. The *logos* has become the bearer of truth and life rather than the embodiment of grace and truth. He has become a motion and principle of reason rather than the inaugurator of a new order of human and cosmic possibilities and purposes. The experience and apprehension of transcendence has shifted from the involvement of humanity and the world with the self-giving self-disclosure of God as Savior, Lord, and Creator of humanity and the world to a participation of humanity through the rational structure of the human reason in the divine reason and its ordering of the world. In short, the Gospel of Jesus, the *logos*, has become the Gospel of the *logos* in Jesus. An inversion of the relations between Gospel and *logos* has occurred. The original impulse and movement from Gospel to *logos* has been turned back upon itself as an impulse and movement from *logos* to Gospel.

We are suggesting that this inversion has fatefully affected the course of Christian theology. The *logos* doctrine, originally designed to give an appropriate shape of words to the Gospel, has actually functioned to distort the communication and interpretation of the Gospel. Behind the Christological impasse of Chalcedon, there lies a defective *logos* of transcendence that has come to a dead end in a "world come of age." To paraphrase a vivid polarization of Dietrich Bonhoeffer's, the *logos* doctrine has actually functioned to repress rather than to attest to the *anti-logos* at whose instance the doctrine was initially included in the theological response of the church to the self-identifying self-communication of God to humanity and the world in Jesus Christ. "How," asks Bonhoeffer, concerning the occasion and object of theological reflection:

> How does the object x fit into the order (that is, of knowledge and experience) already at hand? ... The immanent *logos* of man determines the 'how' of this object according to its own mode of ordering. What happens, however, when somewhere the claim is put forward that this *logos* of man is called into question, put under judgment, is dead? What happens when an "*anti-logos*" appears which the *logos*, according to its own mode of ordering, finds deficient?[7]

It is this question which makes it appropriate, even urgent, in our time, to explore the theological possibility of a reversal of that early inversion of the order of the relation between gospel and *logos* by taking a further look at that turn in the road, as *The New Yorker* inimitably put it, a year or so ago, in the context of an after-five function of the cocktail set. On that occasion, a lady, both wistfully and bibulously, asks, "What I say is, where did we all take the wrong turn?"

III

The New Yorker's question has more than a coincidental connection with the question posed by Bonhoeffer. In our time, as in that original "fullness of time," the problem of the faithful and creative relation between soteriology and intelligibility is decisively up for discussion. Does the Gospel inaugurate and announce a transformation of the shape of things in heaven and in earth that brings experience and meaning together in a new and living or fulfilling way? Does Jesus of Nazareth both make sense of human life in this world and the next and set the limits and the terms for apprehending and interpreting the sense which life makes? In short, grace and truth are in Jesus Christ, or they aren't. *Tertium non datur* [the law of the excluded middle].[8]

Let it not be too easily and too quickly observed that the alternative has been too sharply and rhetorically put. The aim is to try to identify as precisely as possible the point at which the wrong turn was taken. Far more is at stake than the perennial tension between faith and reason, revealed theology and natural theology, redemption and creation, which we have all lived under for so long as to have become all but irremediably conditioned to living with them. More is at stake than the question of the nature of theology, of whether dogmatics requires apologetics or nullifies it. What is at stake is the revision of truth by reason of the advent and power of grace in Jesus Christ and the consequent appropriation of truth by grace for and by Jesus Christ. What is at stake is the scientific possibility and integrity of theology, of systematic theology, in distinction from biblical and historical theology, or from whatever other kinds there may be. What is at stake is whether Christology can be *explicitly* what it has always been *implicitly*, namely, the central and critical instance of Christian theology and on this account also—indeed, just on this account—"the science *katexochen* . . . the unacknowledged and hidden center of the *universitas litterarum*."[9]

These are the stakes that were lost sight of when Christian theology took its erroneous pre-Chalcedonian turn. We are not reproaching the Fathers for this mistake but asking instead whether we are either faithful or wise in overlooking whatever possibilities there may be for turning back and turning around. What these possibilities are and what their implementation involves belong to the major responsibility of theology in a world come of age. At this writing, we have only hints to offer that can only be most sketchily alluded to. These hints take us back to the pre-Chalcedonian turn in the road. They focus upon God's self-identifying self-communication in Jesus of Nazareth as a *new beginning*.

Commenting upon "conflicting elements in the picture of Jesus as the Christ," Professor Tillich remarks:

> One must distinguish between the symbolic frame in which the picture of Jesus as the Christ appears and the substance in which the power of the New Being is present . . . Better for this purpose than any of the others was the symbol of the Logos, which, by its very nature, is a conceptual symbol having both religious and philosophical roots. Consequently, the Christology of the early Church became Logos-Christology. It is unfair to criticize the Church Fathers for their use of Greek concepts. There were no other available conceptual expressions of man's cognitive encounter with the world. Whether or not these concepts were adequate to the interpretation of the Christian message remains a permanent question of theology.[10]

Commenting upon the fact of emergence as "evidence for a purposive activity or nisus in the cosmic order," professor Norman Pittenger has remarked:

> Evolution . . . implies . . . an Eternal Reality in relation to which and by which an "epigenesis" takes place. That Reality is the God of the Christian whose outgoing creative revelatory activity or Word is the nisus or purpose expressed in the cosmic process . . . Through the Word (the Logos) God informs every grade and level of being; but he is not identified with the universe which is creative and derivative . . . The claim which was made for Christ was that he was the 'Word made flesh,' the actualization of the Logos in the human plane and in human form, so far as that may be possible in genuine human nature and mind . . . Thus, our Lord can legitimately, even though not demonstrably, be seen as the decisive expression of the Eternal Reality in human nature, *deitas sub specie humanitatis* [the divine under the guise of humanity].[11]

We are in cordial agreement with these attempts to take up the problem of gospel and *logos* where the Fathers took it up and at the point at which the wrong turn was taken. The Fourth Gospel's preoccupation with the mystery and the reality of the self-identifying self-communication of God in Jesus Christ is the central concern of these contemporary appropriations of the *logos* concept in order to give intelligibility and meaning to salvation. Yet these attempts seem to us to be renewing at the same time the ancient and precarious turn in the road. The effort to "update" the gospel by "updating" the *logos* has changed the language but not the formula with the result that the gospel fails an effective challenge of the *logos*. Truth—whether as "available conceptual expressions of man's cognitive encounter with the world" or "as the actualization of the Logos . . . as far as that may be possible in genuine human nature and mind"—sets the limits and the terms within which the grace and truth in Jesus Christ are apprehendable and communicable. An outdated *logos* cannot serve the gospel in a world come of age.

A singular glimpse of the possibility given to theology to pursue was noted almost on the threshold of Chalcedon itself. It will occur to no one that Augustine of Hippo was inclined to disparage the conceptual tools of the Greeks or to ignore the crucial question of transcendence and mediation focused in Jesus Christ. "Accordingly, when we speak of God," he wrote:

> We do not affirm two or three principles, no more than we are at liberty to affirm two or three gods; . . . speaking . . . of the Father, or of the Son, or of the Holy Ghost, we confess that each is God . . . It was therefore truly said that man is cleansed only by a Beginning, although the Platonists erred in speaking in the plural of *principles* . . . The Beginning, therefore, having assumed a human soul and flesh, cleanses the soul and flesh of believers. Therefore when the Jews asked Him who he was he answered that he was the Beginning." (*Verbum itaque dictum est, non purgari hominem nisi principio, quamvis pluraliter sint apud eos dicta principia . . . Principium ergo suscepta anima et carne et animam credentium mundat et carnem. Ideo quaerentibus Judeis quis esset, respondit se esse principium*).[12]

Perhaps the integrity of theology about the grace and truth in Jesus Christ requires of theology a livelier combination of rhetorical subtlety with conceptual precision. It is the Gospel which liberates the *logos*—not the *logos* the Gospel—for dealing with the problem of transcendence in a world come of age.

NOTES

1. Published in *Theology Today* 21, no. 3 (1964): 274–86; reprinted with permission.

2. For instance, John 1:1–5, 1 John 1:1, and Rev. 10:13. Oscar Cullmann, *The Christology of the New Testament* (Philadelphia: Westminster Press, 1959), 249. W. D. Davies (*Paul and Rabbinic Judaism*) has noted that Paul makes no chronological use of the term *logos* at all, preferring the term *sophia*. [Editorial: W.D. Davies, *Paul and Rabbinic Judaism: Some Rabbinic Elements in Pauline Theology* (Minneapolis: Fortress, 1980).]

3. F. L. Cross, ed., *Studies in the Fourth Gospel* (London: A. R. Mowbray and Co. Ltd., 1957), 11.

4. Alois Grillmeier und Heinrich Bacht, *Des Konzil von Chalkedon*, Bd. I, (Wuerzburg: Echter Verlag, 1951).

5. Justin Martyr, *First Apology*, in *Early Christian Fathers*, Cyril C. Richardson et. al, eds., Library of Christian Classics, vol. 1 (Philadelphia: SCM, 1953), par. 46, 272.

6. Clement of Alexandria, *The Instructor I.2*, in *The Ante-Nicene Fathers, Volume 2: Fathers of the Second Century*, eds. Alexander Roberts and James Donaldson (New York: Christian Literature Publishing Co., 1885), 210.

7. Dietrich Bonhoeffer, *Wer Ist und Wer War Jesus Christus?* (Hamburg: Furche Verlag, 1962), 11–12; translation and parenthesis Lehmann's. [Editorial: See Dietrich Bonhoeffer, "Lectures on Christology (Student Notes)" in *Berlin: 1932–1933*, ed. Larry L. Rasmussen, trans. Isabel Best and David Higgins, DBW 12 (Minneapolis: Fortress Press, 2009), 299–360.]

8. [Editorial: a claim is true or false; there is no third option. Also known as the law of the excluded middle.]

9. Bonhoeffer, "*Wer Ist und Wer War Jesus Christus?*" 10–11. [Editorial: Christology is "the hidden center of scholarship, of the universe of scholarship." See Bonhoeffer, "Lectures on Christology," 301, including footnote 8.]

10. Paul Tillich, *Systematic Theology*, vol. 2 (Chicago: University of Chicago Press, 1957), 138–39.

11. Norman Pittenger, *The Word Incarnate* (New York: Harper and Brothers, 1959), 166–167.

12. Augustine, *De civitate Dei*, X, 24. Modern Library edition, 328–29; *Migne, Pl.*, 40–41, 500–501.

Chapter 30

Dietrich Bonhoeffer and Paul Lehmann Correspondence (1938–1939)[1]

40. TO PAUL LEHMANN, DECEMBER 14, 1938

Dear Paul,
You wrote me last year at Christmas, and I was delighted to receive the greetings! But without an address I couldn't reply. Now I will simply ask R. Niebuhr to forward this card. Hopefully, this will now work. There would be so much to tell that one can't even begin. The best thing would be if you could visit us again or invite me over for a semester. That wouldn't be bad at all! After such a long time, I would so like to see the country people again, and especially my friends. What might you be doing now? Are you already a professor? How is the *theologia sacra* [sacred theology] doing? Probably you have long since written the most voluminous and revolutionary books, and here we know nothing about it. By the way, I enjoy writing books as well, despite Eccl. 12:12. If you want, I will send you my *Discipleship* from last year. But I have no idea what interests you now. Do write me again! How are you doing personally? What are Joe Moor, Franklin Fisher, Klein, Dombrowski doing? I visited Baillie once in Edinburgh. How does Brunner come across in Princeton? I heard something about objections against critical research on the Bible! What noteworthy books are being published at present over there? As you see, there's a great deal I would like to know from you!—I enjoy recalling our time together. I am still in touch with Sutz. Jean Lasserre has gotten married. People like us cannot yet afford to do so. Life is too nomadlike for it. There's much joy in the work, however. Very heartfelt greetings to you and your wife with all good wishes for the new year.

Yours truly,
Dietrich B.
Berlin-Charlottenburg, Marienburger Allee 43

91. FROM REINHOLD NIEBUHR TO PAUL LEHMANN, MAY 11

Dear Paul,
I have finished eight of my ten lectures here and have done as well as could be expected I suppose. Had a good audience all through but don't know much about how my stuff has been received.

I will not bother you with personal news however. My concern is in regard to Bonhoeffer. He came to see me shortly upon our arrival and is anxious to come to America to evade for the time being a call to the colours. I secured an invitation for him for the Union Seminary summer school and also asked the Federal Council to arrange for meetings in church camps etc. He would like to stay through the fall and lecture in colleges and seminaries. As I will not be back until November I am wondering whether you would be willing to constitute a committee with me, call me the chairman and yourself the secretary and send out a mimeographed letter offering Bonhoeffer's services to colleges and universities. Ask them for a nominal fee of $25 to $50 for his services. You could have him give you topics and a description of his activities in behalf of the confessional synod.

I don't like to through [*sic*] this work on you but I think you could do it best. Be sure and hire stenographers for the job and let me have the bill. Bonhoeffer's present address is Marienburger Allee 43 Berlin-Charlottenburg 9. Don't write him too much but if you are willing to do this just tell him that you will get in touch with him as soon as he arrives at Union to work our plans which I have suggested. There will be some difficulty getting him out and if he fails he will land in prison. He has done a great work for the church.

Edinburgh has been very kind to us and we have little time to ourselves. I am staying till May 23rd and then will go to Oxford. After June 13 you can reach me at The Moat House, Wivelsfield, Sussex.
Love from all of us.
Yours,
[Reinhold Niebuhr]

97. FROM PAUL LEHMANN, MAY 27, 1939

Dear Dietrich:

The word that you have been invited to lecture in the summer session of Union Theological Seminary, New York, encourages me to make this urgent request of you. Will you not be good enough to consent and make all possible arrangements accordingly to lecture in the department of Religion here at the college during the forthcoming academic year, 1939–1941? It has long been a concern of mine that your approach to the problems of philosophy and theology should be heard by my students here and by others. Accordingly, I am venturing to plan on your coming and make arrangements for similar lectures on other campuses of my acquaintance. I am sure you will be eagerly received.

More precise details can be agreed upon while you are in residence at Union Seminary. Meanwhile, I shall look forward to your arrival here.
Ever sincerely yours,
Paul
Paul L. Lehmann, Th. D
Professor of Religion

114. TO PAUL LEHMANN, JUNE 17, 1939

My dear Paul,
Nun also bin ich wieder hier! [So now I am here again!] Niebuhr will have written to you about it. There has been some misunderstanding about my trip. I am not a refugee, but I must go back to Germany to take up my work over there. They are in need of teachers. I want to stay until late autumn or spring at the very latest. The first week in August I am delivering lectures for one week at the Summer School of Union. Will I see you at all? Hopefully! Do you think that several more lectures (with salary, for I have no money here!) could be arranged at other universities? Niebuhr was perhaps *too optimistic*. I spent a few days with Coffin in Lakeville. Today I met with Roberts, whom I liked a great deal.

Let me hear from you soon! I am living at Union, Prophet's Chamber.

Give my regards to your wife and accept my warm greetings yourself, from your old
Dietrich Bonhoeffer

123. LETTER OF RECOMMENDATION FROM PAUL LEHMANN TO COLLEGES AND SEMINARIES IN THE UNITED STATES, JUNE 27, 1939

Dear Sir:

A committee of which Dr. Reinhold Niebuhr, Professor of Applied Christianity at the Union Theological Seminary, New York, is chairman, is venturing to bring to your attention, the Reverend Dietrich Bonhoeffer, Licentiate in Theology.

Reverend Mr. Bonhoeffer is one of the ablest of the younger theologians and one of the more courageous of the younger pastors who have undertaken the task of the faithful exposition and perpetuation of the Christian faith in the present critical time in Germany. He comes from a distinguished line of forebears both in the pulpit and in the university. He himself holds a graduate theological degree from the University of Berlin and from Union Theological Seminary at New York. Among the more notable of Mr. Bonhoeffer's contributions to theological learning are three brilliant and profound volumes on "The Communion of Saints," "Act and Being," and one published only recently under the title, "Community Life."

During the academic year, 1930–1931, Mr. Bonhoeffer was a fellow in theology at Union Seminary and after his return to Germany he began a promising theological career as *Privatdozent* [Associate Professor] in the theological faculty at Berlin. Political circumstances have interrupted these hopes. After a pastorate in the German Church in London, Mr. Bonhoeffer returned to his country and assumed the difficult responsibility of teaching the future ministers of the Confessional Church. Some time ago his little seminary was closed by the government and he has been continuing his work since then in a private capacity in the parsonages of Pommern.

Since Mr. Bonhoeffer will be lecturing in theology at the summer session of the Union Theological Seminary, New York, we are anxious to provide for him a wider hearing in American academic and theological circles. Accordingly, we are arranging a schedule of lectures at colleges and seminaries during the academic year, 1939–1940. If your institution has a lecture foundation or lecture series on a variety of problems, will you give favorable consideration to an invitation to Mr. Bonhoeffer to appear? He is in full command of the English language and prepared to discuss in a reliable and challenging manner problems of theology, philosophy, and the contemporary situation of Christianity in Germany. The committee is venturing to suggest an honorarium of not less that twenty-five dollars, and wherever possible, of fifty dollars.

I hope very urgently that we may have some word from you at the earliest possible moment. Correspondence either for Mr. Bonhoeffer or for the committee may be addressed to me at the address below. Your active cooperation in this venture will be a real expression of the spirit of ecumenical Christianity and deeply appreciated.

Respectfully,
Paul L. Lehmann, Th.D.

Elmhurst College,
Elmhurst, Illinois

124. FROM PAUL LEHMANN TO REINHOLD NIEBUHR, JUNE 28, 1939

Dear Reinie:

Immediately upon receipt of your letter of May 11, I got started. I wrote at once to Dr. Press and contacted Pauck and Paul Scherer. The enclosed letter which I am sending out today to some thirty or forty places will speak for itself. I hope replies will not come in too slowly.

Meanwhile a letter has come from Bonhoeffer who is already at Union. I don't quite know what to make of it for he speaks already of going back. He says that he is not a refugee and must go back to Germany to take up his work over there, for Germany needs teachers. "Ich will," he writes, "bis Spätherbst oder spätestens Frühjahr bleiben." ["I want to stay until late autumn or spring at the very latest."]

What occurred to me at once was the Eden Theological lectures at Convocation. I ventured to ask Dr. Press to invite Bonhoeffer. He replied that he knew of Bonhoeffer and that the seminary which adds him to the faculty will indeed get an able theologian. What this has to do with my request, I do not comprehend. So I have written again today asking specifically for the lectureship for Bonhoeffer and saying that you regarded the matter as urgently as I do. Since Press asked me for your address, he may want to write to you about it. Therefore I want you to know what I am doing. We are inviting Bonhoeffer for the four Lenten sermons which come just about Eden convocation time. The two would fit beautifully together. As soon as I get replies to the general letter, I shall make up a schedule.

Richter will be teaching with us next Fall. The Board seems to have been surprisingly cooperative, the faculty mildly impressed. But it will be like a cultural tornado, which is exactly what this place needs.

The Christian Century brings glowing reports of your lectures. For once I can agree with something that they are responsible for. It must be pleasant if pressing to work out the second set amidst the charms of the English country side. I still insist that it is the best thing the British have had in years. The real shame is that you can't take over the foreign office as well while you are there. But they seem to prefer ostriches.

We shall be leaving on Saturday for Columbus for the summer. We are practically exhausted from the ridiculous pace of the past month. Carlson has gone over my manuscript for stylistic touches and that has helped a great deal.

The title is still hanging fire. I hope very much that you will not be bothered with the stuff at the wrong time for you.

Already we are looking forward to your January visit. Meanwhile take our continuing thoughts and good wishes to Ursula, yourself and the children, and if there is any way at any time that I can do something like this, please never hesitate to write. I'm never too busy or tired for your requests.

Affectionately,
Paul

125. FROM PAUL LEHMANN, JUNE 28, 1939

My dear Dietrich,

You cannot know with what joy and relief your letter was received. It came to me just when I had to be away for some days and to take part in a conference here for some days, so that I have had to wait until now to reply. Evidently my letter of May 27th, sent to Berlin will not have reached you. Since that time, Marion and I have been eagerly awaiting word of your arrival at Union. Now that you are there, we can scarcely wait until you are here with us.

Whether or not Dr. Niebuhr has been too optimistic, I do not know. But I do know that it is unthinkable that you should return before America shall have had the fullest opportunity to be enriched by your contribution to its theological hour of destiny. At least, I like to think of it in this way. The tragic political occasion for these disturbed times may have one great and positive overtone in the widening of the American theological understanding by the present cross fertilization with the continental tradition. So that you must see this also as a responsibility as well as the German need for teachers.

And besides, Marion and I need very badly to see you again. Surely you would not deprive us of the hope that we have carried with us since the day when we left the café on Unter den Linden. With your anticipated permission, I have already taken steps to bring this about. The enclosed letter will speak for itself. But meanwhile, there is more definite word for you. I am authorized to invite you to deliver the annual series of Lenten sermons which is a part of our campus religious life program. These occur on four succeeding Wednesdays during Lent and seek to interpret the Cross to the contemporary student mind. There will be one hundred dollars at your disposal for these sermons and you will live with us. At about the same time, Eden Seminary has a theological lectureship at its annual convocation. This is usually about mid-February. I have written asking that you be invited for these. I hope it will work out.

But whatever happens, Marion and I want you to know that our home is yours in every respect for as long a time as you are able and willing to have it so. There is no limit. And you cannot afford us any greater happiness than by acting with complete freedom on this promise.

Whether or not I shall get to New York this summer, I do not yet know. I am trying very hard to arrange some kind of a brief excursion there, specially to see you. We are leaving here on Saturday for Columbus, Ohio, where we are likely to be until the first of September. The address there is 931 Oakwood Avenue. It should be just about that time that you will be ready to come west and we shall await you here. You will let me hear from you in Columbus, won't you?

Sometime between July 9th and 12th, a very good friend of mine and former student, George Kalbfleisch by name, will try to visit you in Union. He is en route to Amsterdam and expects to visit Germany. It was through him that I hoped to send you some word of reply to your earlier letter at Christmas time. Since he expects to visit Germany, there may be some word that you might like to send. I simply mention this in order that you may know that you can have complete confidence in him. I have told him so much of you and am anxious that you meet.

As soon as replies to the letter which I am mailing today to some thirty or forty places come to me, you will hear more. Meanwhile do keep in touch with me and remember how anxious we are to have you with us again.

Marion joins me in kindest greetings and highest regard,
Paul

126. TO PAUL LEHMANN, JUNE 28, 1939

Dear Paul,
I wonder if you received my letter last week. Things have changed for me entirely. I am going back to Germany on August 2nd or even July 25th. The political situation is so terrible. But, of course, I should like to have a word from you before I leave. I am enjoying a few weeks in freedom, but on the other hand, I feel, I must go back to the "trenches" (I mean of the Church-struggle).
Yours ever,
Dietrich Bonhoeffer

128. TO PAUL LEHMANN, JUNE 30, 1939

My dear Paul,
Thank you so much for your good letter which is so full of friendship and hope for the future. I can hardly bring myself to tell you that in the meantime

I have had to decide to return to Germany, already in the next few weeks. Behind my invitation here lay the misunderstanding that I intended to remain in America for good. They wanted to assign me the care of Christian refugees here, a job that would have prevented me from any return to Germany, as necessary as it is in itself. It must, however, be done by a refugee. Now in the meantime everything has been decided and has also been settled with the Confessing Church; I shall travel back in July or August. While I regret this for various reasons, on the other hand, I am also glad to be given the opportunity to help again over there very soon. I am being pulled toward the brothers in struggle. You will understand this! Now I have one urgent request: in your very friendly letter to the Colleges you mentioned my work in Pomerania. Should such a page come into the hands of a German official, the work that in the meantime continues would be at an end. Will you understand my asking you sincerely and urgently to write *immediately* to the same circle that I have already returned and all plans have been canceled, perhaps also (which would be important to me) that a misunderstanding had prevailed in the matter! I hope that the circle is trustworthy enough not to let the letter go further. Now you have had much work, and I thank you for this with all my heart! I am infinitely sorry that we will not see each other. I had expected, especially from a meeting with you, so much toward understanding the situation here and many other things. Now this will not come to pass. It is such a pity! But there is no longer any other way! I am now expected back there soon. The political situation is dreadful, and I must be with my brothers when things become serious. We will then often think of each other and be with each other in prayer, and we will leave it to God as to whether and when he will lead us back together again in a way we can see. In such "final" times everyone should be found at the place where he belongs. May God grant us that we stand firm there.

Forgive the trouble I have put you to! See to it that people tacitly regard the matter as finished. From now on, please do not mention anything at all about Pomerania, etc. in your letter, nor that the matter should not reach any German official; instead it's best to just state that "the inquiry concerning Mr. D.B. in the meantime has been resolved through his return to Germany and that a misunderstanding had prevailed in the matter." That would be my preference and the best thing for my work over there, which is so urgently necessary. To say more could awaken unnecessary interest. And please, do this without delay!

Do not believe that I regret my journey here. I am very happy that I was here and have seen and learned so much in one month. My greatest pain is that I did not get to see you and your wife.

Now be well, dear Paul! May God protect you both and give you strength and joy for the work; may God preserve our fellowship as well, as he has done up to now.
Greetings to you in old faithfulness and gratitude always, your
Dietrich Bonhoeffer
PS I travel presumably already on July 8!

131. FROM PAUL LEHMANN, COLUMBUS, OHIO, JULY 2, 1939

My dear Dietrich:

Your letter was awaiting me when I arrived here this morning. It was of great help in explaining your card which I received in Elmhurst on last Thursday. But I cannot tell you how deeply it troubles both Marion and me. I write now, believe me, with great heaviness of spirit.

I shall, of course, comply immediately with your request. Please know that I do so with great reluctance and out of a full understanding of your situation. On such a basis you are not entitled to speak of effort expended and kindness shown. The principle matter of concern is you and the cause to which you are devoted.

Now, I have the following to propose: we must meet before your return. I simply could not think of you being here and going back without it. Therefore, you must be good enough to let me know by return mail which time will be best for my coming to New York. Since the friend about whom I wrote you is planning to come to New York next Saturday, July 8, arriving Sunday morning, July 9th, I wonder whether or not you could wait long enough to make possible my coming with him. Then I could also be with him when he sails on July 12. On the other hand, if you must sail on the 8th, as you suggest, I shall come at once. We must have some opportunity to talk together.

Will you let me have word by return mail? Do you think also that you could explain my coming to Emmanuel and ask him whether I might have a bed at the Seminary for a few days, I shall be there? Please go to no trouble over this. If it cannot be, I shall arrange when I come.

Meanwhile, I shall look forward to seeing you and Marion joins me in the prayerful commitment of our ways to Him who bringeth all things to pass and in continuing, affectionate regard,
Paul

132. CIRCULAR LETTER FROM PAUL LEHMANN TO COLLEGES AND SEMINARIES IN THE UNITED STATES, JULY 3, 1939.

Dear Sir:

Under date of June 27th, a communication was addressed to you in behalf of the Reverend Dietrich Bonhoeffer, Licentiate in Theology. It concerned the desire of a committee of which Dr. Reinhold Niebuhr is the chairman, to make Mr. Bonhoeffer's visit to America available to colleges and seminaries interested in his lectures.

Word has just come that the circumstances of Mr. Bonhoeffer's visit to the United States have been entirely misunderstood and that the contemplated opportunity of inviting him cannot materialize owing to his return to Germany.

The committee appreciates the courtesy of your interest in its effort and regrets very much the error of its earlier communication.

Respectfully,
Paul Lehmann,
Th.D., Secretary

133. TO PAUL LEHMANN, JULY 3, 1939

My dear Paul,

Many, many thanks for your letter! Of course, I would be *very* happy to still see you, and your offer to come is more than I dared to think. Of course, I can also arrange my schedule as I wish. But I must depart on the evening of July 8. Can you really undertake the long journey for such a short time? Or is that not too much? Please don't overtax yourself! I will probably hear more from you. The enclosed letter was exactly what I had in mind. Sincere thanks!
Always in faithfulness, your
Dietrich Bonhoeffer

136. FROM REINHOLD NIEBUHR TO PAUL LEHMANN

Dear Paul:

Thank you for your kind letter. I am sorry about the trouble you have had at my suggestion with Bonhoeffer. A letter from Van Dusen in the same mail with yours informs me that Bonhoeffer is returning on August 8. I do not understand it at all. He wanted to stay out for a year and [I] don't understand why he changed his plans after we made the arrangements.

I am working on my third lecture right now. Have been at it so long that I feel the whole thing to be stale and unprofitable. I don't find it easy to get material in the libraries in London so the second series will be thin and will have to be reworked. Karl Barth's son Marcus [sic] was at the lectures and he thought them very heretical. A very nice lad but 102% Barthian. He believes that if there were no ten commandments no one would ever have known that it is wrong to kill. That kind of stuff gets me quite madly liberal.

You are quite right about the English countryside. We have a lovely spot in Sussex where we will be till September 1st. The children are doing well. I enclose a photo. I do hope you and Marion will have a good rest of this summer. For goodness sake don't do everything they ask you to do.

Terribly sorry to have increased your work futilely about Bonhoeffer. Please send me a bill for the actual expenses.

Love from Ursula to Marion.
Affectionately yours,
Reinie

142A: FROM PAUL LEHMANN TO TIMOTHY LEHMANN, COLUMBUS, OHIO, JULY 17, 1939

Dear Dad:
Thanks so much for all your bother about the mail and the check. It was a great help to have it since I had finally to go to New York. By this time the letter and the denial will have reached everybody so that I doubt any unfortunate circumstances will result.

It was really very worth my going even though I could not persuade Bonhoeffer to change his mind. I simply could not bring myself to allow him to have come and gone, perhaps without any possibility of meeting again, without seeing him while he was here. The reunion was a great joy to us both. Of the details, I must tell you when we are in Elmhurst again. Meanwhile, I can only note that two important matters are likely to come from my visit. One is a rethinking of my whole theological and ethical position in the light of the current struggle of the Confessional Church; the other is a wholly new appraisal of the National Socialist movement. I am reading just now a book which Bonhoeffer gave me, written by a former Nazi, and the best interpretation of the spiritual and cultural significance of what is now happening in Germany. It is called "the Nihilistic Revolution" and reinforces in a remarkable way the reports from Bonhoeffer himself. I wish everyone might read the work for it makes plain what a vast difference there is between the penetrating and the surface understanding of current affairs and what is more shocking, how the end of a completely pragmatic philosophy is a pragmatic methodology which completely destroys universal forms.

As for Dietrich himself, I can only say that I understand his position completely. He had agreed with his friends that he would come back without fail within one year, unless a mutually agreed upon code formula came to him. This formula was to express their conviction that war was imminent. This formula came and there was no alternative. He fully expects war in September and will thus have one month to make the necessary connections so vital to the ongoing of the Confessing Church. Meanwhile, there had come to Bonhoeffer the clear perception that he who wished to have any voice in the new Germany must live through this worst of agonies with her. It was unthinkable to him to desert his friends and his task simply in order to safeguard his own life. The outstanding impression one gets from being with him and from hearing his account of the work he is doing is that the only power for living in a completely broken world is the Christian gospel. Here is a man and a group who are so completely committed to Christ in life that it has become axiomatic to them that they may have to die for Him. And they are ready. When the New Testament talks about one's "joy being full" it lays down what these men are actually experiencing now. One discovers over against such a witness to the faith that the times of the end are really the time of the only possible beginning and that one's own life and faith securely pursued above these struggles of the end lack all reality. The German Confessional Church is re-enacting the book of the Acts. Therein is its power; therein is the hope for the only possible German future . . .

Marion joins me in warmest greetings and love to you all,
As ever, Paul

151. FROM PAUL LEHMANN TO REINHOLD NIEBUHR, COLUMBUS, OHIO, JULY 31, 1939

Dear Reinie:
After hearing from your mother and Hulda about your tremendously crowded schedule these days, I ought to thank you for taking any time at all to write and for the additional kindness of the photo. I saw your folks, including also Helmuth, when I made a dash to New York the first week of this month to see what all this was about Bonhoeffer. Your mother was kind enough also to let me have the press comments on your lectures. These I have now read with great interest and care and shall return. It was almost as though I had been there myself. I have no doubt at all that the Gifford's have reached a new high. As soon as they will be published, I shall own them myself.

Perhaps you will have heard all about Bonhoeffer by now. His hope was to get a brief glimpse of you on his return through England. In case he did not succeed, I think some explanation is due you, so I shall venture to make it. My own conversation with him convinced me that he was doing the only thing he could do.

You see, his original concern was the avoidance of military duty. The oath to Hitler which this would have involved was intolerable to him. At the same time, he did not welcome the idea of imprisonment on this ground any earlier than absolutely necessary. The visit to America would have secured a postponement of this decision and left him free to continue his work, though at some distance. Meanwhile anything could happen both within Germany and without and the whole problem disappear. The American invitation actually has delayed his obligation to report for duty until Spring.

Bonhoeffer arrived in New York about the tenth of June, expecting to stay for one year. Before he left Germany, he pledged himself to return without fail after this year and, if war seemed imminent, to return at once. The war news was to reach him from his friends in the confessional church by code. He was here scarcely a week when this formula came to him, whereupon he decided to return at once. He reasoned that one month of work before the hostilities would be of strategic importance for the confessional church.

Now there are three other factors which play into this decision. The first is that Bonhoeffer had no definite job over here. The post with Leiper offered him with the Refugee Committee could not be accepted without excluding himself permanently from Germany, which he was pledged not to do. On the other hand, if he had had a definite teaching post, he would have regarded that as a prior obligation and not returned immediately. Occasional lectures seemed to him too dangerous in view of the immanence of war which would certainly prohibit these opportunities to aliens. The second consideration was the discovery during the short time that he was here that he could not hope to make any contribution to the German future, if it were given him to survive, unless he suffered through this present time. This had not been quite so clear to him before his trip. But from the isolation of Coffin's summer home he had looked across the seas and become convinced that voluntary exile was the path to permanent inactivity. Here was an additional ground for not endangering his return by accepting Leiper's offer. And of course, the third factor in his decision was the growing feeling that to remain here would have reduced itself to a violation of the gospel injunction that he that loseth his life shall save it. On this point he could not bring his conscience to rest and in the face of the next few critical weeks, he simply had to return.

I do not feel justified in taking your time now with more than the barest comments. So I shall reserve other remarks about this whole situation until we meet, I hope in January. As for the expenses, please let this be a small contribution of mine to the decencies that still remain in this world. It was not very much and I can and do gladly assume it. If you want to get rid of the money you would have spent, give it to the society for drowning the present Prime Minister, if the British still have enough virility to organize it.

One specific point Bonhoeffer wanted me to mention. It concerns the Union fellowship to Germany. We visited Tyron while in New York and gleaned indirectly that the German appointee was a German Christian. This really disturbed Bonhoeffer greatly. He felt it an unwarranted contradiction in the professed interest of the Seminary in the Confessional struggle, the more especially since he believes it of great importance for Confessional Church students to have the opportunity of the freer air of foreign study for a time. Doesn't it mean that the Seminary ought to revise its German Committee? Why couldn't Bonhoeffer be asked to head such a committee for the future? The International Student Exchange in Berlin is certainly Nazi dominated. I suppose nothing can be done anymore this year. But I think that these awards ought to be thoroughly altered.

Perhaps Eden could help by exchanging students with the Confessional Church. Bonhoeffer says that they are prepared to provide keep over there and passage from Germany to New York for the German student. If Eden could offer keep here plus the fare from New York to St. Louis some arrangement could be made. It would be a real assistance to the Confessional Church . . .

Do you know the book by Hermann Rauschning: "Die Revolution des Nihilismus"? Bonhoeffer gave it to me as the best interpretation of contemporary German affairs. I have just finished it and found it immensely illuminating. I must talk with you about that too when we meet . . . [Paul Lehmann]

NOTE

1. Dietrich Bonhoeffer, *Theological Education Underground: 1937–40,* DBW 15 (Minneapolis: Fortress Press, 2012), 91–92, 164–65, 170–71, 191–92, 201–6, 209–10, 212–14, 216, 252–54, and 262–64; reprinted with permission.

Chapter 31

Dietrich Bonhoeffer[1]

Four Theological Giants Influence Our Faith (1968)

Mrs. Lindsay, ladies and gentlemen. This is a David and Goliath month. You can decide each week who the giants are and who David is. Since the people about whom the discussions are to go on announce that we are the David's. It has occurred to me also on this cold morning, with this magnificent company of people, that it might be singularly appropriate both to the concerns and passion of Reinhold Niebuhr's life and to the concerns and work which Dean Shinn does in this seminary, if this company joined the Peace Parade in Washington and had the meeting and the questions after they had got through with Miss Rankin. If the ladies at Union Seminary took over the reins of foreign policy, we might get somewhere in Vietnam.

Meanwhile, to begin with Dietrich Bonhoeffer, it has seemed to me that we might try to think together about him, in a threefold way: I should like to try to say, first of all, something about Bonhoeffer as a person, then something about Bonhoeffer's pilgrimage as a Christian in the modern world, and finally something about the power of his ideas—why I think they are so suggestive to contemporary students of theology and not only students of theology but contemporary people in the oddest sorts of ways. One of the oddest I learned about only last week when I was talking with a minister from South Dakota who was telling me that he had gone recently to a garage to have his car attended to. The man who was presiding over the garage was at work upon a car way down underneath and he inquired who was there and what the matter was. When the man told him who he was, down from underneath the car came the question, "What do you think about this man, Bonhoeffer?" Now I'm sure that Dietrich himself would never have expected a question about himself to have come out from under the chassis of a Chevrolet. So that this is a kind of sign, of which there are not a few in Dietrich's life, of this curious phenomenon, this curious Bonhoeffer phenomenon of a person catching on in a time beyond his own time. This is the mystery and the temptation of responses to Bonhoeffer. The mystery because it is a kind of ineluctable incitement to further probing, to a kind of restless curiosity, to always new facets of the understanding of oneself, of the faith, of the world in which one lives, around all kinds of unpredictable corners. A temptation on the other hand, as the death of God theologians have demonstrated, a temptation to make Bonhoeffer responsible for the strangest assortment of things cultic and not so cultic, at most of which I think he, himself would have shuddered. This is, however, the risk that any of us takes, particularly those to whom, in the New Testament phrase, "much has been given"; from them, "much will be required." What is being required of Bonhoeffer is all sorts of twisted misinterpretation, partly out of enthusiasm, partly out of respect, and partly out of unwillingness to do one's homework. But in any case, you have been doing your homework, so let me say first some things about him as a person.

I

He was born on the 4th of February, in the year 1906. His life came to a tragic close, as you know, on the 9th of April in the year 1945 when he, along with a number of others, including his own bother and two brothers-in-law, were executed in the course of the last fury of the then German totalitarian government against the conspirators, of whom Bonhoeffer was one, who had sought a change of power in the German state before it was too late.

My own acquaintance with Bonhoeffer began in this seminary. This seminary has had for as long as I have had any contact with it or recollection of it, a tradition of inviting each year to its student body particularly gifted students from abroad. Thus people have come to us from Scotland, from England, from France, from Switzerland, from Germany in a kind of steady succession of theological students. Among these in the year 1930 was Dietrich Bonhoeffer himself. He had just completed his own theological study which led to what in Germany goes by the quaint name of a "licentiate in theology," which is roughly the equivalent of our PhD. And he had come to this country as an interlude before taking up his academic vocation in whatever university would find it possible to engage him. The German system in which you write a dissertation in order to convince the faculty, then you have to write a second dissertation in order to convince any given university that the faculty which had given you the first degree, was not irresponsible.

Bonhoeffer's treatise entitling him to a University appointment had not yet been completed, although his doctoral dissertation had been. So he was here. And what one was immediately, I think, struck by was that, except for the name, one would not off hand have suspected him of being German. He was the most un-german German that I have ever myself met. And this was not because he did not look like a German. He did look like a German—blond, rather solid built and thorough in his bearing, [and German] in his way of saying what was on his mind. But apart from this he was singularly un-German. And I think one could put it this way. As you know, one of the things that the Germans do least well is look at the world from somebody else's point of view. They seem congenitally unable to relate in this way. Probably this kind of single-minded concentration accounts for the fact that the Germans always excel in science, philosophy, theology, and perhaps even in the field of letters. But this single-minded concentration carries with it a great disadvantage, namely that they are really unable to understand how they look, or how the world looks from another point of view. But Bonhoeffer was unique in this respect. In fact, the liveliness of his mind was matched by a lively curiosity about all things human. This took very amusing as well as almost parabolic forms. Among the amusing forms, I think on might note, his almost intuitive desire of long standing to go to Rome. Against the background of a highly cultured German family this desire is especially intriguing. On his mother's side, there were theological scholars and preachers at the court. On his father's side, there were also scholars, but more scientifically minded ancestors. His own father was a distinguished physician and psychiatrist who came to the directorship of the faculty of Psychiatry in Berlin University and of the psychiatric clinic in the city of Berlin. So, this great combination of German aristocracy, learning and German social conservatism filtered through this singularly un-german German. It is one of the ways that God reserves, I suppose, to cause the wrath of humanity to praise God. Children turn out differently form the way their parents either are or expect.

But Rome, for this ultra-German, Lutheran Protestant had a fascination. And he couldn't really rest until he got there, which he did, together with his brother, on a holiday while he was a student. This was in the middle '20s. And while there, he was simply fascinated by Roman Catholicism. This was long before John XXIII. I have thought about that many times since, because this is one of the points at which Bonhoeffer's experience and mine seem to have been at variance. When I first went to Rome I was horrified by Catholicism. When he went to Rome he couldn't let go of it. I have often puzzled about that. It indicates, it seems to me, a kind of incipient openness to what was at the other extreme of one's experience, to try to take it in, not to try to control it, but in order to learn from it what one could learn, for one's own experience.

The still more puzzling and even amusing indication of this openness came out of his Barcelona period. He was for a time a vicar of a German congregation in Barcelona period. As I recall among our own disputes and debates here in the Seminary as fellow students, the thing I never could really get through my mind was that this Lutheran Christian was ecstatic about the bull fights. He thought that the bull fights in Spain were one of the most exciting aspects of what he learned there. And by way of a letter, his biographer reminds us of the fact that somehow, in Bonhoeffer's own imagination, Catholicism and bull fights go together. That helped me to understand that. He wrote that the thing that impressed him most was that in Spain, the most rigidly Catholic land, there should be this wild fury about the bull fight. It almost seems, he said, as if the population which goes to a carefully disciplined mass on Sunday, whose whole life is ordered in a carefully structured way, goes on Sunday afternoon to the Corida to let out its pent up humanity. Now I think this is a measure, not only of Bonhoeffer's openness to that which was distant from him, but a measure also of his intuitive grasp of the human element in what was distant from him. This was, I think, characteristically evident also in the fact that the thing that interested him most during his day at Union was not the theology which was going on in the seminary, which wasn't, but what interested him most was what was going on in Harlem. This was for him the discovery of a new kind of world. And one of my classmates in the seminary at that time, Franklin Fisher, who afterwards became a professor at Howard University and is unhappily no longer among us, alive and at work—Franklin Fisher was Bonhoeffer's almost weekly escort to Harlem. He went very frequently to the Abyssinian Baptist Church, and he had this kind of restless concern about this new kind of people whom he had never known anything about before. I still recall an occasion when Bonhoeffer planned a birthday dinner with Fisher and some other friends including myself, and we were going downtown. This was long before the Supreme Court decision, and we telephonically contacted several restaurants, and on being told that a Negro couldn't be served we had the dinner up here. This was the measure already of the way in which he could relate his convictions to his life, his life to his convictions. Perhaps parabolically. This is why, as I say, the mystery and the temptation, are a little precarious.

Perhaps parabolically one might call attention to two aspects of this mystery and temptation in his life. One is a curious sentence in a sermon, which Bonhoeffer preached in one of the great churches in Berlin, where he had substituted for the incumbent pastor for a time in 1932. There he said, in the course of his sermon:

> We must not marvel, if, for our church, times should come again in which the blood of martyrs will be required. But this blood, if we really still have enough courage and faithfulness to shed it, we must remember that this blood will not be so transparent and so guiltless as the blood of the first witnesses. Our blood carries with it a great guilt of our own, the guilt of the ungrateful servant.[2]

And one can understand why Dr. Bethge, his biographer, wonders about the possibility that here might have been a foreshadowing of later things to come. One thinks, again this is the temptation, so I will just mention it sort of *sotto voce*, one thinks of the New Testament record concerning our Lord, in which almost at his birth the shadow of the cross was experienced, at least as the New Testament suggests, by Mary, his mother.

Another parabolic indication of this singularly un-German German has recently come to public view, I think, in the publication of some of the letters which were exchanged between Dietrich and his fiancée. These letters, as you know perhaps, appeared in the *New York Times* upon the occasion of the November issue of our own seminary bulletin which, it seems to me, is a remarkable tribute to the kind of theological students who are at work in this seminary today.[3] If we have this kind of imaginativeness and resourcefulness ahead, the church is in better shape than it deserves to be. In any case, the engagement has been interesting to me, as I have thought about it, because it cuts in on the temptation to put a premature halo around Bonhoeffer. It is one thing to be celebrated as martyr; you know, when you lay your life on the line. It's another thing to observe when you write letters to your fiancée that the same effort to connect faith concretely with life emerges. In one of the letters, there is an extraordinary reference to the fact that Bonhoeffer believed that their marriage would really take place. This was for him a sign of the providential ordering of his life which he would always be prepared to accept, but never be prepared to "jump the gun on," and say, 'it must go that way, or else providence is called into question.' He never put it that way. Instead, he connected the providential ordering of his life with a remarkable word to his fiancée, as they were discussing what their house might look like and what kinds of things they wanted in it, that they must always give thanks to God and receive their marriage as a gift from him. This is exactly the same faith mentality of obedient surrender in the path of freedom that finally issued in his martyrdom. I think, therefore, that it is not inappropriate to draw parabolic inferences from the life of the man whose life exhibits the central paradox that I have called being un-German as a German. From the beginning, he is being shaped by the situation in which he is to be other than he is, in order to be what he is. This is what usually is called conversion, only the conversionists make it too simple to be interesting. But this is how the flesh and blood conversion goes—being made other than we are, that we may really be what we are. That's the humanity of conversion, whatever the theology is. I might just say one other thing about that. But two things I never could understand about Bonhoeffer—one is his passion to go to India. We spent a whole couple of weeks running around lower Manhattan together trying to persuade some imaginative sea captain to take us abroad a freighter to go to India. Bonhoeffer had $2,500 in the bank, so that he could have paid the passage for both of us.

It was his father's. He wouldn't touch it. I think probably, although he never said so, it didn't escape his attention that having been through inflation once, that world politics might take a curious twist and it wouldn't be bad to have a friend at Chase Manhattan. Anyway, we didn't get to India. And now a monograph is being written, trying to show that Bonhoeffer's passion for India had something to do with what he later came to call "non-religious interpretation." I'll talk about non-religious interpretation later, but even after I talk about it, I don't see the connection. In any case, this is a semi-psychological study and psychologists can draw the strangest conclusions from the strangest evidence, so it may be, there may be something in it. Freud at least knew what Bonhoeffer was up to, if Bonhoeffer didn't.

II

Now, about pilgrimage. Bethge has said, in a very suggestive and impressive way, in his biography, that Bonhoeffer's life is best understood as a movement from the theologian to Christian, and from Christian to contemporary. Now obviously, this movement is not mutually exclusive. There are people, of course, who are always ready to conclude that if you are a theologian you couldn't possibly be a Christian. Just as there are people who, as Christians, get impatient with theology. But in any case, some fresh perspective became the focus of orientation of what he was doing. When Bonhoeffer decided to become a theologian, the focal point of all his aristocratic, cultural, social and political background emerged in a clear and formative way. Not that his family had ever concluded that because there had been distinguished theologians in the past, someone in this large family of ten children had better be a theologian, in order to keep the family record in tact on the contrary, it is a curious thing, really, that Bonhoeffer should be a theologian. Or maybe not so curious, because he grew up in a family which really did believe that "the family that prays together stays together." But they didn't really think that the church was the place where you did your praying. The biography makes it very clear that Bonhoeffer's family maintained a cordial, but "distant" relationship to the church. They went on "state occasions" as a family. They observed the offices of the church—burial, marriage, confirmation and such things. But the view that one's life is nourished by continuing and intimate participation in the church, this was not a part of Bonhoeffer's youth. In this respect, the family was not any different from any other suburban, Berlin family of the time. One's religious life was a matter of family prayers, family devotion, the kind of naturalness which makes for faith and nourishes it. This was before vitamin D in the cereal displaced faith; faith was, as it were, part of one's cereal life, so that it was absorbed directly into the blood stream. The result was an extraordinary kind of naturalness, and no pretension at all, in the life of faith. Well, this was the kind of environment in which Bonhoeffer grew up. At the same time, he was always keenly aware of the power of mind and impact of two older brothers, both of whom had really no interest in the intellectual dimensions of faith. One of them became a distinguished nuclear physicist, the other became a very successful lawyer. It was the lawyer brother who lost his life with the theological brother in 1945.[4] Thus, when Bonhoeffer came with his announcement that he was going to be a theologian, his older brothers roared. And his father and mother, while they found it inappropriate as parents to join in the laughter, were very puzzled. They didn't interfere. Why did he become a theologian? Why did he become a martyr? This has a kind of parabolic, providential dimension to it. The fact, however, that he became not only a theologian, but the formative theologian for a generation after his, is an extraordinary commentary, it seems to me, on the way in which the providence of God orders the unruly wills and affections of humanity.

As a theologian, he was in trouble with the prevailing climate of the faculty in the university. When one thinks how many creative theologians are in trouble with their theological teachers it makes one a little nervous to be a theological teacher. Bonhoeffer was no exception. It was, to be sure, Harnack and Seeberg, who were the great historical and theological giants, to use your language, in the theological faculty in Berlin, which Bonhoeffer attended. But it really was Karl Barth who intrigued Bonhoeffer from the first. Bonhoeffer had (this is another one of these curious parables, not to overwork that imaginative possibility), Bonhoeffer had already done his doctorate without having had any immediate, personal contact with Barth, though he was always keen to meet him. Eberhard Bethge has distinguished four stages of Bonhoeffer's relations with Barth. I mention this because, although it isn't really supposed to be widely noised about, Barth is still the formative theologian of the twentieth century. I notice he's not on your list. But this is an American parochialism. So we are less open to what is at the other extremity from our concerns than Bonhoeffer was. But then, that's my own parochialism, you see, because I happen to have a strong conviction about that, with which very few of my colleagues in this place agree.

Anyway, the four phases of Bonhoeffer's relation to Barth, indicate how a creative theological career develops in relation to the people who are shaping theology in the midst of which one develops. There was a first period from 1925–1929, in which Barth and Bonhoeffer were related to each other chiefly through Bonhoeffer's reading what Barth had written. And Bonhoeffer, already at this stage, evidenced a remarkable interest in and attachment to Barth, but at the same time, a remarkable independence from him. Barth had taken a very strong Calvinistic position about the honor of God, the sovereignty of God, the otherness of God and the sovereign initiative of God in making himself known to humanity. His great formula was that the finite cannot comprehend the infinite. Bonhoeffer, on the other hand found this really problematical. He never really could accept the view. This was due chiefly to his Lutheranism which affirmed that the finite can comprehend the infinite. *Finitum non capax infiniti* [the finite is not capable of the infinite], Barth insisted; Bonhoeffer insisted, *finiti capax infiniti* [the finite is capable of the infinite]. That is to say, there is always an inner, personal appropriation of the life of faith which is related to knowing God, which he found necessary really to stress over against Barth.

Then there was the period between 1931 and 1933, the second period in which each of these people tried in various ways to come together for meeting and for conversation. Bonhoeffer visited one of Barth's seminars on Luther and in the course of the discussion Bonhoeffer introduced Luther's remark to the effect that God has often more pleasure in the rejection of the atheists than he does in the prayers of the believers—"Who said that?" Barth asked. And that was the beginning of their actual confrontation.

Here was another point of tension. The tensions concerned a question which engaged Bonhoeffer all his life, namely, how does what the church has to say about humanity's position and responsibility in the world, how does that become concrete? The question of the concrete stance of the Christian in the world was one which, Bonhoeffer felt, Barth, though he was concerned about this, did not face as clearly and explicitly as Bonhoeffer himself wished.

The third period is the that of theological distance. Here, though Bonhoeffer and Barth worked intimately together in the political struggles of the church vis a vis the mounting totalitarianism of the German state, still in theological matters Bonhoeffer found Barth's doctrine of justification by faith still more acutely lacking in the concreteness necessary for the Christian. Meantime, a change had come into Bonhoeffer's own life. The theologian was already on the way to becoming a Christian. The person who had written highly sophisticated books about the *Communion of Saints* and *Act and Being* was now on the way to writing about *The Cost of Discipleship*. This book which Barth later praised in a very positive way, expressed a major point of difference between them.

The fourth period, dates from 1944 onwards, in which Bonhoeffer, from his prison cell, criticizes Barth in a way which Barth found very painful. Bonhoeffer thought Barth had succumbed to revelational positivism. By this, he meant that Barth takes the word of preaching, the word of the scriptures and affirms them, without giving sufficient account of what goes on the receiving end of the stick.

Now, Bonhoeffer's work on *The Communion of Saints* was ready for publication in 1927. But he couldn't find a publisher. It is interesting to me the way Bonhoeffer's publisher now is cashing in enormously on what he refused to take risks with in 1927. I don't suppose one can be too unhappy about that, but it is another one of the ways in which the providence of God strangely works in the world.

Anyhow, in 1927 this book was available but nobody would publish it. In this book, Bonhoeffer called for an attempt to do theology by taking the church seriously. At the same time, Karl Barth was working on the revised edition of his way of doing theology. And he changed the title from Christian Theology to Church Theology. One wonders what would have happened if Barth had read *The Communion of Saints*, not after Bonhoeffer's death at which point he praised it very highly too, but had read it while he was at work revising his own way of doing theology. The older and the younger theologian might have come together in a comradeship which would have borne rather different fruit in our time than in the nature of the case happened. So Bonhoeffer, the theologian, manifested again this independence of mind with enormous respect for the new theology, new in his time, as it came in the work of Barth.

Then came the movement from theologian to Christian. This is the period of *The Cost of Discipleship*, and of *Life Together*, the period when Bonhoeffer had already left the university behind and was at work in an underground theological seminary on the Baltic Sea. Here something had happened about which he never spoke. His students, however, were aware of a change, shall we say of mood, of an inner appropriation of the ideas of Christ so that the lectures become a kind of diary of the practice of the Christian life. In this period, this is one of the things that makes me nervous still about *The Cost of Discipleship*, Bonhoeffer dreamed of the possibility of a community of faith and discipline as the setting of theological learning in which what one learned about theology and what one practiced in one's life, would be integrated and real. He had given up on the university. He had apparently been influenced to some extent by the Taize community and such other communities as have since taken shape. I may say, that this was for me the most surprising part of my own knowledge of and experience with Bonhoeffer. That he could have been a pacifist was understandable, but as a pacifist how could he have gone in what seemed to be an ascetic direction? Bethge and I have often talked about this. The biography now shows that an inward change was taking place. The precise nature of this change is only evident from a casual letter Bonhoeffer once wrote to a student friend of his, with whom he had no further contact, telling her in explicit language that something had happened to him. But what had happened, he never said. This was characteristic of the family. One didn't talk really about the things that mattered most deeply to one. One just let it come out by being different. So the conservative became the pacifist, the theologian became the Christian.

And then the theologian and the Christian became the contemporary; the conservative and the pacifist became the conspirator. I suppose this is the next great surprise about Bonhoeffer's life. How could a man who started where he started, and who had, as it were, in the chromosomes, a Lutheran aversion to any disorder in the state, how could such a man be a conspirator, take part in a revolution? How is one to understand that? I think one is to understand that with reference to what made him a Christian. One is to understand it with reference to this singular openness and sensitivity to what was at the other pole of one's life. I think one is to understand it with reference to Bonhoeffer's passion, from very early on, with the fact that the Christian life makes no sense unless it is concrete. In the difficult days of the conspiracy, he found himself, as a Christian and a theologian, related to a church that was sitting out the collapse of Christian civilization, and endeavoring to do business at the same old stand, in the same old way when the issues of life and death, of faith and future, of the integrity of humanity were being hammered out by people in law and in politics, in government and in labor unions. Bonhoeffer was unable, as a Christian, to turn his back upon the concreteness of his environment, if his brothers and brothers-in-law and their friends inside the government, and in the positions of leadership in the state, who cared nothing for the church at all, if they were prepared out of human conscience and passion to lay their lives on the line, how could he, as a Christian, sit it out? That was his question. Obviously, he could not. He came to the conclusion that he could not sit it out. So he joined the conspiracy and became one of the emissaries under the protection of the German foreign office going abroad for purposes of contacts with the World Council of Churches, not least with the then government of Anthony Eden through the then Archbishop of Chichester, George Bell, trying to convince through Bell—Bell he did convince—the then Sir Anthony Eden, as British Foreign minister that the unconditional surrender policy was madness, that if the allied governments knew the German situation and responded to it, and were interested in a constructive option, they would see that there was in Germany an important group of leaders, responsible leaders, prepared to take over the government. But the conspirators met only with stony silence from the allied capitals. And it remained for John Foster Dulles to do us all in afterwards.

Now, this identification, with people involved with the burdens of the world, (as a Christian) was the great new change. It has led to one of the most difficult problems in Bonhoeffer interpretation which I just want to mention in passing. It sharply raises the question, whether, and in how far there was a marked shift or change in Bonhoeffer's position. Some indication of the possibility of a shift may be had from these two remarks: (1) In 1943 he wrote: "If we really survive this terrible war, it will be necessary to reestablish the fundamental educational foundations which have come to us on the basis of Christianity. To reestablish these foundations in the life of the peoples inwardly and externally." (2) In 1944 he wrote:

> It will not be the task of our generation to desire once again those great things (that is, the foundations of Christianity), but to save our souls from chaos, and to conserve something that we can recognize as a remnant to which we might tie our lives. We will have rather more to carry our life than to construct it. We will have rather more to hope than to plan, rather more to persevere than to advance. We are convicted of our privileges and we must recognize that we cannot run out on the judgment of history.[5]

Here the theologian and the Christian cross the frontier of radical contemporaneity into a world which has finished with Christianity. If Christianity is to be anything again, it will have to be it on some other basis.

III

This brings me to the power of Bonhoeffer's ideas. I think we could say that the power of Bonhoeffer's ideas is rooted in the inescapable questions to which he tried, in his own way, to give some glimpses of an answer. The first question is: How can one speak in a secular fashion about God? A secular fashion is a worldly fashion. Bonhoeffer was convinced that the world had "come of age." And by this phrase, Bonhoeffer meant not many things, but something quite clearly understandable and identifiable. What he meant was, that a steady course of development since the eighteenth century had in the mid-twentieth century, in the face of the Second World War, come to an end. This was a development which had crossed the threshold from a time which Auguste Comte had described as "the long minority of humanity" to the full majority of humanity. The world of culture has left not only infancy behind, but it has also left adolescence behind. Now one must live as though God did not exist—*ets Deus non daretor*, as if God were not given. The meaning of this is that the Christian had for centuries been proposing to humanity, that God was a necessary condition of human life. God's necessity tended to be experienced and recommended in terms of what God could do for you and for me, to make our life fuller, to make our life richer, to make our life more quiet, to make our life more peaceful, to make real estate safer in suburbia, to make insurance policies dependable. This God, said Bonhoeffer, is the *Deus ex machina* of which idolatry is a specialty. The God whose business it is to bail us out when we get stuck, this God is the God of a world in infancy and adolescence. The fact now is that humanity is prepared to go it alone, can go it alone, so that we are living in a time in which it is very, very difficult to find out where God cuts in, if at all. As Bishop Robinson has put it: "There simply are no vacant places left."

Bonhoeffer's point in a world come of age is, not that God is dead, but that the dead God has been done in, and the God of Christianity, who is the father of Jesus Christ, our Lord, this God is now exposed to view in the integrity and power of his being related to our lives at the center, not on the periphery. God is not an errand boy, but the continuing presence without whom we simply are not what we are. In a world come of age, the God who means anything at all, is the presence at the center, whom we discover, as we go on, to be a cloud by day and a pillar of fire by night, a refuge and a strength, a very present help in time of trouble. But this discovery is not the proof that we need God. It is a sign that God has blessed us with God's presence in our midst. "Non-religious interpretation," therefore, is the attempt to speak in a non-religious way about religious things. And this was the major passion of Bonhoeffer's life. Thus, you see, he moves right into the middle of the contemporary mind and mood, which I discover, with the threat of unemployment hanging over my head, every time I try to do introduction to theology in this seminary.

Three years ago, the students came still with a certain curiosity about what this "Christian bit" was all about. Now they couldn't care less. What they want to know is, what if anything makes sense, Christian or not. How can we speak, in a secular fashion about God? Does God have a worldly name? And we must do it in a nonreligious way, that is to say, we must do it in a way in which the language, the images which have been tarnished by the *Deus ex machina* in our past, have been replaced by another way of speaking. Last week I saw a new play in Minneapolis that I hope will come to New York. Clive Barnes thought it might be a good idea, and I cordially agree. The play is called *Tango*, and in it there is a line which keeps ringing through my ears and mind.[6] I have never understood what the chaos was, before the world was created, but in this seedy household where everything was in disarray, I got some glimpse of it. Anyway, the seediest character in it says at one point under provocation, "Tragedy is impossible, farce bores me. Happening is all that's left." That's what the great deeds of God always have been understood to be in biblical faith. Creation, crucifixion, redemption, or resurrection, the new humanity and the coming again in—"happening is all that's left," in a world that has lost tragedy and is bored by its own attempt to entertain itself.

The second inescapable Bonhoeffer question is: "Who is Jesus Christ for us today?" I think it would be too much of a violation of Bonhoeffer to say, Jesus Christ is God's worldly name. His first lectures at the University of Berlin were on Christology, and he tried already then as a young theologian, to say the same things about Jesus Christ that had always been said, but to say it all differently. Consequently, he started in a quite different way to talk about Jesus Christ in the University. The students were aware of the fresh air in the corridors and in the class room. Never had they heard theology talked about like this. They didn't know whether it was theology. But here was a theologian who brought his life and his theological concerns, the classroom and his students' concerns somehow together in an incarnation of human interchanges. So, as Dr. Bethge has told us in the lecture which he gave in this place last April, Bonhoeffer's characteristic way of speaking about Jesus Christ is, "the man for others." This is for him, a Christological title. Whether it is a good one or not, I think we will all agree that to say that Jesus Christ is the son of God, or Lord and Savior is a religious way of saying it. To say that he is a man for others is a secular way of saying it, a non-religious way of saying it. You don't have to buy it, but you can't avoid your own alternative. Simply reciting the Bible is not going to get us where God's presence breaks through. So, the question: "Who is Jesus Christ for us today?" became the ruling concern of Bonhoeffer.

This concern led him to a major problem. It goes back to his passion for concreteness. Bonhoeffer stresses that in the secular world our real "hang-up" is the problem how, as Christians, to be meaningfully, that is concretely, involved in the world, without losing our identity as Christians. Contrariwise, how shall we focus upon our identity as Christians and not cut ourselves off from the world? The dialectic of identity and identification constantly haunts the Christian amidst the struggles of a world which for the moment has repudiated all [the Christian's] heritage. What this comes to is that the Christian must keep on saying prayers with both eyes open. Bonhoeffer, thus, invites all of us to join his movement from theologian, or believer if you like, to Christian, to being contemporaries in flesh and blood on the frontier of all of those problems in the common life where the humanity of human beings is "up for grabs."

Let us pray: God of our fathers and our God, we give thee thanks for Jesus Christ our Lord, and for the faithful in every generation and in our generation, who testify concerning him. Quicken us in our thankfulness for the life and thought and mind and spirit of thy servant, Dietrich, and for this place in which he sojourned for a time, and by reason of which he also belongs to us. As we severally move wherever thou dost set us down, we may be strengthened in heart and mind and soul to gladness in being faithful as thou givest us to be faithful to Jesus, our Lord.

NOTES

1. Paul L. Lehmann, "Dietrich Bonhoeffer" Four Theological Giants Influence Our Faith" 1968 January Lecture Series, January 8, 1968. When he delivered this lecture, Lehmann was Auburn Professor of Systematic Theology at Union Theological

Seminary in New York. These January lectures, held in James Chapel, had been sponsored by the women of Union Seminary for 17 years at the time of this lecture series. This manuscript is transcribed as delivered and has not been previously published; used with permission.

2. [Editorial: Dietrich Bonhoeffer, "Sermon on Colossians 3:1–4, Berlin, Fourth Sunday after Trinity, June 19, 1932," in *Ecumenical, Academic, and Pastoral Work: 1931–1932*, DBW 11, 459.]

3. [Editorial: Lehmann is referring to the journal *Union Seminary Quarterly Review*, which was staffed entirely by Union PhD students who produced a special issue on Bonhoeffer. See *USQR* 23, No. 1 (Fall 1967).]

4. [Editorial: Dietrich Bonhoeffer's brother, Klaus, was part of the resistance against Hitler. Klaus and their brother-in-law, Rüdiger Schleicher, were executed on April 23, 1945. Another brother-in-law, Hans von Dohnanyi, was also executed for his part in the conspiracy.]

5. [Editorial: No citation is given for these two quotations in the original.]

6. [Editorial: Slawomir Mrożek's *Tango* was first staged in Poland in 1965.]

Chapter 32

Bonhoeffer—Real or Counterfeit (1966)[1]

A former colleague of mine, upon his return from a series of speaking engagements, was wont, ever and again, to remark: "it is not my traducers who bother me; it is my introducers." Just so—Dietrich Bonhoeffer, from the perspective of the nearer presence of God into which, from our perspective, he has been untimely called, must ever and again be saying to himself: "it is not my critics who bother me; it is my commentators and translators."

Bonhoeffer would be amply entitled to these musings. For seldom has an author, living or dead, been so misrepresented by his commentators and translators. *The Cost of Discipleship* (1949), for example, moves from its unexplained modification of Bonhoeffer's title (which was simply *Discipleship*) to the unexplained deletion of two sections, just short of fifty pages in the original, while en route, numerous liberties have been taken by the translator with the text, with particular damage to the poetry. The *Ethics* (1955) is a similar case as regards translation and poetry. The paperback edition of 1965, has the same translation, yet duly reports its base in the sixth German edition of 1963. But without explanation this edition omits Dr. Eberhard Bethge's *Preface to the Newly Arranged Sixth Edition* which is indispensable if the reader is to understand what is going on. The so-called Death of God theologians are perhaps the most conspicuous of Bonhoeffer's misrepresenters. They have seized upon the *Letters and Papers from Prison* with such avid and hasty enthusiasm as to have provided an American parallel to those German enthusiasts who have all but launched a "Bonhoeffer School." On the Continent, "the world come of age," "religion-less Christianity," "true worldliness" have tempted Bonhoeffer's former pupils, now in theological faculties or church administration, towards cultic passions. In the United States, these same phrases have been appropriated as a kind of quintessential "new essence of Christianity" which claims Bonhoeffer for the tradition of Nietzsche and celebrates him as a forerunner of a theology without God. It cannot be too strongly emphasized that both cultic and atheistic celebrations of Bonhoeffer are grievous distortions of his thought and spirit. When the prison papers are read and reflected upon, with due regard for Bonhoeffer's exegetical and theological writings, there's no informed and responsible way of claiming Bonhoeffer for a theology without God. Indeed, exactly the contrary is the case. Bonhoeffer's principal theological concern was with the problem of transcendence, that is, with the task of dissociating the God revealed in Jesus Christ from the *deus ex machina* of religion, including Christianity; and with the task of exploring the Scriptures and the tradition of Christian thought, for light in arriving at a meaningful way of speaking precisely about God in the twentieth century. It is, therefore, an irony worth noting that Dr. Martin Marty's well-intentioned symposium on *The Place of Bonhoeffer* should have failed to make its warning heard. The place carved out for Bonhoeffer turns out to be much too sketchy, and even hasty for the stability necessary to a careful and balanced appraisal of Bonhoeffer's real concerns. Marty's warning thus fell between two stools, the distorted misrepresentation and the episodic presentation, and could scarcely be heeded.

Accordingly, we owe to Dr. Ronald Gregor Smith a great debt of gratitude for proceeding "with deliberate speed" to set Bonhoeffer in perspective by setting the Bonhoeffer record straight. His translation of the *Sanctorum Communio* takes up the work of Bonhoeffer where a responsible interest in him should begin. This applies to the form as well as to the content of the present volume.

Bonhoeffer first published *Sanctorum Communio* in 1930. It was his dissertation submitted to the theological faculty at the University of Berlin. The work earned him the Licentiate in Theology. The aim of this research was to explore the inter-relations between dogmatic theology, social philosophy, and sociology. The argument tries to analyze the basic social relation which underlies the conception of *sociality*. It understands this relation as a relation between Person and Community and characterized chiefly by an activity of willing. At the community level, this activity of willing leads to certain basic social structures. At the level of person, this activity of willing leads to an "I–Thou" relation which is simply fundamental to the reality of personal life. Various philosophical attempts to give meaning to the concept of "person" are discarded, on the ground that, in one way or another, they do not maintain the basic social relation which underlies both community and personal life. The search for an adequate concept of the "person-in-community" and of "community as a community of persons" leads to the Christian understanding both of person and of community as rooted in the transcendent will of God. God wills both persons and persons-in-community. For Bonhoeffer the link between such an abstract analysis of the basic social relation and the empirical forms of community is provided by the reality and the meaning of the Christian church. Hence, his monograph bears the sub-title, "A Dogmatic Inquiry into the Sociology of the Church."

The analysis is difficult reading. For American readers especially, it presupposes a view of sociology and of philosophy which seems scarcely empirical at all. Weber and Troeltsch and Durkheim are more familiar to us than are Simmel and Toennies (especially Toennies) and Vierkandt upon whom Bonhoeffer relies. Similarly, it is difficult for us who are immersed in the dynamics of social change and the diversity of social and institutional structures to summon the patience necessary to pursue in any sustained way the question whether there is a "primal community" that underlies and illuminates the "broken communities" in which human beings concretely live. For Bonhoeffer, on the other hand, the church is unintelligible apart from the willing activity of God as creator, redeemer, and consummator of human beings as persons in community. Jesus Christ, in particular, is unintelligible except as a person who inaugurated a community in the world in a quite discernible and empirical sense. Thus, for him, the church as an idea, that is, as it lends itself to conceptual analysis and description, includes its empirical reality. Contrariwise, as an empirical community, the church among other forms of community continually forces upon reflective attention the question of the possibility and the meaning of authentic community. Indeed, for Bonhoeffer, it is the socio-theological reality of the church that continually provides the concrete occasion for facing, in thought and action, the question both of the meaning and of the redemption of social institutions.

The merit of Professor Smith's clear and smooth and, on the whole, admirable translation is that it not only makes a basic work of Bonhoeffer's available but it also actually restores to the English text all the material which had been excised from the original manuscript when it was first published. In the German edition of 1960, this previously deleted material appears in an appendix. It had been deleted among other reasons because of certain differences between Bonhoeffer and Professor Reinhold Seeberg, his advisor; and for reasons pressed by the publisher. What Professor Smith has given us here is, therefore, a complete original text, the excisions being restored to their original position. Bonhoeffer's thought is thus more readily and correctly available in this English translation than in any extant German text. The publisher too has responded in kind with a handsome typeface and binding.

If it is a considerable gratification to be able to direct the attention of readers to Professor Smith's translation as a way into the *real* Bonhoeffer, it is a considerable disappointment to report that *No Rusty Swords* is a tawdry piece of counterfeit. The integrity between Bonhoeffer and his words which marks *Sanctorum Communio* has here been shattered, and indeed, violated. The words still belong to Bonhoeffer. But they are torn from the matrix of Eberhard Bethge's conscientious attempt to keep Bonhoeffer and his words together. The result is that the reader is continually exposed to the melodramatic intrusions of commentator and translator. Bonhoeffer has been turned into a commercial.

Since the commentator (introducer) and the translator do not identify themselves, one can only surmise by association that Mr. Robertson is connected in some way with Religious Broadcasting in England or Scotland and Mr. Bowden is the same who translated Grillmeier's *Christ in Christian Tradition*. The Introduction is clearly by Mr. Robertson. The translations, being astonishingly misleading, must, in the absence of identification, be assumed to be a shared carelessness. This reviewer has a list of nearly fifty dubious or erroneous translations which obviously cannot be noted here. Many of them could be set down to understandable human oversight. However, it is the pretentious Introduction which haunts the reader with the likelihood that these dubious translations are more egregious than accidental.

Let us begin at the obvious point: the *title.* The phrase has been taken from a remark in Bonhoeffer's *Ethics.* "Yet our business now is to replace our rusty swords with sharp ones" (p. 68 in the paperback edition). The allusion has been to Don Quixote who is for Bonhoeffer the symbol of ethical irrelevance and ineffectiveness. Heedless of this warning, the commentator and translator of the present volume detach the phrase from its context and suggest with touching romanticism that the materials drawn from Eberhard Bethge's *Gesammelte Schriften*, Volume I and chiefly Volume III, are to be understood as a biographical enterprise in weaponry. How else is one to interpret the caption assigned to chapter one: "The Perfect Setting?" How else can one take seriously the biographical summaries which run throughout the volume, except as a re-introduction of Don Quixote? The game of windmills is apparently designed to divert the reader's attention from the "sharp swords" of Bonhoeffer's own writings to the rustically romantic ones of a Hollywood scenario. In a similar vein, we are told that the volume at its close leaves us in some need of "one more glimpse ahead." "It is to a garden in New York at the beginning of July 1939—" Bonhoeffer's letter, written "in Dr. Coffin's garden," is then quoted and annotated as "New York." Unhappily, this reviewer knows that the garden was in Lakeville, Connecticut where Bonhoeffer had gone for a few days visit with President Coffin. A more serious misrepresentation is the judgment, with regard to Bonhoeffer's return to Germany, that "he was right to assume that he would be needed." This is at best a hagiographical retrospect. Having wrestled with Bonhoeffer over that decision, I know that his being needed in the future was farthest from his mind. Such an assumption was totally alien to his mind and spirit. What he did know (not assume) was, that he had committed himself to his brethren in the struggle inside Germany, and that there was no other way for him to honor that commitment but to return.

The introductory scenario continues with at least two further touches, on the boundary between romanticism and melodrama. We are, unfortunately, promised a second volume which will deal with Bonhoeffer's journey to the United States. We are told that his reasons for not remaining in the United States "are clearly seen in the developing theology of the early period." The truth is rather that any connection is purely coincidental. And definitely, "had we studied his letters carefully at that point," we should have been able to forecast *only* his integrity and his theological brilliance, but certainly *not* "that he would return as soon as war was imminent." What the letters show is that the return was a fixed commitment and did not need to be "forecast." If forecasting could be indulged in at this period, it would have been directed to the possibility that he might *not* return. The Introduction concludes with a gratuitous compliment to Eberhard Bethge. "We look forward to the biography which only he can write, because he knew Dietrich Bonhoeffer as no other student did." If this were a candid acknowledgement, it should have prompted the abandonment of the present volume.

We may conclude with a few of the more glaring translation mistakes. On p. 80, Bonhoeffer is describing the adulteration of food during the hunger blockade of Germany. Here we have at best an omission from the English of Bonhoeffer himself; at worst, the translator's too hasty attempt to correct him. Bonhoeffer remarks: "As a matter of fact instead of good meal there was largely sawdust in our bread, etc." He is made to say in this book: "Instead of a good meal there was largely sawdust in our bread, etc." On p 67, there is a note which implies that the last two pages of the manuscript were lost. Actually, it was only the page before the last (die Vorletzte Seite) which was missing. (Comp.GS, III, 83f.) On pp. 121–122, Barth's *bon mots* were not "too feeble (bloed) to repeat"; it was "pointless to repeat them." On p. 319, second line from bottom, "parenthetic" should read "parenetical." One final instance: the Appendix II, on the "Theology of Crisis." Here the commentator explains that Barth's influence on Bonhoeffer can be seen from Bonhoeffer's having to explain to an American audience what the theology of crisis is about. All that Bonhoeffer's address shows is that he knew what the theology of crisis was about and that he thought it important. It does not show whether and to what extent Barth can be said to have influenced Bonhoeffer. Certainly, it is too much to say that this influence is "first seen most clearly" (p. 361) here.

No *Rusty Swords* purports to take us, on the basis of "Lectures, Letters and Notes" from 1928 to 1936. In this way, we are supposed to be able to short-cut the painstaking work of Eberhard Bethge and follow Bonhoeffer from his graduate student days to his directorship of the underground theological seminary at Finkenwalde. From start to finish this book is a contrived piece of work in which commentator, translator, and publisher have confused misrepresentation with interpretation. One of the youngest of the arts has been linked with the oldest of the professions in an enterprise of seductive solicitation. Thanks to the *Sanctorum Communio*, however, the real Bonhoeffer still has a better-than-even chance against the counterfeit.

NOTE

1. Published in *Union Seminary Quarterly Review* 21, no. 3 (March 1966): 364–369; reprinted with permission. The essay reviews two books: Dietrich Bonhoeffer, *The Communion of Saints*, trans. R. Gregor Smith (New York: Harper and Row, 1964); and Dietrich Bonhoeffer, *No Rusty Swords*, ed. Edwin H. Robertson, trans. Edwin H. Robertson and John Bowden (New York, Harper and Row, 1965).

Chapter 33

Called for Freedom (1947)[1]

I do not know whether you members of the class of 1947 have ever read or reflected upon the letter to the Galatians. But I do know that the diplomas, which are soon to come to you, bear the seal of one of the greatest pioneering centers of freedom—intellectual, political, social—in this country. It is, however, an open question whether you imminent alumni will sustain and enlarge the achievements of your Alma Mater for freedom or whether you will succumb to the pressures and the powers now abroad in the earth which use the name of freedom to cloak malignant tyranny. In short, when in the days to come you take your pen in hand to direct the President of this University concerning his duties, what kind of a document will you sign, and what sort of a check will you enclose? Your signature will tell—and even your failure to sign—whether or not you have been engaged in translating your learning and your training into rich and responsible life.

I think you will need the outlook and the convictions and the resources indicated by the letter to the Galatians if you are to be and remain committed to freedom, and if you are to make the heritage and the privilege of your degrees and your diplomas count in that cause. Such a claim sounds rhetorical, I know: just the sort of observation one would expect to hear from a pulpit, especially on Baccalaureate Sunday—and expect to forget. Will you, nevertheless, join me this morning in exploring the letter to the Galatians to see what its outlook, and convictions, and resources are and what they have to do with this kind of life you will be living as you scatter this week from this campus to diverse and changing communities? If we focus upon the question of freedom it is because that question is central to the letter to the Galatians and critical for the future before you. The issue is: will you be coerced and frustrated or cooperative and free?

Galatians has been called the "Christian Declaration of Independence/" The analogy is quite the appropriate if we think of the way in which the Declaration of Independence expresses the essential character and significance of the American Revolution. Just so, the letter to the Galatians expresses the essential character and significance of the Christian revolution. Both revolutions turned on the issue of freedom. But the two freedoms were not the same at all. It makes quite a difference whether freedom is essentially a protest against tyrannical political rule in the name of rights inherent in the nature and dignity of humanity or whether freedom is essentially a new life inherent in the deliverance and the destiny of humans before God. Certainly there is abundant evidence to show that human dignity is no guarantee of human freedom. Otherwise, the Atlantic Charter would scarcely have been required as a supplement to the charter signed at Philadelphia. But it can also be shown that when you and I begin to understand our lives in the context of the freedom for which we were called, quite other and more promising human and political possibilities are open to us—"in the course of human events." For these more promising human and political possibilities emerge from the kind of personal and social revolution effected by the Christian faith. And it is one of the unhappy conditions of our time that we are not surely persuaded that this is so.

Here is this letter to the Galatians. It is one of the earlier of the writings of the Apostle Paul and as it has turned out, it contains the core of his interpretation of the meaning of Christianity.

Toward the end of this letter to the Galatians, Paul somewhat abruptly directs our attention to results. "For freedom did Christ set us free: stand fast therefore, and be not entangled again in the yoke of bondage" (Gal. 5:1). Freedom against bondage—this is the real difference between a person who is a Christian and one who is not. Here is really the upshot of what the life and death and resurrection of Jesus mean. This is what God meant to accomplish in Christ for humanity in the world, and if you are wondering today whether the purpose of God in Christ is working in you consider whether you are free.

What is this freedom in which we are bidden to stand fast? In his very illuminating treatment of the problem of freedom, Mr. Erich Fromm reminds us that two elements at least belong to freedom. He calls them "freedom from" and "freedom to," and by the first is meant, broadly speaking, emancipation from repression; by the second is meant, the relation of belonging. The first is the negative aspect of freedom; the second is the positive aspect of freedom. Now, although Mr. Fromm chooses to ignore the Apostle Paul, I venture to think that it is exactly this distinction between negative and positive freedom, which the Apostle regards as the net result of the work of Jesus Christ. Only, Saint Paul puts the positive side of the matter first. "For freedom did Christ set us free." That is to say, the whole point of the Christian gospel is that it makes it possible for humans to be what they are meant to be by delivering them from everything that stands in the way. Jesus, in a phrase of the Fourth Gospel's, is the "Truth and the Life" (John 14:6) because he makes plain our destiny and delivers us from all hindrance in fulfilling it.

There are many ways in stating what Christian freedom is, the freedom about which St. Paul wrote to the Galatians. We could say, for example, that freedom is "being, in fact, what one have been created to be"; or that, freedom is "being completely at home," with all that you and I, who are not at home, know that we should be if we were. Or, quite briefly, we may say that freedom is "self-fulfillment"—self-fulfillment not as a goal towards which we aspire but as the plain and concrete truth about ourselves here and now. You will see that once that such freedom is quite different from our accustomed way of thinking about it. It is not a question of the will—of whether you and I can choose to be and do what we wish, or whether our choices are illusions which we recognize as such as soon as we get to college and learn how little influence we actually exert upon the course of nature and of history. Such discussions are very useful for sharpening one's wits. But too often they belie one's heart. For you and I know in our hearts—whatever may be the theoretical state of the matter—that if only we could be know, and cared for, and count as everything is us cries out to be—then, we should be free indeed. Then, although we should be bound by every sort of obstacle, and complexity, yes, and even prison walls, we should "mount up with wings as eagles, we should run and not be weary, we should walk, and not faint" (Isa. 40:31). For we should, indeed, be free!

Listen—to these words set down for himself, surely also for you and for me, shortly before he was hanged by his Nazi captors and within two days of the liberation of that prison by American troops in Berlin:

> Who am I? They tell me often, that I come out of my cell at ease, and high-hearted, and firm, like a lord from his castle. Who am I? They tell me often, that I talk with my guards freely and friendly and clear, as though it were I who ought to command. Who am I? They tell me too, that I bear the day of misfortune with equanimity, smiling, and pride, as one accustomed to victory. Am I really what others declare me to be? Or am I only what I know of myself? Restless, aspiring, sick, like a bird in a cage yearning for breath, as though someone were choking me, thirsting for kind words, for the nearness of people, trembling with anger at the caprice and the tiniest discomfort, driven to and fro by the expectation of great events, helplessly worried about friends so far away, too tired and empty to pray, to think, to work, dull and ready to take leave of everything? Who am I? This one or that one? Am I the one today and tomorrow the other? Am I both at once? Before men, a hypocrite and in my own eyes a contemptible suffering weakling? Or is what remains of me, like a defeated army retreating in disorder from a victory already won? Who am I? This solitary asking makes a mockery of me whoever I am. You know me, God, I am yours!"[2]

Was he—in prison—yet free? Are you—free—yet imprisoned? The last words he spoke which reached his parents from him ran as follows:

Please be not troubled about me. I am so sure of God's hand and guidance that I hope forever to be kept in this assurance. You must never doubt that I am thankful and glad to be kept in this assurance. You must never doubt that I am thankful and glad to go the way which I am being led. My past life is abundantly full of God's mercy, and above all sin stands the forgiving love of the crucified. It is those who have come and been close to me for whom I am most grateful, and my only wish is, that they may never have to be sorry for me, but that they, too, may always be thankful for God's mercy and sure of His forgiveness. I wanted to say this once and for all so that you should really be glad to hear it.[3]

Of course, one can only be free—like that—as a believer in Christ. That was Saint Paul's point too. And the reason is, that the entanglements are very great. "For freedom did Christ set us free: stand fast therefore, and be not entangled again in a yoke of bondage." A yoke of bondage—this is what Christ has set us, in Erich Fromm's phrase, "free from." St. Paul was thinking specifically of the yoke of his own religion. He has been brought up on a formula for freedom, which, instead of liberating him, enslaved him. It was, as you know, the Jewish law. Dissension had, in fact, sprung up in the church in Galatia because people were going around with the charge that if Paul was right about the net result of the Christian religion, then, centuries of sincere religious thought and practice were disposed of at a single stroke; and even worse—plain people were left without any sure and practical religious guidance. If religious faith is to get results, people have to know what is required and what is prohibited and be able to check their behavior by definite standards. For a man to declare, as Paul was doing, that the heart of religion was not rules, not even delight in the law of the Lord, but freedom—that seemed like an open invitation to anarchy. On this basis, what was to prevent a believer from saying in effect, "Christ has freed me from all law. I shall now think and act as I please?" Or, as a widely accepted contemporary version has it, "what a man most nobly and deeply senses within himself, is Christ in him. A man's religion is his own affair and one man's religion is as good as another's."

Let us reserve for a moment the matter of religious anarchy and consider the fundamental point at issue between the freedom which Paul had come to know in Christ and the religion of the commandments by which he lived before his conversion. Certainly the line is not to be drawn between what is desirable and undesirable, noble and unworthy in religion. Indeed, would it not make a very real difference in your life and mine—whether we think of the Ten Commandments, or of the remarkable moral and religious precepts of the Mosaic code as a whole, or of the response of a sensitive conscience to the personal and social issues of daily living—if we could say with conviction: "Blesses are they that keep his testimonies, that seek him with the whole heart" (Ps. 119:1, 2)? But we must confess instead that our religious convictions are far less sure and definite than *that*. Indeed we have no clear sense of religious direction and guidance at all!

Paul is on the side of the one who takes seriously the law of the Lord. We are not! Starting from a life that was full of religious prescription and observance, Paul crossed the threshold of a great religious discovery. We have come to look upon religion as the *last* place to look for discoveries of any kind! The real issue between what Paul had come to know in Christ and what he had known under the law is that there is no power in the law to reach the goal that it sets up. This issue is our issue too. And I am venturing to call attention to it, especially today, because we are met together with those who are crossing a threshold from one kind of life to another. Graduation from a university—whether your degree be that of Bachelor or Master or Doctor—is a kind of second chance to make or to fail to make life count. That chance has been yours because leisure and resources have been made available to you so that you might cultivate learning and skill in more adequate relation to your personal interests and capacities. The question is: when the charm and protection of this campus are no longer your daily environment, will the standards and the practices of the society into which you go suck you in and mow you down, or will you stand—rooted and grounded in motives and purposes which give meaning to live no matter what happens and what the fashion is? Nothing less than *your personal integrity* is involved in this question! And your personal integrity is a matter of freedom—for instance, of whether you live by what you were meant to be, or by what it is expedient to be. The first is the road to fulfillment; the second to frustration.

May I suggest, for example, that perhaps the most perilous prospect of the days before you is that people chiefly live by calculation rather than by commitment? This is true of the simplest as well as of the most complex relations in which we live as human beings.

In that fortuitous community who, with me, catches the 8:40 every morning to Philadelphia, I recently encountered an example of what I mean. A woman had decided to take out an insurance policy against the theft of all of the personal effects of her family. Her son had lost his overcoat, causing some considerable irritation on the part of his mother. It was her design to pay the first premium on her policy and report the loss of the overcoat as her first claim. To her husband this seemed a most unconscionable piece of chicanery. At the same time, the husband who had acquired and driven for four months a 1947 Chevrolet was anxious to exchange it for a Buick Eight, when they were available, and was seeking to sell his car at a $400 profit over what he had paid for it. To the wife, this constituted an act of bad faith and a breach of ethics which could not be countenanced. The conclusion was: "it all depends, I guess, on the way you look at things." Now these people are good

Presbyterians, good Republicans, with a good job, a good credit rating, and a 1947 Buick Eight. Yet I am a little uneasy—wouldn't you be?—about the fact that as parents they have the responsibility for the attitudes, values, and destinies of three growing children? There is to be sure precept upon precept which these people wouldn't dream of breaking. They wouldn't rob banks, and teach their children to lie; and they believe that it is the business of the preacher in Church on Sunday morning to tell people straight out what they ought to do, what the law is. But at the same time they believe in treating their maid as though she were not quite a human being, that Henry Wallace is virtually a communist, and that the main business of religion is to tell you what to do but to have nothing to say about whether or not you do it.

> Oh, how the devil who controls the moral asymmetric souls the either-ors, the mongrel halves who find truth in a mirror, laughs, yet time and memory are still limiting factors on his will; he cannot always fool us thrice, for he may never tell us lies, just half-truths we can synthesize. So, hidden in his hocus-pocus, there lies the gift of double focus, that magic lamp which looks so dull and utterly impractical yet, if Aladdin use it right, can be a sesame to light.[4]

W. H. Auden has been a careful student of Saint Paul. Otherwise, it is not too much to say, these lines from his "Double Man" would not have been written. Saint Paul can teach us again that living by calculation is the frustrating of trying to live by precepts and rules, social, moral, and religious. This kind of living blazes no trail to the living God and to self-fulfillment. It destroys, instead, the freedom of belonging to God and of being what you were created to be. There is no power in ourselves, do you see, whereby the desires of our hearts can triumph over their devices. For we are entangled a yoke of bondage!

But—but "be not entangled again." For if the Pauline struggle is our struggle—and we know it is!—so is the Pauline triumph. "The law of the Spirit of life in Christ Jesus made me free from the law of sin and of death" (Rom. 8:2). "For ye, brethren, were called for freedom; only use not your freedom for an occasion to the flesh, but through love be servants one to another."

Our calling, that is, the nature and the logic of our existence are—to be free. Here is the real meaning of the earthly life of Jesus Christ and of his triumph over death. By that life and death our calling for freedom is unshakeable and plain. And by the power which the living and exalted Christ now holds and exercises over and in the world we can be free. "Above all sin stands the forgiving love of the crucified. Who am I?" The question put form under the yoke of the law is now answered, forever. "You know me God, I am yours!"

"Only use not your freedom for an occasion to the flesh, but through love be servants one to another." This is Paul's injunction to those who suppose that Christian freedom involves no discipline. For the sake of freedom, the risk of anarchy must be run. But the risk of anarchy can only be recommended to those who believe Christ. For they discover, once they are out from under the law, not license but love.

Can you still remember when you came to Chapel Hill as a freshman and were tediously, and sometimes even threateningly, introduced to the mores and the regulations of the campus and the university? If you were like I was, you didn't take the "freshman handbook" too seriously. In fact your chief interest in it was probably to prove to yourself how much more wisely you would have compiled the book if you had been the Dean. There certainly would have been less rules. But suppose, as a freshman, you had taken the trouble to read the handbook of two decades ago. That exercise would not only have been a relief. It would have brought you positive exhilaration. But do you suppose that your own freshman handbook, or the one that will be ready for the incoming class in the Fall, were prepared without the benefit of Deans? Are Deans, nowadays, more naïve? It may be that some paragraphs reflect a certain administrative weariness in the face of undergraduate persistence. But the real truth is that the metamorphosis of the freshman handbook is an interesting barometer of the shifts in educational theory in the direction of the considered risks of freedom. Such risks were equally known to Saint Paul, and in the passage succeeding upon our text, he catalogues the dangers he knew to be evident in Galatia: "The works of our flesh are manifest, which are these: idolatry, enmities, strife, factions, revellings, and such like" (vv.19, 20). And his judgment is that "they who practice such things shall not inherit the kingdom of God." For people like *that*, it is simply safer to live under the law. But they do not find self-fulfillment. Self-fulfillment is reserved for those who are free in Christ. And they can be recognized. For they bring forth the fruits of the Spirit: "love, joy, peace, long-suffering, kindness, goodness, faithfulness, meekness, self-control." And Paul's judgment is that "against these such there is no law" (v. 22). But while educational theory has shifted in the direction of the risks of freedom, it has also shifted from the only basis on which that freedom can lead you to be "servants of another." This is not wholly a defection of the university but rather of the times in which we live. The pathos of these times is that you and I as people are not prepared within ourselves to meet the conditions required for living together with ourselves. We tend to use our freedom as an occasion to the flesh, rather than through love be servants of one another. The great social issue of our time is an issue of freedom. It is the question whether the economic anarchies of political democracy and the economic securities of political tyranny can so moderate one another that the institutions of humankind shall become instruments of human freedom—highways of service which fortify our sense of belonging, rather than roadways of destruction born of frenzied isolation. And underneath and intertwined with this great social issue of our time is a perilously personal one—also an issue of freedom. Isabel Bolton puts it breathlessly and painfully, as in her recent novel, she leads us towards its climax, the cocktail party at the Lennie Weeds:

> She looked around the room—nobody was exchanging anything with anyone. And weren't we all engaged in the most melancholy of trysts—communing exclusively with ourselves? . . . would Freddie just look at the various groups and couples? Who was really conversing with any one? They chatted, they laughed, they laid on and off the necessary smiles, they made the appropriate gestures. But couldn't he see that everyone had the roving eye—the travelling attention? Nobody was really listening to anyone? Look at the unappeased, the hungry expressions mantling these faces . . . As Bridget has said this afternoon, it was all of it a nightmare and one from which no one would awake unless we woke from it together (pp. 118, 119, 187).[5]

Miss Bolton calls her novel: "Do I wake or Sleep?" This is exactly the question before you today. For the years that lie open to you are certain to try by fire all that you have studied and learned, struggled and hoped for as members of this graduating class. Your baccalaureate can become for you a forgotten formality of commencement week. But it can also become for you the occasion for remembering that you need not go through life escaping into sleep. You can remember always, with Saint Paul, when and how to keep awake. For Christians have the power to be: not frustrated but free, not self-preoccupied but servants one to another, not restless but fulfilled, belonging to God in Christ. "For freedom did Christ set us free: stand fast therefore, and be not entangled again in a yoke of bondage . . . For ye, brethren, were called for freedom; only use not your freedom for an occasion to the flesh, but through love be servants to another." Amen.

NOTES

1. Baccalaureate sermon delivered at the University of North Carolina in Chapel Hill on June 8, 1947; reprinted with permission. The text was: Gal. 5:1, 13.
2. [Editorial: See Dietrich Bonhoeffer, *Letters and Papers from Prison*, 459–60.]
3. [Editorial: This paragraph is included in a letter written to Eberhard Bethge in August 1944. See Bonhoeffer, *Letters and Papers from Prison*, 517–18.]
4. W. H. Auden, "A Presumptive Joy," in *The Double Man* (Random House, 1941) 11, 820 ff.
5. [Editorial: The title of Isabel's novel is not given in the original essay.]

Scripture Index

OLD TESTAMENT

Genesis, 22–23, 116
   6:4, 98
   37:8, 48

Exodus, 144–146, 208–209, 270
   32:1–14, 271

Leviticus
   19:23, 104
   24:22, 104

Numbers
   13:33, 98

Deuteronomy, 215, 272
   2:11, 98
   2:20, 98
   5:14, 98
   6:4–24, 37
   10:18–19, 98
   26:13, 98
   27:19, 273

Judges
   9, 83

1 Samuel
   3:1, 182
   3:2, 222

Psalms
   103:7, 17
   119, 159
   119:21, 159
   119:71, 308
   130:14, 105
   135:13, 120
   139, 35
   139:14, 36

Proverbs
   26:12, 179

Ecclesiastes
   12:12, 345

Isaiah
   9:6, 117
   11:10, 143
   26:19, 152
   40:31, 381
   52:1, 193
   53:1, 193

Jeremiah

31:34, 143

Lamentations
   3:23, 13

Ezekiel, 143–146
   37, 142, 145, 152
   37:1–3; 11–14, 143

Daniel
   2:2, 152

Jonah, 92

Micah
   4:4, 143
   6:8, 167

Habakkuk, 92

NEW TESTAMENT

Matthew
   6:20–21, 272
   7:13–14, 161
   9:17, 290
   13:52, 235
   17:1–7, 207
   17:2, 208–209
   23:23, 162
   24:43–44, 182
   25:35, 273
   25:44, 162

Mark
   1:15, 117
   2:22, 235
   9:2–8, 207
   9:3, 209
   10:18, 121
   14:62, 56

Luke, 174
   1:17, 180
   1:46ff., 199
   1:51–52
   6:39, 290
   7:35, 179
   9:28–36, 207
   9:62, 56
   11:42, 162
   16:1ff., 52

John, 16, 152, 335
   1:1, 242
   1:1–4, 335
   1:1–5, 343
   1:10–14, 335
   1:12, 291
   1:14a, 242
   1:45, 47
   1:46ff., 199
   3:21, 42
   6:27, 50
   8:32, 201
   10:30, 50
   14:6, 380

Acts, 356
   1:8b, 98
   2, 123
   2:7–8, 272
   17:28, 53, 118

Romans, 165, 231, 237–238, 243, 252
   1:2–4, 145
   1:3f., 237
   5:1f., 237
   6:1f., 237
   6:3–4, 258
   7–8, 238
   8:2, 384
   8:15–16, 51–52
   10:14–15, 182
   12:6, 243
   12:21–13:7, 189
   13:10, 127

Scripture Index

1 Corinthians
    1:24, 37
    1:26ff., 199
    1:26–29, 174
    1:28, 60, 194
    1:29, 147
    1:30, 334
    2:8, 144, 147
    13:2, 33
    14:8, 222, 267

2 Corinthians
    3–5, 185
    4:6, 42, 119, 208
    4:7, 200
    5:17, 42, 119
    6:8, 200
    10:5, 156

Galatians, 379–381
    4:9, 145
    5:1, 7, 302, 380, 386
    5:13, 7, 302
    5:25, 145

Ephesians, 165
    1:3, 37
    1:4, 37
    1:7–12, 37
    2:14, 97, 201, 315
    2:20, 98
    5:5, 37
    2:20, 98
    6:12, 33, 210

Philippians

    3:10, 311
    3:10–11, 151
    2:6–11, 146

Colossians, 165
    1:15–20, 146
    2:10, 146
    3:1–14, 372

1 Timothy
    2:4, 34
    3:16, 146

Hebrews, 114
    12:4, 202
    13:1–2, 280
    13:8, 201, 247
    13:21, 121

1 Peter, 146
    1:20 (3:18, 19, 21d, 22), 153
    3:15–22, 145
    3:18–22, 142, 145–146
    3:22, 146

1 John
    1:1, 343
    1:7, 42
    4:1, 33
    4:18, 280

Revelation
    10:13, 343
    11:15, 117
    20:7, 145

Name Index

Abraham, 37, 98, 114, 227, 273–274
Addams, Jane, 276
Aiken, Charles, 58, 61
Alexander, Archibald, 58
Alexander the Great, 260
Altizer, Thomas J., 330
Alves, Rubem, 5, 108–109
Aquinas, Thomas, 65, 69–70, 82, 198, 231, 282, 284, 286, 297
Arce, Sergio, 5
Arendt, Hannah, 169, 193
Aristotle, 56, 69, 71, 117, 120, 268, 286
Aswell, James B., 276
Athanasius, 86, 142, 147–148, 198
Auden, W.H., 12, 29, 30, 38, 39, 105, 118, 119, 120, 265, 324, 331, 384, 386
Augustine, 70, 78, 80, 82, 85–86, 112, 142, 147–148, 151, 153, 155, 169, 183, 193, 198, 240, 252, 261–262, 265, 284, 286, 289–290, 292, 294–297, 343–344
Aurelius, Marcus, 282–283

Bacht, Heinrich, 343
Baillie, John, 44, 53, 345
Barnes, Clive, 370
Barnes, Harry Elmer, 276

Barth, Karl, 2, 4–8, 11–14, 16, 18–20, 26, 44, 46, 63, 65–67, 69, 71–75, 77–92, 95, 107–109, 139, 177–195, 198, 214–216, 231–253, 272, 283, 296, 299, 311–312, 317, 319, 328, 330, 354, 365–367, 377
Barth, Markus, 354
Bartley III, William, 320–321, 330
Battle, George Gordon, 276
Bell, George, 304, 368
Bengel, J.C., 88
Bennett, James V., 171, 174
Bennett, John C., 41, 154
Berrigan, Daniel, 274
Bethge, Eberhard, 152, 158–159, 169–170, 194, 299–300, 302, 304, 310–311, 313, 316–317, 322–323, 325–331, 363–365, 367, 371, 377, 386
Blease, Cole, 276
Bloch, Ernst, 187–188
Blumhardts, the, 183
Bock, Kim Yong, 5
Boesak, Alan, 5, 108, 109
Bolton, Isabel, 386
Bonhoeffer, Dietrich, 1, 4, 6–8, 14, 79, 107, 109, 142, 148–149, 152–53, 157–59, 162, 166, 169–170, 184–87,

193–94, 198, 213, 217, 228, 272,
    299–331, 337–341, 344–378, 386
Bonhoeffer, Klaus, 299, 372
Braun, Herbert, 319
Bretal, Robert, 89
Brinton, Crane, 211–212
Broun, Heywood, 276
Brown, Raymond E., 152
Brown, William Adams, 177, 191
Brunner, Emil, 2, 6–7, 11, 13–14,
    16, 18, 20, 23–24, 63, 65–67, 69,
    71–75, 79, 123, 126, 133–140,
    245, 248–249, 251–255, 265, 284,
    292, 296, 345
Buber, Martin, 133, 192, 291, 297
Bultmann, Rudolf, xiii, 2, 3, 13, 14,
    48, 50, 51, 97–105, 146, 153, 249,
    250, 253, 319
Busch, Eberhard, 77, 86

Calvin, John, 39, 43, 47, 50–54, 65, 78,
    88, 91–92, 114–115, 120, 123, 130,
    133–134, 138–139, 151, 174–175,
    177, 191, 198, 200–201, 234, 240,
    251, 262, 285–286
Carlyle, A.J., 260, 265
Casalis, Georges, 180, 184, 187, 192
Chagall, Marc, 271–272
Chi-ha, Kim, 109
Cicero, 86, 260–261, 281, 292, 296
Clement of Alexandria, 49, 339, 344
Cochrane, Charles, 55, 61, 86, 147,
    153, 195, 297
Coffin, William Sloane, 347, 357, 376
Colwell, Stephen, 58–61
Comte, Auguste, 285–286, 337, 369
Cone, James, 4, 5, 6, 14, 107, 195, 205
Conzelmann, Hans, 272
Cross, F.L., 343,
Cullmann, Oscar, 343
Cummings, E. E., 12, 54, 296

Davies, W.D., 343
Deloria, Jr., Vine, 108
Descartes, René, 94

Dewey, John, 42, 314
Dibelius, Otto, 304
Dionysius, 289
Dodd, C.H., 335
Dostoevsky, Fyodor, 38, 164, 170, 183
Durkheim, Emile, 375

Ebner, Ferdinand, 133
Eliot, T.S., 29, 267, 272
Ellul, Jacques, 183, 193
Emerson, Ralph Waldo, 31–32
Erasmus, 16

Falk, Richard, 79, 272
Fanon, Frantz, 107, 197, 200
Feuerbach, Ludwig, 183–186, 188, 193
Fisher, Franklin, 300, 314–315, 345, 362
Fletcher, Joseph, 13, 14
Frank, Erich, 113
Freud, Sigmund, 183, 211, 239, 285,
    289, 296, 320, 322, 325, 330, 364
Fromm, Erich, 380
Fuller, Reginald, 152
Funk, Robert, 97, 105

Gandhi, 312
Garvey, Marcus, 202
Gilson, Etienne, 283, 296
Gompers, Samuel, 276
Green, Abner, 106
Green, William, 276
Grillmeier, Alois, 336, 343, 376
Gustafson, James, 79

Hamilton, Alexander, 156, 169
Hamilton, William, 301, 321, 330
Hammelsbeck, Oskar, 159, 170
Hays, Arthur Garfield, 276
Hegel, G.W.F., 184–188, 193–194
Herberg, William, 217–225
Herrmann, Wilhelm, 66, 70, 80, 232,
    235, 246–247
Herzog, Frederick, 188, 194, 205
Hitler, Adolf, 77, 157–159, 202,
    319, 356, 372

Name Index 393

Hobbes, Thomas, 105, 212, 282, 286, 293, 295
Holmes, John Haynes, 276

James, Colin C.W., 305
James, William, 314
Jaspers, Karl, 159
John XXIII (Pope), 361
Jones, Harry W., 264–265
Jüngel, Eberhard, 191, 195

Kant, Immanuel, 99, 124–126, 140, 245, 285–286
Käsemann, Ernst, 7, 10, 387
Kay, James F., xi, 2–4, 9
Kegley, Charles, 89
Kennedy, Edward, 279
Kerr, Walter, 269, 272
Kierkegaard, Søren, 43, 50–51, 93, 178, 183, 239, 251, 328
Kohlbruegge, Hermann, 183
Küng, Hans, 82

La Follette, Suzanne, 276
Landes, George, 106
Lasserre, Jean, 308, 345
Lefever, Ernest, 149, 151, 154
Lehmann, Marion, 1, 3–4, 9, 299–300, 302, 308, 315, 350–351, 353, 355–356
Lehmann, Peter, 3, 9
Lehmann, Timothy, 1, 355
Leiper, Henry, 304, 357
Locke, John, 286
Luther, Martin, 35, 39, 43, 45, 53, 63–65, 69, 75, 78, 91–92, 122–123, 128–129, 131, 133–134, 138–140, 151, 198, 234, 241, 262, 284, 286, 326, 366
Lyman, Eugene W., 310, 313–314, 317

Mackay, John A., 5, 6, 8, 10
Madison, James, 169
Marty, Martin, 223, 374
Martyn, J. Louis, 3–5, 7, 153

Marx, Karl, 89, 183–186, 193, 214, 229, 291
McCarthy, Joseph R., 150, 163, 172–173
McNiell, John T., 45, 191, 296, 310
Melanchthon, Phillip, 281, 296
Melano Couch, Beatriz, 5, 108, 109
Menzel, Martha Emilie, 1
Meuss, Gisale, 331
Mill, John Stuart, 57
Milosz, Czeslaw, 165
Milton, John, 164, 170
Mirabeau, Marquis de, 208, 212, 169
Moltmann, Jürgen, 187–188, 190, 194, 201–205
Moor, Joe, 345
Morris, John D., 175
Morse, Christopher, xi, 1, 4–5, 8–12, 14
Mozart, Wolfgang Amadeus, 83, 86, 247, 252
Murray, Father John Courtney, 224
Müller, Julius, 183
Müller, Ludwig, 77

Niebuhr, Reinhold, 79, 84, 87–96, 138, 151, 234, 249–250, 291, 300, 302, 304, 305, 311, 321, 346, 347, 349, 353, 354, 356, 359
Niebuhr, Richard H., 45, 53, 94, 105, 178, 191, 249, 253
Niemoeller, Martin, 168, 170, 279
Nietzsche, Friedrich Wilhelm, 183, 191, 218, 225, 248, 373
Nixon, Richard M., 162, 274
Nygren, Anders (Bishop), 81

Origen, 235
Oster, Hans, 157
Overbeck, Franz, 183

Palmer, A. Mitchell, 106, 276
Pascal, Blaise, 20, 24, 41–44, 50, 53, 112, 119–120, 291, 297
Pauck, Wilhelm, 178, 192, 317, 330, 349

Paul, Saint (of Tarsus, the Apostle), 32, 43, 87, 114, 119, 174, 193, 237–238, 270, 272, 319, 380, 382, 384–386
Peabody, Francis Greenwood, 32
Pelagius, 240
Perry, Ralph Barton, 314
Pilate, Pontius, 145, 323
Plato, 56, 71, 80, 126, 286
Plutarch, 268
Pope, Paul IV, 82
Przywara, Erich, 82

Quixote, Don, 376

Reagan, Ronald, 106, 154, 170
Reich, Charles, 193
Reichwein, Adolf, 159
Rilke, Rainer Maria, 191, 195
Ritschl, Albrecht, 44–45
Robertson, D.B., 89
Robertson, Edwin, 169, 376, 378
Robinson, Gene (Bishop), 370
Roosevelt, Theodore, 104
Russel, Bertrand, 155, 169, 314
Rust, Bernard, 77

Sabbath, Adolph J., 172
Saxon, Wolfgang, 9
Schaff, Philip, 251
Schlatter, Adolf, 183
Schleicher, Rüdiger, 372
Schleiermacher, Friedrich 25, 35, 44–45, 66, 70, 184, 198, 246–248
Scholz, Heinrich, 82
Seeberg, Reinhold, 365, 375
Segretti, Daniel, 162
Shaull, Richard, xi, 5, 108–109
Simmel, George, 375
Smart, James, 177
Smith, Louise Pettibone, 98–106
Smith, Ronald Gregor, 95, 372, 375

Socrates, 52, 80, 245, 286, 288
Stoppard, Tom, 161, 170
Sutz, Erwin, 310–311, 345

Taft, William Howard, 104
Thaumaturgus, Gregory, 235
Thomas, Aquinas, 65
Thucydides, 57, 61
Tillich, Paul, 6, 27, 44, 249–250, 253, 321, 342, 344
Toennies, Ferdinand, 375
Toynbee, Arnold, 19, 211, 283
Troeltsch, Ernst, 60, 79, 94, 121–123, 138, 181–182, 187, 192–194, 255, 265, 290, 296–297, 375
Truman, Harry, 211

van Buren, Paul, 27
Velde, Harold H., 172
Vierkandt, Alfred, 375
Virgil, 78, 86, 286
von Balthasar, Hans Urs, 82
von Dohnanyi, Hans, 372
von Harnack, Adolf, 45–49, 53, 75, 178, 192, 198
von Hindenburg, Paul, 77
von Rad, Gerhard, 144, 152

Watson, J.B., 314
Weber, Max, 286–288, 296, 375
Weigel, Father (Gustave), 225
West, Charles, 69, 170
Whitman, Walt, 280
Wilkinson, John, 183, 193
Will, George F., 149–150, 154, 161
Williams, George, 38
Williams, Tennessee, 269
Wise, Steven, 300

Yeats, William Butler, 85–86

Subject Index

Abyssinian Baptist Church (138th St., Harlem), 362
advent, 208
Alexandria, 335–336
Alien Registration Act (1940), 278
Alien Registration Act (1950), 275
American Civil Liberties Union, 2
American Committee for Protection of Foreign Born, 14
American Committee on Cultural Freedom, 150, 163
American Committee Opposed to Alien Registration, 276
American Federation of Labor, 276
American Society of Christian Ethics, 150
Anabaptism, 60
analogia entis, 67, 72, 82, 241, 243
analogia fide, 82
analogy, 26, 83. *See also analogia entis*; *analogia fide*
anarchy, 261–262, 385; economic, 135; moral, 23; of Anabaptism, 60; religious, 382
Anglo-Saxons, 97–98; theology, 90
anthropology, 5, 11, 72, 184, 241–245, 249, 251; theological, 91
anti-communism, 84, 150, 163
anti-democratic surveillance programs, 215
anti-establishment, 188
anti-immigrant, 2, 277–279
anti-intellectual, 193
anti-union, 276
Antioch, 335–336
apartheid, 108
apologetics, 26, 58–59, 61, 341
Apologists, the, 64, 336, 339
apostolic, 46–52, 94, 141, 177, 185, 270
Apostolic Fathers, the, 336, 339
apperceptive, 336–339
asceticism, 140, 164, 286, 289, 367
atheism, 320
authoritarianism, 65, 160, 167
authority, 18, 24, 81, 148, 156, 209; and contextual theology, 27–28; and dialectical theology, 21; and freedom, 155; and wisdom, 292–295; biblical, 7, 17, 18, 80; divine, 271, 327; liberal conceptions of, 21; obedience to, 122–123, 131; of Christ, 146, 151; of established power, 84, 103–104, 146–147; of love, 292; of special revelation, 69; religious, 17, 18, 64
autonomy: economic, 135; of faith, 65; of human reason, 65, 241

395

Aztec civilization, 118

Baalim, 98
Baker Library (Dartmouth), 118
Baltimore, 1
baptism, 77, 101, 153, 258–259, 264
Barcelona, 361
Barmen Declaration, 165, 170, 319; Synod of, 159, 189
Basel, 78, 82, 88, 90, 177, 191, 252; University of, 231
believers and unbelievers, 3, 85, 174, 261, 343, 366
Berkeley, 181
Berlin, 77, 159, 299, 304, 315–316, 346, 348, 350, 358, 361, 362, 364–365, 372, 381; University of, 361, 370, 374
Bethlehem, 9, 85, 189
Bible, 7, 17–23, 55–56, 65, 69, 71–73, 79, 90, 104, 115–117, 173–174, 179, 192–193, 198, 214, 232, 234–235, 238, 241–242, 250–251, 262, 288–291, 297, 307, 326–329, 335, 345, 371
biblical criticism, 22, 250
Bill of Rights, the, 104, 166, 172–174
Black Power, 107
body of Christ, 271
Bonn, 2, 77–78, 177
book burning, 171
Brazil, xi, 108
Buchenwald, 313

Cambridge, England, 15, 16, 22
Cambridge, MA, 224
canon, 47, 116
capitalism, 84, 135, 137, 286
Carolus Magnus, 11, 77–85
catechism, 35, 92, 120, 259
Catholicism, 223–224, 258; Catholic ethics and moral theology, 126, 224; Roman Catholic Church, 69, 220, 224–225, 290, 362; Roman Catholic theology, 68–72, 82, 122, 126, 179, 224–225, 241; Roman Catholic tradition, 27, 64, 215, 238, 257
Chalcedon, 82, 85, 336, 339–343
charity, 3, 59–60
Christ, 35, 37, 42–52, 55–56, 59, 64–65, 69, 85, 92, 108, 119, 121–124, 127–128, 132, 139, 156, 161, 173, 185, 188, 190, 191, 201, 240, 243, 245, 247, 250, 271–272, 313, 315, 316, 323, 325, 334, 337, 339–343, 356, 367, 370–371, 374–375; Adam/Christ typology, 146; and anthropology, 244; and forgiveness, 258; and freedom, 382–386; and history, 26, 189; and justification, 135; and neighbor, 134, 324; and redemption, 23, 133, 228, 380; and worldliness, 326; as crisis of human existence, 239; as God's self-revelation, 16, 22, 54, 65–66, 71–73, 239, 242, 245–246, 249, 327, 336–338; as Jesus of Nazareth, 209, 291, 301; as king, 53, 147, 149; as Lord, 13, 237, 326; as symbol, 27; as white, 200; church of, 3, 52, 60, 229, 307; crucifixion and resurrection of, 145, 264; obedience, 163; preaching of, 117, 145; resurrection of, 148, 151, 153; sufferings of, 145. *See also* Jesus
Christian ethics, 9, 13–14, 58–61, 121–122, 150
Christmas, 39, 82, 119–120, 158, 275, 345, 351
christology, 13, 28, 72, 87, 89, 152–153, 188, 242–243, 246, 249, 301, 341, 343–344; and religionless Christianity, 323; Bonhoeffer's lectures on, 370; *logos*, 333–342
church, 3–5, 7, 9, 15, 17, 21–22, 26–27, 37, 41, 45, 55, 59–60, 79–82, 84, 88–90, 122, 136, 141–142, 147, 150, 177, 179, 194, 201, 203, 211, 214, 219, 220, 227, 232–236, 238, 239, 241–242, 270, 283–284, 326–329,

334, 340, 346, 363–364, 367–368, 373, 375, 382, 384; ancient, 60, 333, 338, 342; and humanity, 323; and ministry, 155–170; and racism, 229–230; and revolution, 111–112, 115–116; and state, 155–156; and world, 325; Black, 314; bureaucratic structure of, 94, 227–228; early, 336; Eastern, 142; German, 77, 303, 308, 348; in Safenwil, 19, 231; in South Africa, 151; in the United States, 307; Mennonite Church (USA), 5; of Jesus Christ, 307; Presbyterian Church (USA), 4; Protestant, 19, 60, 246–249, 252, 307; Reformed, 167, 299; Riverside Church (New York), 220; struggle against Hitler, 319, 348, 351, 366; triumphant, 309; United Presbyterian Church, 167; visible, 52, 329. *See also* body of Christ; community of faith
Church and Society in Latin America (ISAL), 108
civil liberties, 2, 7, 103, 107, 171–175, 214, 221, 222
Civil Rights Movement, 107
clergy, 32, 117, 230, 257
colonialism, 6, 203
Commission on Institutional Racism, 229
Commonweal, 276
communion of saints, 45, 262
Communism, 84, 89, 95, 167
Communist Party, 103, 168, 174–175, 219, 384
community of faith, 16, 21, 26–28, 37–38, 41, 45–50, 60, 143, 144, 148, 159, 162–163, 174, 190, 201, 262, 264, 273–274, 294, 329, 348, 367, 374–375
compromise, 91, 94–95, 122
concreteness, 6, 19, 25–27, 36, 38, 44, 47, 51–52, 93, 126, 128, 130, 132, 134–135, 137, 139, 163, 172, 184–188, 192, 197–199, 201, 204–205, 208–210, 220, 222, 263–264, 280, 288–289, 326–327, 329, 335, 366, 368, 371, 375
conformity, 123, 126, 130, 151, 282; in relation to God, 124, 128; with Christ's death, 151–152
conscience, 15, 58, 68, 82, 99, 102–105, 109, 139, 167–168, 173–174, 180, 273–274, 357, 368, 382
context, 26, 28, 143, 148, 209, 262, 288, 337; of ethics, 123; of human activity, 128; of Jesus, 97; of freedom, 118, 380; of human history, 326; of reality, 35; of the Bible, 327; of theology, 31–39, 43–48
Confessing Church, 351–352, 355–358
Constitution (U.S.), 169, 278–279
contemporaneity, 26, 91, 282, 320, 369
Corinth, 269
covenant, 142–144, 153, 208–209, 259–260, 271, 273
creation, doctrine of, 12–13, 16, 23, 63, 68–74, 121–124, 128, 130, 132–137, 148, 189, 326
Creed, 35, 334–335; Apostles, 153; Nicene, 236
Cuba, 219
culture, 7, 15, 17, 19–22, 26, 46, 55, 65, 79, 94, 114, 119, 135–137, 154, 156, 163, 166, 168, 178, 181–183, 186–187, 192–194, 197, 209, 213–215, 217–219, 221–222, 229, 246–250, 256, 268, 270, 286, 290–291, 311, 325, 327, 333–334, 336–338, 349, 355, 361, 364, 369; aboriginal, 118; cultural positivism, 26, 217; cultural religions, 67; European, 299; Greek, 113; liberalism, 93; modern culture, 90; pluralism, 222; post-Christian, 218; scientific, 296; western cultural history, 56, 79

Dahlem Synod, 159
Decalogue, the, 2, 9, 122, 139, 259–261, 285, 292

398

Subject Index

Declaration of Independence, the, 65, 379
deportations, 215, 276–279
deus absconditus, 63–64
deus ex machina, 337, 369–370, 374
deus revelatus, 63–64
dialectic, 18, 25–28, 35, 47, 63–66, 72–74, 81, 85, 121, 122, 127–129, 136, 139, 178–179, 184, 245, 301, 323–329, 371
dialogical confessionalism, 29
discernment (theological), 4, 6, 32–33, 37, 56–57, 59, 74, 80, 85, 129, 141, 147, 190, 252, 291–292, 295, 323, 338, 375
Disciples of Christ (denominational), 168, 317
discipleship, 273, 315, 323, 326
docetism, 49
doctrine, 6, 34, 82, 94–95, 201, 224–225, 241, 261, 293, 340; false, 165
dogma, 29, 32, 45, 80, 85, 122, 333
Duke Divinity School, 23
duty, 125, 129–140, 286

Easter, 119, 141–153
ecclesiastical, 15, 65, 158–159, 218, 303
ecumenism, 2, 150, 213, 220–221, 227–229, 300, 304, 334, 348
Eden Theological Seminary, 2, 349–350, 358
Edinburgh, 44, 345, 346
Eighth International Conference on the Unity of the Sciences, 150
election, doctrine of, 52, 82, 187, 189, 199, 209
Elmhurst College, 2, 348, 353, 355
Emergency Civil Liberties Committee, 2, 9, 107
Enlightenment, the, 65, 70–71, 74, 182, 286
epistemology, 65, 75, 94, 125, 240, 242–243, 249
eschatology, 48–50, 89, 136, 138, 140, 145, 181–182, 188

establishment, 188, 191, 209–210, 212
ethics, xi, 1, 2, 4, 6–10, 13–14, 26, 29, 44, 55–61, 65, 69, 79, 82, 90, 94–95, 123, 159–160, 204, 211, 215, 247, 252, 269, 281–290, 296, 301, 321, 323–329, 355, 373, 376, 383; absolutism, 283; and dogmatics, 28; Catholic, 126; contextual task of, 109; Lutheran, 262; medieval, 122; political, 260; Protestant analysis of, 121–140; relationality, 301; relativism, 283; revolutionary, 107–109, 137
Ethics and Public Policy Center (Georgetown University), 149–150, 153–154
Eucharist, 219, 329
evil, 33, 95, 132, 139–140, 147, 158, 160, 164–165, 173, 210
exile, 142–144, 357
existentialism, 257
exodus, 144–146, 208–209, 270–271
experience, 1, 17, 19–20, 25, 32, 34, 37, 45, 54, 56, 63, 65, 78, 92–94, 114–115, 119, 125, 130, 138, 142–143, 146–147, 149, 151, 158–162, 165, 190, 199, 207–208, 214, 228, 241, 244, 246, 264, 271, 274, 279–280, 301, 314–315, 327–328, 333–334, 338, 340–341, 361, 367; black, 198, 201, 203; German, 202

faith, 12, 16–21, 23, 27, 33, 41–46, 55, 57, 60, 65, 67, 69, 71, 73, 78, 82–85, 87, 90–91, 105, 129, 131–134, 140–141, 147–149, 162–163, 166, 168, 171, 174, 179, 194, 198, 220, 234, 236, 238–239, 243, 246, 255, 273, 294, 313–314, 320, 324, 337, 348, 356, 360, 363–365, 368; and behavior, 257, 259; and commitment, 223; and culture, 178; and doctrine, 13; and doubt, 41, 105, 300, 320; and ethics, 26; and ethnic traditions, 225; and hope, 143, 146, 270; and

humor, 311; and learning, 41, 55; and obedience, 80, 82, 142, 151, 155, 162, 227–229; and prayer, 310; and reason, 70, 258, 341; and resurrection, 142; and revolution, 111–119; and works, 132, 257; and worldliness, 301–302, 323–331; articles of, 286; bad, 149, 383; biblical, 22, 245, 370; ecumenical symbols of, 334; *fides qua creditor* and *fides quae creditor*, 198; *fides salvifica*, 236; knowledge of, 34–38, 49–51, 69, 239–241, 246 270, 294; leap of, 50–51; messianic, 291; of the Reformation, 6; power of, 213, 221; Protestant, 107, 213, 222–223; rational, 294; religious, 168, 292, 382; risk of, 204; rule of, 49; secret discipline of, 329; seeking understanding, 314
fascism, 137
Federalist Papers, 169
Finkenwalde, 311, 315, 377
Flossenbürg, 313, 315
forgiveness, 2, 5, 20, 60, 64, 138, 204, 215, 245, 255–265, 323, 382
freedom, 7, 10, 104–105, 118, 143–144, 159–160, 165, 190, 193, 199, 202, 204, 208, 210, 215, 219, 229, 270, 274, 295, 302, 313, 315, 326–328, 330, 350–351, 363, 379–386; and authority, 155; and responsibility, 132, 260, 268; gift and practice of, 102; meaning and purpose of, 112; of God, 12, 25, 117, 134, 189, 200, 238; of humanity, 46, 73, 80, 93, 113–114, 131, 146–147, 166, 183, 199, 212, 241, 274; of inquiry, 65; of obedience, 85, 293; of speech, 214, 279; of systematic theology, 27; of the Christian, 131; of the will, 292
French Revolution, 184, 193

Geneva Conference on the Church and Society (1966), 149

Gentiles, the, 319
Germany, 156–158, 165, 170, 202, 258, 299–300, 302–303, 305–306, 308, 330, 347–349, 351–352, 354–358, 360, 368, 376–377
Gestapo, 313, 316
Gettysburg, 90
Gifford Lectures, 44, 138
glory, 42, 52, 85, 114, 119, 137, 144, 146–149, 152, 156, 178, 208, 220, 227, 236, 258, 335
gnosticism, 45, 49, 146
God, 5, 16, 18, 20, 22–23, 25–28, 33–38, 42–43, 45–46, 49–51, 56, 60, 63–73, 78–79, 81–84, 88–89, 91–93, 101, 104–105, 108, 115–119, 121–138, 141–153, 159–160, 162, 164, 167–168, 170, 174, 177, 180, 185, 188, 198, 203–204, 211–212, 220, 228, 237–241, 245, 256, 258–260, 262, 268, 271, 281, 283–285, 291–294, 301, 310, 316, 321–322, 324–325, 327, 329, 334, 336–337, 339, 342–343, 352, 361, 363, 365, 369–371, 373, 380–382, 384–385; absence of, 338; action of, 47, 123, 137, 247, 336; activity in the world, 3, 6, 13, 45, 125, 128, 238; and humanity, 19–20, 25–26, 36, 63–67, 70–74, 116, 123–124, 155, 183, 185, 189–190, 201, 236, 237–238, 241, 245, 249, 255, 260, 339–340; and liberation, 191, 204; and love, 84, 127–128, 131–133, 148, 166, 174, 238, 245; and reconciliation, 203, 301; and the church, 248; and the election of Israel, 199; and the future, 56, 191; and the world, 36, 63–65, 68, 71, 136, 138, 185, 189, 198, 237, 259, 291, 323, 335–336, 338; as creator, 17, 38, 114, 125, 129, 137, 228; as creator and redeemer, 46, 70, 74, 138, 215, 375; children of, 52, 137, 291; claim of, 190; command of, 125, 132,

135–136, 148, 326; commandments of, 271; communication of, 240, 242, 245, 335, 337, 339, 342; death of, 218, 301, 320, 322–323, 352, 373; doctrine of, 7, 244; dynamic and rejuvenating activity of, 222; economy of, 228; faith in, 174, 238; forgiveness of, 20–21; freedom of, 12, 134, 189; glory of, 42, 52, 114, 137, 178, 208, 220; grace of, 13, 21, 23, 67, 100, 284; hiddenness of, 63, 199; holiness of, 271; honor of, 365; humanity of, 85, 191; humanizing presence and activity of, 3, 4, 117, 119, 189, 191, 209; immanence of, 70, 271; in American society, 218; in Jesus Christ, 13, 16, 23, 21–22, 45, 55, 65, 71–72, 108, 127, 189–190, 201, 244, 249, 270, 295, 335–336, 370, 386; judgment of, 123, 168, 173; justice of, 84, 273; law of, 116, 128, 293; mercy of, 382; mountain of, 270; moving strength of, 56–57, 60; of the Bible, 19, 173; of the oppressed, 146; order and purpose of, 262; otherness of, 12, 178, 238, 242–243, 366; people of, 56, 115, 144, 165, 173, 187; politics of, 117, 119, 197, 209; power of, 25, 37, 51, 56, 87, 174, 250, 270; presence and activity of, 189–190, 198, 371, 373; providence of, 41, 92, 100, 365, 367; purpose of, 173, 215, 326, 380; right hand of, 145–146, 151, 153, 236; righteousness of, 124–125, 133, 173, 174, 209, 229, 273; self-disclosure, 25–26, 37–38, 68, 198–199, 291, 301, 335, 340; self-revelation of, 65, 188, 191, 239, 241, 247; sovereignty of, 239, 246, 366; transcendence of, 12; trinity of, 26, 60; trust in, 260–261; will of, 21, 124–129, 131, 134–135, 163, 173, 190–191, 215, 233, 240, 259–260, 282, 285, 293, 327, 339, 374; wisdom of, 37, 87, 250, 270; with us, 218. *See also* image; kingdom of God; knowledge; revelation; Trinity

gospel, 1, 7, 10, 18, 21–22, 27, 42, 50, 59–64, 74, 79, 85, 109, 117, 126, 128, 139, 156, 178–182, 188, 190, 198, 200, 203–204, 208, 221, 233, 237–238, 255–262, 301, 310, 328, 333–343, 356–357, 380

Göttingen, 78, 82

government, 77, 156, 166, 172, 208, 220, 275, 277, 279, 348, 360, 368

grace, 13, 20–21, 35, 37, 67, 69, 82, 85, 93–94, 99–101, 128, 138, 148, 164, 177, 201, 237, 242, 252, 271, 284, 289, 315, 335, 340–341, 343; and baptism, 77; and faith, 124, 238, 243; and forgiveness, 64; and justification, 159–160, 222; and law, 122, 126; and nature, 70; and sin, 23, 70, 74, 93

Greek Orthodoxy, 15

Greeks, 56, 80, 113–115, 343

guerilla groups, 149

guilt, 142, 158–161, 164, 197, 278, 362

Harlem, 307, 314–315, 362

Harvard Divinity School, 2, 6, 31–32, 38, 102, 219, 272, 300, 303, 305

Hellenism, 55; Hellenic, 334; Hellenistic Greek, 38; Hellenization, 45

hermeneutics, 215, 249–251, 319

heteronomy, 27

Hiroshima, 210–212

history, 2, 7, 17, 20, 22–23, 26, 37, 56, 66, 79, 89, 113–116, 125, 133, 141, 144, 149, 187, 189–190, 193–194, 209, 229, 248, 270, 286, 291, 301, 326–327, 334, 369, 381; and hope, 208; consciousness, 94, 273; historical, 16, 17, 21–23, 37, 43, 46, 48–52, 63, 67, 92, 94, 109, 116–118, 137, 141, 147, 168, 180–181, 187, 234, 242, 259, 287; historicality, 326; Jesus, 45–47, 186, 237; meaning of, 237; of black people in the U.S., 199; of Bonhoeffer's influence, 300, 304; of Christian ethics, 121; of Christianity, 222, 225; of ethical thought, 138; of Lutheranism, 131; of Protestant thought, 121, 186; of Roman Catholicism, 225; skepticism, 48–50; theology, 341

Holy Spirit, 17, 22–23, 29, 49, 51, 55–56, 63, 145, 165, 177, 228, 230, 243, 262, 274, 384–385

hope, 33, 51, 57, 74, 79, 82, 85, 99, 105, 108, 109, 125, 138, 142–144, 147, 152, 157, 187, 190, 194, 197, 199, 202, 204, 208, 219, 231, 239, 257–258, 270–271, 280, 285, 312, 329, 348–352, 355–357, 369–370, 382, 386

House Un-American Activities Committee, 104

human fulfillment, 37, 59, 74, 80, 113–115, 119, 127–128, 144, 146, 156, 173, 185, 190–191, 199, 208, 210, 258, 260, 267, 270, 273, 294, 326, 330, 381, 383–385

humanism, 3, 66, 71, 285

humanistic, 52, 92, 214, 222, 323

humanization, 3, 9, 10, 14, 28, 84, 85, 108, 109, 115, 119, 183, 191, 199, 211, 215, 229, 268, 292, 294, 326, 387

humanizing, 3–5, 9, 29, 113, 117, 182, 184, 189, 190, 209, 211, 215, 228, 267, 272, 274, 289, 291–293, 295

Hungary, 84–85, 89

hypocrisy, 84, 283, 381

iconoclasm, 29, 91

idealism, 26, 91, 94–95, 180

ideology, 108, 199–201, 205, 289, 330

idolatry, 17, 29, 91, 103, 174, 200, 229, 237, 330, 369, 385

ignorance, 28, 52, 75, 80, 99, 118

image(s), 143, 146, 200, 217, 270–271, 319, 370; *imago dei*, 69; of Bible, 116; of God, 68, 70, 72–73, 241, 258; of life, 268–269; of spirit, 268; of the revolutionary figure, 112; political, 116–117

imagination, 57, 60, 98–100, 102, 111–112, 115–118, 167, 218, 262, 362

immigration, 2, 7, 175, 215, 275, 277, 278

imperialism, 28, 137

incarnation, 13, 68–70, 117, 119, 123, 137, 141, 146–147, 179, 198–199, 265, 339, 371

individualism, 21, 144, 255, 290; individual, 50, 59–60, 135–136, 142, 148, 180, 235; individuality, 136

inerrancy, 17, 49

injustice, 84, 100, 144, 163, 165, 211, 229, 263

Internal Security Act (1950), 174, 275, 278

Islam, 79, 223

Israel, 36, 142–144, 209, 222, 271, 291; election of, 199; Israelite, 137, 199, 271; messianic faith of, 291; people of, 17, 142–143, 273; prophets of, 89

Jerusalem, 142, 145, 207

Jesus, 49–50, 69, 114, 117, 236, 268–270, 301; and atonement, 117; and black theology, 198–201; and conflict, 174, 238; and hospitality to the stranger, 274; and love, 295; and Moses, 271, 273; and the neighbor, 324; and the prophets, 173; as Christ, 291; as object of faith, 21; crucifixion and resurrection of, 141–142, 145, 153, 270–271, 380; death of, 255; ethic of, 290; life and message of, 21, 333, 384; person and work of, 16, 20; preaching of, 117; presence of, 147, 294, 334; relation with God, 141, 244, 334–343; transfiguration of, 207–212; virgin birth of, 81. *See also* Christ

Judaism, 223, 343; Jewish law, 382; Jew(s), 168, 217, 223, 225, 269, 343
judgment, 20, 57, 59, 103, 116, 123–124, 128, 134, 137–138, 162, 168, 173, 199, 236, 238–239, 245, 281–282, 287, 295, 340, 369, 385; and forgiveness, 20; last, 148
justice, 14, 81, 84–86, 91, 93, 100, 104–105, 108, 117, 120, 143–144, 147–149, 155–156, 162–168, 180, 193, 204, 211, 215, 229, 245, 255–265, 273, 275, 279
justification by faith, 14, 23, 60, 107, 121–140, 159–160, 366

kingdom of God, 21, 56, 88, 117, 178, 273, 328, 385
koinonia, 5, 10, 387
knowledge, 2, 8, 17, 21, 25, 29, 33–38, 43, 45, 47–48, 55, 59, 61, 90, 95, 100, 123, 125, 186, 193, 198, 236, 238–252, 269, 271, 340, 367; of faith, 20, 34–38, 45, 49, 51, 82, 238–252, 270, 294; of God, 32–38, 45, 66–78, 91, 124, 127, 129, 138, 236, 238–52; of good, 127; of humanity, 78, 91, 244–252; saving, 23, 34–38, 45; scientific, 45

law, 13, 47, 58, 104–105 126, 132, 139, 143, 154–156, 162, 171–174, 208, 215, 224, 255–265, 275–279, 294, 301, 368, 383–385; and covenant, 259–260, 262; and divine activity, 128, 209; and forgiveness, 255–265; and gospel, 59–60, 63, 74, 139, 190, 257, 260, 262; and grace, 122; and justification, 139; and love, 128, 133, 209, 256–257, 261, 292, 295; and providence, 294; and order, 84, 144, 295; and sin, 64; and the good, 126; and the prophets, 47, 209; biblical, 257; Christian, 122; eternal, 155, 284, 290; fulfillment of, 127; Jewish, 382; *lex aeterna*, 290; of God, 116, 143, 293, 382–383; of historical life, 117–118; of nature, 60, 121, 127, 256–257, 260–262, 281–298; of the state, 139; three-fold use of, 261–262
legalism, 128
liberalism: political, 57–58, 93; theological, 7, 16, 17, 20–22, 71, 79, 93, 214, 234–236
liberation, 36, 52, 81, 85, 108, 146, 180, 188, 191–192, 195, 198–204, 208, 268, 274, 280, 381
liberty, 104, 131, 165, 167, 262, 274, 276, 278, 343
literalism, 48; biblical, 65, 250; crude, 49; naïve, 48, 51, 54; orthodox, 81; textual, 17
liturgy, 27, 163
London, 86, 159, 303, 306, 312, 348, 354
love, 36, 38, 59, 84–85, 101, 104, 122–123, 128–129, 131–133, 148, 156, 158, 160, 166–168, 177, 210, 219, 238–239, 245, 260, 262–265, 270, 280, 290, 292–293, 295 323–324, 346, 355–356, 382, 384–386; and faith, 324; and forgiveness, 64, 264, 323, 384; and holiness, 20; and justice, 93, 148–149, 156, 215, 255–259, 262, 264; and law, 128, 133, 256–257, 261, 285, 292, 295; as fulfillment of the law, 127–128, 260; community of, 81; foolishness of, 93; gospel of, 256, 261; of glory, 149; of God, 127–128, 132–134, 148, 174, 239; of neighbor, 132–134; of power, 148, 262
Lutheranism, 122, 131, 134, 326, 366

Manichaeism, 84
martyr, 362–363; martyrdom, 307, 315, 320
Marxism, 301, 288–89, 319
Marxist-Christian dialogues, 2
matrix, 375; of black experience, 201; of sovereignty, 289; political, 141–148

McCarran Act, (Walter), 104,
171–174, 278
McCarthyism, 2, 107
Messiah, 48, 123, 145
messianic, 48, 52, 119, 144, 156, 192,
207–209, 291–295; messianism, 145,
153; politics, 145
metaphysics, 44–45, 65, 69, 257
moral obligation, 125, 149–150; nature
of, 125, 129–130, 132, 134
Muslim, 223

Natural Law, 60, 121–122, 215, 257,
260–262, 280–297; *lex naturae*,
121–122, 126, 260, 294
Nation, 276
nature, 23, 70, 93, 101, 127, 135, 141,
167, 173, 209, 256, 281, 287–288,
290, 296, 334, 380–281; human, 12,
67–68, 79, 95, 99, 126, 133, 241,
258, 260, 281, 288, 290, 334, 380,
381; law of, 58, 127, 256, 260, 284–
285; of authority, 21–22; of God,
21, 68, 243, 273, 293; of religious
authority, 17, 22; of the good, 125,
132, 134, 136
Neo-Orthodoxy, 7, 12, 14, 16–22, 178,
231–236, 249–250
New Haven, 223
New Jersey, 9, 172, 223
New Republic, 276
New Testament, 3, 4, 7, 13, 34, 37–37,
48, 54, 56, 86, 140, 143, 152–153,
165, 208, 250, 291, 333–334, 343,
356, 360, 363
New York, 1–8, 53, 171, 182, 220, 223,
227, 274, 299–302, 304–309, 312,
346–348, 350, 353, 355–358, 370,
376; College of the City of, 181
New York Review of Books, 268,
272, 320, 330
New York Times, 9, 163, 170, 175, 227,
272, 276, 280, 363
New Yorker, 161, 170, 193, 340
Newsweek, 268, 272

ontology, 36, 79; ontological, 79, 94,
241, 244–245, 250
orthodox, 21, 65, 71, 74, 81, 179,
235, 246, 276; Greek, 15;
Protestant, 34, 71

Pelagian, 240
permanence, 31, 113–114, 190
phenomenology, 26–28, 43, 45, 47–48,
211, 244; phenomenon, 47, 51, 67,
211, 221, 227, 360
philosophy, 2, 6, 31, 50, 52, 59, 69,
74, 124, 159, 168, 184, 193, 250,
257, 287–290, 296, 306, 313, 338,
347–348, 355, 361, 374–375
philosophical, 13, 14, 27, 45, 47, 54,
69, 90, 95, 121, 134, 211, 269, 314,
321, 342, 374
piety, 41, 91, 118, 141, 155–
160, 292, 311
politic, body, 104, 210, 222
political(ly), 1, 4–5, 7, 23, 32, 57–60,
80–81, 84, 89, 106, 107 116–117,
119, 137, 140–154, 156, 159, 160,
173–174, 179–189, 207, 211–212,
213, 217–219, 222, 247, 252, 260–
261, 265, 268, 272, 285, 288, 290,
294–295, 310–312, 348, 350–352,
364, 366, 368, 379–380, 385;
messianism, 145
politics, 2, 10, 12, 14, 55–58, 79,
84–85, 89, 93, 108, 117, 120,
141–153, 155–169, 184, 188, 190,
193, 197, 207–212, 215, 268, 274,
280, 283, 285–288, 295, 326–327,
338, 364, 368
platonism, 81; platonic, 89, 188, 343
positivism 28, 282, 285, 295; cultural,
26; political, 294; positivistic, 25, 26,
257, 262, 285; revelational, 185, 328,
366; theological, 28
post-Christian, 7, 213, 217–226, 329
power(s), 8, 16, 27–28, 33, 37, 56–57,
77, 83, 91, 95, 98, 100, 103–104,
117, 137–138, 144–153, 155–170,

172–173, 180, 182, 184–185, 189–190, 199, 204, 207–213, 215, 221–222, 224–225, 229, 243, 262, 268, 271–275, 280, 284–286, 289–292, 295, 310, 313, 315, 320, 323, 341–342, 356, 359, 260, 265, 369, 379, 383–386; and authority, 81, 84, 327; and piety, 118, 155; and principalities, 165, 210, 274, 280, 301, 334; apperceptive, 339; (de)sacralization of, 186–190; formative, 25, 94, 283; of darkness, 145; of God, 6, 10, 25, 29, 51–52, 56, 68, 87, 119, 174, 246, 250, 270, 311, 370; of obedience, 137; of particularity, 13, 44–54, 51–52; of politics, 165; of redemption, 117; of resistance, 144, 160, 276; of the Word, 104; of the world, 144–145, 189; of transformation, 115, 186
Presbyterian, 2, 15, 61, 98, 108, 162, 163, 167, 168, 299, 384
Presbyterian Church (USA), 4, 5, 170
Princeton Seminary, 55, 58–59
Principle of New College (Edinburgh), 44
process, 135, 188, 225, 279, 285, 295, 342; and God, 115; creative, 125; Thought, 79
proleptic, 26, 78, 197
prophetic, 7, 26, 29, 33, 52, 71, 81, 161, 178, 209, 216, 221
proposition, 34, 244, 291, 296; propositional, 44, 81, 238
Polytheism, 46, 79
Program to Combat Racism, 149
Protestant(ism), 7, 45, 59, 63, 66, 74, 122, 139, 213–214, 216–225, 234, 314, 317; American, 307; Church, 19, 66, 246, 307; contemporary, 68, 108, 123, 234–235; modern, 60, 68, 70–73; post-, 217, 221
public, 171, 174, 276, 285, 363; Law, 171, 174; liberty, 165; life, 225, 328; interest, 277; places, 99, 275; relations, 116; trust, 166
Puritan, 286

race, 199, 202, 314, 339
racial, 263
racism, 6–7, 214, 229–230, 300
ratification, 155–156, 159, 161–169
reason, 26, 34–36, 38, 44–52, 56, 70, 121, 124–127, 151, 239–245, 258, 260, 281–295, 336, 339–341
redeemer, 43, 46, 70, 74, 138, 146, 152, 199, 215, 271, 375
redemption, 16, 38, 70, 72, 74, 117, 121, 123 198, 210, 212, 238, 245, 334, 341, 370, 375
referential, 26–27, 184, 337
Reformation, 6, 8, 12–13, 18–19, 21, 37, 44, 63–65, 67, 72, 91–92, 107, 121–140, 214, 221, 225, 231, 233–236, 242, 257, 262, 290, 292, 314, 317, 326, 329; ethics, 55–61; ethos of, 262; post-, 45; protestant, 16, 35, 58, 232
Reformers, 6, 12, 20, 26, 35–37, 45, 59–60, 63, 64, 66, 71–74, 122–123, 130–134, 136, 139, 214, 222, 234–238, 240, 262–263, 292, 296
relativism, 262, 282–283, 293
religion, 2, 10, 16–17, 19–20, 31–32, 35, 39, 42–43, 46, 54, 59, 65, 67, 70, 74–75, 89, 92, 96, 98, 122, 138, 168, 186, 190, 193–195, 205, 223, 267, 270, 272, 272, 288, 290–291, 296, 314, 317, 320, 322, 329, 337–338, 347, 374, 382–384
religionless Christianity, 300, 323
renaissance, 65, 285
responsibility, 16–17, 19–23, 27, 29, 33–38, 43, 50, 55, 57, 60, 68, 73–74, 79–84, 99–102, 112, 114, 125, 131, 144, 150, 154, 156–158, 166, 172, 202, 213, 232, 247–248, 256, 258, 260, 264, 270, 272–273, 286,

288, 326, 341, 348, 350, 366, 384; theological, 23
resurrection, 143, 147–148, 278; of Jesus Christ 13, 20–21, 23, 69, 81, 117–119, 141, 143–146, 151, 153, 264, 311, 380; of the dead, 98, 370
revelation, 23, 25, 65–73, 79, 192, 198, 237, 248–249, 259; and history, 189; and philosophy, 50; and reason, 26; and revolution, 190; and sin, 68; as creation and saving knowledge, 23; biblical, 250; content of, 125; contextual character of, 301; concept of, 178–179; general, 68; meaning of, 23, 242; of God, 7, 21–22, 46, 65, 67, 82, 188, 191, 199, 238–239, 241, 247, 325, 338; of Jesus, 21, 327; special, 69–70, 138; theology of, 68; truth of, 246
revolution(s), 4, 184, 191, 208, 210–212, 355, 380; and emancipation, 109; and reconciliation, 192; and transfiguration, 212; and violence, 201; black, 197, 202; social, 380; theological, 111–112; truth of, 7
revolutionary, 6–7, 10, 12, 60, 107, 111–112, 114, 116–117, 134, 137, 147, 168, 182–183, 186–189, 193, 195, 203, 345; a-revolutionary, 204; character of human life, 112; dimension of the gospel, 109; environment of human life, 117; ethic, 107, 123, 137; movements, 147; politics, 207–212; social change, 119; theology, 107, 193; thrust, 183, 185, 193, 202, 204
risk of particularity, 41–54
Ritschlians, 79
Roman Catholic Church, 64, 68. *See also* church

Sabbath, 314
Sache, Sachkritik, 99
Scholasticism, 65
science(s), 44, 52

scientific, 34, 45, 81, 90, 218, 240, 285, 296, 341; character of theology, 179, 192
scripture(s), 20, 80–82, 36, 124, 140, 142, 147, 161, 165, 333–335. *See also* Bible; Word of God
secular, 3, 27, 32, 66, 71–72, 117, 220–222, 247, 260, 320, 328, 369–371
self-conscious(ness), 45, 93, 220, 271, 311
self-disclosure of God, 16, 25–26, 29, 37–38, 68, 115, 127, 188, 191, 198–199, 238–247, 301, 335, 339–342
sin, 20, 23, 64, 68–70, 73–74, 93–94, 122–123, 128, 135–137, 141–142, 149, 151, 201, 224, 245, 284, 382
situation, 8, 18–20, 26–27, 29, 64, 90, 113, 136–137, 158, 167–168, 180, 188, 221, 223–225, 235, 240, 245, 247, 255, 257–258, 263, 308, 325, 327, 348, 357; cultural, 22, 213, 218, 246–249, 338; ethics, 13, 247; in Germany, 348, 351, 353, 363, 368; political, 15, 294, 352
skepticism, 19, 48–51, 179
Sloan Fellow, 1, 299
sociological, 230, 327; analysis, 221; concreteness, 198–202; reality, 203; reality of the Church, 329; religion, 223; situation, 225
sociology, 6, 149, 151, 224–225, 229, 326–327, 374–375
sola gratia-sola fide, 124, 133, 236
sophia, 146, 343
spirit, 15, 20, 26–27, 58–59, 67, 74, 94, 122, 131, 142–143, 146, 151, 153, 168, 218, 268, 286, 289, 296, 311, 320, 329, 348, 353, 371, 374, 376; Absolute, 164; of the age, 31–33, 38
Survey, 276
syncretism, 79, 98, 268, 270

theology: and the death of God, 218, 225, 301, 320, 322–324, 330, 260, 373; as practical discipline, 43; as

speculative, 44, 52; biblical, 22; black, 195, 197–205; catalytic, 29, 52, 203, 289–290; Christian, 3, 6–9, 14, 43–44, 47, 49, 51, 78, 92, 183, 193–194, 197–205, 216, 233, 239, 247, 251, 332, 334–337, 340–341, 367; contextual, 13–14, 25–30, 36, 38; dialectical, 20–23 11, 12, 14, 18, 20–23, 184, 192, 245, 251, 257; dogmatic, 44–45, 374; liberal, 12; liberation, xi, 5, 12, 108, 109, 230; of crisis, 23, 214, 234, 236, 248, 251, 377; of revelation, 68, 80; practical, 43, 52; speculative, 44, 52; systematic, 2, 5–6, 25–29, 35–36, 44–45, 53–54, 191, 234, 239, 249, 253, 272, 299, 341, 344, 371; task of, 13, 22, 29, 35, 43–44, 49, 188, 338; *theologia naturalis*, 69; *theologia revelata*, 68–69; *theologia specialis*, 69; today, 1, 7–8, 10–11, 13, 15–23, 48, 50, 109, 170, 184, 213, 243, 251
theophanies, 67
Time, 168
totalitarian(ism), 160, 166–167, 316, 360, 366
tradition, 4–6, 12–13, 27–28, 46, 60, 99, 198, 223, 247, 261–262, 271, 282–283, 287–288, 290, 292, 296–297, 329, 337, 360, 373–376; and Scripture, 82; continental, 350; covenantal, 79; doctrinal, 33–34; dogmatic, 65, 201; of the Reformation, 214, 231, 234, 257; Protestant, 215; Roman Catholic, 27, 215, 225, 257; theological, 67, 107, 141, 147, 151, 178, 239, 241, 320
Trinity, 26, 55–58, 80, 245; *tri-unity*, 242. *See also* God
truth, 12, 18–20, 28–29, 35, 37, 45, 59, 70, 82, 93, 98, 107, 112–113, 135, 146, 151, 158, 160–161, 163, 168, 173, 177, 182–185, 193, 198–201, 208, 210, 212, 219, 233–234, 237–239, 242, 245, 250, 265, 268, 280, 288–289, 314–315, 317, 320–321, 335, 340–343, 377, 380–381, 385; apprehension of, 36; knowledge of, 34, 45, 55; of faith, 85, 91; of revelation, 246; prophetic, 7; religious, 65
twentieth-century, 1, 20, 118, 182, 365, 374
II Clement, 49

Union Presbyterian Seminary (New York), xi, 1–2, 4–9, 11, 53, 78, 154, 194, 214, 272, 299, 304, 306, 308, 316–317, 346–348, 371
Union Presbyterian Seminary (Richmond), 4, 95, 230
Unitarian, 15
United States, 79, 84, 97, 103–104, 107, 154, 167–171, 197–203, 219–221, 236, 249, 268, 274, 276, 300–301, 305–308, 314, 317, 320, 347, 353–354, 373, 377
unity, 4, 15, 69, 136, 228, 316; of the German Evangelical Church, 165
universal, 17, 46, 126–127, 137, 186, 222, 257, 279; forms, 355; moral, 281; principle, 260, 282
university (as institution), 32–34, 37, 77, 156–157, 161, 171, 214, 222, 231, 248, 260, 360, 365, 367, 370, 383, 385

Walter-McCarran Act, 104, 174, 278
Washington, D.C., 153–154, 175, 305, 359
Wellesley College, 2–3, 14, 97–106
wisdom, 18, 46, 93, 98, 102, 120, 130, 168–169, 179, 201, 212, 261, 270, 283, 290, 293, 295, 336, 339–340; of God, 37, 87, 250
Word of God, 8, 20, 26, 165, 179, 216, 233, 240, 242–244, 339. *See also* Bible; Jesus; revelation
worldliness, 300–302, 319–331, 373

world come of age, 79, 81, 92, 213, 300–302, 319, 319–330, 333–343, 370, 373
World Council of Churches (WCC), 15, 149, 151, 154, 368
World Presbyterian Alliance, 30
World War I, 19, 178, 257, 275
World War II, 97, 157, 275, 310, 312, 369
wrath: divine, 64; of humanity, 361

Yale University, 58, 162, 269

About the Editors

Nancy J. Duff is the Stephen Colwell Associate Prof. of Christian Ethics Emerita, Princeton Theological Seminary, Princeton, NJ. She is the author of *Humanization and the Politics of God: the Koinonia Ethics of Paul Lehmann* (Grand Rapids: Eerdmans, 1992) and *Making Faithful Decisions at the End of Life* (Louisville: Westminster John Knox, 2018).

Ry O. Siggelkow is the director of the Leadership Center for Social Justice at United Theological Seminary of the Twin Cities, St. Paul, MN. He is the editor of Ernst Käsemann's *Church Conflicts: The Cross, Apocalyptic, and Political Resistance* (Grand Rapids: Baker, 2021) and the author of *Apocalyptic and the Call to Freedom: Ernst Käsemann's Theology of Liberation*, forthcoming with Baylor University Press.

Brandon K. Watson is the academic assistant for Systematic Theology at the Protestant University Wuppertal, and a researcher at Heidelberg University. He is the translator of Markus Mühling's *Post-Systematic Theology II: Ways of Thinking—A Theological Philosophy*, forthcoming with Brill.